Glencoe

Discovering
Life Skills

Mc
Graw
Hill
Education

mheducation.com/prek-12

Copyright © 2016 McGraw-Hill Education

Send all inquiries to:
McGraw-Hill Education
8787 Orion Place
Columbus, OH 43240

ISBN: 978-0-02-140049-2
MHID: 0-02-140049-0

Printed in the United States of America.

3 4 5 6 7 8 QVS 21 20 19 18 17

Educational Reviewers

LeeLinda Baggett
Family and Consumer
 Sciences Teacher
Trickum Middle School
Lilburn, Georgia

Melinda Chambers
Family and Consumer
 Sciences Teacher
Romney Middle School
Romney, West Virginia

Tammy Clow-Kennedy
Family and Consumer
 Sciences Teacher
Hendrix Junior High School
Chandler, Arizona

Dawn Gary
Family and Consumer
 Sciences Teacher
Lafayette Parish
School Board
Lafayette, Louisiana

Janet Hartline
Family and Consumer
 Sciences Teacher
Fort Payne High School
Fort Payne, Alabama

Judy Henry
Family and Consumer
 Sciences Teacher
ROCORI Middle School
Cold Spring, Minnesota

Georgia Lash
Student Council Advisor
Family and Consumer
 Sciences Department
Hillcrest High School
Simpsonville, South Carolina

Angie Lustrick
Nutritionist–Personal
 Trainer
Angie's World
Riverside, California

Valerie Morgan
Family and Consumer
 Sciences Teacher
Water Valley High School
Water Valley, Mississippi

**Teddy Mwonyonyi-
Nantambi**
Family and Consumer
 Sciences Department
 Chair
Cleveland Municipal
School District
Cleveland, Ohio

Kimberly Myers
Family and Consumer
 Sciences Teacher
Aynor High School
Aynor, South Carolina

Bettie J. O'Shields
Family and Consumer
 Sciences Teacher
Durham Public Schools
Durham, North Carolina

Mary Lu Pennington
Family and Consumer
 Sciences Department
 Chair
Guion Creek Middle School
Indianapolis, Indiana

Jeanine M. Pope
Family and Consumer
 Sciences Teacher
Fort Morgan High School
Fort Morgan, Colorado

Marcia Jean Ritter
Family and Consumer
 Sciences Teacher, Retired
Pleasant Lea Middle School
Lee's Summit, Missouri

Patti Sanchez
Family and Consumer
 Sciences Teacher
Preston Junior High School
Fort Collins, Colorado

Jill Tolleson
Family and Consumer
 Sciences Teacher
Delight School System
Delight, Arkansas

Anne Weiss
Family and Consumer
 Sciences Teacher, Retired
Kimball Middle School
Elgin, Illinois

Technical Reviewers

Vikki Jackson
Family and Consumer
 Sciences Teacher
Kathleen Middle School
Lakeland, Florida

**Gina Marie Montefusco,
BSN**
Travel Staff Nurse/
Pediatrics Nurse
Los Angeles, CA

Kathryn Oliver Russell
Family and Consumer
 Sciences Department
 Chair
Chickasha, Oklahoma

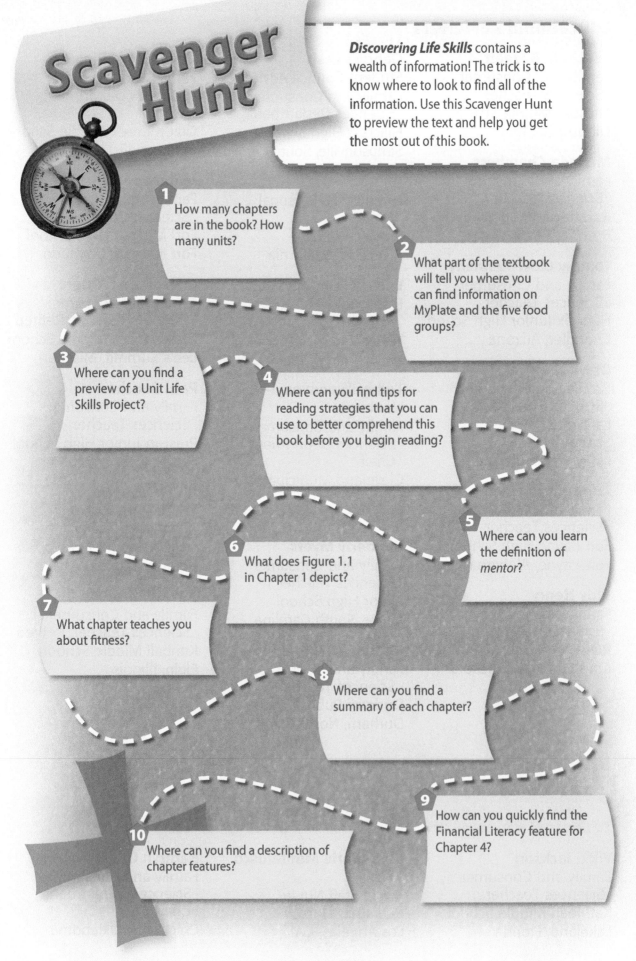

Scavenger Hunt

Discovering Life Skills contains a wealth of information! The trick is to know where to look to find all of the information. Use this Scavenger Hunt to preview the text and help you get the most out of this book.

1 How many chapters are in the book? How many units?

2 What part of the textbook will tell you where you can find information on MyPlate and the five food groups?

3 Where can you find a preview of a Unit Life Skills Project?

4 Where can you find tips for reading strategies that you can use to better comprehend this book before you begin reading?

5 Where can you learn the definition of *mentor*?

6 What does Figure 1.1 in Chapter 1 depict?

7 What chapter teaches you about fitness?

8 Where can you find a summary of each chapter?

9 How can you quickly find the Financial Literacy feature for Chapter 4?

10 Where can you find a description of chapter features?

Table of Contents

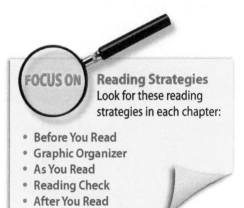

FOCUS ON Reading Strategies
Look for these reading strategies in each chapter:

- Before You Read
- Graphic Organizer
- As You Read
- Reading Check
- After You Read

Table of Contents

Table of Contents

FOCUS ON

Academic Success
To help you succeed in your classes and on tests, look for these academic skills:

- Reading Guides
- Writing Tips
- Math You Can Use
- Science You Can Use

Siede Preis/Getty Images

Table of Contents

FOCUS ON

Project-Based Learning
Projects throughout the book can help you use your skills in real-life situations:

- Real-world scenarios
- Step-by-step instructions
- Independent and group activities

Siede Preis/Getty Images

Table of Contents

Mazer Creative Services

Table of Contents

FOCUS ON Assessment
Look for review questions and activities to help you remember important topics:

- Reading Checks
- Section Reviews
- Chapter Reviews
- Life Skills Projects

Siede Preis/Getty Images

Table of Contents

Features Table of Contents

Academic Skills for Life!

How much money can you save by recycling? How can you avoid the dangers of second-hand smoke? Do you know how to compare products to get the best value for your money? Use these academic features to succeed in school, on tests, and with life!

MATH YOU CAN USE

SCIENCE YOU CAN USE

Financial Literacy

D. Hurst/Alamy

Tips for Success Throughout Your School Years

Where can you go for extra help in a difficult subject? How can you organize your study space more effectively? What can you do to reduce your stress level? Look for the Succeed in School tips in every chapter to help you in every class you take.

SUCCEED IN SCHOOL!

What Do You Want to Do?

What career options are open to you? What do professionals in the Family and Consumer Sciences fields really do? Discover a world of possibilities!

Discovering Careers
Focus On Careers In...

Features Table of Contents

Life Skills for Every Day

Do you know what it is like to set up a business? How can you keep a young child entertained while you baby sit? What can you do to help the environment? How can safety practices help you in the kitchen or while you are online? These activities and ideas show you how to apply your new skills to everyday life.

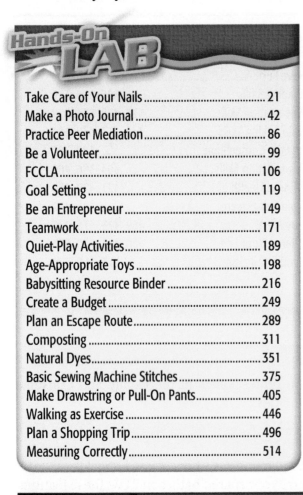

Hands-On LAB

Safety Check

How To...

Connect to Your Community – All Over the World!

Your world goes beyond your home and school. As you prepare to enter adulthood, you are learning that others can be affected by your actions. Community Connections gives you ideas for helping your community. Discover International shows how people all over the world are connected through common bonds.

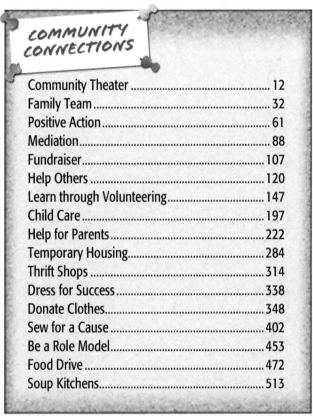

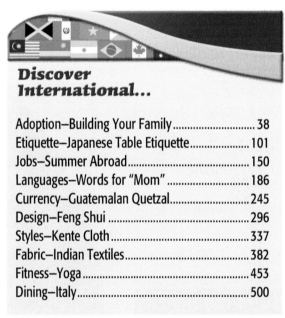

Take on New Responsibilities

What would you do if your coworker would rather chat on the phone than do his job? What if you and your sister could not agree on how to organize your shared bathroom? Use these features to develop your sense of responsibility for yourself and others.

Character Counts

Unit Preview

This unit is about the factors that make us who we are. In this unit, you will learn about:

- How you will develop your unique personality.

- Why grooming and personal care are important.

- The structure and comfort that families provide.

- The types of changes families might experience.

- How to be a good friend.

- How to recognize positive and negative peer pressure.

Explore the Photo

Everyone develops their own unique personality. *What are some of the factors that affect your personality and help you develop into the person you are?*

Steve Mason/Getty Images

Your Role Models

When you are done studying this unit, you will complete a project in which you will:

✓ Take and collect photographs of people you admire.

✓ Interview one of the people in your photographs.

✓ Create and share a collage of the photos and descriptions of your role models with your class.

The prewriting activity below will help you get started.

My Journal

Prewriting Activity
Make a List

Think about the stories, cartoons, books, and imaginary friends you enjoyed when you were a small child. Create a list of the characters you enjoyed the most. Next to each one, write a brief description about why the character appealed to you.

● What traits do the characters in your list have in common?

● What do these characters have in common with the real people in your life today?

Chapter 1

Discover Yourself

Section 1.1

You Are Unique

■ **Main Idea** Many parts of your life come together to make you a unique person.

Section 1.2

Grooming and Personal Care

■ **Main Idea** To look your best, it is important to practice good grooming skills and present a positive attitude.

©KidStock/Blend Images LLC

Freewriting

Dependability Dependable people can be counted on by family and friends. Show that you can be trusted by keeping your word, meeting responsibilities, and being supportive. Freewrite about a time when you, or someone you know, showed dependability.

Writing Tips To freewrite effectively, follow these steps:

1. Let your thoughts run free and simply begin writing whatever comes to mind.
2. Write without stopping to reread, rephrase, or rethink what you are writing.
3. Set a definite time limit.

Potapova

Section **1.1** You Are Unique

Reading Guide

Before You Read

Preview Read the Key Concepts. Write one or two sentences predicting what the section will be about.

Read to Learn
Key Concepts

✓ **List** factors that influence who you are.

✓ **Name** the qualities that make people unique individuals.

✓ **Analyze** why it is important to understand emotions.

✓ **Describe** the physical changes that happen during adolescence.

Main Idea
Many parts of your life come together to make you a unique person.

Content Vocabulary

○ heredity
○ culture
○ self-concept
○ self-esteem

○ constructive criticism
○ self-actualization
○ adolescence

Academic Vocabulary
■ respect   ■ potential

Graphic Organizer

As you read, list the supporting details for the four main topics in this section. Use the graphic organizer like the one shown to help you organize your information.

Heredity and Environment	What Makes Me Unique?	Emotional Changes	Physical Changes

⬆ **Graphic Organizer** Go to ConnectED. mcgraw-hill.com to download this graphic organizer.

As You Read

Connect How do you think your parents are responsible for your personality?

During your teen years, you enter the stage of life when you start to become your own person. As you leave childhood behind, you will begin to discover what makes you unique. Your unique personality will continue to grow and change. You will also experience many emotions and physical changes. You will develop your own value system, and you will start to see how your values fit into the world around you.

Heredity and Environment

No two people act, think, or feel the same way. Everyone comes from a different background and has different experiences. Everything you do, everywhere you go, and everyone you know influence who you are. Your family members and friends probably have the most influence on you. **Figure 1.1** describes some of the major influences on the person you are becoming.

Figure 1.1 You Are One of a Kind

Unique Qualities Many factors influence who you are. *How have some of these factors affected you?*

Heredity Genetic traits, such as the color of your hair and eyes, come from your parents.

Family Your family is usually your first influence.

Roles You fill many roles: student, daughter, son, brother, sister, or friend.

Environment You learn about your world from the people and conditions that surround you.

Culture Traditions you enjoy may be influenced by your culture.

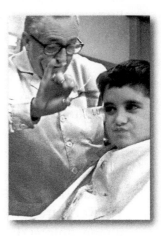

Experiences Knowledge and skills build over a lifetime to create a unique set of life experiences.

◆ **Vocabulary**

You can find definitions in the glossary at the back of this book.

Some of what makes you an individual is a result of heredity. **Heredity** (hə-'re-də-tē) is the passing on of traits, or characteristics and qualities, from parents to their children. Some of these traits are physical, such as your eye color, your facial features, and your body build. Heredity also can play a part in your intelligence.

You have other qualities that make you a unique individual. These traits are a result of your environment. Some of your interests and abilities are learned from the people and things in your environment. Perhaps your sister taught you how to skate. Maybe a friend got you interested in technology.

Family Roles

Your family is one of the strongest influences on the person you are becoming. Are you an only child, the oldest child, the youngest child, or a middle child? What activities do you do with family members? These questions suggest some of the ways you are influenced by your family.

The roles you have determine how you relate to other people and how you act in various situations. A role is your position in a group or situation. You have many roles. At home you may be a daughter or a son, a brother or a sister. At school you may be a student, a best friend, and a team member. In the community you may be a volunteer or a member of a club. Your roles vary, depending on the people with whom you interact and the situations involved. You learn your roles by talking to and watching people who are important to you. Role models are people who help you see what is expected of you in certain situations. Role models can be parents, older siblings, relatives, teachers, coaches, or religious leaders. Who are some of your role models?

Positive Focus
Discover Learning Skills Every person has his or her own best way of learning. Some students learn best by listening to their teacher speak. Others learn best by reading. Many students learn well through hands-on projects. Ask your teacher or guidance counselor how to find out which ways of learning are best for you.

Culture

Your culture also influences who you are. Ways of thinking, acting, dressing, and speaking shared by a group of people is called **culture**. Cultures may be based on ethnic group, geographic location, or social class. Culture often determines certain traditions people follow. You may not even think about your culture until you meet someone who speaks another language, enjoys different foods, or celebrates different holidays from yours.

> **Reading Check** *Define* What is culture?

Role Model You may be a role model for someone younger. *How can you make sure the example you set is a positive one?*

What Makes Me Unique?

Although you share some common qualities with other teens, you are an individual. What personal strengths and abilities do you have that make you different from your friends? Whether you are shy, outgoing, funny, or serious, there is no one else like you. You are unique.

Personality Traits

Personality is the combination of the attitudes, interests, behaviors, emotions, roles, and other traits that make you who you are. Your personality shows in the way you look, the way you communicate, and the way you act. It is the part of you that you show to other people. Your personality continues to change as you experience new things and meet new people. You can become a more interesting person when you develop skills and talents, gain more knowledge, and join in school and community activities.

Everyone's personality is different. Take a look at your personality traits to see how other people relate to you. How dependable are you? Can people count on you to be true to your word? Are you easy to get along with? Can you be trusted? Personality traits such as dependability, cooperation, and honesty help determine the type of relationships you will have with other people. When friends and family members know they can count on you to follow through, you will be trusted to do more on your own. When you learn more about yourself, you can appreciate yourself and other people more.

© Ian Shaw/Alamy

A Positive Self-Concept

If you have a positive self-concept, you are more likely to succeed in life. A **self-concept** is a mental picture of yourself. Self-concept includes your views about your personality traits and about what activities you perform well. Your self-concept is also influenced by the people around you. It can give you the confidence to try new things. If you have a positive self-concept, you are more willing to make new friends, go to new places, and try new things.

Your self-concept does not always stay the same. It may change as the situation you are in changes. When you help a neighbor, for example, you feel really proud of yourself. On the other hand, if you have an argument with a friend, you may not feel as good about yourself. Even people with a strong self-concept get discouraged when something does not work out as they planned.

It is possible to improve your self-concept. Try to do something each day to help build the qualities you want to improve. Work to achieve your goals and be recognized for your achievements to give your self-concept a boost. In what situations might your self-concept improve?

Here are some qualities that can help you build a positive self-concept:

- **Honesty** Tell the truth and be sincere to show your honesty. Honesty is the quality of communicating truthfully.
- **Thoughtfulness** Think about how your actions affect other people. Help others without being asked. Remember to say "please" and "thank you."
- **Cheerfulness** Being cheerful means being happy, friendly, and seeing the bright side of life. Cheerful people are pleasant and optimistic.
- **Responsibility** Show that you are responsible by doing your homework and chores, and being home on time. It also means being accountable, or accepting the consequences of your actions.
- **Self-Control** Think before you act, and set limits to practice self-control. Use your knowledge of right and wrong to guide your actions.

- **Adaptability** If you are adaptable, you can adjust to different situations at school, at home, or at work.
- **Compassion** Care about others when they are hurting. Let them know that you care to show compassion.
- **Cooperation** Doing what a teacher or parent asks you to do is cooperation.
- **Courtesy** Be considerate and respectful to others.
- **Dependability** Being a person others can count on shows dependability.
- **Enthusiasm** Show that you are willing and eager to do you part at school, at home, and at work.
- **Friendliness** Say hello and smile to show your friendliness to others.
- **Generosity** Be willing to give what you can to others.
- **Sincerity** Always be yourself.

Building Self-Esteem

When you have a positive self-concept or self-image, you like yourself. In turn, you will develop self-esteem. **Self-esteem** is a sense of confidence and self-worth. If you have respect, or value, for yourself, you can use your own judgment, resist peer pressure, and achieve your goals. Learn to recognize the things you do well. Be realistic about your expectations. No one does everything well. Give yourself credit for your success. Look at your mistakes as opportunities to learn and grow.

How do you feel when someone criticizes you? Do you become defensive? The ability to accept criticism is vital, or very important, to your success in life, at home, at school, at work, and in the community. **Constructive criticism** is helpful advice. It is meant to help you grow and improve and often includes suggestions for solutions. For example, if your music teacher suggests a different song to fit your voice, you could improve your performance by following that advice. Learning to accept constructive criticism is a good way to improve your self-esteem.

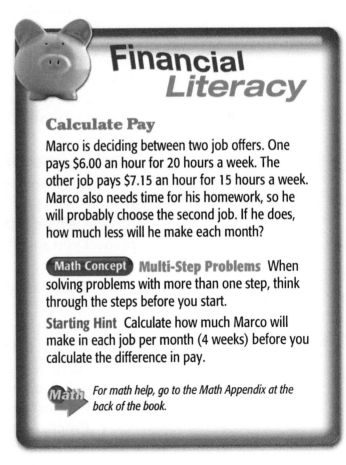

Financial Literacy

Calculate Pay

Marco is deciding between two job offers. One pays $6.00 an hour for 20 hours a week. The other job pays $7.15 an hour for 15 hours a week. Marco also needs time for his homework, so he will probably choose the second job. If he does, how much less will he make each month?

Math Concept **Multi-Step Problems** When solving problems with more than one step, think through the steps before you start.

Starting Hint Calculate how much Marco will make in each job per month (4 weeks) before you calculate the difference in pay.

For math help, go to the Math Appendix at the back of the book.

D. Hurst/Alamy

Show Responsibility

Each day you make many choices. You are responsible for your own behavior and actions. You can show responsibility by making wise choices. For example, you can take care of your health by choosing to eat healthful foods, to exercise, and to get enough rest. At school you can choose to complete your school-work on time and to try to do your best. The more you show responsibility, the more freedom and trust you may be given in the future. Here are a few ways you can show responsibility:

- **Obey rules.** Families, schools, and communities have rules that help maintain order and keep people safe. You act responsibly when you follow the rules.
- **Help others.** Responsible people look out for their families, friends, and neighbors, not just for themselves. If you see someone in trouble, try to get help.
- **Keep your promises.** If you told a friend that you would help him study for a test, you need to keep that promise. In this way, you will show friends and others that they can count on you.
- **Carry out tasks.** If it is your job to clear the table, do it without being told. When you see other tasks that need to be done, do them. Do not wait to be asked. This shows maturity.

Being responsible is one of the most important qualifications for success in any job. Being responsible means getting to work on time, even when you would rather sleep late or spend time with friends. It means being familiar with the tasks of your job and doing them correctly.

Learning Responsibility

Not everyone has the same responsibilities, and your responsibilities will change over time. Learning responsibility can be hard, but it has many rewards. Other people will respect you and start treating you like an adult. Follow these guidelines for success:

- **Understand expectations.** Find out what is expected of you. Listen carefully. Ask questions if you do not understand.
- **Get advice from role models.** Ask good adult role models to help you learn the right thing to do.
- **Take on new tasks.** You can avoid stress if you take on new tasks gradually and do not take on too much at once.
- **Practice patience.** Be patient with yourself. If you forget to do something or do it wrong, learn from your mistake and try harder the next time.

Certain characteristics go along with being responsible. Which of these characteristics do you have? Responsible people:

- Are reliable.
- Keep their word.
- Show respect for other people and their property.
- Are trustworthy.
- Admit their mistakes and do not blame others.

Your Value System

The way you meet your needs and wants is based on your values. Values are your beliefs about right and wrong and about what is important in life. Most people share some common values, such as a good family life, trust, freedom, and health. Other values are individual, such as being a good student and playing a sport well.

Needs

You have the same basic needs that all people have. Physical needs are basic to your survival and well-being. They include food, clothing, and shelter. You also have emotional needs such as feeling safe and secure. These needs also include a sense of belonging and the need to be loved and accepted by other people. When your emotional needs are met, you feel good about yourself.

Positive Focus
Avoid Comparisons
You can learn from other people by observing their successes. Remember that each person is unique, and each person has his or her strengths. Do your best without comparing yourself to your friends, family, or other students in your classes.

Brand X Pictures/Alamy

Be Responsible Helping others shows responsibility. *What can you do to show that you are a responsible person?*

According to psychologist Abraham Maslow's Hierarchy of Human Needs, you also need self-actualization (see **Figure 1.2**). **Self-actualization** (self-ˌak-ch(ə-w)ə-lə-ˈzā-shən) means to reach your full potential. When you aim to reach your full potential, you increase your chances for success. Use your skills, talents, and abilities to achieve your goals in life.

Personal strengths and abilities have a direct impact on the choices you make. For example, a courageous person is more likely to take risks. A creative person is likely to choose a career in the arts. What are your personal strengths and abilities?

Figure 1.2 Abraham Maslow's Hierarchy of Human Needs

Level of Needs Maslow's theory of basic human needs suggests that needs are defined by stages. *Which stage are you in right now?*

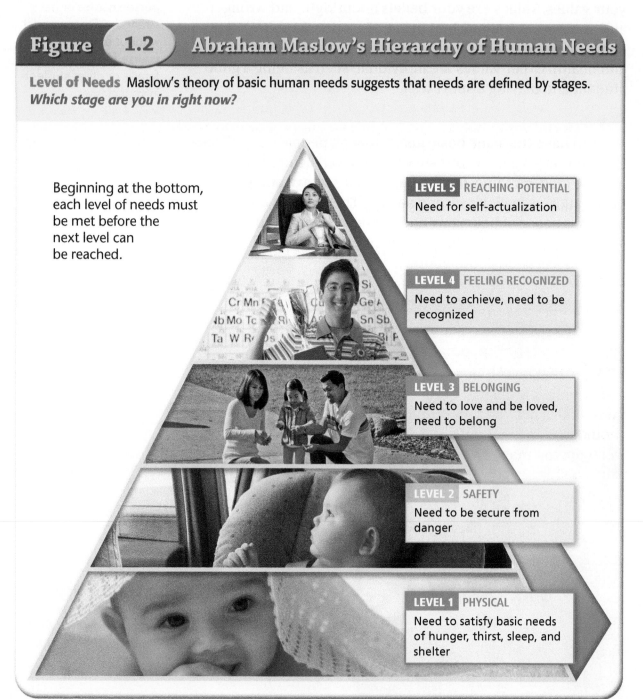

Beginning at the bottom, each level of needs must be met before the next level can be reached.

LEVEL 5 REACHING POTENTIAL
Need for self-actualization

LEVEL 4 FEELING RECOGNIZED
Need to achieve, need to be recognized

LEVEL 3 BELONGING
Need to love and be loved, need to belong

LEVEL 2 SAFETY
Need to be secure from danger

LEVEL 1 PHYSICAL
Need to satisfy basic needs of hunger, thirst, sleep, and shelter

Wants

Wants are different from needs. Wants are things that you would like to have, but are not necessary for survival. You may want the latest movie or video game, but you can live without it.

Sometimes people confuse wants and needs. Have you ever wanted something so much that you convinced yourself that you really needed it? Perhaps you felt that you could not live without a new outfit. Did you really need it, or was it something you simply wanted to have?

Values

Like most people, you probably grew up sharing your family's values about tradition, culture, religion, education, and marriage. Your values are the beliefs and principles you choose to live by. Your values define who you are, shape your attitudes and your choices, and help you identify your priorities. Values are usually influenced by family, religious beliefs, teachers, friends, society, and personal experiences. Perhaps your family places a value on how birthdays and holidays are celebrated. A good family life is a common value shared by most people.

People have different values because their interests and experiences are different. People come from a variety of backgrounds. The way you prioritize your values may also be different from the way others prioritize their values. Prioritize means to rank or order things by their importance. For example, some people put a high priority on regular exercise and healthful eating.

You should respect other people's values, even though their values may be different from yours. Other people should also respect your values. Knowing what you value will help you make good decisions. As you develop your value system, you may notice that some of your values are in conflict with each other. For example, you may spend the afternoon finishing a math assignment because you value good grades. What if your friends invite you to the movies that same afternoon? You will have to decide which value is more important. Is it completing your math homework or is it being with your friends? What you value says a lot about you.

Reading Check *Contrast How are wants different from needs?*

Emotional Changes

An important part of your personality is related to your emotions. An emotion is a strong feeling about someone or something. If you understand your emotions and why they change, you will better understand yourself.

You have many emotions. You may feel pleased and excited when you do something well. You may feel sad or frustrated when things do not go as expected or hoped.

One of the difficult things about emotions is that you may experience more than one at the same time. You may feel both excited and scared about being in a school play. You may feel proud that a college accepted your sister, yet sad that she will be going away. Having two different emotions at the same time can make it hard to sort out your feelings.

Adolescence (a-də-ˈle-sən(t)s) is the period of great growth and change between childhood and adulthood. During adolescence you will be adjusting to many physical and emotional changes. For example, your emotions will seem stronger and harder to control. This is because your body is developing and changing. Your feelings may be hurt more easily. You may also feel ignored or become irritated easily. Sometimes you will feel happy and want to be with your friends. At other times you may want to be alone and not talk to anyone. Adjusting to new emotions can be challenging. When your moods are constantly changing, it may seem as if you lack control over your life. Instead, you can learn to handle your emotions.

Dealing with Your Emotions

Even though these new and changing emotions are difficult to understand, you should not let them rule your life. For example, everyone feels angry at times. However, it is the way you handle your emotions that is most important. Try these healthy ways to deal with your emotions:

- Admit how you feel and why you feel that way.
- Talk about your feelings with a family member, friend, teacher, or counselor.
- Write down your feelings in a journal.
- Work off your feelings by doing something physical, such as taking a walk.
- If you are angry with another person, wait until you have cooled off before speaking to him or her. Tell the person how you feel and what you need or want.

Reading Check *Identify What is one healthy way to deal with your emotions?*

Physical Changes

Physical changes in height, weight, and body shape occur during adolescence. You may notice that you or your friends seem to grow inches overnight. Sometimes the different parts of your body do not all grow at the same rate. It can be frustrating when your body is constantly changing and growing. Just when you get used to it one way, it changes again. These rapid changes can make you feel awkard and clumsy. Remember that everyone grows at his or her own rate. Your classmates are growing and changing, too. A positive self-concept can help you adjust to the changes that happen during adolescence.

↑ Understand
Emotions Two people can have different emotions about the same news. *Why is it important to understand your emotions?*

Section 1.1 After You Read

Review What You Have Learned

1. **Name** two examples of inherited traits.
2. **Explain** how personality is shown.
3. **Describe** ways your emotions are affected during adolescence.
4. **Name** two physical changes that can happen during adolescence.

Practice Academic Skills

English Language Arts

5. Talk with your family about the traits that you and your family share. Write a list of traits, and next to each trait write whether it is inherited or cultural.

Social Studies

6. Imagine that you have a younger brother or sister. Write a paragraph to describe what you and your family can do to help the child develop a positive self-concept.

✦ Check Your Answers Check Your Answers at ConnectED.mcgraw-hill.com.

Section 1.2 Grooming and Personal Care

Reading Guide

Before You Read

Preview Look at the photos and figures in this section and read their captions. Write one or two sentences predicting what the section will be about.

Read to Learn

Key Concepts

✓ **Describe** the importance of personal grooming.

✓ **Explain** the significance of first impressions.

Main Idea

To look your best, it is important to practice good grooming skills and present a positive attitude.

Content Vocabulary

○ grooming
○ hygiene
○ acne
○ dermatologist
○ cavity

Academic Vocabulary

■ durability
■ opinion

Graphic Organizer

As you read, list the five areas that you should care for when grooming. Use a graphic organizer like the one shown to help you organize your information.

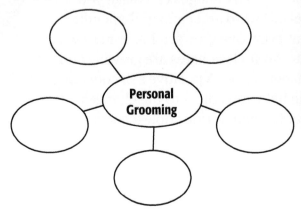

Personal Grooming

Graphic Organizer Go to ConnectED. mcgraw-hill.com to download this graphic organizer.

Taking care of your physical appearance affects the way other people see you. It also affects the way you feel about yourself. When you look your best, you feel more self-confident and you are more likely to make a positive impression on people. Grooming and personal care includes caring for your skin, hair, hands, feet, and teeth. Being clean contributes to your health. You will learn how being well-groomed can help you make a good impression when you meet people.

Personal Grooming

How many ads have you seen about grooming aids for teens? **Grooming** includes the things you do to care for your physical appearance. Advertisements may lead you to believe that it takes time, money, and certain products to look good. The fact is that you can look your best by following a basic grooming and hygiene routine every day. **Hygiene** is keeping yourself clean. Take care of your skin, hair, hands, feet, nails, and teeth. Make sure your clothing is neat and clean. Although there are physical features that you cannot change, such as your height, you can still look your best.

As You Read

Connect How can taking care of yourself now be important to your future?

Your Skin

During the teen years, the oil glands in your skin begin to work harder. The extra oil can clog your pores and cause skin problems such as acne. **Acne** is a common skin condition that occurs when pores are clogged with oil, dead skin cells, and bacteria. This can cause pimples on the face, back, and chest. Teens with severe acne may need to see a **dermatologist**, a doctor who treats skin disorders. To take good care of your skin, follow these tips:

Vocabulary

You can find definitions in the glossary at the back of this book.

- Get enough rest and exercise.
- Drink six to eight glasses of water each day.
- Bathe every day.
- Wash your face and neck with mild soap and water at least twice a day.
- Use deodorant or antiperspirant daily.
- Do not pick at or squeeze pimples.
- Choose grooming products that do not irritate your skin. Look for products that are labeled *mild* or *hypoallergenic*.
- Protect your skin from the sun. Use a sunscreen with a sun protection factor (SPF) of at least 15. Reapply the sunscreen after you swim or if you perspire, or sweat.

Your Hair

For many teens, hair is a way to express personality. Whatever hairstyle you prefer, your hair is most attractive when it is clean and healthy. Here are some ways to care for your hair:

- Wash and brush or comb your hair regularly.
- Choose a shampoo made for your type of hair. Is your hair curly, fine, or chemically-treated?
- Shampoo your hair gently. Use your fingertips to work the lather through your hair. Rinse thoroughly.
- When using a conditioner after shampooing, follow the directions on the bottle.

Safety Check

Sunscreen
Being outdoors without sunscreen can cause painful sunburn and can lead to skin cancer with continued exposure. Use these tips for applying sunscreen:

- Always use a sun protection factor (SPF) of at least 15.
- Reapply after swimming or other physical activity.

Your Hands and Feet

Good grooming includes taking care of your hands and feet. Keep your nails clean and shaped to help prevent injuries and disease. To care for feet and hands:

- Wash your hands, feet, and nails with soap and water to remove dirt, dead skin, and germs.
- After washing, be sure to dry your feet thoroughly.
- Do not wear wet socks or shoes. This can cause bacteria to grow.
- Moisturize your hands and feet with lotion. Powder your feet to control odor.
- Trim and file your fingernails to shape them. Trim your toenails straight across to keep nails from growing into your skin.

Your Teeth

Your teeth affect not only your appearance but also your health. Your teeth help you chew food. Teeth shape your mouth and your smile. Taking care of your teeth can help prevent cavities and gum disease. A **cavity** is an area of decay in a tooth. The best way to avoid these problems is to keep your teeth clean. Follow these tips for healthy teeth:

- Choose a brush with soft bristles, and use a toothpaste that contains fluoride.
- To brush, use gentle up-and-down strokes to clean between the teeth and massage your gums.
- Floss your teeth once a day. Ask your dentist to show you the proper technique.
- Keep sweets to a minimum, especially between meals.
- Eat a balanced diet with nutritious foods.
- Get regular dental checkups.

Your Clothing

Clothing is form of self-expression. Clothing choices should be based on function, style, and durability, or how long it will last. You will learn more about clothing in Chapter 16. Here are some basics:

- Clothing should be clean and changed daily.
- Treat stains as soon as possible.
- Fix any rips or tears before they can get worse.
- Choose the appropriate clothing for each occasion.
- Mix and match separate pieces for new combinations.

Reading Check *Examine* *What should you do in your daily grooming routine to look your best?*

Take Care of Your Nails

In this activity you will work with a partner to give each other a manicure. Before you begin, read through the entire Hands-On Lab assignment. Write down any questions you may have about the activity. Reread the text or ask your teacher for help if you need it.

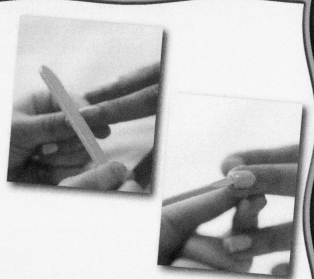

Supplies

✓ Nail polish remover (optional)
✓ Cotton balls
✓ Hand or cuticle cream
✓ Cuticle stick
✓ Nail clippers
✓ Nail file
✓ Nail buffer
✓ Nail brush

Develop Your Plan

- Gather your supplies and clean them according to your teacher's instructions.
- Partner with someone to give and receive a manicure.
- Review and discuss the steps below to give a manicure.
- Discuss what you and your partner will include in the manicure.

Implement Your Plan

- Remove any nail polish with the nail polish remover and cotton balls.
- Wash hands with a mild hand soap and warm water.

- Gently push back cuticles with a cuticle stick. If the cuticle does not move, soften it with cuticle or hand cream.
- Clip nails if necessary.
- Shape and file nails. File in one direction. Going back and forth can create small tears in the nail that may split.
- Use the nail buffer to buff and shine the nails. Gently rub the buffer back and forth across the top of each nail.
- Wash hands and nails again.

Evaluate Your Results

Describe your manicure experience. How do your nails look? What would you change if you were to do the manicure again? Write a paragraph to explain your answer.

Projects and Activities Go to connectED.mcgraw-hill.com.

(l & r)Ingram Publishing

First Impressions

All people show certain personality traits, such as polite or rude, accepting or judgmental. Most people show a little bit of all of these traits at one time or another. It is natural to express different traits in different settings. For example, strangers may be more likely to judge each other than they judge friends. How do you want new people to see you? **Figure 1.3** offers tips for how to make a good first impression with a positive attitude.

People form an **opinion**, or judgment, about you the first time they meet you. This instant opinion is called a first impression. It is based on the way you look, dress, talk, and behave. First impressions are important because they help people decide whether they want to know you better. What type of first impression do you make when you are considerate of others? In contrast, what do people think if you use poor table manners?

Figure 1.3 Make an Impression with Your Attitude

Build a Positive Attitude It is not always easy to think positively, but when you make the effort, the results can be worthwhile. *What can you do to turn your attitude around when you are feeling negative?*

- **Take positive action.** Just taking the first steps toward improving your attitude can make you feel better.

- **Talk positively.** If things do not go as planned, remind yourself that you can learn from the experience. Say to yourself, "What can I do better next time?"

- **Accept yourself.** You have weaknesses as well as strengths. Forgive yourself for mistakes and learn from them. Reward yourself for the things you do well.

- **Stay open to learning.** Learning new skills and knowledge increases your self-esteem.

- **Reach out to others.** Develop good relationships with lots of different people. Seek role models who are positive thinkers. Do not try to be exactly like other people. Instead, adjust your attitude to match their positive qualities.

- **Assert yourself.** You have a right to speak up and act on your beliefs. Maintain a positive environment by saying what you think and feel in ways that are not offensive or hurtful.

- **Accept and respect others as they are.** By treating people with respect, you show that you think of them as worthwhile individuals.

© Pascal Broze/SuperStock

First impressions are not always accurate. When people have a chance to get to know you better, they may change their opinion. Sometimes, however, the first impression is the only chance you have to make a good impression.

Attitude and Your Appearance

Have you ever met an attractive person who became unattractive to you because he or she was mean, had bad manners, or did not treat you well? Perhaps you have met a person you first thought was unattractive, but he or she started to look better to you because of a great personality. This is because your attitude can affect the way you look. If you are often unhappy, angry, or bitter, it can show on your face and in the way you carry yourself. People are not attracted to negativity. On the other hand, if you smile, feel happy, and have a positive self-concept, you will probably find that people are drawn to you because you have traits they admire.

Looking Your Best Practice good grooming to help you make a positive first impression. *What other habits can help you make a good first impression?*

Section 1.2 After You Read

Review What You Have Learned

1. **List** five things about your personal appearance that require daily care.
2. **Describe** what may be noticed when someone makes a first impression.

Practice Academic Skills

English Language Arts

3. Create a poster that shows how to care for your skin, hair, hands and feet, or teeth. Use information from your text and pictures clipped from magazines.

Social Studies

4. Write a paragraph about the first impression you had of someone. What did you notice about his or her appearance and personality? What could you tell about his or her culture? What opinions did you form about him or her based on your first impression? Did your opinions change later? If so, why?

· ·

Check Your Answers Check Your Answers at connectED.mcgraw-hill.com.

Discovering Careers

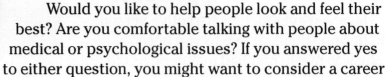

Would you like to help people look and feel their best? Are you comfortable talking with people about medical or psychological issues? If you answered yes to either question, you might want to consider a career in personal health and hygiene. The following chart explores several careers in the personal health and hygiene industry.

Career Activities ▼

At School

1 Select three of the careers listed. Research the education, training, and work experience required for each career. Write a summary of your results.

At Home

2 Prepare a pamphlet for your family that explains the importance of properly caring for teeth and gums. Use images from magazines as illustrations. Share the pamphlet with your classmates.

At Work

3 A positive self-concept can help you perform well on the job. How can honesty, thoughtfulness, cheerfulness, responsibility, and self-control benefit you at work? Write one sentence for each quality and discuss them with your classmates.

In the Community

4 Contact and interview someone in your community who works in the personal care industry. Ask this person to describe what his or her typical work day is like. Share what you learned with your class.

Job Title	Job Description
Psychologist	Provides counseling. Assists individuals in achieving personal, social, educational, and vocational adjustments. Collects data through interviews and observation.
Dermatologist	Diagnoses and treats diseases of the skin, hair, and nails. Requires medical degree with specialization.
Dentist	Diagnoses and treats diseases, injuries, and malformations of teeth, gums, and related oral structures. Provides education in oral and dental hygiene.
Theatrical Makeup Artist	Applies makeup to performers to enhance appearance. Consults with photographers and stage and motion picture supervisors.
Cosmetologist	Provides beauty services for customers. Styles hair by cutting, trimming, and tapering. Suggests current styles or listens to customer's instructions.

Chapter Summary

Section 1.1 You Are Unique

During your teen years you start to become your own person. You experience emotional and physical changes, and you develop your own values. Family, friends, and culture influence who you are. Your personality shows in your appearance and your actions. A positive self-concept helps you cope with life. You are responsible for your own behavior and actions.

Section 1.2 Grooming and Personal Care

Taking care of your physical appearance contributes to the way other people see you. Grooming and personal care include caring for your skin, hair, hands, feet, and teeth. When you are clean, you are more likely to be healthy. Being well-groomed can help you make a good impression when you meet people for the first time. A good attitude can affect the impression you make.

Words You Learned

1. Use each of these content vocabulary words and academic vocabulary words in a sentence.

Content Vocabulary
- heredity (p. 8)
- culture (p. 8)
- self-concept (p. 10)
- self-esteem (p. 11)
- constructive criticism (p. 11)
- self-actualization (p. 14)
- adolescence (p. 16)
- grooming (p. 19)
- hygiene (p. 19)
- acne (p. 19)
- dermatologist (p. 19)
- cavity (p. 20)

Academic Vocabulary
- respect (p. 11)
- potential (p. 14)
- durability (p. 20)
- opinion (p. 22)

Review Key Concepts

2. **List** factors that influence who you are.

3. **Name** the qualities that make people unique individuals.

4. **Analyze** why it is important to understand emotions.

5. **Describe** the physical changes that happen during adolescence.

6. **Describe** the importance of personal grooming.

7. **Explain** the significance of first impressions.

Critical Thinking

8. **Describe** how your actions reveal which values are most important to you.

9. **Compare and contrast** needs and wants.

Real-World Skills and Applications

Problem-Solving

10. Choose Hair Care Products Sarah needs to buy products for her hair. She likes the way her friends do their hair, so she asked them what products they like to use. One friend has thick, curly hair, and her other friend's hair is fine and straight. Sarah has curly hair, but she uses a straightener at least once a week. How should Sarah decide what products she should buy for her hair?

Interpersonal and Collaborative

11. Research Adolescence Follow your teacher's instructions to form into teams. Work together to research the physical changes teens experience during adolescence. How do these changes affect relationships with family and friends? How can teens cope with these changes? Present your findings to your class.

Financial Literacy

12. Comparison Shopping There is an almost endless supply of personal care products available. Some are necessary, such as shampoo and toothpaste, and others may not be necessary. Think before you buy. Ask yourself if you really need the product. Maybe you want it because your friends use it or the advertising looks good. Also think about prices and your budget. Visit the hair care section of a supermarket or drugstore. Pick three different shampoos that you would consider using for your hair. Calculate and compare the price per ounce of each product. Which product is the best buy? Why? Share the information with your class.

13. Positive Self-Concept Much of your success depends on developing a positive self-concept. Cut out images from magazines and create a collage that represents the way you see yourself. Include images that show influences on your personality, such as heredity, environment, your experiences, and your culture. Share your collage with your class.

14. Stain Removal To care for your clothing, you may need to treat stains. Think about your daily activities. What kinds of stains might cause problems for you? Pen ink, grass, mud, or salad oil? Make a list of common stains. Then conduct research to find ways to remove stains from clothing. Write a one- or two-page guide that explains how to remove stains. Use graphics or drawings to illustrate your guide.

15. International Cultures Sometimes people do not think about their own culture until they experience other cultures. For example, you may not have tried *kielbasa* (sausage) or *pierogis* (dumplings) unless you have been to a traditional Polish wedding. Conduct research to become familiar with another culture of your choice. Write two or more paragraphs to describe what you learned about the other culture. Include information about traditions, foods, and beliefs.

D.Hurst/Alamy

Academic Skills

English Language Arts

16. Constructive Criticism Role-Play
Follow your teacher's instructions to form small groups. Work with your group to develop situations in which constructive criticism would be helpful. The situation might be helping a sibling develop a new skill, or helping a friend practice an oral presentation. Each group member should play a part. Write a script and act out the role-play for the rest of the class.

Science

17. Examine a Problem Taking care of your teeth can help prevent cavities and gum disease.
Procedure Conduct research on the results of poor dental hygiene. Find out about ways to maintain the health of your teeth.
Analysis Make a chart to show what can happen if you do not take proper care of your teeth and gums. Write a list of tips to keep your teeth healthy.

Mathematics

18. Calculate a Budget People who maintain budgets can often avoid money troubles. Imagine that you are living on your own and need to make a personal budget that includes your needs and wants. After making a list of the things you need and the things you want, you determine that your basic needs require 75 percent of your monthly income. Your wants cost 15 percent. If your monthly income is $2,000, how much are you spending on wants?

Math Concept **Multiply Dollars by Percents** A percent is a ratio that compares a number to 100.

Starting Hint To multiply percentages, first rewrite the percent (15%) as a fraction. The numerator is 15 and the denominator is 100. Convert the fraction to a decimal. Multiply this decimal by the number ($2,000). Remember to put the decimal point in the correct place in your answer.

Standardized Test Practice

Timed Writing
Read and answer the question in five minutes. Use a separate sheet of paper for your answer.

Test-Taking Tip When taking a timed writing, first read the question carefully to see what needs to be included in your response. Then write a quick plan or outline to follow as you write.

19. A person's self-concept includes many qualities. Choose a quality from this chapter that you think is the most important for your own self-concept. Explain why the quality is important to you and give examples of how you show that quality in your own life.

Chapter 2

Your Family

Section 2.1

Family Characteristics

■ **Main Idea** Families come in many forms, but each family provides structure, comfort, and a place to learn about the responsibilities of life.

Section 2.2

Changes in the Family

■ **Main Idea** Families experience different kinds of changes, but they can use positive strategies to adjust.

Explore the Photo

Families are the building blocks of your future. *What word best describes what family means to you?*

Prewriting

Support A supportive person helps others by offering service, assistance, or encouragement. Imagine that you need to write an essay about how your family supports one another. Prewrite to help you organize your thoughts. Make a list of qualities that supportive families have. Choose the qualities that are most important to you to use in a future essay.

Writing Tips To prewrite effectively, follow these steps:

1. Freewrite as many qualities as you can.
2. List the qualities and see how they relate to each other.
3. Underline the most important qualities only after you have finished your list.

29

Section 2.1 Family Characteristics

Reading Guide

Before You Read

Preview Choose a Content or Academic Vocabulary word that is new to you. When you find it in the text, write down the definition.

Read to Learn

Key Concepts

✓ **List** seven different family types.

✓ **Identify** four skills that can help you get along with people.

✓ **Explain** ways to show responsibility.

Main Idea

Families come in many forms, but each provides structure, comfort, and a place to learn about the responsibilities of life.

Content Vocabulary

○ environment
○ tradition
○ stereotype
○ sibling
○ responsible

Academic Vocabulary

■ reserved
■ enrich

Graphic Organizer

As you read, list ten ways family relationships can be improved. Use a graphic organizer like the one shown to help you organize your information.

Improve Family Relationships
1. _____
2. _____
3. _____
4. _____
5. _____
6. _____
7. _____
8. _____
9. _____
10. _____

Graphic Organizer Go to **connectED.mcgraw-hill.com** to download this graphic organizer.

What comes to mind when you think of family? How do you define family? Is it being together for a holiday? Is it the group of people living next door? Perhaps you think of a large family with lots of children. There are many kinds of families.

Family Structures

The form a family takes is called a structure. The structure can affect the way a family functions. Family structures change over time. Describe each person in your family and his or her relationship to you. Your description will probably match one of the family types in **Figure 2.1.**

The conditions that surround you are your **environment**. No matter what family structure you have, a healthy family environment can be a source of happiness and growth for its members. As you read about families, you will notice that families are as different as the people in them. What really matters is what happens inside the family. Within the family, people gain skills, strength, and knowledge to help them succeed in society.

Healthy families care about each member and work together as a team. Family members work together to:

- Provide food, clothing, and a place to live.
- Create a loving and welcoming environment.
- Encourage independence.
- Teach values and life skills.
- Give friendship, guidance, and support.

As You Read

Connect How does your family structure affect the relationships within your family?

Vocabulary

You can find definitions in the glossary at the back of this book.

Figure 2.1 Family Types

Unique Family Structure Families can be as different as the people in them. *What can happen to change a family's structure?*

Nuclear Family	Includes two parents and one or more children.
Single-parent Family	One parent and one or more children.
Blended Family	Formed when two people marry and at least one person has a child or children from a previous marriage.
Adoptive Family	A family with a child or children who are made a permanent part of the family through legal action.
Foster Family	A family that temporarily takes care of a child or children.
Legal Guardian	A person who has financial and legal duties to care for a child or children.
Extended Family	One or two parents and children as well as other relatives, such as grandparents or aunts and uncles.

Celebrate Traditions The traditions you follow as a family can strengthen your values and relationships. *What traditions do you enjoy with your family?*

COMMUNITY CONNECTIONS

Family Team Organize a family team to raise money for a community cause. Your family can spend time training and preparing for the event. Working together for a good cause will help your family bond and will help your community as well.

Your Unique Family

The people who make up your family have different skills, talents, and personalities. For example, your father may be an artist. Your sister may play on the soccer team and enjoy reading. Your brother may play in a band and have an outgoing personality. The skills, talents, and personalities of its members make each family unique.

People within families have different ways of expressing, or showing, their emotions. Some show their love for each other openly. They may hug one another and say "I love you" to show affection. Others may be more reserved, or shy. This does not mean that families who do not hug feel less love. They just show it in different ways.

A **tradition** is a custom or belief. Traditions are often passed from previous generations, such as your grandparents and their families. Traditions can influence holiday celebrations, food choices, and religious practices. It is important to understand that customs and traditions can be different without being wrong. An idea about the qualities or behavior of a certain group of people is a **stereotype**. Do not let negative stereotypes keep you from getting to know people and letting them get to know you.

Reading Check   *Define What is a family structure?*

Family Relationships

Families can become closer when family members spend time together. Get involved in each other's daily lives. Share your activities, hobbies, and interests. Characteristics of positive family relationships are easy to spot. Does your family have these positive characteristics?

- Support one another.
- Laugh and play together.
- Share responsibilities.
- Trust one another.
- Respect one another.

Think about the activities you like to share with your parents. Are there things you enjoy doing with your siblings? A **sibling** is a brother or a sister. Share daily events, such as talking about what happened at school, to help strengthen and promotoe satisfying family relationships. Other ways to enrich, or improve, family life include:

- Attend religious services.
- Create new traditions.
- Plan special celebrations.
- Discuss books, movies, and current events.
- Sit down together for meals as often as possible.

Family Ties Spending time together can bring family members closer. *What are some activities that family members can enjoy together?*

Family members do things to help each other. When her mother had a baby, Maya helped out by making dinner each night. Maya's actions increased the bonds of the family unit. Strong family relationships are especially helpful during difficult times. For example, when a family member becomes ill, it is helpful when the rest of the family pitches in to help and is supportive. It is also important to have fun and enjoy each other's company. **Figure 2.2** illustrates just a few ideas for fun activities families can do at home.

Figure 2.2 Family Activities

Enrich Your Family Life Families can find a variety of ways to spend quality time together at home. *What kinds of activities do you and your family do at home?*

Family Meals It is not unusual in American society to feel too busy for regular sit-down meals with your family. However, it is important to share meals to encourage family closeness.

Movie Night Make popcorn, turn out the lights, and enjoy a movie together at home. Discuss the movie as a family afterwards.

Game Time If weather allows, go outside and play a game. If that is not possible, play cards or a board game inside.

(t)Radius Images/Alamy; (c & b)Hero/Corbis/Glow Images

Getting Along with People

Within your family, you learn and develop the character skills of consideration, cooperation, reliability, and respect. These skills can help you get along with family members. These skills also can help prepare you for relationships with people at school, at work, and in the community.

- **Consideration** Think about other people and their feelings. Treat people the same way you would like to be treated.
- **Cooperation** When you cooperate, you work with others to achieve a common goal. It means doing what is asked of you, and doing what needs to be done to finish a task or a project.
- **Reliability** Do you do what you say you will do? People like to know they can depend on you. Prove to them that you will keep your word. When you are reliable, people will trust you to do what is expected of you.
- **Respect** Think about someone you admire. It may be a friend, a family member, a teacher, a coach, or a community leader. How would you treat such a person? If you have respect for someone, it shows in your behavior. You are kind, you listen to opinions, and you consider the thoughts and feelings of others.

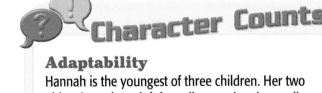

Character Counts

Adaptability

Hannah is the youngest of three children. Her two older sisters have left for college and no longer live at home. She finally has her room and her parents all to herself! Then, her parents announce that they are going to have another child. It is a surprise to everyone, but they will all have to adapt. Hannah was expecting to be the center of attention with her sisters being away. Now a baby is on the way, and she feels resentful and angry that the baby will be the new focus of the family.

You Make the Call

Should Hannah keep her feelings to herself? Write a paragraph that explains what you think Hannah should do.

Share Space

How can the character skills listed above help you at home? Whether you are sharing a bedroom, a bathroom, or the kitchen, you must work with other family members to keep shared spaces organized and clean. Sharing space will be easier if you follow these guidelines:

- **Be considerate of others.** Show your consideration by not leaving your belongings in someone else's way. When you finish using the kitchen or the bathroom, be sure to clean up after yourself.
- **Cooperate with family members.** Is there a "morning rush hour" at your house? This can happen when several family members try to get ready for work or school at the same time. The morning will go more smoothly if everyone agrees on a schedule.

MATH YOU CAN USE

Schedule Your Morning

Four people in your home need to be ready for breakfast by 7:30 A.M. Each person needs the bathroom for 15 minutes. Make a schedule for the bathroom so that everyone can be ready in one hour.

Math Concept **Adding Up Time** When you add time, remember that there are 60 minutes in 1 hour.

Starting Hint Start by subtracting 60 minutes, or 1 hour, from 7:30 to determine that the first person would get the bathroom at 6:30.

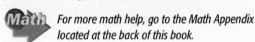 For more math help, go to the Math Appendix located at the back of this book.

- **Show that you are reliable.** As a member of a family, you are expected to participate in the activities that keep a household running smoothly. Family members need to rely on each other to do their share of the work, such as washing dishes, caring for pets, and remembering to turn out the lights.
- **Respect other people's privacy.** If someone's door is closed, knock and wait for a response before entering. Keep your music or television turned low, or use headphones at a safe volume if another person wants to sleep or study. Never read another person's mail or look through someone else's belongings without their permission.

Rights of Family Members

Each family member has the right to expect support, understanding, trust, and respect from other family members. Supportive families make sure each member's rights are respected and expectations are met. When these basic needs are not met, relationships suffer. It is important to support each family member's emotional needs.

Your Parents

As you move toward independence, it helps to understand that your parents are people, too. They, too, are working toward goals. Perhaps they are going back to school, or saving for a family vacation or their retirement. Sometimes parents face work problems, financial difficulties, or health issues. Just like you, they have good days and bad days. It helps to recognize your parents' point of view. If you give your parents love and understanding, family life is more likely to go smoothly.

Communication with your parents is especially important during your teen years. Talk openly to them about your problems, thoughts, and concerns. People who know each other well, such as parents and their children, may believe that they can read each other's minds. This can lead to misunderstandings. Do not try to guess what your parents are thinking. Talk to them and listen to them. Open communication can help both you and your parents understand one another's feelings.

Your Siblings

You love your brothers and sisters. However, there are times when you may not get along. Here are some suggestions to help you get along with your siblings:

- Avoid teasing them.
- Speak kindly.
- Respect their rights as family members.
- Give them compliments and encouragement.
- Share your belongings with them, and ask permission before you use or borrow their belongings.
- Do your share of the chores.

Older Relatives

Grandparents and great-grandparents are part of your extended family. They may live with you, nearby, or far away. You can benefit when you interact regularly with your older relatives. Perhaps your grandparents enjoy taking you out to the movies, to sporting events, or on a camping trip. Some grandparents take on a parenting role by caring for grandchildren while parents work.

Whether young or old, everyone can enjoy shared activities such as board games, gardening, or cooking. Take advantage of the time you have with grandparents and older relatives. They can share family stories, traditions, and history. Ask an older relative if they have family photo albums you can look at. When grandparents live far away, letters, phone calls, and e-mails can maintain a long-distance relationship.

Reading Check   *Explain* *How can you respect the space of other family members in your home?*

Blend Images/Alamy

Share Activities
Your grandparents and other older relatives have many experiences and much knowledge to share. *How can you learn about their life experiences?*

Family Responsibilities

Society works in many ways to help families with their
needs. Society provides resources such as education, health
care, and law enforcement to help strengthen and protect
families. However, these resources cannot do everything.
Families and the individuals within each family need to take
active roles as well. Strong families can help society grow
stronger. What can you do? Being part of a family means being
responsible for yourself and also showing responsible behav-
ior to your family. If you are **responsible**, you are dependable
and you make wise choices. The values you learn from your
family can be applied to your life away from home.

At Home

The people who care for you work hard to provide food,
to pay for utilities, and to offer the comforts of home. You can
show responsible behavior as well as respect when you take
care of the things in your home. There are little things you can
do, such as remember to turn off lights and keep your room
clean and neat. Regular chores are not punishment. They are
part of being in a family, and every member has to do his or
her share. Follow your family's rules, and do your chores with-
out being asked and without complaining. These actions can
help show your family that you are responsible and on your
way toward more independence.

Discover International...

Adoption

Building Your Family

There are many parents in developing
nations who do not have the means
to support a child. Parents in difficult
situations, such as extreme poverty or
unfair government practices, may choose
to allow a family in another country to adopt their child.
For the adopting family, it can be a difficult, emotionally
draining, and expensive process. It requires patience and
perseverance, and a willingness to accept risks. However, it
can be very rewarding. Not only do they have a new family
member to love, they also enrich their lives with the culture
of the child's native country.

perseverance
['pèr-sə-'vir-ən(t)s] steady and
continued course of action or belief
over a long period of time, usually
accompanied by difficulties, dangers,
or setbacks.

Science Photo Library/Alamy

Away from Home

If you learn respect, consideration, cooperation, dependability, and reliability from your family, you are likely to show these qualities away from home, too.

When you are at school, respect your teachers, coaches, and other students. Make smart decisions about avoiding drugs, tobacco, and alcohol. If you are going to be late, call home to let someone know. As you get older and move toward independence, you will probably get a job. The responsibilities you learn at home can help you to be responsible at work.

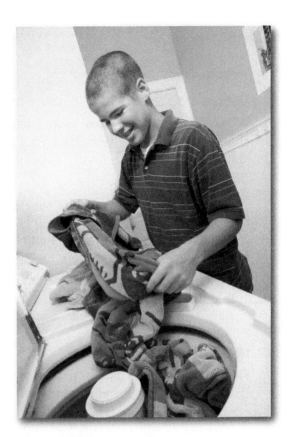

Show Responsibility Doing your chores without being asked shows responsibility. *What are some other ways you can show responsibility at home?*

Section 2.1 After You Read

Review What You Have Learned

1. **List** two examples of family traditions.
2. **Identify** at least three activities you can do with your family to help you learn and have fun.
3. **Explain** how your family prepares you to deal with responsibilities when you are away from home.

Practice Academic Skills

English Language Arts

4. Interview your parents, grandparents, or other relatives about a tradition in your family. How did the tradition start? Who was there when the tradition began? How does your family continue that tradition today? Write a paragraph about what you learned.

Social Studies

5. Conduct research to learn about the way another culture celebrates the birth of a new family member. How is it similar to the way you and your family celebrate? How is it different? Discuss how learning about other cultures can benefit you.

Check Your Answers Check Your Answers at connectED.mcgraw-hill.com.

Reading Guide

Before You Read

What You Want to Know Write a list of what you want to know about adjusting to family changes. As you read, write down the heads in this section that provide that information.

Read to Learn

Key Concepts

✓ **Outline** six changes that can happen in family life.

✓ **Describe** ways to adjust to the changes that can affect families.

Main Idea

Families experience different kinds of changes, and they can adjust through positive strategies.

Content Vocabulary

○ divorce
○ disability

Academic Vocabulary

■ adapt
■ advance

Graphic Organizer

As you read, identify four actions you can take to adjust to changes in your family. Use a graphic organizer like the one shown to help you organize your information.

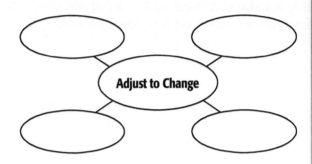

Adjust to Change

Graphic Organizer Go to connectED.mcgraw-hill.com to download this graphic organizer.

Change is a normal part of life. Think of how you have changed since you were a baby. Think of how your family has changed. Some changes are cause for celebration. Other changes may create hardships and challenges. As we grow, we learn to adjust and adapt to all kinds of changes with support from our families.

Changing Family Roles

As each person grows and changes, the rest of the family needs to **adapt**, or adjust to, the changes. Your roles change as family members grow and change. If your older sister leaves for college, you may find that you have more chores to do at home. You may also find that you have more time to spend with your parents. Sometimes the changes are planned or expected. Other times they come as a surprise. New family members may be born or adopted. Older brothers or sisters may move out of the home, or back home again. A grandparent may move in with your family. **Figure 2.3** describes the four stages of the family life cycle.

As You Read

Connect What part of the life cycle are you entering now?

Figure 2.3 The Family Life Cycle

Families Grow and Change Families experience common stages. *What are the changes that a family might go through at each stage?*

Beginning Stage Newly married couples get to know each other before children are born.

Parenting Stage Couples who choose to have children dedicate the parenting years to meeting the needs of their children.

Launching Stage Children grow older and more independent and leave home.

Senior Stage Parents adjust to being a couple again. People in the senior stage may retire, enjoy more leisure activities, and some may have grandchildren.

Make a Photo Journal

In this activity, you will create a photo journal about a special time you shared with your family. Before you begin, read through the entire Hands-On Lab assignment. Write down any questions that you may have about the activity. Reread the text or ask your teacher for help if you need it.

Supplies

- ✓ Scrapbook paper (one for each person, and one for the cover)
- ✓ Photographs and mementos of the special event or vacation
- ✓ Pens, markers, crayons
- ✓ Ribbons, yarns, or twine
- ✓ Glue stick
- ✓ Scissors or hole punch

Develop Your Plan

- ■ Set a time and place to do the project together.
- ■ Gather your supplies.
- ■ Ask your family to choose a special event or vacation.
- ■ Brainstorm memories about the occasion.

Implement Your Plan

- ■ Give each family member a sheet of scrapbook paper.
- ■ Have each person select 2 or 3 photos and glue them to the paper.

- ■ Add mementos, such as ticket stubs or postcards.
- ■ Have each person write captions for the photos.
- ■ Add bits of ribbon or yarn to decorate the pages.
- ■ Create a cover.
- ■ When everyone is finished, punch holes in the pages and add the cover.
- ■ Thread ribbon or yarn through the holes to tie the journal together.

Evaluate Your Results

Did your family members enjoy making the photo album? Did it turn out as you had planned? Why or why not? Is there anything you would change if you did the project again? Write one or more paragraphs to explain your answer.

Projects and Activities Go to **connectED.mcgraw-hill.com**.

Divorce

Families must learn to accept changes, even when they are painful. A **divorce** is the legal end to a marriage. When changes are the result of divorce, you may have to deal with one parent moving out. You also may also have to deal with a parent going to work for the first time. You may have to take on more responsibilities. You may feel more alone. Tell both of your parents how you are feeling. They are probably worried about the changes, too. You can reassure each other. Always remember that when parents divorce, it is not the fault of their children.

◤◇ Vocabulary

You can find definitions in the glossary at the back of this book.

Remarriage

After a divorce, one or both parents may remarry. This brings more changes. New stepbrothers or stepsisters may join the family. The newly formed couple may decide to have a child together. You are blending a new family and need to share games, space, and parents. You may also have to get used to a visitation schedule, which means going from one parent to the other. This may be difficult, but it will allow you to spend time with both of your parents.

When Justin's father remarried, his stepmother brought her two young children to live with Justin and his father. Now Justin has found himself in a new role as an older brother, and sometimes as a babysitter. What roles do you have within your family? How have your roles changed since you were in grammar school?

Job Loss

A parent may lose a job and the family may have less money to spend. When a parent loses a job, you may fear what will happen to your family. Your routine may be upset and you should discuss your feelings about it. You may not be able to provide money, but you can do your part. Be understanding if you have to cut back on your activities or purchases. Your parents will appreciate your efforts.

⟳ **Family Roles** As family roles change, you may find yourself with different responsibilities. *How might the addition of a younger stepbrother or stepsister change your responsibilities?*

Ingram Publishing

Special Challenges It can be difficult to know how to behave with someone in your family who is disabled. *What can you do to show support and understanding?*

Disabilities

You may have a sibling or parent with a disability. A **disability** is a permanent or temporary physical, mental, or emotional condition. Your family member may act out in a way that brings attention to your family. Understand that your family member cannot control his or her condition. Be supportive and loving. Look for ways to be helpful. Depending on the person's condition, encourage independence to help boost his or her confidence and self-esteem.

Serious Illness

When a family member is seriously ill, it can be very stressful for the whole family. Perhaps your brother or sister has cancer, or your mother has diabetes, or your father has heart disease. Constant trips to the doctor, reactions to medications, and dealing with constant pain are common.

Confide your fears in someone you trust, such as a parent, grandparent, religious leader, teacher, or another responsible adult. Find out what you can do to help. Perhaps you can choose quiet activities when the ill person is sleeping, take on extra chores, or read to the person.

Death

One of the most difficult changes for a family to deal with is the death of a family member. People can find it almost impossible to accept that a part of the family is gone. They sometimes feel guilty about what they did not say or do when the person was alive. These reactions are normal. Everyone in the family can support and comfort one another. Some families seek professional counseling to help them deal with the loss of a family member.

Get Feedback
Ask Your Teacher
Your teacher is most likely the best source to offer feedback on your schoolwork. He or she knows what you do best and how you can improve.

Reading Check *Explain How can you support family members during change?*

Realistic Reflections

Adjusting to Change

Not all changes are negative. Getting your own bedroom or making a new friend are examples of positive changes. No matter what changes occur in your life, you will have to adjust to them. Here are some positive ways to accept change:

- **Plan ahead.** If you know about a change in advance, or ahead of time, prepare for it even if you do not want it to happen. For example, if you are going to a new school, visit the school before your first day. You might even make a new friend before school starts.

- **Talk.** Discuss your feelings. Your family and friends can be a great source of strength and encouragement. Teachers, counselors, coaches, religious leaders, and family service workers can also help you understand and handle the change.

- **Be supportive.** When your family faces changes, you can help just by being there. If your brother is nervous about a new job, point out his strengths.

- **Look for the positive.** Remember that changes are a normal part of life. How you deal with changes can help you grow. It does not help to dwell on what is wrong or different. What can you learn from the experience? Every change brings a new experience that can help you prepare for future changes.

Section 2.2 After You Read

Review What You Have Learned

1. **Name** the four stages of the family life cycle.
2. **Explain** how an unexpected change can be positive.

Practice Academic Skills

English Language Arts

3. Choose a change that your family experienced. Write a journal entry about the change. What was the event? Describe how the event affected you and your family.

Social Studies

4. Work with family members to collect information about the life experiences of an older relative. Did you learn something about the person that you never knew before? What effect has this person's life had on you? Write a paragraph about what you learned, and attach photos if available.

Check Your Answers Check Your Answers at connectED.mcgraw-hill.com.

Discovering Careers

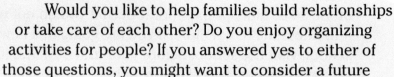

Would you like to help families build relationships or take care of each other? Do you enjoy organizing activities for people? If you answered yes to either of those questions, you might want to consider a future career in family health. The following chart explores several careers in the family health industry.

Career Activities ▼

At School

1 Select three of the careers listed. Research the education, training, and work experience required for each career. Write a summary of your results.

At Home

2 With the help of a parent, write out the characteristics of a good teacher. Then prioritize the characteristics by what is most important to you.

At Work

3 Confidentiality means to keep personal information private. Write a paragraph that explains why you think confidentiality is important for the careers listed on this page. Share your paragraph with another classmate and discuss your ideas.

In the Community

4 Contact and interview someone in your community who works in the family health industry. Ask this person to describe what his or her typical work day is like. Share what you learned with your class.

Job Title	Job Description
Family Counselor	Provides individual and family counseling. Helps clients with personal and family problems.
Family Practitioner	Examines patients, orders tests, and diagnoses condition of patient. Advises patients about diet, hygiene, and disease prevention.
Recreation Aide	Assists with recreation activities at community center or other recreation facility. Posts activity schedules and registration requirements.
Elementary School Teacher	Teaches elementary school students. Writes lesson plans. Assigns activities and corrects papers. Works with parents to support children's learning.
Coach	Works with children and/or adults in a specific sport. Encourages teamwork and skill development.
School Guidance Counselor	Provides counseling. Helps with college and career planning for students and parents. Works with teachers and students to achieve academic success.

Chapter Summary

Section 2.1 Family Characteristics

A healthy family life can be a source of pleasure and growth for its members. Healthy families care about each other and work together as a team even though they have different skills, talents, and personalities. Families may have various traditions and beliefs handed down from one generation to another. Families can become closer when they spend time together. Within your family, you practice the skills of consideration, cooperation, reliability, and respect.

Section 2.2 Changes in the Family

Families change and adapt for many reasons. Some changes result from divorce. Some divorced parents remarry and new siblings may join the family. Family members may live with a disability or develop a serious illness. Other changes result when a parent loses a job. One of the most difficult changes for a family is death. Not all changes are negative, but whether negative or positive, everyone in the family must learn to adapt. Families can be a source of strength and support during change.

Words You Learned

1. Write each of the vocabulary words below on an index card. Write the definitions on separate index cards. Work in pairs to match each word to its definition.

Content Vocabulary

○ environment (p. 31)
○ tradition (p. 32)
○ stereotype (p. 32)
○ sibling (p. 33)
○ responsible (p. 38)
○ divorce (p. 43)
○ disability (p. 44)

Academic Vocabulary

■ reserved (p. 32)
■ enrich (p. 33)
■ adapt (p. 41)
■ advance (p. 45)

Review Key Concepts

2. **List** seven different family types.

3. **Identify** four skills that can help you get along with people.

4. **Explain** ways to show responsibility.

5. **Outline** six changes that can happen in family life.

6. **Describe** ways to adjust to the changes that can affect families.

Critical Thinking

7. **Evaluate** why it is important for families to provide more than food, shelter, and clothing.

8. **Explain** how learning about different customs can help you avoid stereotyping people.

9. **Determine** which stage of the family life cycle is the most difficult for people. Why? Which stage do you think is the easiest? Why?

Real-World Skills and Applications

Problem-Solving

10. Obtain Information About a New School Gordon has found out that he and his family are moving this summer. He will attend a new school. Develop a list of resources Gordon could use to gather information about the new school.

Technology Applications

11. Design a Web Page Using information from your text and other resources, design a Web page that includes tips for getting along with your family and other people. Include at least four tips, and provide a real-life example to show how following the tips can help families get along. Come up with a name for your Web site. Use fun language and graphics to communicate the tips.

Financial Literacy

12. Fun for Less Franklin and Norma are looking for activities outside the home that they can share with their four children, ages 14, 12, 8, and 5. They feel that it is important that the family spends quality time together, but they do not have a lot of money to spend on family outings. After researching different types of activities, they have found two that sound promising. Tickets to a local cultural festival are $6.00 for people over age 12, and $3.00 for ages 12 and under. On the same day, the local children's museum, where admission is normally $7.00, is offering 2-for-1 admission. Which activity is less expensive?

13. Create a New Tradition Talk with your family about creating a new tradition that would show who you are as a family. Consider holidays or birthdays as a time to include the new tradition. Discuss with your family how this tradition will be meaningful for your family and when you can first honor it together. Prepare a short presentation to share with your class.

14. Research Your Heritage Talk to your parents, grandparents, and other family members about your heritage, or family history. See how far back you can trace your roots. Prepare a family tree to present to the class. The family tree should include dates and interesting historical details about your family.

15. Genealogy Geneology is information about your ancestors, or the people in your family from previous generations. With permission from your parents or teacher, go online to research your family geneology. Use search words such as your last name, genealogy, or family history. Where did your family name originate? What nationalities and ethnicities are represented in your family? What can you find out about your ancestors? Include this information in your Life Skills binder.

D.Hurst/Alamy

Academic Skills

English Language Arts

16. Persuade A recent article in your local newspaper points out resources, agencies, and support services that can give children what they need for growth and development. "Families are not the most important part of child development," according to the article. Do you think this statement is correct or incorrect? Write a letter to the editor of the newspaper to explain your opinion.

Social Studies

17. Geography Choose an extended family member who lives some distance away from you. If you do not have a family member who lives far away, choose one of your friends. Use a map to plan a route to get to their home if you went by car. Use the map legend to find out how many miles the trip is.

Mathematics

18. Create a Graph Some of your classmates may be the youngest people in their families. One or more may be the oldest child in their household, while others may be only children. Go to ten of your classmates and ask them the ages of each of their brothers and sisters. Write down their responses, and show the number of siblings at each age in a bar graph.

Math Concept **Bar Graphs** A bar graph uses vertical bars to display data. Typically, the vertical axis will indicate quantity, while the horizontal axis can show time periods or other categories.

Starting Hint The horizontal scale in your bar graph should show ages in years (from the lowest age you wrote down to the highest). The vertical scale should show the number of siblings. Draw a bar above each age that indicates how many siblings had that age.

Standardized Test Practice ● ● ● ● ● ● ● ● ●

True/False

Carefully read each statement. Decide if each statement is true or false.

> **Test-Taking Tip** For true/false questions, pay attention to key words like always or never. These mean the statement must be true all of the time or none of the time.

On a separate piece of paper, write T for true statements or F for false statements.

19. Changes in the family always result in negative outcomes.
20. An adopted child is a permanent member of his or her family.
21. Only the parents in a household have rights and responsibilities.

Chapter **3**

Your Friendships

Section 3.1

Friends

■ **Main Idea** Friendships grow, develop, and change throughout your life.

Section 3.2

Peer Pressure

■ **Main Idea** Recognizing the difference between positive and negative peer pressure can help you make smart decisions.

Oliver Rossi/Fancy Collection/SuperStock

Explore the Photo

Friends add value to your life. *How do you think your life is better because of your friends?*

Write a Journal Entry

Your Best Friend A journal is a book in which you can write down your thoughts and record memories. It is an informal way to write. It can help you get into the routine of writing regularly.

Write about your best friend. What do you have in common? What activities do you do together? What makes him or her a good friend?

Writing Tips Follow these steps for effective journal writing:

1. Pick a specific topic.
2. Write several times a week.
3. Read back over your entries to see how you have changed.

Section 3.1 Friends

Reading Guide

Before You Read

Predict Before starting the section, browse the content by reading headings, bold words, and photo captions. Do they help you predict the information in the section?

Read to Learn

Key Concepts

✓ **Describe** ways to make a new friend.

✓ **List** the qualities of a good friend.

✓ **Predict** how change can affect friendship.

Main Idea

Friendships grow, develop, and change throughout your life.

Content Vocabulary

○ acquaintance ○ compromise
○ diverse ○ expectation
○ peer ○ jealousy

Academic Vocabulary

■ benefit
■ confide

Graphic Organizer

As you read, identify what you know, what you want to learn, what you learned, and how you can learn more about friendship. Use a graphic organizer like the one shown to help you organize your information.

What I Know	What I Want to Find Out	What I Learned	How Can I Learn More

🖑 **Graphic Organizer** Go to connectED. mcgraw-hill.com to download this graphic organizer

---

Who are your friends? Are they people you can talk to about your secrets and goals? Are they other teens who like to watch the movies you like to watch? Are they your teammates or the people in your science club? You probably cannot define your friends in such simple words. Friends may be all those things, but they are also much more.

What Is a Friend?

As You Read

Connect When you think of your best friend, what is the first word that comes to your mind?

A friend is someone you like and who likes you. A friend is someone you can talk to. A friend is a person who shares similar interests and goals. For example, you may enjoy going to the mall on a Saturday afternoon with your friends. Perhaps you study with your friends. You and your friends may have similar career goals or college plans. The most important quality that friends have in common is that they care about each other's lives.

How Do Friendships Begin?

Friendships begin and grow when people meet and like each other. You do not instantly have a friend just because you meet someone. Some people are only acquaintances. An **acquaintance** (ə-'kwän-tᵊn(t)s) is a person you greet or meet fairly often, but with whom you do not have a close relationship. It may be a classmate, a neighbor, or the librarian at school.

Friendships usually develop from the acquaintances that you have. They are formed with people you are interested in getting to know better. They can grow into lasting friendships as you learn more about each other.

 **Vocabulary**

You can find definitions in the glossary at the back of this book.

Develop Friendships As you get to know people better, friendships often develop. *How did you meet your friends?*

Brand X Pictures/Alamy

MATH YOU CAN USE

(+) (−) (×) (÷) (ENTER)

How to Split a Bill

You and four friends took Sabrina out for her birthday. The bill is $57.00, and you want to include a 15 percent tip. You agree to split the bill and tip equally among you and your four friends so that Sabrina does not have to pay. How much does each person owe?

Math Concept **Find a Percent of a Number** To calculate a certain percentage of a number, change the percent to a decimal by moving the decimal point two places to the left. Then multiply the number by the decimal.

Starting Hint To find 15% of $57.00, multiply 57 by 0.15. Add this number to $57.00 and divide by 5 to determine what each person owes for the birthday dinner.

 For more math help, go to the Math Appendix located at the back of this book.

Give and Take

A give-and-take relationship means that each person in a friendship benefits, or gains something positive, from the other person. Some people are casual friends. You may enjoy their company at school or skating with them in the park. Others may become close friends and with whom you share the details of your life. All friends can learn from each other. They have something to offer each other. Friends can improve your life, and you can improve the lives of your friends. If you ask ten people to describe what they like most about their friends, you will probably get ten different answers. However, certain qualities are basic to all good friendships. Good friends:

- Enjoy each other's company.
- Share good times.
- Support and help each other through difficult times.
- Accept each other as they are.
- Listen when the other needs to talk.
- Are honest with each other.
- Encourage each other to avoid harmful behavior and situations.
- Depend on each other.

Make New Friends

It is not always easy to begin a new friendship. You can be successful if you make an effort. Everyone has to make new friends at times. Old friends may move away, or friend-ships may change as you grow and develop new interests. For example, you may want a new buddy to go swimming with or to find a person who shares your interest in crafts. Making new friends is a skill that you can learn.

As you go through life, you will have many chances to develop new friendships. Some friendships may begin easily. Others take more effort, and you may need to keep trying. However, not all friendships will work out. The person you thought might make a good friend may be too busy or have different interests. With experience, you can learn to recog-nize which friendships are worth pursuing, or working for.

Diversity

You live in a diverse society. **Diverse** means made up of many different parts. Most of your friends are probably similar to you in many ways, but different in other ways. You may even have friends who are very different from you. Throughout your life, you will have friendships with a variety of people. Some will be older, and others will be younger. You will have male friends and female friends. You may have friends from different religious or social backgrounds.

Imagine how boring the world would be without diversity. What if everyone had the same hobby or played the same sport? What if all the movies you watched had the same story? What if you never had the chance to learn something new? It would be a very dull world. Differences make life interesting, and differences make people interesting. Do not pass up a possible friendship because someone is a different age, ethnicity, or gender, or has a different cultural background. Diversity can enrich your life. If you establish a relationship with someone different from you, you can learn about new ideas, experience new activities, and become a more interesting person. Developing an appreciation for diversity can help you in school, at work, and in all of the relationships you develop throughout your life.

Reading Check *Recognize How can friends share and contribute to each others' lives?*

Tom Merton/Getty Images

Connect with Others These friends have many differences, but they enjoy spending time together. *What qualities can diverse people bring to your friendships?*

What Makes a Good Friend?

Good friends are supportive, caring, trustworthy, dependable, and reliable. Good friends do not ask or expect you to participate in harmful activities. Good friends accept you as you are. You confide in, or tell secrets to, a good friend. It is important that your friends have these qualities. However, it is just as important for you to have these qualities, too. Listen to your friends and offer your help when it is needed. Praise your friends when they do well, and encourage them when things are not going so well.

Being Part of a Group

Adolescence is a time when most teens seek approval from their peers. **Peers** are people the same age as you. Acceptance and recognition from your peers help you develop a sense of belonging. Being accepted by your peers can increase your self-esteem.

Your peer group helps to fill your needs for companionship and support. Within the group, you can learn and practice social skills, such as communication, conflict resolution, and compromise. A **compromise** ('käm-prə-ˌmīz) is an agreement

🔊 **Shared Interests** When you have something in common with someone, you have the start of a possible friendship. *What interests do you share with your friends?*

in which each person gives up something in order to reach a solution that satisfies everyone. Each person gives a little, and each person takes a little. These skills will be useful throughout your life.

Changes in Friendships

Your friendships will probably change over the years. Some of your friends may move away or attend a different school. Some of your friends may have new responsibilities after school. Friendships can also change when you and your friends discover new interests and activities.

Try not to be discouraged when you and a friend grow apart. You will have many chances throughout your life to develop new friends. It is important to remember that changes in friendships can help you grow and learn. You may not choose for these changes to happen, but you can use what you learn from the changes to understand more about yourself and others.

Differences in Expectations

Has there ever been a time when a friend let you down? Some changes in friendships are due to changing expectations. An **expectation** is a person's idea about what should be or should not be.

Character Counts

Honesty

Alex and Jamie have been friends since the first grade. Last year, Jamie joined the volleyball team and made several new friends. His new friends are very active in sports, and Jamie spends a lot of time with them now. Alex is not very athletic and does not have much in common with Jamie's new friends. Alex feels like he is losing Jamie as a friend. Alex asked Jamie to quit the volleyball team and stop spending so much time with his new friends so they can do the things they used to do.

You Make the Call

Should Jamie quit the team and stop hanging out with his new friends? Write a paragraph that explains what you think Jamie should do.

➡ **When Friendships Change** Problems can arise when your expectations do not match those of your friends. *What changes in friendships are common during the teen years?*

Dynamic Graphics Group/Creatas/Alamy

A common expectation in friendships is to have and to be a best friend. Best friends expect to trust each other and share common interests. Changes in friendships may occur when someone who was your best friend develops different interests and no longer spends as much time with you. Problems may arise when one friend expects more from the relationship than the other friend wants to give. Changes in best friends are common. You can learn what to expect from your friends and what your friends expect from you.

Expectations between boys and girls also change often during the teen years. Sometimes a boy and girl who were friends develop a boyfriend-girlfriend relationship. This usually means that they have romantic feelings for each other.

Jealousy

Jealousy is when a person feels unhappy about someone else's possessions, accomplishments, or luck. Jealousy can occur when you do not want to share something or someone with another person. It can also happen when someone has something that you want. People often feel jealous when they are unsure of themselves or about their relationship with someone else. When you feel jealous of a friend's achievements, do something that makes you feel good about yourself.

Section 3.1 After You Read

Review What You Have Learned

1. **Compare and contrast** an acquaintance with a friend.
2. **Explain** why peers are so important to teens.
3. **Describe** the common expectations of a best friend.

Practice Academic Skills

English Language Arts

4. In small groups, determine what qualities make a good friend. Write a list of questions to ask other classmates about successful friendships. Interview classmates, and present your findings to your class.

Social Studies

5. Write a list of suggestions to help make a new foreign-exchange student in your school feel welcome.

➤ **Check Your Answers** Check Your Answers at connectED.mcgraw-hill.com.

Reading Guide

Before You Read

Use Color As you read, use different colored pens to take notes. This can help you learn new material and study for tests. Try red for vocabulary words, blue for explanations, and green for examples.

Read to Learn

Key Concepts

✓ **Evaluate** how peer pressure can affect the decision-making process.

✓ **Explain** how saying no to high-risk behavior promotes teen safety.

✓ **Describe** how being assertive can help you be more in control of your life.

Main Idea

Recognizing the difference between positive and negative peer pressure can help you make smart decisions.

Content Vocabulary

○ peer pressure
○ refusal skills
○ addiction
○ abstinence
○ assertive
○ bully

Academic Vocabulary

■ acceptance　　■ resist

Graphic Organizer

As you read, list three effects of positive peer pressure and three effects of negative peer pressure. Use a graphic organizer like the one shown to help you organize your information.

Positive Peer Pressure	Negative Peer Pressure

↗ **Graphic Organizer** Go to connectED. mcgraw-hill.com to download this graphic organizer.

Everyone wants to be accepted and liked by his or her peers. The desire to belong to a peer group can be positive. There are times, however, when peers can have a negative impact on your life. Learn to recognize the differences between positive and negative pressures. It can help you decide if you should go along with the group or act as an individual.

Peers and Decision Making

The support and confidence peers give you can help your self-confidence and increase your self-esteem. At times, your peers may expect you to join in their actions and activities. **Peer pressure** is the influence you feel to go along with the behavior of your peers. Peer pressure can be negative or positive.

As You Read

Connect Think about the last time you felt pressured into doing something or not doing something. How did it make you feel?

Positive Peer Pressure

Acceptance, or approval, from your peers can help you feel good about yourself. A peer group can give you a sense of belonging and encourage positive behavior. Suppose that you were competing in a tennis match. It would feel good to know that your friends were there to cheer you on. You would feel confident and want to do your best. It can motivate you to try new activities. This type of peer pressure is a positive force.

◆ Vocabulary

You can find definitions in the glossary at the back of this book.

Negative Peer Pressure

Peer pressure can also be a negative force. Some groups make outsiders feel uncomfortable, unpopular, or unwanted. If one member of a group is critical or has a bad attitude, it may influence the entire group. Social media can be used to influence negatively as well. If the group has decided to exclude someone, you may feel pressured to avoid that person even if you like him or her.

Another negative kind of peer pressure is when you feel pushed to participate in activities that go against your values. Maybe someone tried to get you to skip school, smoke, drink alcohol, join a gang, or do something else that you know is dangerous or illegal. Always remember that true friends will not put you in dangerous positions.

Reading Check   *Predict What can happen if one person in a peer group has a bad attitude?*

Positive Influence Spending time with your peers can have a positive influence on you. *How can spending time with your peers make you feel good about yourself?*

Pascal Broze/SuperStock

Handle Peer Pressure

Everyone at one time or another is faced with decisions about following the group or following their own conscience, or sense of right and wrong. When this happens, ask yourself: Are the wishes of a few people more important than what I believe is right? If I do something because of peer pressure, will I be sorry about it later?

Here are some ways to deal with negative peer pressure:

- **Think ahead.** Decide ahead of time what you will do if certain situations come up. You might even practice what you will say and do.
- **Suggest other activities.** Think of things to do that are fun, healthy, safe, and legal. Let your friends know that you would like to be with them, but not if it means doing something wrong, unsafe, or illegal.
- **Choose your friends carefully.** Develop friendships with peers who share your values and interests.
- **Talk to parents and counselors.** Let them know if you are having problems. They can give you the support and encouragement you need to resist, or fight against, the pressure.

Practice refusal skills. If your friends ask you to do something that is wrong or against your values, use refusal skills. **Refusal skills** are communication tools that can help you say no when you feel pushed to take part in activities that are unsafe or unhealthful, or that go against your values (see **Figure 3.1**).

COMMUNITY CONNECTIONS
Positive Action To help avoid negative peer pressure, it is important to have alternatives, or other choices. Put together a list of ten positive community activities for teens. Share the list with your class.

Figure 3.1 Refusal Skills

Peer Pressure Everyone faces negative peer pressure at some point. *What are some ways that you can stand firm against negative peer pressure?*

- State exactly how you feel, directly and honestly.
- Do not apologize for your decisions or for your values.
- Use direct eye contact to show that you mean what you say.
- Use a firm yet friendly tone of voice.
- Use the other person's name.
- Suggest an alternative, or other option.
- Avoid compromise, which can be a slow way to saying yes.

PhotoAlto

How To...

Say "NO"

You will be faced with many choices and situations. Some are about choosing the way you behave toward others. Some are about reacting to how others behave toward you. Some situations will make you feel uncomfortable or put you in danger. Remember to say "NO" in these situations.

Tobacco, Alcohol, and Other Drugs True friends will not ask their friends to do things they do not want to do. You know what is right and wrong. Do not offer tobacco, alcohol, or drugs to anyone. Refuse any offers of these things from others. Stand up to peer pressure. Say "NO."

Shoplifting Shoplifting is stealing, and the penalties can have a long-term impact on your life.

Gangs Joining a gang can be very dangerous. You may be asked to do illegal things for the sake of other gang members.

Bullying Never try to bully or cyberbully anyone, and do not allow yourself to be bullied. Bullies should not be allowed to hassle anyone. Cyberbullying can occur in various ways, including social media . Get an adult to help if you are being bullied or if you see someone else being bullied.

Guns You know that guns are not toys and are dangerous. Never try to bring a gun to school. If someone wants to show you a gun at school, just walk away. Report the situation immediately to an adult.

Robert Daly/age fotostock

Avoid Harmful Substances

Everyone wants to be liked and accepted, but some people feel that gaining popularity is more important. Some teens think that they will be popular if they smoke cigarettes, use alcohol or other drugs, or sniff substances. They may do these things to impress friends or because their friends have dared them to do it. It is important to learn to use refusal skills when you feel pressured to join in activities that you believe, or know, are wrong.

If you have ever thought about trying alcohol or other drugs, think again about the reasons why. Carefully consider the long-term effects of such a decision. Using alcohol and other drugs does not make a person popular, build self-confidence, or solve problems. What alcohol and other drugs do is trap a person into a cycle of self-abuse. These harmful substances slow down your ability to act and think normally. They weaken your ability to make wise decisions. If you are faced with negative peer pressure, it is best to say "no" and walk away.

Many people who try tobacco, alcohol, or other drugs soon find themselves addicted. **Addiction** is a person's physical or mental dependence on a drug or other substance. Many people die each year from substance abuse. Excessive use of alcohol, drugs, and even over-the-counter (OTC) medications that you can buy at the supermarket can result in death. In addition, substance abuse often tears families apart and creates problems in the community. Substance abuse often leads to violence, crime, job loss, and suicide. The best way to avoid substance abuse is to never even try to use these substances.

Avoid High-Risk Behaviors

Negative peer pressure can cause more than regrets. Accepting a ride from someone who has been drinking alcohol can result in injury or death from a serious accident. Sexual involvement can result in pregnancy. It can also have harmful, even life-threatening, results in the form of AIDS and other sexually transmitted diseases (STDs).

Responsible people avoid such risks. They know that a healthy future is at stake. **Abstinence** ('ab-stə-nən(t)s) is a decision to avoid high-risk behaviors, including sexual activity and the use of tobacco, alcohol, and other drugs. Abstinence is the only sure way to protect yourself against the potentially dangerous consequences of high-risk behaviors. By saying "no" to behaviors that go against your values, you can feel better about yourself and have more self-respect.

Problem Solving
Ask for Extra Help
If you do not understand an assignment or homework problem, ask your teacher for extra help after school. Most teachers welcome the chance to provide guidance, and they will be glad to see that you are making an effort to solve your problem.

● ● ● ● ● ● ● ● ● ● ● ● ● ●

Driving
You may have siblings or friends who drive. Before you ride in a car with someone, it is important to do more than just buckle your safety belt. Remember these tips:

● Never get into a car with someone who has been drinking or using other drugs. Even a small amount can impair one's ability to drive safely.

● Call a parent or trusted adult to pick you up if you do not have a safe ride home.

Second-Hand Smoke

Being around people who smoke is harmful to your health. Second-hand smoke is a combination of a smoker's exhaled smoke, and the smoke from the burning end of a cigarette. Both parts contain chemicals that are harmful to everyone, especially children and teens.

Procedure Conduct research to find out more about the harmful effects of second-hand smoke.

Analysis Write a list of steps a teen can take to reduce his or her exposure to second-hand smoke.

Think about your values. Doing something that goes against your values is never a good idea. Here are some ways to say "no" to peer pressure:

- This goes against my values.
- I don't want to get hooked on alcohol or drugs.
- I don't smoke.
- I value my life too much to do that.
- I have too much self-respect to take that risk.
- I'm not into that. Go away.
- I'm not ready. I want to wait until I'm married.
- I don't want to get AIDS or an STD.

Reading Check **Define** *What is abstinence?*

Assert Yourself

You will be better prepared to handle negative peer pressure if you learn how to use refusal skills and to act assertively. When you are **assertive**, you express your views clearly and respectfully in positive ways. You speak in a confident manner. You do not give in to others when you believe something is wrong. You stand up for what you believe. Assertive teens do not wait for someone else to decide what the group is going to do. They suggest safe, responsible activities. Learn to be assertive to help you feel more in control.

You Have Options Always think about the consequences of high-risk behaviors. It is never worth it, and there are always other choices you can make. *Can you name two situations in which you or someone you know had to say "no" to high-risk behaviors?*

©Moxie Productions/Blend Images

Handle Bullies

A **bully** or cyberbully is a person who physically or verbally abuses someone to cause injury or discomfort through a variety of ways, including social media. People may become bullies because of the need for attention, feelings of low self-esteem, abuse in their own lives, or even peer pressure. Help prevent bullying by following these tips:

- Tell your parents, a teacher, counselor, or another trusted adult if someone bullies you or another person.
- Do not get angry and strike back.
- Either respond firmly or walk away.
- Stick up for another person who is being bullied.
- Stay away from bullies and the places they hang out.

When faced with a threatening situation, your brain automatically triggers your adrenal glands to release more adrenaline (ə-'dre-nə-lən). This will increase your heart rate, pulse, and respiration rate, which causes you to want to fight back or to get away from the threat. The "fight-or-flight response" is your body's physical and mental response to a threat. You have the power to choose between fighting back or getting away. Choose wisely and walk away from bullies.

Section 3.2 After You Read

Review What You Have Learned

1. **Give** an example of positive peer pressure.
2. **Describe** the best way to deal with negative peer pressure.
3. **Identify** the characteristics of a bully.

Practice Academic Skills

English Language Arts

4. Using the tips for handling a bully, create a public service announcement, poster, or skit to present to elementary-age students. Make it fun and educational for this age group.

Social Studies

5. Think about a situation in which you were faced with negative peer pressure. How did you react? How did the pressure affect you? How did the group or individual react to you? After reading this chapter, what could you do differently next time? Write a paragraph to answer these questions.

Check Your Answers Check Your Answers at connectED.mcgraw-hill.com.

Discovering Careers

Do you have the desire to help others in unsafe situations? Can you help others make the right decisions? If you answered yes to either of those questions, you might want to consider a future career in public safety. The following chart explores several careers in the public safety industry.

Career Activities ▼

At School

1 Select three of the careers listed. Research the education, training, and work experience required for each career. Write a summary of your results.

At Home

2 Create an escape plan for your family to exit your home in case of an emergency. Use your home's floor plan to show how to exit all areas in the home.

At Work

3 Make a list of at least five things an employee can do to help keep his or her work area safe. Ask a friend or relative who works if you need help with ideas.

In the Community

4 Contact and interview someone in your community who works in the public safety industry. Ask this person to describe what his or her typical work day is like. Share what you learned with your class.

Job Title	Job Description
Police Officer	Patrols assigned areas. Controls disturbances of the peace, and arrests violators. Reports hazards. Directs traffic around fires or other disruptions.
Postal Clerk	Sells stamps and postage. Registers and insures mail and computes mailing costs. Checks suspicious mail or packages for safety.
Nurse Practitioner	Performs physical examinations and preventative health care within prescribed guidelines. Helps assess patient's clinical problems and health care needs.
Firefighter	Responds to fire alarms and other emergency calls. Administers first aid and artificial respiration to injured persons.
Security Guard	Checks buildings and personnel for any suspicious or dangerous activities. Protect customers in public or commercial buildings.
Airport Security Agent	Checks luggage for suspicious items. Checks passengers for weapons or illegal substances. Helps passengers safely arrive at their gate.

George Doyle & Ciaran Griffin/SuperStock

Chapter Summary

Section 3.1 Friends
Friendships begin and develop when people meet and like each other. Good friendships are based on a give-and-take relationship. Friends enjoy good times together, help each other in bad times, accept each other as they are, and encourage and support each other. Good friends are supportive, caring, trustworthy, dependable, and reliable. Your friendships will grow, develop, and change throughout your life.

Section 3.2 Peer Pressure
Positive peer pressure gives you a sense of belonging and encourages positive behavior. Negative peer pressure encourages participation in unsafe or unhealthful behaviors that go against your values. When faced with negative peer pressure, say "no" and walk away. Negative peer pressure can cause more than regrets. You will be better prepared to handle negative peer pressure if you learn how to use refusal skills and to act assertively.

Words You Learned

1. Label each of these content vocabulary words and academic vocabulary words as a noun, verb, or adjective.

Content Vocabulary
- acquaintance (p. 53)
- diverse (p. 55)
- peer (p. 56)
- compromise (p. 56)
- expectation (p. 57)
- jealousy (p. 58)
- peer pressure (p. 60)
- refusal skills (p. 61)
- addiction (p. 63)
- abstinence (p. 63)
- assertive (p. 64)
- bully (p. 65)

Academic Vocabulary
- benefit (p. 54)
- confide (p. 56)
- acceptance (p. 60)
- resist (p. 61)

Review Key Concepts

2. **Describe** ways to make a new friend.

3. **List** the qualities of a good friend.

4. **Predict** how change can affect friendship.

5. **Evaluate** how peer pressure can affect the decision-making process.

6. **Explain** how saying no to high-risk behavior promotes teen safety.

7. **Describe** how being assertive can help you be more in control of your life.

Critical Thinking

8. **Compare and contrast** positive and negative peer pressure.

9. **Explain** how those who abuse drugs and alcohol can be a burden on society.

Real-World Skills and Applications

Problem-Solving

10. Make Decisions about Drinking
Lucas has been asked by one of his acquaintances, Jolie, to go to a party on Friday night. Jolie has a reputation for sneaking alcohol into parties. Develop a plan for Lucas to decide what he should do.

Interpersonal and Collaborative

11. Practice Refusal Skills Follow your teacher's instructions to form teams. With your team, come up with a list of situations in which negative peer pressure can be a factor. Then pick one of the situations and write a script for a realistic scenario. Include planning ahead and using refusal skills. Make sure everyone in the group has a part to play. Perform the scenario in front of the class. After all class members have performed their scenarios, discuss what worked well and what could be improved.

Financial Literacy

12. Calculate an Entertainment Budget Cole makes $150 per month at his after-school job. He would like to set aside 50% of his monthly income in his savings account. He has budgeted another 30% of his income for paying various expenses, such as food and bus fare. The remainder of his income is available to use on entertainment and fun activities. Cole and his friends like to go to movies on weekends. Movies cost $10 per ticket. They also like to go bowling, at $3 per game. Given his budget, how many movies could Cole see in one month? How many games could he bowl in one month? If he bowls three games, how many movie tickets could he then buy in the same month?

13. Friendship T-Shirt To communicate your care for a friend, make a Friendship T-Shirt. Use a clean, light-colored T-shirt, fabric markers, and cardboard. Slip cardboard inside the T-shirt. Use fabric markers to decorate the front and back of the shirt with drawings and words that describe your friend. Give your shirt to a friend when you are finished.

14. Research Friendship Poets and writers have described friendship in a variety of ways throughout history. Choose a historical period, such as the Renaissance, and look up poems or other writings about friendship. How was friendship described or symbolized? What kind of words did they use? Would you use the same words to describe your own friendships today? Why or why not? Prepare a short presentation for your class.

15. Peer Pressure in the Past Under the supervision of a parent or teacher, go online to research movies about life in the 1940s or 1950s. Choose a movie with a theme of friendship. If possible, watch the movie. If you cannot watch the movie, find online summaries of the story. Write a one-page essay that describes the story. Compare the peer pressures faced by teens in the movie to the pressures teens face today. Keep your essay in your Life Skills Binder.

D.Hurst/Alamy

Academic Skills

English Language Arts

16. Write a Persuasive Letter Imagine that one of your good friends has started hanging out with some teens who use alcohol, drugs, and cigarettes. Write a letter to your friend to convince her to stop hanging out with these teens.

Science

17. Risks and Benefits An action plan is a step-by-step strategy to identify and achieve your goals. Create an action plan for abstaining from the use of alcohol.

Procedure Conduct research about the consequences of alcohol abuse.

Analysis Make a list of negative consequences of alcohol. Next to each consequence, write a way to say "no" to help you avoid the consequence.

Mathematics

18. Calculate Interest Your friend Gary wants to borrow $100 from you to buy a new MP3 player. You know that he is responsible, and that he will receive a paycheck from his part-time job in a month. You decide that it will be okay to lend him the money for one month. If you charge 8 percent interest, how much money will Gary owe you when he gets paid?

Math Concept **Simple Interest** To calculate simple interest, multiply the amount borrowed by the interest percentage.

Starting Hint Multiply the amount of the loan ($100) by the interest rate (8%, or 0.08) to calculate the interest amount. Add this number to $100 to come up with the total due at the end of the month.

Standardized Test Practice

Short Answer

Answer each of the questions in one to three sentences.

Test-Taking Tip When answering a short answer question, it is important to read the question carefully so that you respond with only the information it is asking.

19. Describe what kind of friend you are.
20. How can friendships change during your teen years?
21. How can practicing abstinence keep you healthy?

UNIT 1 Life Skills Project

Your Role Models

Like everyone else, there are people in your life who influence you. Famous people may have achieved goals that you admire. Friends and family members may have values that are important to you. This project will help you explore the traits you wish to develop.

My Journal Complete the journal entry from page 3, and refer to it to complete your list of role models.

Project Assignment ▼

In this project, you will:

- Create a list of people you consider role models.
- Choose, take, or collect photographs of your role models.
- Describe admirable traits that your choices possess.
- Interview one of your role models.
- Create a collage that displays photographs and descriptions of your role models.
- Present your findings to your class.
- Include this project in the first section of your personal Life Skills binder.

Step 1 Make a List of Your Role Models

To figure out the kind of person you hope to become, think about people you already admire. List the names of people in three categories of your life: Family, Friends, and Celebrities. Then describe the traits that you find admirable.

Step 2 Find Photographs of Three Role Models

Find photographs in magazines if you have famous role models. Look through family albums or take your own photographs of friends and family role models. Think about how you will prepare each photo to display in a collage. Then write two or more paragraphs that answer these questions:

- ✔ What traits do you find admirable about each person?
- ✔ How does their photograph reflect those traits?
- ✔ Why did you choose each specific picture?
- ✔ How do these role models reflect your own values?

Step 3 Interview Someone You Admire

Interview one of your role models. Ask these questions:

- ✔ What do you think makes you unique?
- ✔ What would you consider your most important values?
- ✔ Who are your role models?

Use these interviewing skills when conducting your interview and these writing skills when writing the summary of notes from your interview.

Interviewing Skills
- Record interview responses and take notes.
- Listen attentively.

Writing Skills
- Use complete sentences.
- Use correct spelling and grammar.

Step 4 Create and Present Your Collage

Use the Life Skills Project Checklist on the right to plan and complete your collage and give an oral report on it. Before you speak, ask other students to describe your pictures to see if they accurately depict your role model.

Use these speaking skills when presenting your final report.

Speaking Skills
- Speak clearly and concisely.
- Be sensitive to the needs of your audience.
- Use standard English to communicate.

Step 5 Evaluate Your Presentation

Your project will be evaluated based on:

✔ Completeness and organization of your list of role models.

✔ Your photographs and descriptions that represent your role models' traits.

✔ The creativity of your collage.

✔ The summary written from interview notes.

✔ Grammar and sentence structure.

✔ Presentation to the class.

✔ Creativity and neatness.

🖝 **Evaluation Rubric** Go to connectED. mcgraw-hill.com for a rubric you can use to evaluate your final project.

Amos Morgan/Getty Images

Life Skills Project Checklist

Research Your Role Models

✅ Create your list of role models.

✅ Collect photos or take photos of your choices.

✅ Interview one of your chosen role models.

Writing Skills

✅ Describe the traits you find admirable.

✅ Describe the role models in your photographs.

✅ Write a summary from your interview with your role model.

Present Your Findings

✅ Prepare a collage and a short presentation to share the photographs of your role models and the descriptions of their traits that you admire.

✅ Invite the students of the class to ask any questions they may have. Answer these questions with responses that respect their perspectives.

✅ Add this project to your Life Skills binder.

Academic Skills

✅ Conduct research to gather information.

✅ Communicate effectively.

✅ Organize your presentation so the audience can follow along easily.

✅ Thoroughly express your ideas.

Take Charge of Your Life

Unit Preview

This unit is about being in control of your own life. In this unit, you will learn about:

- Using verbal and nonverbal skills to communicate efficiently.
- Recognizing the causes of conflict.
- The duties of being a responsible citizen.
- The importance of leadership skills.
- Why setting goals is essential.
- Making smart decisions.

Explore the Photo
Achieving a goal can be a very fulfilling experience. *What are some of the things you should think about when setting goals?*

© Tetra Images/ Alamy

Your Point of View

When you are done studying this unit, you will complete a project in which you will:

✓ Discover an issue in your community that you care about.

✓ Interview someone who holds an elected office.

✓ Share your opinion on the issue with your class.

The prewriting activity below will help you get started.

My Journal

Prewriting Activity
Research Newspaper Stories

Find and read stories in your local newspaper about local issues that you care about. Cut out these stories for your journal, and write a summary of the article beside each one.

● What are the facts and issues discussed in each article?

● What are the different opinions about each issue? There are often two sides to an issue. If this is the case, summarize the opinion of each side.

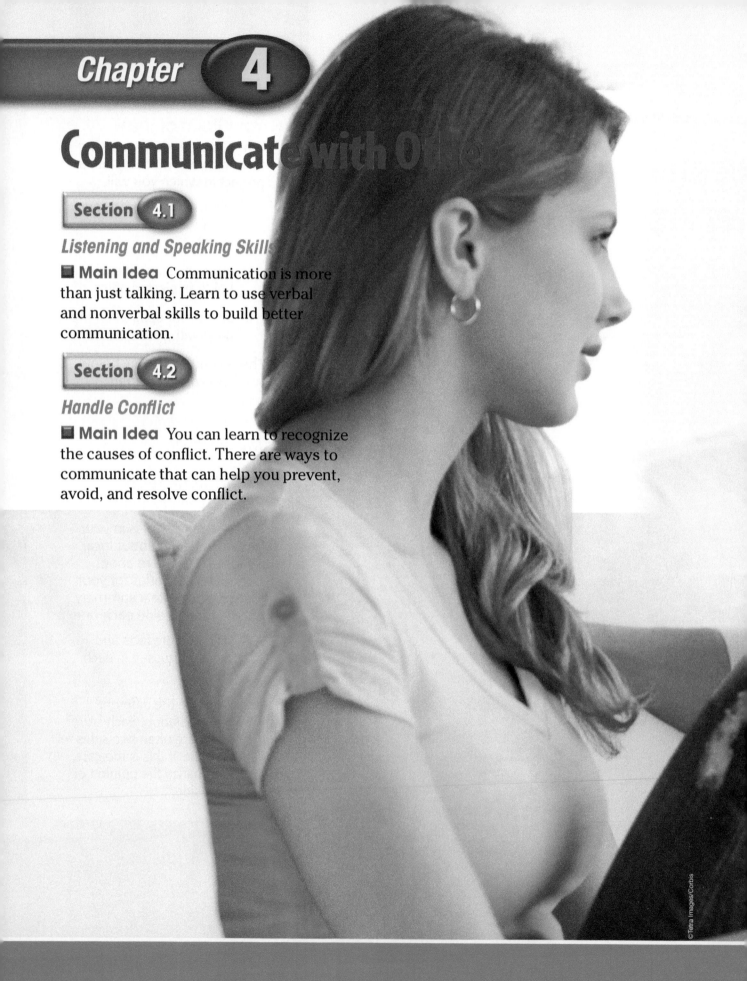

Chapter 4

Communicate with Others

Section 4.1

Listening and Speaking Skills

■ **Main Idea** Communication is more than just talking. Learn to use verbal and nonverbal skills to build better communication.

Section 4.2

Handle Conflict

■ **Main Idea** You can learn to recognize the causes of conflict. There are ways to communicate that can help you prevent, avoid, and resolve conflict.

©Tetra Images/Corbis

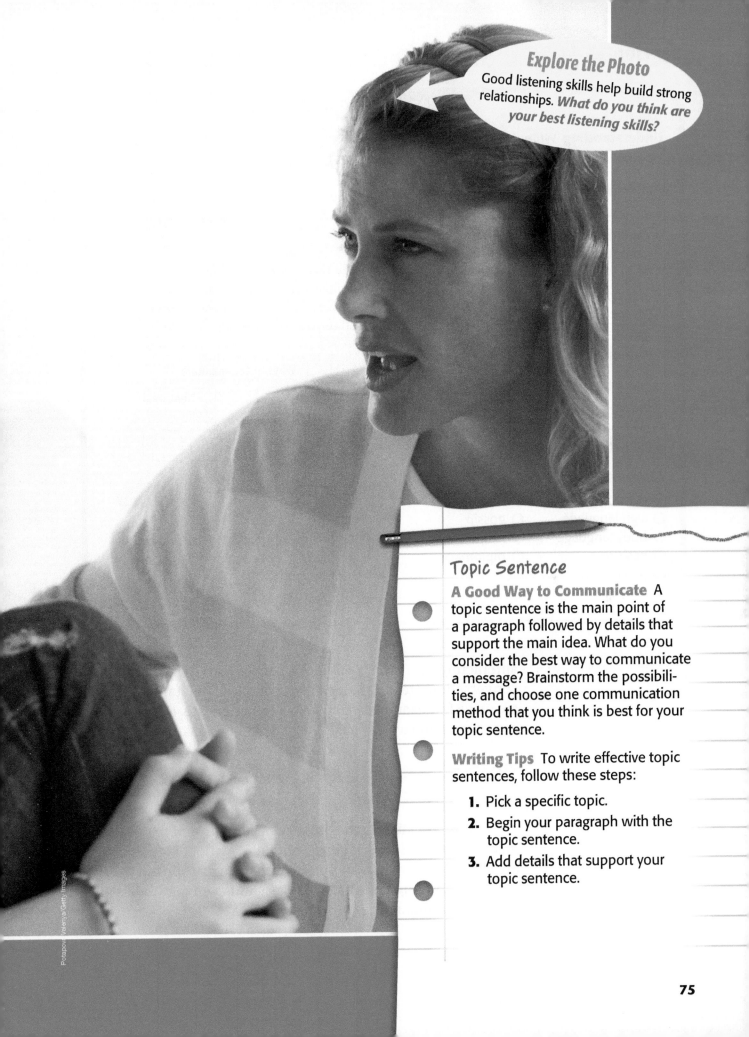

Explore the Photo

Good listening skills help build strong relationships. *What do you think are your best listening skills?*

Topic Sentence

A Good Way to Communicate A topic sentence is the main point of a paragraph followed by details that support the main idea. What do you consider the best way to communicate a message? Brainstorm the possibilities, and choose one communication method that you think is best for your topic sentence.

Writing Tips To write effective topic sentences, follow these steps:

1. Pick a specific topic.
2. Begin your paragraph with the topic sentence.
3. Add details that support your topic sentence.

Before You Read

Understanding Write down questions while you read. Many of them will be answered as you read. If not, you will have a list ready for your teacher.

Read to Learn

Key Concepts

✓ **Describe** how verbal and nonverbal communication can show how you feel about yourself and others.

✓ **Recognize** that listening is as important as speaking.

✓ **Show** how asking questions can improve communication.

Main Idea

Communication is more than just talking. Learn to use verbal and nonverbal skills to build better communication.

Content Vocabulary

○ communication
○ sign language
○ body language
○ gesture
○ perception
○ feedback
○ gossip
○ rumor
○ diplomacy

Academic Vocabulary

■ signal
■ exchange

Graphic Organizer

As you read, look for verbal and nonverbal guidelines for effective communication. Use a web like the one shown to help you organize your information.

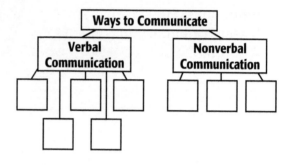

Graphic Organizer Go to connectED. mcgraw-hill.com to download this graphic organizer.

Interacting with other people is a part of your daily life. Phone conversations, talking face to face, e-mail, and instant messages are just a few examples of how you communicate. Improve your communication with speaking and listening skills.

Verbal and Nonverbal Communication

Communication is the process of sending and receiving messages about ideas, feelings, and information. Messages are sent with words and without words. We use spoken words, written words, sign language, images, and even our bodies and faces to communicate.

Verbal Communication

Verbal communication can be spoken or written. Carefully select the right words to express yourself. Say what you think and feel, but always be polite. Effective verbal communication guidelines include the following:

- **Speak for yourself.** Share your own experiences and feelings. Do not assume that other people know what you think, how you feel, or what you want.
- **Avoid speaking for others.** Do not assume that you know what other people think, how they feel, or what they want. Ask them. Let them speak for themselves.
- **Be clear and direct.** Tone of voice can reveal your feelings. You can send mixed messages if your tone does not match the words you are using.
- **Be aware of your listener.** Check to see that your listener understands what you are saying. Social media or texting can make this difficult.
- **Ask questions.** Ask "who," "what," "when," "where," and "how" questions. These questions help others share their thoughts and feelings.

As You Read

Connect How has technology changed the way people talk to each other?

Vocabulary

You can find definitions in the glossary at the back of this book.

Be a Good Listener
Listening is just as important as speaking. *How does it make you feel when someone really seems to listen to what you say?*

Nonverbal Communication

Nonverbal communication is communication without using words. You may think of sign language when you think of nonverbal communication. **Sign language** is a system of hand signs used by or for people who have a hearing impairment. However, there are many other ways people communicate without words. Think about the common greeting, "It is nice to meet you." Now, think about that greeting spoken with a handshake and a smile. Nonverbal communication can add to verbal communication and make it more effective. **Figure 4.1** describes common nonverbal communication signals. We communicate without words in the following ways:

- **Body Language** You communicate a lot through body language. **Body language** is nonverbal communication through gestures, facial expressions, behaviors, and posture. A **gesture** ('jes-chər) is the use of body movements to communicate meanings or emotions. Sometimes you use body language instead of words without being aware of it.

- **Posture** Your posture can signal, or show, your interest level. Tense posture may indicate that you are nervous, angry, or worried. Folded arms can show that you do not want to listen. If you appear relaxed, people are more likely to open up to you.

- **Personal Space** Some people prefer that others do not stand or sit too close to them. Others are more comfortable with physical closeness. The space in which you feel comfortable is your personal space. The amount of personal space you require can communicate your feelings. For example, if you keep your distance from people, it can show that you are not interested in conversation. If you allow people to be closer to you, you appear open to conversation.

Reading Check *List* *What are three types of nonverbal communication?*

Be an Active Listener

The ability to listen is just as important as the ability to speak. Listening is not the same as hearing. When you hear, you are aware of the words being said. When you listen, you make an effort to understand the message. An active listener restates what the speaker says to make sure he or she understands the message.

You can improve your listening skills by using the following guidelines:

- Give your full attention to the speaker.
- Do not interrupt.
- Concentrate on what the speaker is saying, not on what you will say next.
- Listen for the overall meaning, not just the details.
- Pay attention to nonverbal signs.
- Avoid making quick judgments.
- Try not to become distracted.
- When the other person is finished, ask questions to show that you understand.

SUCCEED IN SCHOOL!

Seek Encouragement
Family and Friends
Seek out friends and family members who are supportive of your efforts in school and who encourage you to do your best.

Figure 4.1 Nonverbal Signals

Communicate Without Words Watch people when they are not speaking and you can see that they are still communicating. *How can you show a person that you are interested in the conversation without using words?*

Body Signals Folded arms can signal disinterest or anger. Hands on your hips can show impatience. Lean forward and face the speaker to show concern and interest.

Nod or Shake Your Head You can nod your head and smile to show approval or that you agree. You can shake your head to show that you disagree or do not understand.

Eye Contact Look the other person in the eye to show interest and caring. If you do not look at the other person, it could make him or her think you are bored, distracted, or uninterested.

(tl)© Pascal Broze/SuperStock; (cr) ©PhotoAlto; (bl)Glow Images

Is Body Language Affected by Gender?

To complete a scientific investigation or experiment, you collect data. Scientists collect data as numbers and descriptions, and then organize the data in different ways. Use your science skills to determine whether or not gender plays a part in body language.

Procedure Choose a locations to observe teens, such as at your school, a community center, or a favorite place to meet your friends. Using the examples in Figure 4.1 as a guide, create a chart to record the types of nonverbal communication used by boys and the types used by girls.

Analysis What body language did you see most often? Did boys make certain gestures more often than girls? Did girls use different kinds of body language from boys? Draw conclusions from the data to share with classmates.

Perception and Communication Styles

How well you listen affects your perception. **Perception** (pər-'sep-shən) is using your senses to get information about what is around you. Perception can be influenced by where you grew up, your education, your values, and your cultural heritage. These factors can affect the way verbal and nonverbal messages are sent and received.

Just as people's perceptions can differ, so can communication styles. Assertive communicators make sure their points get across. Passive communicators often listen more than they speak. Aggressive communicators may offend other people by taking over the conversation. Remember to consider the other person's perception and communication style when listening to what they are saying to you.

Reading Check **List** *What are three styles of communication?*

Conversation

Conversation involves the exchange, or sharing, of ideas, thoughts, and feelings. It is a two-way street. You must be willing to express yourself as well as listen to others.

For a conversation to be interesting and effective, it is important for each person to have a chance to talk. A good way to start is to ask the other person about his or her interests. Most people like to talk about their own experiences.

Ask Questions

It is important to give and receive feedback during a conversation. **Feedback** is the response given to a message sent. Ask questions to help you find out about other people's interests. Think about the following example: Rena asks, "Do you like baseball?" Eric answers, "Yes." That is the end of the conversation. This kind of closed-end question means that the answer is either "yes" or "no." There is no room for further discussion. Rena could get a better response if she asks, "What did you think of the game today?" Eric might say, "My favorite player scored three runs!" This is an example of an open-ended question. It leaves the possibility for more to talk about.

Gossip Hurts No one benefits from gossip. *What can you say to a friend who wants to gossip?*

Avoid asking "why" questions such as "Why did you change your mind?" This type of question forces the other person to explain or defend his or her actions. You also should avoid questions that lead the other person to answer the way you think he or she should answer. For example, if you ask, "Don't you think vegetarian pizza is the best?" is really a statement of what you think. It is a way to get the other person to agree with you. Instead ask, "What kind of pizza do you like best?"

Avoid Gossip

Do you know people who gossip? **Gossip** is talking to people about someone else's personal life or private business. It is often done in an unkind way and can lead to rumors. A **rumor** is a statement spread from one person to another without knowing whether or not it is true. The information spread through gossip may be hurtful. It can damage friendships and ruin reputations. When you avoid gossip and rumors, you can show that you are a mature, caring, and responsible person.

Financial Literacy

Cell Phone Costs

Anna would like to purchase a cell phone so she can better communicate with friends and family. After doing some research, she finds that the phone will cost $39.45, the prepaid minutes will cost $19.99, the activation fee will be $15.50, and a case to hold the phone will be $16.65. How much will Anna need to buy the phone?

Math Concept **Adding Decimals** To add decimals, list the numbers vertically, being sure to line up the decimal points. Add normally from right to left, carrying when necessary. Be sure to bring the decimal point down into the answer.

Starting Hint: List the numbers ($39.45, $19.99, $15.50, and $16.65) in a vertical line with the decimal points lined up. Then add, starting with the hundredths place. Be sure to place the decimal point correctly in the answer, and label the answer.

 For math help, go to the Math Appendix at the back of the book.

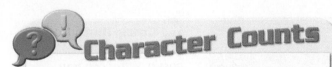

Character Counts

Integrity

Shanda has just moved to a new town and school. She really wants to fit in and get to know people. Two girls in her neighborhood offered to walk to school with her, introduce her to their friends, and show her around. On the first day of school, she walked with her new acquaintances. The girls started gossiping about some other girls that Shanda has not met. Shanda does not know whether or not the things they said are true.

You Make the Call

Should Shanda continue walking with the girls and participate in the gossip? Should she find someone else to walk to school with? Write a paragraph that explains what you think Shanda should do.

Be Diplomatic

When you say things in a way that will not embarrass someone or cause hurt feelings, you are being diplomatic. **Diplomacy**, (də-'plō-mə-sē) also called tact, is being honest without being hurtful. It is important that negative comments focus on the issue, not the person. For example, imagine if your teacher said, "There is only one day left before the test. What can I do to help you prepare?" How would you react to that question? Most likely, you would feel glad or relieved that your teacher wants to help. Now imagine if the teacher said, "Why aren't you ready for the test yet?" How would you react to that question? You would probably feel defensive or angry and less willing to answer. Think before you speak. Sometimes, the way you say something can be even more important than what you say.

Section 4.1 After You Read

Review What You Have Learned

1. **List** the guidelines for effective verbal communication.
2. **Describe** ways to improve your listening skills.
3. **Explain** why gossip can be destructive to other people.

Practice Academic Skills

English Language Arts

4. Observe interactions between two of your friends. Then write a paragraph to describe what was said, how it was said, and to evaluate whether or not they effectively used any of the communication skills from this chapter.

Social Studies

5. How has technology changed the way people talk to each other? Do you think these changes are positive or negative? Explain your answers.

. . . .

Check Your Answers Check Your Answers at connectED.mcgraw-hill.com.

Reading Guide

Before You Read

Buddy Up for Success One advantage to sharing your notes with a buddy is that you can compare notes before you start quizzing each other.

Read to Learn

Key Concepts

✓ **Identify** factors that can cause conflict.

✓ **Explain** how you can prevent conflict.

✓ **Suggest** ways to resolve conflict.

Main Idea

You can learn to recognize the causes of conflict. There are ways to communicate that can help you prevent, avoid, and resolve conflict.

Content Vocabulary

○ conflict
○ prejudice
○ negotiation
○ peer mediation

Academic Vocabulary

■ escalate
■ neutral

Graphic Organizer

As you read, list five causes of conflict. Next to each cause, write something you can do to prevent the conflict. The first one is completed for you. Use a graphic organizer like the one shown to help you organize your information.

Causes of Conflict	Ways to Prevent the Conflict
1. Misunderstandings	Listen closely. Repeat what the other person said.
2.	
3.	
4.	
5.	

Graphic Organizer Go to connectED. mcgraw-hill.com to download this graphic organizer.

Do you get along with everyone all of the time? If you are like most people, your answer is probably no. In fact, you might even find that lately you get into more arguments than you did when you were younger. That is because you are developing opinions of your own. Learn how to handle and communicate your opinions in positive ways. This is an important part of becoming an adult.

Face Conflict

A **conflict** is a disagreement or struggle between two or more people. Everyone experiences conflict at one time or another. You have probably had disagreements with both friends and family members.

Causes of Conflict

As You Read

Connect Think about the skills you have or want to learn to help you resolve conflicts.

Think about the last time that you had a disagreement. Can you remember the cause? Conflict with friends and peers is not unusual, especially during the teen years.

- **Misunderstandings** Conflicts often occur when people do not communicate effectively. Take the time to listen closely to what the other person is saying.
- **Differing Opinions** You have your own opinions about a wide range of topics. You might feel a need to defend your opinions. It is important to remember that each person has the right to his or her opinion. Do not let this become a power struggle. Conflicts over control can hurt the people involved.
- **Gossip** If a group of teens started gossiping about your best friend's parents going through a divorce, your friend would probably feel hurt and angry. You might feel angry, too. Avoid gossip when using social media and texting as well.
- **Jealousy** If you and a friend both tried out for the lead in the school play and your friend got the part, you might feel jealous. Do not waste your energy being jealous of others. Focus on your own accomplishments and goals instead.
- **Prejudice** Some conflicts are caused by **prejudice** ('pre-jə-dəs), an opinion about people that is formed without facts or knowledge. Prejudice causes people to judge others without taking the time to get to know them. Remember that just because someone is different from you does not mean they are bad or wrong. Get to know people for who they are. Do not allow stereotypes to keep you from forming friendships.

Vocabulary

You can find definitions in the glossary at the back of this book.

Damage Control

Unresolved conflict can damage relationships. *What can happen if you do not resolve a conflict with one of your parents?*

Reading Check *Define* *What is conflict?*

Design Pics/Don Hammond

Take Time Out Sometimes it helps to be alone to think over a situation. *How can you help prevent conflict by examining your behavior?*

Prevent and Avoid Conflict

You can prevent some conflicts by heading off problems before they start. The best way to do this is to pay attention to your own behavior. How do you treat others? Why do you say or do certain things? When you explore your actions, you may find that there are some qualities you can improve in yourself. Try to look at situations from their point of view.

Control Anger

A conflict can escalate, or get worse, if you get angry. Learning to control your anger is an important way to prevent conflicts. When you or another person is angry, it can be easy for things to get out of hand. If you are angry, follow these tips to keep your anger from making a conflict worse:

- **Write in a journal.** Put your feelings on paper in a journal.
- **Listen to or play music.** Music can have a calming effect.
- **Find a creative outlet.** Draw, paint, write songs or poetry, or start a scrapbook project.
- **Exercise.** Use your energy for a long walk or run, or work it off at the gym.
- **Get some rest.** Anger can drain your energy and make you feel tired. Take a break, a nap, or go to bed early. Sleep helps you focus.
- **Talk to someone.** Talk about your feelings with a trusted adult.

Reading Check *Understand What can you do to help control your anger in conflict situations?*

Practice Peer Mediation

In this activity you will practice the steps in peer mediation. If time permits, practice once as a mediator and once as a person with a conflict. Before you begin, read through the entire Hands-On-Lab assignment. Write down any questions that you might have about the activity. Reread the text or ask your teacher for help if you need it.

Supplies
✓ Paper
✓ Pen or pencil

Develop Your Plan

■ Come up with a set of rules for the process. Write them down.

■ Assign two students to be in the conflict and another to be the mediator.

■ Each student should tell his or her side of the story or complaint. If necessary, the mediator can meet with each person separately.

■ Create and discuss possible solutions.

■ Once a solution is reached, both students should sign a "contract" stating that they agree to the solution.

Implementation

■ Each student should listen quietly until the other finishes his or her side of the story.

■ The mediator should ask any questions he or she has.

■ The mediator should paraphrase, or tell the story in his or her own words, what was said to make sure the issues are clear.

■ Each side should offer several solutions to the conflict.

■ The peer mediator should choose the best solution.

■ Both students should sign a contract agreeing to the solution.

Evaluate Your Results

What problems did you have in this exercise? Were you able to work out a solution to which both students agreed? If so, what was the solution? What would you do differently next time? If you are ever in a conflict at school, would you seek out a peer mediator for help? Why or why not? Write one or more paragraphs to explain your answer.

Projects and Activities Go to connectED.mcgraw-hill.com.

Resolve Conflict

People who handle conflict well use good communication skills. You do not have to wait for a conflict to practice these skills. In fact, if you work on these skills every day, you may have fewer conflicts in the first place. However, conflicts can occur in spite of your best efforts. When they do, you and the other person can work out your differences in a way that satisfies both of you. Use the communication skills in **Figure 4.2** on page 88 to help you resolve conflicts.

Compromise and Negotiation

Resolving a conflict often means reaching a compromise. A compromise is an agreement in which each person gives up something in order to reach a solution that satisfies everyone. This is also called a give-and-take solution. Even if you are not involved in a conflict yourself, you can help other people solve conflicts. Instead of taking sides, try to get the people involved to talk to each other about compromise. This kind of support can help them see that they do not have to fight to come to a resolution.

Negotiation is one of the best ways to compromise. **Negotiation** (ni-ˌgō-shē-ˈā-shən) is the process of talking about a conflict and deciding how to reach a compromise. This requires a lot of give-and-take, in which both sides give up some demands and both sides get some of what they want.

For negotiation to work, both sides must be willing to stop asking for certain things or at least change their demands. For example, Rachel gets angry when her younger brother, Mark, borrows her CDs without asking. Mark, however, cannot always ask because Rachel is at basketball practice when he has time to listen to them. Perhaps Rachel could agree to let him borrow certain CDs when she is not home. In return, Mark could let her borrow his handheld electronic game without asking when she wants to play it after he has gone to bed.

- **Follow up.** When you negotiate you must make sure that you can follow through with your promises. If you agree to behave differently, you must actually do so. Otherwise, your agreement is worthless.
- **Get help.** Sometimes compromises can best be reached with the help of a third person who is neutral. To be neutral means to not take sides. This person may be a parent, teacher, school counselor, or other trusted adult. Sometimes this third person is a peer.

SUCCEED IN SCHOOL!

Seek Encouragement
Your Community
Look for sources of support in your community. The local library and other educational resources may provide tutoring.

Figure 4.2 Skills to Help Resolve Conflict

Conflict Resolution Resolving a conflict with an important person in your life can lead to a stronger relationship. *What are some different ways you have successfully resolved disagreements?*

- **Open communication lines.** Choose a quiet location where there will not be any interruptions or distractions. Be willing to listen to each other and to explain your point of view.
- **Use "I" statements.** When you speak, avoid sentences that start with "you." The other person might feel attacked and stop listening. Start sentences with the word "I" and give a description of how you feel. For example, say "I feel like I am not being respected," instead of "You don't respect me."
- **Listen carefully.** When you speak, you want the other person to listen. You should do the same. Do not interrupt. If you have questions, wait until the other person has finished. It can be helpful if you repeat back the other person's point of view to make sure that you understand it.
- **Control your anger.** Take deep breaths. Count to ten. Do not allow anger to take over. If you feel that you cannot control your anger, excuse yourself and try again when you feel ready.
- **Negotiate a solution.** Each person should decide what is most important about the outcome. Use these priorities to negotiate.
- **Compromise to reach an agreement.** Give-and-take can help you and the other person come to a solution. A compromise helps both people get some of what they want.

COMMUNITY CONNECTIONS

Mediation Find out if there are organizations in your community that train teens to mediate or negotiate. Identify an organization you can work with to help others resolve conflict.

Peer Mediation

Many schools use peer mediation to help resolve conflicts among students. **Peer mediation** is a process in which trained students help other students find a solution to a conflict before it becomes more serious. Students are often successful with peer mediation because the mediators are students themselves. Peer mediators can often see solutions that those involved in the conflict are too angry or emotional to see. An important part of making any kind of mediation successful is confidentiality. This means the people involved can trust that no one else will hear what is said. This helps students feel free to talk openly and honestly.

Walk Away

Suppose that you made every effort to head off problems before they could lead to a conflict. You tried to resolve problems through communication, negotiation, and compromise. Still, a conflict is growing to a dangerous point. You are at school and a classmate is bullying you. What do you do? Sometimes the best response is to walk away. In such situations it is helpful to seek out and talk to an adult at school or at home. You cannot solve every problem alone. What is important is that you do your best to behave in a way that reflects your values.

Peer Mediator A peer mediator helps his or her peers resolve conflicts. *What personal qualities does a peer mediator need to have?*

Section 4.2 After You Read

Review What You Have Learned

1. **Predict** ways gossip can lead to conflict.
2. **Identify** ways to control anger.
3. **Describe** how negotiation can lead to agreement.

Practice Academic Skills

English Language Arts

4. Write an e-mail to a friend with whom you have had a disagreement. Write what you think started the conflict. Suggest ideas for you and your friend to find a resolution.

Social Studies

5. Predict what could happen if the new student in your class makes false assumptions about you based on your ethnicity or cultural background.

· ·

Check Your Answers Check Your Answers at **connectED.mcgraw-hill.com**.

L. Mouton/PhotoAlto

Discovering Careers

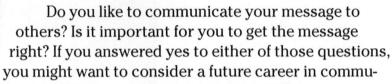

Do you like to communicate your message to others? Is it important for you to get the message right? If you answered yes to either of those questions, you might want to consider a future career in communication. The following chart explores several careers in the communication industry.

Career Activities ▽

At School

❶ Select three of the careers listed. Research the education, training, and work experience required for each career. Write a summary of your results.

At Home

❷ Put together a list of events and activities that will be happening at home or with your family in the next few days. Use the list to create a newscast. Play the role of newscaster and read your story to your family members.

At Work

❸ Make a list of what you think are the three most important qualities in a good journalist. Share your list with your classmates and discuss your choices.

In the Community

❹ Contact and interview someone in your community who works in communication. Ask this person to describe what his or her typical work day is like. Share what you learned with your class.

Job Title	Job Description
Speech Pathologist	Evaluates speech and language skills as related to educational, medical, social, and psychological factors. Plans, directs, or conducts treatment programs.
Newscaster	Broadcasts news items of local, national, and international significance. Prepares or assists in preparation of scripts.
Actor	Plays roles in dramatic productions, commercials, or other media. Interprets or presents characterization to audience.
Public Relations Specialist	Plans and conducts programs designed to create and maintain a favorable public image for employers or clients. Prepares press releases.
Journalist	Gathers and researches information from a variety of sources. Writes articles with accuracy. Uses correct grammar and punctuation
Copy Editor	Edits articles or books for grammar, punctuation, and style. Makes sure written materials communicate clearly and accurately.

Chapter Summary

Section 4.1 Listening and Speaking Skills

Communication is sending and receiving messages about ideas, feelings, and information. Nonverbal communication can show how you feel about yourself and others. Listening is just as important as speaking. People use different styles of communication, sometimes based on their personality or background. Communication through conversation is the sharing of ideas, thoughts, and feelings

Section 4.2 Handle Conflict

Conflicts happen. You can prevent some conflicts by heading off problems before they start. Pay attention to your own behavior. Learn to control your anger. Conflict resolution often means reaching a compromise. Negotiation skills can help you find a compromise. This requires give-and-take, in which both sides give up some demands and both sides get some of what they want.

Words You Learned

1. Write your own definition for each content and academic vocabulary word.

Content Vocabulary

- communication (p. 77)
- sign language (p. 78)
- body language (p. 78)
- gesture (p. 78)
- perception (p. 80)
- feedback (p. 80)
- gossip (p. 81)
- rumor (p. 81)
- diplomacy (p. 82)
- conflict (p. 84)
- prejudice (p. 84)
- negotiation (p. 87)
- peer mediation (p. 88)

Academic Vocabulary

- signal (p. 78)
- exchange (p. 80)
- escalate (p. 85)
- neutral (p. 87)

Review Key Concepts

2. **Describe** how verbal and nonverbal communication can show how you feel about yourself and others.

3. **Recognize** that listening is as important as speaking.

4. **Show** how asking questions can improve communication.

5. **Identify** factors that can cause conflict.

6. **Explain** how you can prevent conflict.

7. **Suggest** ways to resolve conflict.

Critical Thinking

8. **Predict** how you will use communication skills the next time you have a disagreement with a family member.

9. **Analyze** the factors that could cause a small disagreement to become a large conflict.

Real-World Skills and Applications

Problem-Solving

10. Action Plan Paul is starting high school next year. He has noticed that in the past six months or so, he has had more arguments with his parents. He also finds that he loses his temper more than he used to with his younger brother. He wants to go into high school with a good attitude, but he is worried that his temper will have a negative effect on him. Develop an action plan for Paul to help him with his attitude. Present your plan to your classmates.

Interpersonal and Collaborative

11. Evaluate Ways to Communicate
Should you have a conversation or write a letter? Follow your teacher's instructions to team up with another student. Have a face-to-face conversation about your favorite athlete or musical group or another topic of your choice. Then, write a letter to each other on the same topic. Exchange your letters. With your partner, compare your face-to-face conversation to the letters. Which worked better? Explain why.

Financial Literacy

12. Communicating with Shoppers
Visit a mall shop, a supermarket, a convenience store, or a general merchandise store. How does the store communicate to shoppers about the things they want you to buy? What do you notice when you first enter the store? Is it a selection of new products? Are they having a big sale? Are they offering special promotions, like "buy one, get one free?" Does a salesperson approach you to give you information? Make a list of the forms of communication you notice in the store. Do you think they are effective? Do you think they help you save money or spend more money? Do you think shoppers will buy something they were not planning to buy? Write one or more paragraphs to explain your answer.

13. Conflict Handbook Write and illustrate a Conflict Handbook for teens. Develop guidelines for facing, preventing, avoiding, and resolving conflict. Use graphics to illustrate the handbook. Present the Conflict Handbook to your classmates with an eye-catching presentation.

14. Conflict in History Pick a well-known historical conflict. It can be a war, a battle, or a court case. What were the circumstances? Who or what was involved? What were the conflicting issues? How was the conflict resolved? Present this information to your classmates.

15. Give Feedback Imagine that you worked for two weeks on a history project. You put a lot of hard work into it, and you are eager to find out what your grade is. Now imagine that your teacher accepts your project, but does not offer feedback. How do you know what you did well? How do you know where to improve? With permission from your teacher or parents, go online to learn more about how to provide feedback. Create a list of tips to keep in your Life Skills Binder.

D.Hurst/Alamy

Academic Skills

English Language Arts

16. Teach Imagine that one of your elementary school teachers invites you and a partner to speak to her 4th grade class about communicating without words. You and your partner will have five minutes to teach the younger students about body language, facial expressions, and gestures. Make your presentation fun, engaging, and appropriate for this age group.

Social Studies

17. Research Conduct research to find examples of groups and agencies that help people resolve conflicts. Choose the group you think is the most interesting. What specific conflict resolution strategies does the group use? Do they mention the importance of negotiation, compromise, and mediation? Share what you learned with the class in a one-paragraph summary.

Mathematics

18. The Cost of Compromise Dale suggests playing baseball in Benjamin's backyard after school. Benjamin hits a line drive. Harry does not catch it and the ball smashes a window. The three boys negotiate a compromise to split the $168.21 replacement cost of the window, with Benjamin paying twice as much as Harry, and Harry paying twice as much as Dale. How much will each boy need to pay?

Math Concept **Solving Algebraic Equations** You can write an algebraic equation and find the solution. Use a variable to represent an unknown amount.

Starting Hint Let x stand for Dale's share. Harry's share is $2x$. Since Benjamin owes twice as much as Harry, his share is $2 \times 2x = 4x$. You then know that $x + 2x + 4x = \$168.21$. Solve from there.

Standardized Test Practice

Multiple Choice

Read the paragraph. Then read the question and the answer choices. Choose the best answer and write it on a separate sheet of paper.

> **Test-Taking Tip** In a multiple-choice test, read the question and try to answer it before you read the answer choices. This way, the answer choices will not confuse you.

19. Jacob came home and found that his brother used his portable music player again without asking. Now the battery needs recharging, and Jacob wants to use it while doing his homework. What should Jacob do?

   a. Wait until he calms down to talk with his brother.
   b. Confront his brother right away since this happens all the time.
   c. Go tell his parents how mad he is at his brother.
   d. Go take something of his brother's to show him what it feels like.

Chapter 5

Citizenship and Leadership

Section 5.1

Good Citizenship

■ **Main Idea** Citizenship comes with rights and responsibilities.

Section 5.2

Leadership Skills

■ **Main Idea** Leaders demonstrate leadership skills and motivate team members to work together to achieve goals.

Gene Chutka/Getty Images

Explore the Photo

Strong leaders must have good technical skills, people skills, and thinking and planning skills. *Why does a good leader also have to be a good team player?*

Paragraph Development

Leadership Qualities Think about someone who is a strong leader. What qualities does the leader have? Pick the quality that you think is most important, and write a paragraph about that quality of leadership. Include specific examples that show how this quality contributes to strong leadership.

Writing Tips To write a strong paragraph, follow these steps:

1. Write a topic sentence that clearly expresses the main idea of the paragraph.

2. Include one or more details in each sentence that supports the main idea.

3. Link all of your sentences clearly and logically.

Section 5.1 Good Citizenship

Reading Guide

Before You Read

Stay Involved One way to stay involved when reading is to turn each of the headings into a question, then read the section to find the answers. For example, Rewards and Responsibilities of Citizenship might be "What are the rewards and responsibilities of citizenship?"

Read to Learn

Key Concepts

✓ **Name** one responsibility you owe to your community.

✓ **Summarize** the rewards of citizenship.

Main Idea

Citizenship comes with rights and responsibilities.

Content Vocabulary

○ citizen
○ citizenship
○ volunteer

Academic Vocabulary

■ entitled
■ thrive

Graphic Organizer

As you read, identify five ways that you can be responsible in your community. Use a graphic organizer like the one shown to help you organize your information.

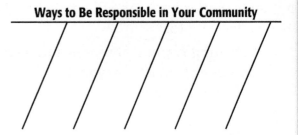

Ways to Be Responsible in Your Community

Graphic Organizer Go to connectED.mcgraw-hill.com to download this graphic organizer.

To be a member of your community, you need to do your share and be responsible. Communities need people who are willing to step up and meet responsibilities such as voting, caring for others, and helping neighbors. When you contribute, or give back, to your community, you can feel a sense of pride and belonging.

Citizenship

The first unit of this book is about discovering who you are, taking care of yourself, and developing your friendships. However, that is just the beginning. Personal growth activities do take up most of your time, but you have another purpose in life. You can make a difference in the lives of others. For example, Sandra and her mom help at the soup kitchen at least once a month. Eric helps his elderly neighbor with her gardening chores.

As an infant, you were completely dependent on others to care for your needs. As a preschooler, you probably were taught to share your toys. Gradually, you learned that what you did or did not do affected others around you. Now you are learning to share your time and talents to improve the lives of others. There are many opportunities for you to make a difference at home, at school, at work, and in your community.

A **citizen** is a member of a community such as a city, state, or country. Citizens are entitled to, or allowed to expect, certain rights. For example, the Bill of Rights gives United States citizens the right to:

- Vote for government representatives.
- Express opinions freely and publicly.
- Receive an education.
- Travel freely within the country.
- Receive a fair and speedy trial.
- Enjoy equal protection under the law, regardless of gender, race, or ethnic group.

As You Read

Connect What are some ways to participate in your government?

Vocabulary

You can find definitions in the glossary at the back of this book.

Volunteer Activities Volunteering can improve your self-esteem. *How can volunteering help you feel good about yourself?*

© mangostock/age fotostock

MATH YOU CAN USE

Teamwork

Deenie has formed a team with her classmates to design a garden for the school library. They must determine how much fencing they need to enclose the garden. The garden is in the shape of a triangle. The sides measure 6 yards, 8 yards, and 10 yards. How much fencing is needed to enclose the garden?

Math Concept **Finding Perimeter** The perimeter of any polygon (a closed shape with 3 or more sides) is calculated by adding the length of all of the polygon's sides.

Starting Hint The fencing will run along the perimeter of the garden. Calculate the perimeter by adding the 3 side lengths: 6 yards + 8 yards + 10 yards.

 For more math help, go to the Math Appendix located at the back of this book.

In return for the rights you enjoy, you have responsibilities to your community. You are required to obey laws and rules. Communities benefit when everyone plays a positive role.

The way you handle your responsibilities as a citizen is called **citizenship**. One of those responsibilities is to give back to the community. Volunteer work can be a valuable experience. When you **volunteer**, you give your time and energy without pay to help others. Volunteering is a good way to demonstrate your citizenship skills. Working with others who share your concerns can be a good way to make friends. As a volunteer, you may come into contact with people you may not meet otherwise. These people may be hungry, homeless, or lonely. Helping people can make you a more compassionate, or caring, person. It can be very satisfying to know that something you do helps someone else.

There are many ways you can volunteer your talents and skills:

- Read to people in a hospital or nursing home.
- Volunteer for an organization that records reading materials for people with visual impairments.
- Join efforts to clean up parks and recreation areas.
- Offer to take care of pets when your neighbors go on vacation.
- Pick up litter and put it in the proper place.
- Return lost items to the lost-and-found department or to the rightful owner.

Whether you demonstrate your citizenship skills alone or in a group, being a good citizen can give you a sense of belonging. You can also develop work experience and skills that you can apply to future jobs. What other ways can you think of to show your citizenship skills?

Reading Check *Define What is a citizen?*

Hands-On LAB

Be a Volunteer

In this activity you will research opportunities to volunteer in your community. Then you will volunteer for one of these opportunities based on your interests and availability. Before you begin, read through the entire Hands-On Lab assignment. Write down any questions that you have about the assignment. Reread the text or ask your teacher for help if you need it.

Supplies

✓ Newspapers
✓ Telephone directory
✓ Computer with Internet access (optional)

Develop Your Plan

- Make a list of volunteer activities that interest you.
- Search newspapers, telephone directories, and the Internet for local volunteering opportunities.
- Call your public library and ask about various organizations that meet there.
- On a sheet of paper, list several organizations that use volunteers.

Implement Your Plan

- Find out what type of help each organization needs from its volunteers.
- Make a list of what you find out and compare it with your values.

- List the days and times each organization needs volunteers. Are you available? Do you have transportation?
- Choose one volunteer opportunity from your list that works with your schedule.
- Contact the organizer and make a commitment to volunteer.

Evaluate Your Results

Describe the opportunity for which you volunteered. Why did you choose that opportunity? What did you learn from the volunteer experience? Would you volunteer with the same organization again? Why or why not? Write one or more paragraphs to explain your answers.

Projects and Activities Go to connectED.mcgraw-hill.com.

Design Pics/SW Productions

Responsibilities and Rewards of Citizenship

Being responsible to your community can bring rewards for you. The sense of pride you can feel when you help and support others in your community can give you a strong connection to your community. You can feel like you are part of something more than yourself.

Be Responsible in Your Community

A community can be a neighborhood, a workplace, a school, a city, and a state. A community will thrive, or survive and improve, only if each person works to make it a better place for everyone. Good citizens look out for other people in the community. Look for ways to care for others and to offer help where it is needed.

Remember Your Manners

When you live and work with other people you need to respect them and yourself. Your home is where you first learn to respect yourself. Your parents probably taught you at an early age to share your toys and say "please" and "thank you." That was just the beginning of good manners. Here are just a few ways to demonstrate your good manners at home, at school, and in your community.

- When you bump into someone, say "Excuse me."
- Do not cut in line. Wait your turn.

Clean Up Your World Good citizens are aware of their responsibility to keep the environment clean. *How do you think the efforts you make can help the environment?*

Japanese Table Etiquette

In Japan, it is common to share several dishes of food at the table rather than serving each person his or her own meal. Chopsticks may be provided specifically for serving food. If not, it is polite to move some food from the common dishes onto your plate with the opposite end of your own chopsticks. After eating, return all of your dishes to the same position they were in when the meal began. Replace the lids on dishes. Put your chopsticks on the chopstick holder or back into their paper slip.

chopsticks A pair of slender sticks held between the thumb and fingers used primarily in Asian countries or Asian restaurants to lift food to the mouth. Chopsticks can be made of wood, bamboo, metal, bone, and plastic. Chopsticks can be plain and functional, or decorated and engraved as works of art.

- If you knock something over, pick it up. Do not leave the mess for someone else to clean up.
- Apologize when you make a mistake.
- Do not interrupt someone when he or she is speaking. Wait until the person is finished speaking.
- Open doors for other people when you reach the entryway first.
- Whether you win or lose, always be courteous when playing sports or games.
- Practice good table etiquette, or manners. This shows respect for other people seated at the table.

Do Your Share

Offer to pitch in and help. Look for ways that you can lend a hand to family members, neighbors, teachers, and friends. Volunteer to help at school or in your community. Get involved in a community-sponsored event, such as a park clean-up or recycling campaign.

Show Respect for Others

Treat others as you would like to be treated. For example, wait your turn instead of trying to get to the front of a line. Give others in your family a chance to use the computer or telephone. Speak respectfully to adults, including parents, grandparents, teachers, and law enforcement officers. Remember to show respect for everyone, not just people you know well or especially like.

©Steve Lupton/Corbis

Help Other Students

Make new students feel comfortable, and introduce them to other people. If you meet someone with different values from your own, be willing to listen and understand. When you disagree with someone, give that person a fair chance to explain his or her opinion.

Take Care of Shared Property

Be as careful with library books or park equipment as you would be with your own belongings. Then the next person will be able to use and enjoy them, too. The same is also true for recreation areas, school buildings, and streets and sidewalks.

Good Manners Always be considerate and polite when sharing meals with family and friends. *Why is using good manners appropriate in every situation?*

Section 5.1 After You Read

Review What You Have Learned

1. **Name** three rights that a U.S. citizen has.
2. **Suggest** ways you can volunteer in your community.

Practice Academic Skills

English Language Arts

3. Conduct research to develop a public service announcement (PSA) that tells teens about local volunteer opportunities. Share your PSA with the class.

Social Studies

4. Conduct research to find a copy of the Bill of Rights. Choose one of the ten amendments. What does the amendment mean? Why do you think the amendment is important?

✈ **Check Your Answers** Check Your Answers at connectED.mcgraw-hill.com.

Section 5.2 Leadership Skills

Reading Guide

Before You Read

Prior Knowledge Look over the Key Concepts at the beginning of the section. As you read, write down what you already know about each concept, and write down what you want to find out by reading the lesson.

Read to Learn

Key Concepts

✓ **Describe** how a leader can guide a group to accomplish goals.

✓ **Define** two different leadership styles.

✓ **Give** examples of teamwork.

Main Idea

Leaders demonstrate leadership skills and motivate team members to work together to achieve goals.

Content Vocabulary

○ leadership
○ leader
○ motivate
○ autocratic leader
○ democratic leader
○ teamwork

Academic Vocabulary

■ elect   ■ delegate

Graphic Organizer

As you read, identify five qualities that a good leader should have. Use a graphic organizer like the one shown to help you organize your thoughts.

Good Leadership Qualities

Graphic Organizer Go to **connectED.mcgraw-hill.com** to download this graphic organizer.

Have you ever been in a group where no one was in charge? It probably seemed disorganized and confusing. Groups need leadership to direct the way tasks are accomplished. There are skills that help leaders guide groups successfully. When the leader is effective, so is the group.

Leadership

Leadership is the direction or guidance that helps a group accomplish its goals. Every group needs a **leader**, a person with the ability to guide and motivate others. Leaders can be found in front of the team to show the way, or they may be in the background to encourage others. Leaders must use good communication skills and know how to work with people.

As You Read

Connect How do you practice teamwork at home?

Sometimes people **elect**, or choose, leaders. For example, the captain of your hockey team and the mayor of your community were probably elected. At other times the job of a leader is not a formal job. When you organize a birthday party for a friend or get your siblings to help rake the leaves, you are in a leadership role. You can become a good leader when you motivate and encourage others, share responsibilities and rewards, have a positive attitude, and make smart decisions.

Motivate Others

When you are the leader, you need to help your group members be enthusiastic about the tasks you want to accomplish together. When you **motivate** someone, you make him or her feel enthusiastic, interested, and committed to a project or task. Motivate the group by being upbeat about the tasks and challenges you need to accomplish together. Set a good example. Be the first person to jump in and work on a project.

Encourage Others

It is easy for group members to become discouraged about the task and their part. Encourage others with positive words. Point out what they are contributing to the group. Be specific, "Thanks for jumping in on that task. I appreciate the way you offer your ideas to others." You can always find something nice to say. Listening is also a good way to encourage someone to share his or her ideas.

Share Responsibilities

You do not have to do it all yourself. Know when to **delegate**, or hand over, some of the responsibilities. Let others have a role in the task you are trying to accomplish. The group will feel good about what they accomplish, and you can feel good about teaching them something new. Share the work and the fun. Work cooperatively with others.

Have a Positive Attitude

Group members will look to you to set the tone for your tasks. Have a positive attitude about every task. Your enthusiasm can have a positive effect on the other members.

▶◇ **Vocabulary**

You can find definitions in the glossary at the back of this book.

Success Is What You Make It!

Achieve Your Goals

After you determine what success means to you, set goals to achieve your success. Break these goals into steps that will help you keep track of your progress.

• • • • • • • • • • • •

A positive attitude can make the difference in how well a job gets done and how well your group works together. Resolve any conflicts in a positive, affirming way.

Make Sound Decisions

Get all of the facts before making a decision. You should never make a snap decision. Investigate the details first. Make sound decisions on behalf of your group to help build your trustworthiness as the leader. Identify clear goals for the group.

Reading Check

Explain How can a leader encourage group members?

Character Counts

Tolerance

Luke is running for the student council where students will work together to lead and accomplish projects for his school. Some of his friends are actively campaigning against Lian, who has been critical of the way the student council has been run in the past. Luke's friends want him to join in the campaign against Lian. He knows that Lian has very different opinions and ideas about the way things should be done on the student council.

You Make the Call

Should Luke campaign against Lian in the student council election? What should Luke tell his friends? Write a paragraph that explains what you think Luke should do.

Work with Your Team When you work together with other people on your team, you set common goals. *How would your team be affected if you did not have goals?*

FCCLA Connection

In this activity, you will explore the benefits of joining FCCLA (Family, Career and Community Leaders of America). Before you begin, read through the entire Hands-On Lab assignment. Write down any questions that you have about the assignment. Reread the text or ask your teacher for help if you need it

Supplies
✓ Computer with Internet access
✓ FCCLA Mission Statement

Develop Your Plan
- Go to the FCCLA Web site (www.fcclainc.org), and read the benefits of joining FCCLA.
- Copy the FCCLA Mission Statement in your notebook.
- List the five steps of the FCCLA Planning Process.
- Share examples of good leaders and the qualities that you think make them good leaders.

Implement Your Plan
- List the leadership qualities that you already have, then list the qualities that you want to develop.
- Set a personal leadership goal and write it down in your notebook.
- Use the FCCLA Planning Process to create a plan for meeting your personal leadership goal.

- In an essay, explain the following:
  — How joining FCCLA could help you develop as a leader.
  — How being a better leader could help you in your relationships.
  — How FCCLA can help you develop character, creative and critical thinking skills, interpersonal communication skills, practical knowledge, and career preparation skills.

Evaluate Your Results
Exchange your FCCLA essay with a classmate and read his or her essay in return. Give each other feedback. Ask your teacher to evaluate your FCCLA plan for your personal leadership goal and provide feedback.

Projects and Activities Go to connectED.mcgraw-hill.com.

Leadership Skills and Styles

Leaders need to have certain basic skills to be successful. They must have technical skills, which means they need to have the ability to do specific tasks. For example, knowing how to use a computer application is a technical skill. Leaders need to be willing to learn new skills when technology changes. Leaders must also have good people skills. People will have a variety of opinions and personalities. Leaders need to communicate effectively with all types of people, and to respect the differences among them. A person who can help solve problems makes a good leader. Leaders also need good thinking skills. A good leader thinks critically and creatively, and knows how to make and carry out plans. It is not always easy to learn these skills. It takes practice to become a good leader.

Leaders often have distinctive or unique leadership styles. Think of a leader in a group you were in. What characteristics of his or her leadership did you notice?

Leaders who dictate are called **autocratic leaders**. This type of leader runs the show, from the smallest details to the big picture. Leaders who involve everyone in the decision-making process are **democratic leaders**. This type of leader helps the group in making decisions. The leader and the group make decisions together. How do you lead? What leadership style do you think works best?

COMMUNITY CONNECTIONS

Fundraiser Look for ways to help out with a local fundraiser in your community. You and your family could participate together in a walk-a-thon, relay, or other community project.

© Image Source

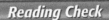

Reading Check

Contrast How do autocratic leaders and democratic leaders differ?

Leadership Opportunities A leader motivates others to accomplish goals. *What leadership opportunities does your school offer?*

Figure 5.1 Effective Interaction

Teamwork When you interact with other people, you will find that they have a variety of personalities, opinions, and ways of doing things. *Why is it beneficial to work in teams?*

Whether you are the leader or a team member:

- Let group members help set goals and make decisions.
- Keep an open mind about the opinions and ideas of others.
- Invite shy team members to get involved.
- Let others make some of the decisions.
- Be enthusiastic and positive.
- Encourage team spirit.
- Ask for everyone's opinion.
- Get everyone involved.
- Be respectful of others.
- Say thank-you.
- Be positive.

- Be considerate of other people's feelings.
- Use effective communication skills.
- Take every opportunity to compliment others.

Teamwork

A group such as a family, a school, or a community needs all of its members to work together. The most effective groups are those that function as teams. When people use **teamwork**, everyone works together to reach a goal. Teamwork means that people in the group help each other and share information. Teams can accomplish more as a group than individual members can accomplish alone. **Figure 5.1** lists several ways you can work effectively with others. Without the cooperation and support of all members, a team cannot operate effectively. For example, you demonstrate teamwork when you:

- Participate in a school fundraiser.
- Play on a sports team.
- Join the student council.
- Pitch in to help your family with yard work.
- Take part in a walk-a-thon.

Be a Strong Team Member

Not everyone can be a leader. In fact, if everyone wanted to be in charge, there would be nothing but conflict. The right combination of team leaders and team members is what makes a team effective.

Help the Team Succeed

A team's success depends on good leadership and good followers. If the followers do not do their share, how can the leaders get anything accomplished? The role of leader requires a lot of time and effort. If the leader has dependable followers, he or she has more time to spend on managing the team's goals. The team is more likely to succeed when the leader has a strong support system.

Do Your Part

If you join a team, be prepared to do your fair share. When everyone does a little work, no one has to do a lot of work. Have fun with your fellow team members, but remember to fulfill your duties as well.

Section 5.2 After You Read

Review What You Have Learned

1. **Explain** why the ability to motivate others is important for good leadership.
2. **Identify** three skills that a good leader should have.
3. **Summarize** the importance of teamwork.

Practice Academic Skills

English Language Arts

4. Imagine you have been asked to interview a person who is running for president of your school's student council. Write three questions to ask the person that would help you find out about his or her leadership skills.

Social Studies

5. For one day, keep a list of what you put in the trash and what you recycle. List and describe at least two actions you could take that would help you reduce waste on a long-term basis.

Check Your Answers Check Your Answers at connectED.mcgraw-hill.com.

Discovering Careers

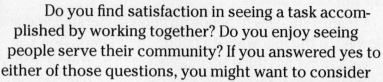

Do you find satisfaction in seeing a task accomplished by working together? Do you enjoy seeing people serve their community? If you answered yes to either of those questions, you might want to consider a future career in community service. The following chart explores several careers in the community service field.

Job Title	Job Description
State Legislator	Helps establish laws and policies in accordance with the state constitution and by-laws. Addresses the concerns of citizens.
Park Naturalist	Plans, develops, and conducts programs to inform public of historical, natural, or scientific features of parks. Schedules programs.
Election Clerk	Compiles and verifies voter lists from official registration records. Distributes ballots to voters and answers questions about procedures.
Little League Coach	Plans practice and play for young baseball players. Works with parents to organize play. Works with team on skills.
County Commissioner	Works with other commissioners to establish policies within a county. Works with citizens and their concerns.

Career Activities ▼

At School

❶ Select three of the careers listed. Research the education, training, and work experience required for each career. Write a summary of your results.

At Home

❷ Plan an informational program about your family's history. Include details about your heritage, places where you have lived, and interesting stories that are unique to your family. Present an outline of the program.

At Work

❸ Make a list of the community concerns that a legislator or commissioner might need to address. Prioritize your list based on what is most pressing for your community.

In the Community

❹ Contact and interview someone in your community who works in community service. Ask this person to describe what his or her typical work day is like. Share what you learned with your class.

Chapter Summary

Section 5.1 Good Citizenship

A citizen is a member of a community and is entitled to certain rights. In return, citizens have responsibilities to their community, such as obeying the law. A good way to demonstrate citizenship skills is to be responsible to your community. Citizens feel pride when they help and support others in their community, which can lead to a strong connection to the community. Citizens care about what happens to family, neighbors, and their community.

Section 5.2 Leadership Skills

Leadership is the direction that helps a group to accomplish its goals. Every group needs a leader. Good leaders motivate and encourage others, share responsibilities and rewards, have a positive attitude, and make smart decisions. Leaders have different leadership styles, and a successful group needs all of its members to work together. When people use teamwork, everyone works together to reach a goal.

Words You Learned

1. Use each of these content vocabulary words and academic vocabulary words to create a crossword puzzle on graph paper. Use the definitions as clues.

Content Vocabulary
- citizen (p. 97)
- citizenship (p. 98)
- volunteer (p. 98)
- leadership (p. 104)
- leader (p. 104)
- motivate (p. 104)
- autocratic leader (p. 107)
- democratic leader (p. 107)
- teamwork (p. 108)

Academic Vocabulary
- entitled (p. 97)
- thrive (p. 100)
- elect (p. 104)
- delegate (p. 104)

Review Key Concepts

2. **Name** one responsibility citizens owe to their community.

3. **Summarize** the rewards of citizenship.

4. **Describe** how a leader can guide a group to accomplish goals.

5. **Define** two different leadership styles.

6. **Give** examples of teamwork.

Critical Thinking

7. **Analyze** how much of a role popularity plays in leadership.

8. **Describe** who must pay when public property is damaged or destroyed.

9. **Explain** why some people may not want to participate in volunteer activities.

Real-World Skills and Applications

Problem-Solving

10. Which Is Better? Find a time to observe two different teams in your school or community, such as a sporting event, group project, or school assembly. What kind of leadership style do you observe in each group? List the pros and cons of each style you observe. Do you think one group has better leadership than the other? Share your observations with your class.

Interpersonal and Collaborative

11. Work Together to Get Involved Follow your teacher's directions to form groups. Work in groups to come up with a list of community groups for which you could volunteer. How could you make a difference? Put together a list for your class with your recommendations and ways to get involved.

Financial Literacy

12. Compare Nonprofits Like any corporation or organization, charities have expenses that must be paid. Non-profit organizations have administrative expenses, which means paying for employee salaries, office locations, and supplies. They also must spend money on mailings, phone calls, Web sites, and special events in order to raise more money. As a result, when you donate to a charity, only a certain percentage of your donation goes to the actual cause. Select two non-profit organizations you would consider donating money to. Conduct research to find out how each one uses the money it collects. Choose the organization that uses the higher percentage of donations for the cause.

13. Build Awareness Spend a day being more aware of people than you usually are. Introduce yourself to people you do not know. Smile and say hello. Ask questions to learn more about the people around you. Write a report about the reactions you got. Was this an easy or difficult task for you? Explain your answer in your report.

14. Research a Leader Choose a current or historical world leader and conduct research to learn about his or her leadership style. Find two examples of how he or she worked with other countries. Create a presentation for your class that explains whether or not you think the leader's style is or was effective.

15. Famous Quotes With permission from your parents or teacher, go online and choose a search engine. Type in a phrase such as "leadership quotations" or "motivational quotes." For example, you may come across this quote from fomer First Lady Rosalynn Carter: "A leader takes people where they want to go. A great leader takes people where they do not necessarily want to go, but ought to be." She probably means that great leaders have the skill and ability to encourage others to do their very best. Read several more, then list three quotations that you think apply to the types of leadership described in this chapter or in your class.

Academic Skills

English Language Arts

16. Create a Children's Book Partner with a kindergartener, a young neighbor, or younger sibling and read a book together. Then, ask the child to help you come up with an idea for a short children's story. Write the story and draw pictures to go with it. Bind the book with yarn or ribbon. Write a paragraph that describes your experience. Give the book to your partner to enjoy again later.

Social Studies

17. Voting Records Contact a local election office to find out how many registered voters live in your district or precinct. How many of them voted in the last election? What percentage of registered voters actually voted? Do you think this is an acceptable percentage? Why or why not? Write a paragraph to explain the information you find.

Mathematics

18. Calculate Claire is a supervisor at a non-profit company that raises money to build homes for low-income families. She has taken her employees out for a team-building lunch. During lunch they discussed their goals and the ways they want to work together to meet them. Claire decided to pay the bill herself so that the company can use more of their funds for the home-building efforts. The final bill is $92.50. If Claire leaves $110 including tip, what percentage did she leave as a tip?

Math Concept **Finding a Percent** To find what percent a number is of a second number, divide the first number by the second number. Multiply the result by 100 and add the percent symbol.

Starting Hint Figure out the amount of the tip by subtracting $92.50 from $110. Divide this tip amount by the original bill amount ($92.50), and multiply by 100 to get the percent.

Standardized Test Practice

Essay

Read the paragraph. Write your answer on a separate piece of paper.

Test-Taking Tip Brainstorm ideas before you begin writing. Use graphic organizers such as a web diagram to put your ideas on paper before you start to organize the essay.

19. You will soon have the opportunity to vote in a presidential campaign. What qualities will you look for when voting for the leadership of our country? Prioritize these qualities and write an essay that describes the kind of leader you would vote for.

Chapter 6

Goals and Decision Making

Section 6.1

Goals

■ **Main Idea** You can accomplish your goals when you are focused and positive. Learn to set short-term and long-term goals to achieve success.

Section 6.2

Decisions

■ **Main Idea** You make decisions every day. Decisions can be big or small. Making responsible decisions now can have a positive impact on your future.

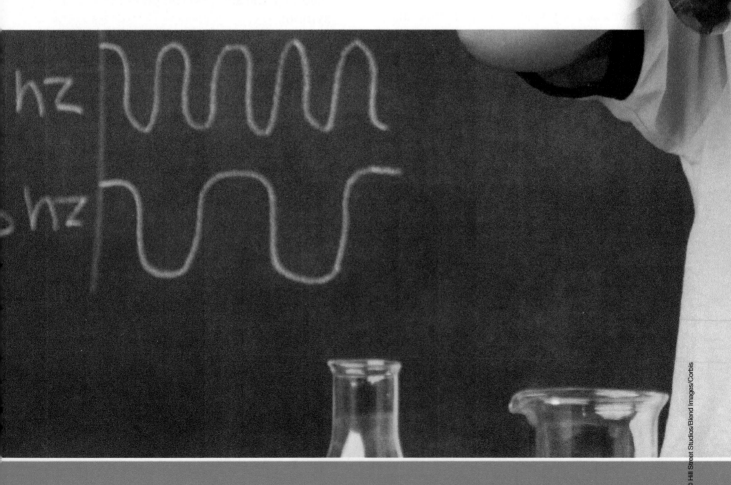

© Hill Street Studios/Blend Images/Corbis

Explore the Photo
Throughout your life, you will set goals and make decisions along the way. *What goals did you set for yourself this week?*

Autobiography

Who Are You? An autobiography is a story about who you are. Writing about yourself may seem like an easy thing to do. However, it can be challenging to write about yourself because there is so much to tell. To write your autobiography, focus your ideas into three areas: your personality, your hobbies and activities, and your job goals.

Writing Tips To write a strong autobiography, follow these steps:

1. Write an introduction that states your name and what you will write about.

2. Write three short paragraphs with details about each of the three areas.

3. Write a conclusion that ties the paragraphs together.

Section 6.1 Goals

Before You Read

Predict Before you start the section, browse the content by reading headings, bold terms, and photo captions. Do they help you predict the information in the section?

Read to Learn

Key Concepts

✓ **Differentiate** between long-term and short-term goals.

✓ **Explain** how attitude helps achieve goals.

Main Idea

You can accomplish your goals when you are focused and positive. Learn to set short-term and long-term goals to achieve success.

Content Vocabulary

○ goal
○ long-term goal
○ short-term goal
○ attitude
○ priority
○ trade-off

Academic Vocabulary

■ worth
■ accomplish

Graphic Organizer

As you read, list and explain five qualities of realistic goals. The first one has been done for you. Use a graphic organizer like the one shown to help you organize your information.

Realistic Goals should be...	Why?
Specific	So you can follow your progress and keep yourself on track.

🏹 **Graphic Organizer** Go to connectED. mcgraw-hill.com to download this graphic organizer.

Having something to aim for can give you purpose and direction in your life. It takes planning and skill to reach goals. You can learn these skills with time and practice. If you know what is important to you, it is easier to set goals and make decisions that can help you reach your goals.

Goal Setting

Goals are essential, or necessary, for success in life. A **goal** is something you want to achieve or accomplish. You will have many goals throughout your life. Some goals will be big, such as learn to fly a jet or get a college degree. Other goals will be smaller, such as pass tomorrow's math test or finish one more chapter in the book you are reading. Many other goals will fall somewhere in between. Personal goals can help you do your best and achieve the things you want and need.

Long-Term and Short-Term Goals

You may not think often about setting goals, but it is something you do almost all the time. Some of your goals may take months or even years to reach. This kind of goal is called a **long-term goal**. Your long-term goals may include marriage, owning a car, going to college, or saving enough money to buy a new computer.

A **short-term goal** can be reached quickly, perhaps in a few days or weeks. Your short-term goals might include complete a science project, pass a math test, or make the cheerleading team.

Sometimes short-term goals can help you achieve a long-term goal. Set short-term goals, such as completing a CPR course, to prepare yourself for your long-term goal of becoming an emergency medical technician. What are your short-term goals? What are your long-term goals?

Set Realistic Goals

When you set goals, you need to make sure that they are realistic. If your goals are too hard to reach, you may become discouraged and give up. If they are too easy, you may lose interest in them. Realistic goals are both reachable and challenging. **Figure 6.1** on page 118 offers guidelines for setting realistic goals.

As You Read

Connect What resources might you need to reach your goals?

Vocabulary

You can find definitions in the glossary at the back of this book.

Corbis/SuperStock

Personal Goals It can be very rewarding to reach a goal.
What do you think of first when you hear the word goal?

Goal setting requires planning. Identify a long-term goal and make a list of what must be done to reach it. Each step you take toward that long-term goal could become a short-term goal. A plan that includes short-term goals as well as long-term goals can provide you with the guidance you need to be a success. A written plan can help you see progress.

Reading Check   *List   What are three examples of a short-term goal?*

Achieve Goals

Achieving your goals is not something that just happens. You need to plan how you can reach each goal. For a good first step, write down the goal. This can help you get a clear picture of what you want to accomplish.

You also need to figure out what resources will be needed to reach your goal. Resources include your time, money, energy, knowledge, and skills. Your family and friends are also resources that are available to you. Use your resources wisely to achieve your goals.

Figure 6.1 Realistic Goals

Plan and Prepare The way you plan your goals and prepare to reach them has a lot to do with your success. *How can being prepared for a problem help you reach a goal?*

To be realistic, your goals should be:

- **Specific** Give yourself a very clear idea of your goal. That way, you can follow your progress easily and keep yourself on track.

- **Challenging** It is good to push yourself to reach a big goal. However, you should be practical about your abilities.

- **Active** Do something every day to work toward your goal.

- **Thought-out** Try to imagine possible problems. Plan positive, creative ways to deal with them. Being prepared for problems can keep you from being caught off guard if your plan hits a snag.

- **Flexible** Even with planning, the unexpected can happen. Be flexible so you can change your plans if you need to.

Goal Setting

In this activity you will use a past goal to learn the process of making short-term and long-term goals. Before you begin, read through the entire Hands-On Lab assignment. Write down any questions that you have about the assignment. Reread the text or ask your teacher for help if you need it

Supplies
✓ 2 sheets of paper
✓ Pen or pencil

Develop Your Plan

■ Fold a sheet of paper in half. On the left side, write down a long-term goal that you have already achieved. Perhaps it was getting a part-time job, earning a place on an athletic team, or joining a club.

■ On the right side of the paper, list what you did to reach that goal. You may not have realized it, but these were your short-term goals.

■ On the back of the paper, write how achieving the goal made you feel. Did you feel proud of yourself? Did you feel inspired to make an even bigger goal next time?

Implement Your Plan

■ Fold a second sheet of paper in half. On the left side, write down a new long-term goal that you want to achieve. For example, you may want to buy a car, get a full-time job, or attend college.

■ On the right side of the paper, list what you will do to reach that goal. For example, if attending college is your long-term goal, you would need to finish high school, research college options, and gather information about requirements. These steps are some of your new short-term goals.

■ On the back of the paper, write how you think you will feel when you reach the goal.

Evaluate Your Results

What did you learn from this exercise? How can you use this process to help you reach your future goals? Write one or more paragraphs to explain your answers.

 Projects and Activities Go to connectED.mcgraw-hill.com.

©Comstock/Corbis

Financial Literacy

Working to Meet Goals

Toni set a long-term goal for herself to rent an apartment. She is comparing rent costs to help make her decision. She found a one-bedroom apartment downtown that rents for $600. She found a one-bedroom apartment in the suburbs that rents for 75% of the cost of the downtown apartment. What is the rent of the apartment in the suburbs?

Math Concept **Multiplying by Percents** To determine the cost of the apartment in the suburbs, multiply the cost of the apartment in the downtown area by 75%.

Starting Hint: To multiply by a percent, you must change the percent to a decimal. To do this, move the decimal point two places to the left. In this problem, 75% becomes .75, which you will multiply by $600.

 For math help, go to the Math Appendix at the back of the book.

You may need to plan more than one way to reach your goal in case your first plan does not work. For example, suppose that you want to take up a new sport. If you find that you do not like team sports, you could try an individual sport such as swimming, jogging, or biking.

Attitude Counts

A positive attitude can go a long way toward helping you achieve your goals. Your **attitude** is the way you feel about something. A positive attitude can help you do your best, even if the task is something you may not enjoy. It can inspire you to keep working toward your goal even if you hit snags or make mistakes along the way. A positive attitude can help you tackle a difficult job rather than put it off. It also can help you be flexible when things do not go exactly as you planned.

Set Priorities

Some of your goals will be more important to you than others. You may even find that two or more goals are in conflict with each other. When this happens, you need to set priorities for your goals. A **priority** is something ranked high in importance. Putting tasks in order of importance can allow you to focus on the goals that mean the most to you.

Setting priorities for your goals may involve making trade-offs. A **trade-off** is something that you give up in order to get something more important. For example, if being on the debate team is very important to you, you may need to put off trying out for the band.

Success and Disappointment

As you experience success in reaching your goals, you can feel good about yourself. Successful experiences can help you grow and develop during your teen years and throughout the rest of your life. When you accomplish a goal, it can inspire you to set new goals and to try new things. This can add to your sense of personal worth, or value.

There may be times when you do not achieve a goal you set for yourself. If you fail to reach a goal, try to figure out what went wrong. Was your goal realistic? Did you have a clear picture of what you wanted to **accomplish**, or achieve? Did you use your resources wisely and plan other ways to reach your goal? Did you have a positive attitude? Did you set priorities? You may be disappointed, but if you know what went wrong, you can learn from it and improve your chances for success the next time.

Learn from Disappointment No one likes to fail, but sometimes it happens. *How can you turn a goal that was not reached into a positive experience?*

Section 6.1 After You Read

Review What You Have Learned

1. **Identify** the importance of setting a realistic goal.
2. **Explain** how a positive attitude can help you reach your goals.

Practice Academic Skills

English Language Arts

3. Write a paragraph to explain how you can use resources to accomplish a short-term goal. Identify the goal, the resources you would use, and how you would use the resources to reach your goal.

Social Studies

4. Conduct research to learn about a major historical accomplishment, such as the invention of the television or the Internet, that changed the way people lived. Or, choose an event such as the moon landing or the civil rights movement in the United States that changed the way people think. Who was responsible? What kinds of goals do you think the individuals or groups had to reach on their way to achieving the accomplishment?

Check Your Answers Check Your Answers at **connectED.mcgraw-hill.com**.

© Pascal Broze/SuperStock

Section 6.2 Decisions

Reading Guide

Before You Read

Check for Understanding If you have questions as you are reading, that means you are checking your understanding of the material. To get the most out of the text, try to answer those questions as you read.

Read to Learn

Key Concepts

✓ **Name** the different ways that decisions are made.

✓ **Recognize** how decisions you make now can affect your future.

Main Idea

You make decisions every day. Decisions can be big or small. Making responsible decisions now can have a positive impact on your future.

Content Vocabulary

○ decision   ○ proactive
○ alternative   ○ consequence

Academic Vocabulary

■ outcome   ■ integrity

Graphic Organizer

As you read, identify six resources you can use when making decisions. Use a graphic organizer like the one shown to help you organize your information.

Graphic Organizer Go to connectED. mcgraw-hill.com to download this graphic organizer.

You may find that success in life depends a lot on your ability to make smart decisions. Learning to make responsible decisions now can help you make more complicated or difficult decisions as you get older. The ability to make responsible decisions can give you a sense of pride and help increase your independence.

Decision Making

You will make many decisions in your life. A **decision** is something that you choose or make up your mind about after thinking over all possible choices. Each day you decide what to eat for lunch, what to do with your free time, and how hard to study. Other decisions require much more thought and planning, such as whom to marry, whether or not to have children, or whether or not to attend college. Here are some different types of decisions:

As You Read

Connect What are some of the small decisions you make every day?

- **Everyday Decisions** Some decisions are choices that you make every day. They usually do not require a lot of time or thought. Deciding what clothes to wear is an everyday decision. It may be important to you at the moment, but it does not change your life.

- **Decisions with Long-Term Effects** Decisions that have long-term effects on your life are major decisions. Some of the major decisions you will make as a teen are what courses you choose to take in high school and whether to get a part-time job.

- **Decisions that Become Habits** Some decisions become habits. These are decisions that you repeat without thinking about it. Brushing your teeth and doing your homework are decisions that become habits.

- **Life-Changing Decisions** Some major decisions, such as whether or not to go to college, can be life-changing. They require much time and thought and may be difficult to make. They are decisions that will affect you throughout your life.

Daily Decisions Simple things people do every day involve decision making. *What did you decide to eat for breakfast this morning?*

Fancy Collection/SuperStock

Sometimes you make decisions by responding to something that has happened. For example, you decide to start an exercise program after doing poorly in gym class. You also make decisions that can cause something to happen. For example, you decide to take on more responsibilities at home so that your family will give you more freedom. Sometimes you can choose to not make a decision at all. For example, you can ignore an invitation to a party. However, not making a decision is actually a decision in itself. When you do not make a decision, you leave the outcome, or result, up to chance or, in some cases, up to other people.

Decisions are made in several different ways:

- **Planned Decisions** Weigh all the facts before making a choice.
- **Default Decisions** Let someone else, or the circumstances, make the decision.
- **Impulse Decisions** Take the first choice available.
- **Emotional Decisions** Pick the choice that feels good without thinking it through.
- **Resistance Decisions** Pick the choice that will result in the least amount of conflict.

The outcome from decisions you make now can affect your future choices in positive and negative ways. For example, if you decide now to drop out of school, you will have fewer job options later. On the other hand, if you decide now to stay in school, you increase your chances of finding a good job in the future. An **alternative** is a choice between two or more different things or actions. Why do you think it is good to have several alternatives when making an important decision?

Make Proactive Decisions

You are more likely to make good decisions and choices if you are proactive. **Proactive** people think ahead about possible decisions or problems and take action right away. They do not ignore a problem, hoping that it will go away or resolve itself. They act as soon as they know something needs to be done. For example, Adam heard about a job opening in a sporting goods store near his home. It was so close he could walk to work. He immediately went to the store to fill out an application. By being proactive, he helped himself get the job. If he had put if off for a few days, the job might have gone to someone else.

Reading Check *Define What is a decision?*

Make Decisions and Solve Problems

The Decision-Making Process To make decisions and solve problems, you need a process to help you make smart and responsible choices. Everyday decisions, such as what to order for dessert or which shoes to wear do not require a process. However, more complicated decisions do need to be thought through with care. Follow the steps below to deal with difficult problems and choices.

1. **Identify the decision or problem.** The first step in making a choice is to identify what needs to be decided. Break big problems or choices into parts. Then you can tackle one part at a time. Start at the beginning and patiently work through the issues.

2. **Consider the alternatives.** Once you have a clear idea about the problem you need to solve, look for ideas about what you can do. The more alternatives you can identify, the better prepared you are to make a choice or solve a problem.

3. **Choose the best alternative.** Think about the advantages and disadvantages of each alternative. Ask yourself, "What would happen if I ...?" Consider your needs, wants, and goals. Thinking through all the possibilities can help you make a better decision. Use your values as guidelines to make your decision.

4. **Act on the decision.** After you have decided what to do, put your decision into action. Keep in mind that it is all right to change your mind if you figure out that you made the wrong choice. Sometimes new information or more thought can lead you in a different direction.

5. **Evaluate the decision.** When you evaluate, you study the results of your actions. Ask yourself these questions: Were my actions effective? Did my decision solve the problem? If not, why? What can I do better next time? Do I feel good about the outcome and the steps I took to reach it? By evaluating, you can improve your decision-making skills for future problems and choices.

Reduce Stress
Ask Your Family
Talk to your family members about any stress you are feeling. Often, all you need to do is tell someone about it to feel better. Someone in your family may have experienced similar feelings and may have advice to offer.

Make Responsible Decisions

Learning to make responsible decisions can give you a sense of control over your life. Instead of accepting whatever happens to you, you can help control how things happen.

Here are some suggestions to help you make responsible decisions:

- **Use good timing.** Make your decisions at the right time. Avoid making quick decisions. Give yourself time to consider all the facts. On the other hand, do not put off a decision too long. If you do, you may find that some of your options are no longer available.
- **Consider the consequences.** A **consequence** (ˌkän(t)-sə-ˌkwen(t)s) is a result of your choice. Think about how your decision can affect your life now and in the future. How will your decision affect you, your family members, or your friends?
- **Be willing to make mistakes.** Any time you make a decision, there is a chance that you will make a mistake. Be willing to make mistakes and to learn from them.
- **Seek advice when you need it.** Advice from family members, teachers, and friends can help you make decisions. Sometimes they have had to make similar decisions. Listen to others and use their advice if it is helpful.

- **Accept responsibility for your decisions.** When you make your own decisions, you must accept responsibility for the consequences. You cannot make excuses or blame others when you make a poor decision. To accept responsibility for your decisions and the consequences of those decisions is a sign of maturity.

Experience Counts Your parents and teachers have had their share of choices to make. *How can their experiences help you make decisions?*

Tim Pannell/SuperStock

Take Responsibility for Decisions

It would be easier to let someone else take the blame when things go wrong. However, you are the only one responsible for the decisions you make. If your decisions or choices do not turn out well, you show **integrity**, or honor and truthfulness, when you admit that you made a mistake. When decisions turn out well, you feel proud. Take responsibility for your decisions because:

- Making mistakes is part of the process. Use the opportunity to learn from them.
- People do not respect you when you make excuses or blame others.
- People do respect you when you try to fix a mistake.
- When things go well, you get to accept the praise and recognition.

 **Character Counts**

Courtesy

Jane's friend Carrie is getting married in two weeks. Jane was invited to the wedding two months ago. Jane did not respond to the invitation because she was thinking about attending another event that ended up being canceled. Carrie does not know if Jane is coming to the wedding. The reception is being catered, and the caterer needs to know how many guests will attend so he can prepare the right amount of food. Jane wants to go to the wedding, but she thinks it is too late to respond.

You Make the Call

Is it too late for Jane to respond to the invitation? Write a paragraph that explains what you think Jane should do.

Section 6.2 After You Read

Review What You Have Learned

1. **Explain** what can happen if you choose not to make a decision.
2. **Identify** ways to make responsible decisions.

Practice Academic Skills

English Language Arts

3. Conduct research to find a literary character who had to make a difficult decision. Was the character's process effective? What was the outcome? What would you have done differently if you were faced with the same decision as the character? Write a paragraph about how the character used the decision-making process.

Social Studies

4. Choose a leader in world history. Research information about the person to find an issue he or she had to decide upon. Prepare a presentation that includes the leader you chose, the factors that led to the decision, and the outcome of the decision.

Check Your Answers Check Your Answers at connectED.mcgraw-hill.com.

Discovering Careers

Do you work well under pressure? Are you able to make quick decisions? Do you want to help people in crisis? If you answered yes to any of those questions, you might want to consider a future in an emergency response career.

The following chart explores several careers in the emergency response field.

Job Title	Job Description
Firefighter	Protect life and property from fires. Often the first emergency responders at traffic accidents. Firefighters are often required to treat injuries as well as fight fires.
Police Officer	Investigates complaints, maintains order, helps individuals, and identifies criminal offenders. Makes quick decisions in emergency situations.
Emergency Room Nurse	Cares for patients in various states of illness or injury. Helps decide which patients are in the most need of immediate care.
9-1-1 Operator	Answers calls from people in distress. Consults detailed manual to provide quick and often life-saving instructions to callers. Coordinates with fire, ambulance, and police services as needed.
Emergency Medical Technician (EMT)	Responds to emergency situations. Makes split-second decisions about patient care. Administers health care for accidents, injuries, and illness.

Career Activities ▼

At School

1 Select three of the careers listed. Research the education, training, and work experience required for each career. Write a summary of your results.

At Home

2 Create an emergency plan with your family in case of fire or other crisis. Make a map of your home with a planned escape route, and agree with your family on a specific place to meet.

At Work

3 Make a list of at least five jobs that require strong decision-making skills. Next to each job listed, write an example of a decision that might need to be made on the job.

In the Community

4 Contact and interview someone in your community who works in an emergency response career. Ask this person to describe what his or her typical work day is like. Share what you learned with your class.

Chapter Summary

Section 6.1 Goals

A goal is something you want to achieve. When you set goals, you need to make sure that they are realistic. Goal setting requires planning and a positive attitude. Some goals will be more important to you than others. As you experience success in reaching your goals, you can feel good about yourself. If you do not achieve a goal, you can learn from the experience and improve your skills for the next goal.

Section 6.2 Decisions

Decision making is an important part of daily life. Sometimes you make decisions by responding to something that has happened. Other times you make decisions based on what you have already planned or considered. The decisions you make now can affect the choices you have in the future. Learning to make responsible decisions can give you a sense of control over your life.

Words You Learned

1. Use each of these content vocabulary words and academic vocabulary words in a sentence.

Content Vocabulary

- goal (p. 117)
- long-term goal (p. 117)
- short-term goal (p. 117)
- attitude (p. 120)
- priority (p. 120)
- trade-off (p. 120)
- decision (p. 123)
- alternative (p. 124)
- proactive (p. 124)
- consequence (p. 126)

Academic Vocabulary

- worth (p. 120)
- accomplish (p. 121)
- outcome (p. 124)
- integrity (p. 127)

Review Key Concepts

2. **Differentiate** between long-term and short-term goals.

3. **Explain** how attitude helps achieve goals.

4. **Name** the different ways that decisions are made.

5. **Recognize** how decisions you make now can affect your future.

Critical Thinking

6. **Assess** Is putting off making a decision always negative? When might it be better to put off making a decision?

7. **Evaluate** Why is it possible for someone who grew up with limited resources to still be successful?

8. **List** Write a list of the steps in the decision-making process. Next to each step, write a tip that can help you make your next important decision.

9. **Predict** Why should you be flexible when setting goals for your future career?

Real-World Skills and Applications

Problem-Solving

10. Prioritize Jacob wants to play football and be in the band. During the fall, both activities hold their practices at the same time, so he has to choose one of the activities. How should he decide which activity to be involved in? What should Jacob consider as he prioritizes his activities?

Technology Applications

11. Design a Template A template is a model or an outline. Use word-processing or spreadsheet software to create a template people can use when they want to achieve a long-term goal. Refer to the steps in the decision-making process. Include helpful tips for each step they should take.

Financial Literacy

12. Set Career Goals You may already know what career you wish to have when you are finished with school. Even if you do, you may have the opportunity in the coming years to reconsider your decision. While money is not the only factor that should guide your career decisions, salaries do play a part in goal setting. Identify three jobs that you might like to have when you have completed your education. Conduct research to find out the typical starting salary for each of the three jobs you selected. How might those salaries affect other long-term goals that you may have? What trade-offs might you have to make?

13. The Impact of Your Choices Choose five decisions you have made in the last week. For each decision, make a list of all the people affected by your choice, including yourself. Put a plus sign next to each name if your choice had a positive effect on the person, or a minus sign if your choice had a negative effect. Rate yourself on how well you consider the consequences of your choices. Are you satisfied with the results?

14. Identify and Evaluate Resources Knowing how to gather information from various resources can help you make decisions and solve problems. Do you plan to attend college? Maybe you want to join a branch of the military, or perhaps you plan to enter the job market right away. List three things you want to do after high school. Then identify sources of information for each. Rank the information sources on your list from most useful to least useful and give reasons for your ranking.

15. Goal Setting Online With permission from your parents or teacher, go online to search for information about how to achieve goals. What advice can you find? Are there tips available online that apply to specific goals? Are there any Web sites about goal setting that you would recommend to a friend? If so, explain why you would recommend them. Write down useful goal-setting tips to share with your classmates and to include in your Life Skills Binder.

DJHurst/Alamy

Academic Skills

English Language Arts

16. Advertise Your student council is launching a campaign to encourage students to make wise decisions by using the decision-making process. Create a pamphlet that that will teach your class-mates how to use the decision-making process. What information will you include? What will the design be?

Science

17. Collect Data An important part of the scientific method is collecting data and studying it to see what it reveals about something. Collect your own data about what people do when they make decisions.

Procedure Choose a place, like a fast food restaurant or movie theater, to record the body language you observe while a person makes a decision.

Analysis Organize your findings in a chart. What conclusions can you draw?

Mathematics

18. Calculate Elena is going to give a speech about setting goals at a luncheon for business executives. Her speech will be accompanied by a slide show. The presentation time limit is 15 minutes, and Elena figures she will use 25 slides. What is the average number of seconds she should spend on each slide without going over the time limit?

Math Concept **Performing Calculations with Time** When performing calculations with time, it is helpful to convert all numbers to the same units prior to calculating. Since a minute has 60 seconds, to convert minutes to seconds, multiply by 60. To convert seconds to minutes, divide by 60.

Starting Hint The average is the total time divided by the number of slides. Convert the number of minutes for the speech (15) to seconds by multiplying by 60. Divide the answer by the number of slides (25). Label your final answer with the correct unit of time.

Standardized Test Practice

Reading Comprehension Read the passage, then answer the question.

Test-Taking Tip Read the passage carefully, underlining key statements as you go. Answer the questions based only on what you just read in the passage, not based on your previous knowledge.

English has thousands of words borrowed from French. However, most of our basic English vocabulary is more similar to German. Compare English *house* and German *Haus* or English *finger* and German *Finger*. In fact, English is much more closely related to German than it is to French. English and German are both part of the Germanic language family.

19. According to this passage, why does English have many words that are similar to German?

Your Point of View

Forming your own opinions shows a sense of responsible citizenship. Local newspapers may highlight issues that are important to your community. Your parents and teachers may have opinions on topics that you can consider. This project will help you explore your own point of view.

My Journal Complete the journal entry from page 73, and refer to it to write your current events summary.

Project Assignment ▼

In this project, you will:

- Clip a news story about an important issue in your community.
- Describe the opposite points of view about the issue.
- Write about your own opinion.
- Interview someone who holds elected office.
- Present a campaign poster and speech about your topic to the class.
- Include this project in the second section of your personal Life Skills binder.

 Step 1 **Research News Stories of Current Events**

Forming your own opinion is easier when you know a lot of information about the issue. Read the local newspaper and clip a story that discusses local topics. Write a summary of the facts of the story and describe the opposing viewpoints.

Step 2 **Select an Issue and a Slogan**

Choose an issue that interests you. Pick a viewpoint that you agree with. Develop an idea for a poster with a slogan that supports your opinion. Then prepare to write a speech that answers these questions:

✔ What are the facts about your issue?
✔ What do the opponents of your position believe?

✔ What facts can you give to support your opinion?
✔ How would you convince others to agree with you?

Step 3 **Interview an Elected Official**

Interview someone in your community who was elected to their position. Ask these questions:

✔ What methods did you use to get people to vote for you?
✔ What is your opinion about the issue I am studying?
✔ How do you prepare to give a speech?

Use these interviewing skills when conducting your interview and these writing skills when writing the summary of notes from your interview.

Interviewing Skills
- Record interview responses and take notes.
- Listen attentively.

Writing Skills
- Use complete sentences.
- Use correct spelling and grammar.

Step 4 Create and Present Your Poster and Speech

Use the Life Skills Project Checklist on the right to plan and complete your poster and write and deliver a two-minute speech about your opinion on this issue.

Use these speaking skills when presenting your final report.

Speaking Skills
- Speak clearly and concisely.
- Be sensitive to the needs of your audience.
- Use standard English to communicate.

Step 5 Evaluate Your Presentation

Your project will be evaluated based on:

- ✔ Completeness and organization in the description of your opinion of the issue you chose.
- ✔ The poster that reflects your opinion on an issue.
- ✔ Your speech about your point of view on an issue.
- ✔ The summary written from interview notes.
- ✔ Grammar and sentence structure.
- ✔ Presentation to the class.
- ✔ Creativity and neatness.

Evaluation Rubric Go to **connectED. mcgraw-hill.com** for a rubric you can use to evaluate your final project.

Life Skills Project Checklist

Research News Stories

- ✔ Read the newspaper and then clip a chosen article.
- ✔ Write down facts and opinions from the article.
- ✔ Create a poster about your topic.
- ✔ Interview an elected official in your community.

Writing Skills

- ✔ Describe the viewpoints and facts in your news story.
- ✔ Write a speech that communicates your point of view.
- ✔ Write a summary from your interview with an elected community member.

Present Your Findings

- ✔ Prepare a short presentation to share your poster and deliver a speech that reflects your point of view.
- ✔ Invite students to ask any questions they may have. Answer these questions with responses that respect their perspectives.
- ✔ Add this project to your Life Skills binder.

Academic Skills

- ✔ Conduct research to gather information.
- ✔ Communicate effectively.
- ✔ Organize your presentation so the audience can follow along easily.
- ✔ Thoroughly express your ideas.

Amos Morgan/Getty Images

Unit Preview

This unit is about preparing for a career. In this unit, you will learn about:

- Why it is important to start thinking about your career now.

- The different reasons people work.

- Skills that are important in the workplace.

- Being a responsible worker.

Explore the Photo

Setting a career goal now can help you attain it later. *What career goals do you have, and what can you do now to help you attain your dream career?*

Jacqui Hansia/moodboard/SuperStock

You in Ten Years

When you are done studying this unit, you will complete a project in which you will:

- ✓ Explore your skills and talents.

- ✓ Interview someone who has a job you want to learn about.

- ✓ Imagine what you will do for a living and describe it to your class.

The prewriting activity below will help you get started.

My Journal

Prewriting Activity
Prepare an Outline

Are you good at math? Do you love children? Are you very artistic? Maybe your friendly nature is appealing to people. Write an outline about jobs or careers you could be doing in ten years.

- What kind of jobs might be suitable to your personality and talents?

- What would you most like to do for a living?

Chapter **7**

Explore Careers

Section 7.1

Plan Your Career

■ **Main Idea** It is important to research and plan your career path.

Section 7.2

Prepare for Work

■ **Main Idea** People work for many reasons and prepare for work in different ways.

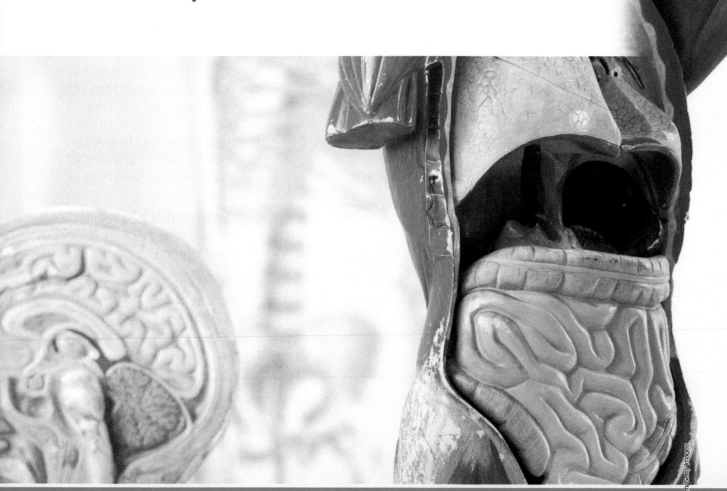

Jolostorm/Getty Images

Explore the Photo
The options for careers are endless as you think about your interests and dreams. *What are you learning about the world of work as you grow older?*

Summary

Work in the News A summary is a shortened version of something that has been said or written. A summary focuses on the main points. Find an article from a news source about the world of work. Write a one-paragraph summary of the article that sums up the main points.

Writing Tips Follow these steps to write a summary:

1. Identify the topic of each section to focus your reading.
2. Identify and list the most important details that support each topic.
3. Review your details and decide what the main points of the section are.

Reading Guide

Before You Read

Check for Understanding If you have questions as you are reading, that means you are checking your understanding of the material. To get the most out of the text, try to answer those questions.

Read to Learn

Key Concepts

✓ **Describe** how to create a career plan.

✓ **Recognize** the importance of researching careers.

Main Idea

It is important to research and plan your career path.

Content Vocabulary

○ aptitude
○ portfolio
○ job shadowing
○ apprentice
○ networking
○ mentor

Academic Vocabulary

■ modify
■ reveal

Graphic Organizer

As you read, identify six factors to review when researching a career. Use a graphic organizer like the one shown to help you organize your information.

Job Research
1.
2.
3.
4.
5.
6.

Graphic Organizer Go to connectED.mcgraw-hill.com to download this graphic organizer.

"**W**hat do you want to be when you grow up?" You have probably heard that question before. Have you really thought about your answer? Perhaps you are interested in becoming a gourmet chef or an astronaut. You have many choices. Whether you choose to be an attorney or a musician, it is not too soon to start thinking about the career you might want to have one day.

Explore Your Options

As You Read

Connect What skills do you have now that can help you in your future career?

It is a good idea to start exploring career opportunities now. That way you will be better prepared to make a career choice. When you think about your options, consider your strengths, interests, abilities, values, and goals. Decisions based on these factors can lead you to work you enjoy. Ask other people how they got started in a career to get ideas for your own career path.

Career Planning

It is a good idea to begin thinking ahead about some of the specific skills that will help you get a job. What are the careers that interest you? It is important to learn about the kind of education and training you will need for the career you choose. It is also important to collect occupational and labor market information about each career. For example, Marissa loves to draw and paint pictures, but she learned through research that the demand for traditional artists is not as high as it used to be. Marissa decided she would need to learn how to use computer graphics software to become a digital artist.

When considering a career, you should also think about your values and goals. What is important to you? What do you want to do with your life? Do you want to help other people? Consider a career in health services. Do you like to build things? Look into construction or architecture. Knowing your values and goals can help you focus on an area that fits your personality. Review your career plan often and modify, or change it, as needed.

Choose What You Enjoy Have you ever noticed that when you are doing something you enjoy, it does not seem like work? *What activities or hobbies do you enjoy that might lead to a career?*

KidStock/Getty Images

Family and Consumer Sciences Teacher Teaching Family and Consumer Sciences involves much more than cooking and sewing. *What other subject areas are involved?*

◆ Vocabulary

You can find definitions in the glossary at the back of this book.

If you need help deciding, there are special tests that can help you discover your aptitudes. An **aptitude** is a natural talent or ability for something. You may not even know about it yet. An aptitude test can help predict your ability to learn certain skills. A test of this kind can help reveal, or show, your strengths. However, this only one of many things you can do to help you decide. You also need to think about your interests. For example, the field of family and consumer sciences includes a wide variety of career options, such as cooking, nutrition, sewing, job preparation, fashion design, caring for children, and money management.

Career Portfolio

As you study and gain work experience, it is a good idea to create a **portfolio**, which is a neatly organized collection of your skills, experiences, and qualifications. Employers view career portfolios as presentations of your skills and abilities. For example, Martin is interested in a career in photography. He has selected prints of his best photos to put in his career portfolio. He also included certificates he earned from the Digital Photography Club. Later, Martin will add letters of recommendation and a list of the knowledge and skills he has gained. Think of a career portfolio as a way to show off your best efforts. Portfolios can be created online, too. Ask your teacher or school librarian for help if you want to get started on your portfolio.

School Resources
School Library
Librarians or media center specialists can help you conduct research and find reading materials. They can also help you locate online tutorials and other learning programs.

● ● ● ● ● ● ● ● ● ● ● ● ●

Reading Check *Identify How can you discover your natural abilities, strengths, or talents?*

Fuse/Getty Images

Research Careers

Talk about career possibilities with your parents, family members, school counselors, and teachers. They can offer you advice and answer questions. Choose a few careers that interest you and do some basic research. **Figure 7.1** lists six important factors to review when researching career possibilities.

Reading about jobs on the Internet and hearing about jobs from others is useful. However, if you want to get a more direct experience, try job shadowing. **Job shadowing** is spending a day or a few hours with someone to observe him or her on the job.

Character Counts

Work Ethic

Clarence works part-time at a local grocery store. He has a variety of responsibilities, from stocking shelves to bagging groceries. His friend Jake drops by almost every day to visit and chat. Often when Jake comes to the store, Clarence finds himself talking with him in the storage room or on an aisle when he is stocking shelves for fifteen or twenty minutes at a time. Clarence knows that he does not get as much done when Jake is there.

You Make the Call

What should Clarence do to use his time at work wisely? Write a paragraph that explains what you think Clarence should do and why.

Figure	7.1	Job Research

Know What to Expect When you know what to expect from a job, it will be easier to decide which ones interest you and match your personality. *Do you think your first job will be in the same field as your career? Why or why not?*

- **Educational Requirements** What education is required for the job? You may need a college degree or certification in the field.

- **Job Responsibilities** What responsibilities or duties are performed on the job? Your work day may include a variety of tasks, or you may do the same tasks every day.

- **Salary Potential** What is the average income of entry-level workers in this position? Know ahead of time what the starting salary is, and what you can expect to earn as you gain more experience.

- **Promotion Opportunities** What opportunities for promotion exist? You may earn a promotion after demonstrating expertise. Some companies require further training to help you move forward.

- **Working Conditions** What are the working conditions? You may be required to attend safety training on the job.

- **Future of Field** Will there be a need for more workers in this field in the future? You may have to upgrade your education or training to keep your job, or find a new job if necessary.

JUPITERIMAGES/Comstock Images/Alamy

If you find a job that you believe would be worth the investment of time and money, an apprenticeship may be a good route to take. An **apprentice** works under the guidance of a skilled professional in order to learn an art, craft, or trade. Once the new skill is mastered, the apprentice may become a professional. Electricians, carpenters, mechanics, sculptors, plumbers, and barbers are just a few professions that may offer apprenticeships.

Networking

If you ever followed up on a job tip you received from a family member or friend, you practiced networking. **Networking** means using your personal connections to help achieve your goals. When you seek job information from people you know, you have a good chance of going into the job application process informed and confident.

Networking is one of the most direct ways to find a job. In addition to networking with your family members you can also network with:

- friends and classmates.
- teachers and mentors.
- employers and coworkers.
- national organizations such as FCCLA (see **Figure 7.2**).
- community organizations.
- recruiters at job fairs.
- Social Media.

Apprenticeship Many skilled workers learn their trade in formal apprenticeship programs. *How can both the apprentice and trainer benefit from an apprenticeship?*

When you network, be courteous. Do not pressure people for information. If you are given a job lead, follow up in a responsible manner. It is important to follow up when someone passes on information that can help you. Your behavior reflects on you and on the person who recommended you.

Mentor

A **mentor** is someone with experience who supports, advises, and encourages the progress of a less experienced person. To identify a mentor, think about a person you admire and respect who has talents and skills you would like to learn. Then arrange to meet with this person and discuss your goals. Mentors can keep you from getting discouraged. Their experience can help you avoid common mistakes. Your mentor may also be able to help you network.

Professional Organizations

Another source of job postings is professional organizations. These organizations are made up of people already employed in a field. You usually need to pay a membership fee to join professional organizations. The services they offer include employment listings, job placement services, scholarships, and network opportunities.

School Resources
Guidance Counselors
Guidance counselors are excellent resources at your school. They can help you choose classes and plan a career path.

• • • • • • • • • • • • • •

Figure **7.2** **FCCLA**

The Ultimate Leadership Experience Middle and high school students can develop their leadership skills in many ways. *Why is it important to join a professional organization such as FCCLA?*

Family, Career and Community Leaders of America (FCCLA) is a national organization of middle and high school students enrolled in family and consumer sciences courses. FCCLA activities provide opportunities for leadership development. Student members benefit from programs that include individual projects which strengthen critical thinking and decision-making skills. Members also participate in team projects to improve cooperative learning.

The Internet

You can also learn about careers through the Internet. You can go online to get ideas, find out what jobs are available, and research specific job requirements. When you are ready, you can submit your résumé online. You will learn more about résumés in the next chapter.

Ask your parents, librarian, or teacher to help you:

- Search *The Occupational Outlook Handbook* or the *Dictionary of Occupational Titles.*
- Find job postings and job descriptions.
- Post a résumé.
- Locate professional organizations.
- Register with online employment agencies.

Find a Mentor Think about a person you admire and respect who has talents and skills you would like to learn. *How can a mentor help you with your career goals?*

Section 7.1 **After You Read**

Review What You Have Learned

1. **List** the factors you should consider when you think about career options.
2. **Explain** why it is important to network.

Practice Academic Skills

English Language Arts

3. Should a person ever choose a career that does not match his or her interests? Why or why not? Explain your answer in a short speech.

Social Studies

4. Locate professional organizations for a career that you are considering. What kinds of benefits do they offer for their members? Write a summary of how the organization could help you prepare for your career.

Check Your Answers Check Your Answers at connectED.mcgraw-hill.com.

Reading Guide

Before You Read

Predict Before starting the section, browse the content by reading headings, bold words, and photo captions. Do they help you predict the information in the section?

Read to Learn

Key Concepts

✓ **Explain** why people work.

✓ **Identify** steps you can take to prepare for work.

Main Idea

People work for many reasons and prepare for work in different ways.

Content Vocabulary

○ job satisfaction
○ entrepreneur
○ franchise

Academic Vocabulary

■ technology
■ credit

Graphic Organizer

As you read, identify four ways that part-time work can prepare you for full-time work. Use a graphic organizer like the one shown to help you organize your information.

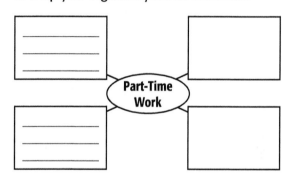

Part-Time Work

⬥ **Graphic Organizer** Go to **connectED.mcgraw-hill.com** to download this graphic organizer.

Just about everyone works. Jobs provide income for homes, cars, food, and other things, like vacations and recreation. Since you are going to spend most of your adult years working, it is important to consider how you can best plan and prepare for the world of work. Take advantage of the many resources available to help you find ideas and opportunities.

The World of Work

You will have several jobs during your lifetime. One of the first steps in finding a job that satisfies you is to consider your skills. Do you have special skills that could be useful in a particular type of work? For example, do you love to read? Are you creative? Do you think science is fascinating? Would you volunteer or work part-time to strengthen those skills?

As You Read

Connect Why is it important to think about your career goals now?

Why People Work

People work for many reasons. The main reason is to earn a living, but there are many other benefits. People take pride in their work and enjoy job satisfaction. **Job satisfaction** is a feeling of accomplishment from a job well done. Every job helps another person in some way. This can help people feel good about themselves and feel satisfied about what they do for others. Work is also a way to meet people and make friends.

Vocabulary

You can find definitions in the glossary at the back of this book.

Enjoy What You Do

Most people choose jobs based on their interests and skills. Some people enjoy physical tasks, such as installing machinery. Others prefer artistic work, such as digital photography or home design. Still others want jobs in which they can help people, such as responding to medical emergencies, or caring for young children.

Most people spend 40 or more years in the workforce. It is worth the effort to research and learn as much as you can about your work options.

Reading Check *Examine How do most people make decisions about what job they want to do?*

School Resources
Ask Your Teacher
If you are having problems in a particular subject, ask your teacher for additional help. He or she may be able to provide after-school tutoring or other activities to help you tackle specific problems.

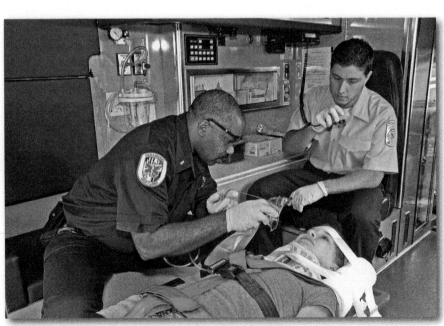

Draw on Your Interests A person who is interested in the medical field and wants to help others may choose a career as an emergency medical technician. *What kind of education or training do you think this person needed?*

Rick Brady/McGraw-Hill Education

Future Plans Education and training continue beyond high school. *What plans do you have after high school graduation?*

Get Ready to Work

Without a high school education, your job opportunities will be limited. Your school counselor will have a lot of information about how you can finish school successfully. There are many ways to continue your education and training after high school. You may choose to:

- **Attend college.** Community colleges, four-year colleges, and universities offer degrees in a wide variety of fields.
- **Enroll at a career and technical center.** A technical training program can train you for specific occupations, such as computer programming, automotive technology, or the culinary arts.
- **Get on-the-job training.** Some companies offer on-the-job training. Others will help you go to school while you are working. Many offer formal apprenticeship programs that require both coursework and work experience.
- **Join a branch of the military.** You can get training in specified fields and save money for college. You may even decide to choose a military career.
- **Volunteer.** Volunteer work is work without pay, but it can provide valuable and rewarding work experience and improve your self-esteem as you help others.

Calculate Average Pay

José enjoys working with people, and is considering going to nursing school to become a nurse. Curious about how much beginning nurses typically make where he lives, he surveys a few local hospitals and doctors' offices. One pays its starting nurses $17.65 per hour, another $18.95 per hour, a third $18.30 per hour, and fourth $17.90 per hour. Based on these figures, what is the average hourly pay for beginning nurses in José's area?

Math Concept **Find the Mean** When you have a series of values, calculate the average (also known as mean) by finding the sum of all of the values, and dividing that sum by the number of values.

Starting Hint Find the average pay rate by adding up all four hourly amounts discovered by José, then divide by the number of values. In this case, the number of values is 4.

 For more math help, go to the Math Appendix located at the back of this book.

Part-Time Work

Before you look for a full-time job, you will probably have part-time jobs. You can get valuable experience by babysitting or delivering newspapers and by working in restaurants, businesses, and stores.

A part-time job can provide you with spending money. However, you might also consider saving a percentage of your money to use toward future education costs. Part-time work plus ongoing education can increase your chances of finding well-paying full-time work in the future. Aside from providing you with an income, part-time employment also helps you:

- **Learn** to get along with your supervisors and coworkers.
- **Find** out if a certain type of work matches you personality.
- **Gain** work experience that will be helpful when you apply for a full-time job.
- **Understand** job requirements and other qualities that you need to have for full-time work.

Fancy Collection/SuperStock

⊃ **Work Experience** Part-time jobs provide valuable work experience. *What kind of part-time work would be useful for someone who wants to own a restaurant?*

Be an Entrepreneur

In this activity you will imagine that you are an entrepreneur starting a new business. Before you begin, read through the entire Hands-On Lab assignment. Write down any questions that you have about the assignment. Reread the text or ask your teacher for help if you need it.

Supplies
✓ Calculator
✓ Computer with Internet access (optional)
✓ Paper and colored pens

Develop Your Plan

■ Choose a business such as babysitting, dog walking, or lawn mowing.

■ Find out what other teens would charge for the same jobs, or what clients would be willing to pay.

■ Gather supplies to create flyers, posters, and business cards to advertise your business.

■ If possible, access a computer graphics program to plan an imaginary Web page.

Implement Your Plan

■ Use graphics to create a fun and colorful flyer.

■ Create business cards with your name, contact information, and a brief list of your services.

■ Design an imaginary Web page to advertise your business.

■ Figure out how many hours you can spend on your business and what you will charge for your services.

■ Calculate the costs of maintaining your business, such as additional flyers and business cards, transportation, and Web site maintenance.

■ Multiply the hours you can work by your hourly rate. Subtract the costs to find your profit.

Evaluate Your Results

What did you learn about starting a business? Is there anything you would change if you could do it again? Do you think you would enjoy being your own boss? Write one or more paragraphs to explain your answer.

⬀ **Projects and Activities** Go to connectED.mcgraw-hill.com.

Discover International...

Jobs

Summer Abroad

International summer expedition programs for teens are becoming popular. Australia, Costa Rica, Ecuador, France, Peru, South Africa, Spain, Thailand, the United Kingdom, Hawaii, and Vietnam are just a few of the places offering wilderness and nature programs. Tour companies are looking for responsible, enthusiastic leaders to guide tours and teach about the host country. Most wilderness programs require certification in First Aid, CPR, and Wilderness First Responder. Programs involving marine expeditions often require SCUBA or sailing experience. Most programs also require language skills and knowledge of the culture in the host country. Successful applicants usually have prior outdoor leadership experience. Some programs require special training before leaving for the expedition.

expedition |ˌek-spə-'di-shən| a trip made by a group of people for a specific purpose, such as exploring unknown territory, or to do scientific study.

Effective Use of Technology

At work, you can use technology as effectively as you use any other resource. Depending on your job, this may mean knowing how to operate anything from a copy machine to an electronic ordering system to an aerospace production line. Here are some tips to keep in mind:

- **Do not expect technology to do your job.** Technology can assist you a great deal, but it cannot think or solve problems. Learn the technology that applies to your job, but remember that you are the one who makes decisions about how to use it.

- **Apply your computer skills.** If you know how to work standard computer software, you can adapt your knowledge and skills to a variety of uses. Many software applications offer free online tutorials to help you improve your skills and learn new ones.

- **Use your computer responsibly.** When you are at school or on the job, remember to use technology and electronic communication only for school or work purposes. Personal e-mail, Web surfing, online chatting, and computer games are inappropriate uses of your school's or employer's resources.

Andersen Ross/Getty Images

Entrepreneurship

For some people, the way to begin a career or to advance is to strike out on their own. An **entrepreneur** (ˌän-trə-p(r)ə-ˈnər) is a person who starts and runs his or her own business. Running your own business has many advantages. You are your own boss. You get credit, or praise and recognition, for all of your successes. Of course, when you are an entrepreneur you are also responsible for every part of the business. If the business does not do well, you could lose a lot of money. This type of work requires a lot of planning and preparation beyond just finding something you enjoy.

Be Your Own Boss Some people get a great deal of job satisfaction from owning their own business. *What kind of personality traits and skills would an entrepreneur need to have?*

Entrepreneurs generally run independent businesses. There are many other types of businesses. A **franchise** (ˈfran-ˌchīz) is an agreement or license to sell a company's products or to operate a business that carries that company's name. It is a common form of ownership used by many chain stores and restaurants.

Section 7.2 After You Read

Review What You Have Learned

1. **Name** the benefits of working part-time.
2. **Explain** the advantages of running your own business.

Practice Academic Skills

English Language Arts

3. Gather information about education and training in your area. What colleges and universities are near your home? Are there trade and technical schools nearby? Can you find apprenticeships offered in your area? What are the costs and requirements of each? Write a summary of your findings.

Social Studies

4. Research a successful entrepreneur who went against the norm to find a new way to do something, or to create a new product. Prepare a short presentation about how this entrepreneur's success affected his or her society.

Check Your Answers Check Your Answers at connectED.mcgraw-hill.com.

Discovering Careers

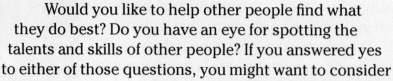

Would you like to help other people find what they do best? Do you have an eye for spotting the talents and skills of other people? If you answered yes to either of those questions, you might want to consider a future career in employment services. The following chart explores several careers in the employment services industry.

Job Title	Job Description
Recruiter	Informs individuals of opportunities, incentives, benefits, and advantages of different careers. Interviews people to determine their suitability for positions.
Human Resources Generalist	Within a specific company, works to fill a variety of positions following hiring guidelines. Interviews candidates and recommends possible hires.
Career Counselor	Supports career exploration. Helps individuals sort out appropriate careers for interests and skill set.
Résumé Writer	Create résumés that present an individual's strengths, skills, and experience in the best possible manner.
Creative Agency Executive	Works with a variety of individuals to place them in appropriate projects based on talents, skills, and experience.
Talent Manager	Represents an individual in the music, movie, or television industries. Locates possible roles or opportunities for performance.

Career Activities ▼

At School

1 Select three of the careers listed. Research the education, training, and work experience required for each career. Write a summary of your results.

At Home

2 Write a job description for the job that one of your family members does at home.

At Work

3 Look through the local classified ads and make a list of jobs that match your career interests.

In the Community

4 Contact and interview someone in your community who works in the employment services industry. Ask this person to describe what his or her typical work day is like. Share what you learned with your class.

Ariel Skelley/Getty Images

Chapter Summary

Section 7.1 Plan Your Career

When you think about your career options, consider your strengths, interests, abilities, values, and goals. Begin thinking about the specific skills and the education and training you will need for the career you choose. As you study and gain work experience, put together a portfolio of your skills, experiences, and qualifications. Talk about career possibilities with your parents, family members, school counselors, and teachers.

Section 7.2 Prepare for Work

One of the first steps in finding a job is to consider your interests. Most people choose jobs based on their interests and skills. Without a high school education, your job opportunities will be limited. There are many options for education after high school. Part-time employment is part of your preparation for full-time employment. Some people go out on their own as an entrepreneur, starting and running their own business.

Words You Learned

1. Use each of these content vocabulary words and academic vocabulary words in a sentence.

Content Vocabulary
- aptitude (p. 140)
- portfolio (p. 140)
- job shadowing (p. 141)
- apprentice (p. 142)
- networking (p. 142)
- mentor (p. 143)
- job satisfaction (p. 146)
- entrepreneur (p. 151)
- franchise (p. 151)

Academic Vocabulary
- modify (p. 139)
- reveal (p. 140)
- technology (p. 150)
- credit (p. 151)

Review Key Concepts

2. **Describe** how to create a career plan.

3. **Recognize** the importance of researching careers.

4. **Explain** why people work.

5. **Identify** steps you can take to prepare for work.

Critical Thinking

6. **Compare and contrast** careers and jobs. Give examples.

7. **Analyze** which is more important: working in a job you love, or working in a job that earns you a lot of money. Why?

8. **Predict** how you will use the Internet to research and find your career.

9. **Assess** the values and interests you might need for a career in middle school counseling. Share your lists with your classmates.

Real-World Skills and Applications

Problem-Solving

10. Take an Aptitude Test Go to your school counselor and ask about aptitude tests that may be available for you to take. Your teacher may direct you to the school counselor, or there may be tests available online. Take at least one test. What were the results? What did you learn about yourself that you did not know before? How can you use the information to plan your career path? Write a summary of your discoveries.

Interpersonal and Collaborative

11. Career Goals Checklist Follow your teacher's directions to form groups. As a group, choose two different careers to research. Create a checklist for each career to show the steps involved in achieving the career goal. Include education, certification, apprenticeships, and special training. Compare the two checklists. Which career would be the most challenging to obtain? Discuss your results with the class.

Financial Literacy

12. Employee Benefits When comparing jobs, it is important to look at the total compensation you will receive for working. Compensation is the salary plus the value of any benefits offered, such as paid vacation, holidays, and sick time. Many positions come with health insurance, while some jobs include additional insurance, and other benefits such as tuition. Determine total compensation by adding the value of each of these benefits to the salary. Gustavo has received a job offer. In addition to his $26,000 per year salary, he will receive a health insurance plan worth $5,000, two weeks of paid vacation, five paid personal days, and five sick days. Assuming that there are 52 weeks in a year, and 5 work days in a week, how much is Gustavo's employment package worth if he accepts this job?

13. Job Application Obtain a job application from a place where you might consider working. Fill out the application. If you do not have experience or job skills yet, fill out the form with what you think would be required for the job. Follow your teacher's instructions to form pairs. Read each other's applications and offer feedback. Use this exercise to help you learn what you need to work on before applying for a job.

14. Military Training Conduct research to find out what the military can offer in terms of job training. Select a branch of the U.S. Armed Forces and create a list of jobs you can pursue with training in the military. How can you use this job training outside of the military?

15. Start Your Portfolio With permission from your parents or teacher, go online to gather information about a career that interests you. Find out the education required for jobs in that field, responsibilities or duties to be expected, working conditions, and the employment outlook. Create a computer-generated career portfolio to include in your Life Skills Binder.

D.Hurst/Alamy

Academic Skills

English Language Arts

16. Conduct an Interview Follow your teacher's instructions to form pairs. With your partner, create a list of interview questions that you might expect during a job interview. Take turns interviewing one another about your aptitudes, abilities, interests, and values. Take notes on your partner's responses. Write a one-paragraph summary describing what you learned about your partner.

Science

17. Describe a Biome Biologists study the features of different areas around the earth called biomes. A biome is an area of the earth that has related geographic features, temperatures, moisture, plants, and animals. **Procedure** Research what kind of plants and animals live in a desert biome. **Analysis** Is it similar to or different from the biome where you live? In which kind of biome would you like to live and work? Explain your answer in a one-page report.

Mathematics

18. Compare Numbers Volunteer work is important to Sheila. Of the 2,400 hours she works each year, she spends 400 hours doing volunteer work at the animal shelter and at the assisted living facility where her grandmother lives. The rest of her work time is spent doing paid work in a legal office. What is the ratio of Sheila's volunteer work time to her paid work time? What is the ratio of her volunteer time to her total work time?

Math Concept **Ratios** A ratio is a comparison of two numbers, typically written as a fraction (with one number over the other number). Make sure that you write the ratio in the order suggested by the question, and always simplify it to lowest terms.

Starting Hint If Sheila spends 400 hours doing volunteer work, then she spends 2,400 − 400 = 2,000 hours doing paid work. The first ratio will include the numbers 400 and 2,000. Write it as a fraction, and reduce it to the lowest terms.

Standardized Test Practice

Multiple-Choice

Choose the phrase that best completes the statement.

Test-Taking Tip In a multiple-choice test, the answers should be specific and precise. Read the questions first, then read all the answer choices. Eliminate answers that you know are incorrect.

19. An employer looks for an employee who has initiative. Initiative means
a. to follow someone else's example.
b. to do what needs to be done without being told.
c. to get going.
d. to prohibit from doing something.

Chapter 8

Enter the Workplace

Don Mason/Getty Images

Explore the Photo
Working together with fellow employees can be rewarding and fun. *What else adds to success and satisfaction in the workplace?*

Write a Cover Letter

Sell Yourself You are applying for a job for which you believe you are well qualified. You have your résumé, but you need to write a cover letter to go with it. A cover letter is a tool you use to "sell" yourself to a potential employer. Write a letter that explains why you are the best candidate, or applicant, for the job.

Writing Tips Follow these steps to write a cover letter:

1. Explain why you are writing. Include how you found out about the job.

2. Highlight personal qualities, skills, and experiences that make you a good candidate.

3. End the letter with a thank-you statement and include how you will follow up with the employer.

Section 8.1 Your Job Search

Reading Guide

Before You Read

Create an Outline Use the section's heading titles to create an outline. Make the titles into Level 1 main ideas. Add supporting details to create Level 2, 3, and 4 details.

Read to Learn

Key Concepts

✓ **Examine** the importance of developing basic employability skills.

✓ **Identify** the paperwork you need before you begin a job search.

✓ **Describe** what to do to apply for a job.

Main Idea

Reading, writing, math, science, speaking, listening, and technology skills contribute to success in the workplace.

Content Vocabulary

○ employability skill
○ comprehend
○ reference
○ résumé
○ orientation

Academic Vocabulary

■ persuade   ■ essential

Graphic Organizer

As you read, identify seven employability skills. Use a graphic organizer like the one shown below to help you organize your information.

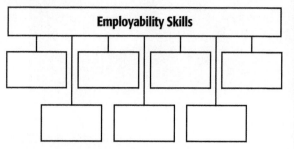

Employability Skills

Graphic Organizer Go to connectED.mcgraw-hill.com to download this graphic organizer.

To prepare for getting a job, you need to practice your skills and gain experience. Preparation starts at home and at school. Getting a job requires reading, writing, math, science, speaking, and listening skills. You use these basic skills when applying for a job, interviewing with employers, and interacting with customers and coworkers.

Develop Your Skills

As You Read

Connect What can you do to present your qualifications to a potential employer?

The most important key to your success is developing basic employability skills. **Employability skills** help you function in life and at work. Reading, writing, math, science, speaking, listening, and technology are some of the most important

 **Employability Skills** You may not realize that you use basic employability skills every day. *How do you use employability skills in your daily activities?*

skills you can have. Each one is necessary for almost every part of your life.

You need reading and writing skills to fill out a job application. You need speaking and listening skills for your job interview. To understand the information on your paycheck and to budget your money, you will need math skills. Science skills will help you understand how technology affects people and their environment. Listening and speaking skills are necessary to communicate with people at home, school, work, and in the community. Technology skills help you do things efficiently. Using basic employability skills every day is the best way to develop them.

Reading Skills

Reading provides a basis for most of the other employability skills. Without reading skills, you could not write, read directions, understand and solve math problems, or use a computer.

 **Vocabulary**

You can find definitions in the glossary at the back of this book.

Build your vocabulary to help develop your reading skills. You can use a dictionary to learn to pronounce words correctly and find out what they mean. You must learn how to follow written directions. The main goal of reading is to comprehend information. When you **comprehend** what you are reading, you understand the words and what they mean. With practice, you can improve your comprehension. **Figure 8.1** explains a reading comprehension technique called SQ3R.

Writing Skills

Writing is a way to express your ideas. When you develop your writing skills, you can feel good about yourself and make a positive impression on others. The ability to express yourself clearly in writing can improve your chances of getting and keeping a job.

You can improve your writing skills by taking time to organize your thoughts. Think about the purpose of what you are going to write. Perhaps you are writing a letter to a potential employer. How can you persuade, or convince, the employer to call you in for an interview?

Outline the major points you want to make. Write a rough draft of your letter, and reread it to see if it can be improved. Proofread, or check for errors in your grammar. Use a dictionary to be sure that you use the right words and spell them correctly. Check to be sure that your work is neat and accurate, or correct. You want to make a good first impression with your letter. Ask a parent or guardian to proofread your letter. Having another person look over your work can help you find errors you may have missed. You can avoid making the same errors the next time you write.

Math Skills

You use math and science skills every day in ways you may not realize. For example, you use math and science when you compare prices, prepare a meal, or remove stains from your clothes.

Check Your Work Ask someone to read what you have written. *How can this help you improve your writing?*

Figure **8.1** **SQ3R**

Reading Comprehension Like any other skill, reading takes practice. *What techniques do you use to help you better understand what you read?*

- **Survey** Skim the headings and summaries to get an idea of what will be covered.

- **Question** Ask yourself questions about what you are reading.

- **Read** Read to answer your questions.

- **Recite** After reading, recite what you read in your own words.

- **Review** Go back over your reading to make sure all your questions were answered. Ask yourself what you learned.

Some of the math skills you must develop are addition, subtraction, multiplication, and division. You also need to master fractions, decimals, and percentages. These math skills will help you figure your weekly earnings. Correct use of a calculator is another necessary math skill. Developing good math skills now can open the door to many opportunities later.

Science Skills

You use science skills every day, too. Knowing how chemical and physical reactions occur is useful in many practical situations. For example, think about what happens when food is cooked or frozen. Science skills can also help you develop an appreciation for your environment. Something as simple as knowing how to select clothing to protect you from the weather is scientific knowledge.

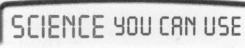

Calculate Speed

Have you ever thought about becoming a pilot and flying faster than the speed of sound? The speed of sound is about 761 miles per hour, or Mach 1. Calculate the speed of a pilot flying at Mach 3.

Procedure Mach is the ratio of an object's speed to the speed of sound. If a jet is going twice the speed of sound then it is moving at Mach 2.

Analysis To figure Mach 3, take the speed of Mach 1 (761 miles per hour) and multiply it by 3.

Blend Images/Alamy

Speaking Skills

Speaking is just as important in the workplace as reading and writing. Developing the ability to express your thoughts verbally can help you perform well on the job, no matter what career you choose. There are many ways to improve your speaking skills:

- **Think** before you speak in order to organize your ideas.
- **Speak** in a direct and straightforward manner.
- **Pronounce** words clearly and correctly.
- **Make** sure that the other person understands what you are saying.
- **Find** a different way to express your idea if your listener does not understand you.

Listening Skills

To be an effective listener, you need to hear, think about, and respond to what the speaker is saying. On the job, you will need to make a real effort to understand what others say to you. If you do not understand what your employer wants you to do, you may not be able to do your job correctly. Here are several ways to improve your listening skills:

- **Concentrate** on what the other person is saying.
- **Let** the other person know that you are listening.
- **Allow** the other person to finish speaking without interrupting.
- **Listen** even if you do not agree with everything the other person is saying.

Ask Questions
Do not be afraid to ask questions as you learn about your job duties. *What might happen if you do not ask questions about your job responsibilities?*

© Purestock/Alamy

Computer Skills
Technology helps us do our jobs. *How do you think technology will help you at work?*

Technology Skills

Technology makes life easier. You can stay in touch by using cell phones and e-mail and by accessing the Internet for information and resources. Computers have changed the way we live and work. Knowing how to use a computer is essential, or absolutely necessary, in today's work world. If you have not spent much time using a computer, now is a good time to practice your keyboarding, or typing, skills. Most computer software is user-friendly, which means it is created to be easy for beginners to use.

Reading Check   *Explain Why is reading such an important skill?*

Get Organized

Before you look for a job, you need to get organized. First, decide what kind of job you want. Next, decide when and for how many hours you can work. Now, decide when you should look for a job. If you want a summer job, start looking in the spring.

Labor Laws

The Fair Labor Standards Act (FLSA) sets requirements for wages, hours, and safety for workers under age 18. As a general rule, the FLSA sets 14 as the minimum age for employment, and limits the number of hours that people under 16 can work. Check the U.S. Department of Labor and the laws in your own state for more information.

moodboard/Alamy

Legal Documents

If you were born in the United States, your parents may have applied for you to have a social security card shortly after you were born. If you do not have a social security card, you must get one. You will need a copy of your birth certificate or other proof that you are a United States citizen. You may also need a work permit or employment certificate if you are under the age of 16 or 18. Once you have the necessary papers, you are ready to begin your job search.

Reading Check *Recall* *How can you find out more information about labor laws?*

Apply for Jobs

When you find a job opening that interests you, fill out a job application. The way you fill out a job application will make an impression on your potential employer. Here are some guidelines to follow:

- **Read** the application form carefully. Follow the instructions exactly.
- **Print** as neatly as possible, using blue or black ink.
- **Check** that you answered every question. If a question does not apply, write "NA" (not applicable).
- **Be prepared** to describe your education, skills, past work experience, and references, even if you already provided this information on an application.

On an application form you may be asked to list several references. A **reference** is a responsible adult who can tell an employer about your character and quality of work. You might choose teachers, counselors, coaches, previous employers, or religious leaders. Be sure to ask each person for permission before you use his or her name as a reference.

Many employers also require a résumé. A **résumé** ('re-zə-'mā) summarizes your qualifications, work experience, education, and interests. **Figure 8.2** shows a sample of a completed résumé. References may be added to a résumé or listed as "available upon request."

The Job Interview

If the employer who reviews your application or résumé thinks that you might be suitable for the job, you will be invited to an interview. A job interview is a meeting between an employer and a job applicant to discuss qualifications. The interviewer will ask many questions. Be prepared to answer such questions as:

First Impression
Your job application may be the first impression you give to a potential employer. *How can the appearance of a job application affect your chances for consideration for a job?*

© Robert Daly/age fotostock

Figure 8.2 Your Résumé

All in One Your résumé allows potential employers to view your qualifications, work experience, education, and activities all at once. *What information is included on a résumé?*

R O B I N   S A N D E R S

208 Denver Way
Anytown, CA 55555
(555) 555-4996
robin@555email.net

CAREER OBJECTIVE
• A professional sales position in the foods industry.

SKILLS AND ABILITIES
• Stocked groceries
• Tracked incoming deliveries
• Prepared inventory reports for supervisor
• Assisted customers in finding groceries
• Provided assembly service for bicycles
• Created customer feedback program

WORK EXPERIENCE
• Stock person: Super Discounts, May 20-- to present

EDUCATION
• Currently attending Chandler Junior College
• Graduate, Chandler High School, May 20--

ACTIVITIES
• Served as Student Council Vice President
• Coordinated Student Council car wash
• Coordinated charity fundraiser, which resulted
  in $21,000 in donations
• Honor Roll student

REFERENCES
• Available upon request.

• "Why do you think you can do this job?"
• "Can you tell me more about your experience?"
• "What do you hope to accomplish in this job?"
• "What are your career goals?"

The interview also gives you a chance to learn more about the job by asking questions of the employer. For example, you might ask what your job duties would be. You should also ask about company benefits, such as vacation, insurance, and pay schedules. You may also want to ask about holidays, overtime, training, and employee assistance programs.

After an interview, you need to follow up. Send a thank-you letter to the employer, even if you decide you are no longer interested in the job. He or she spent time reading your application and speaking to you, so it is professional and courteous to show your appreciation. If you are asked to contact the employer on a specific date, be sure to do so.

SUCCEED IN SCHOOL!

Listening Skills
Focus Your Mind
Avoid distractions when you are listening to someone speak. Do not let your mind wander. Concentrate on making eye contact with the speaker to help you focus.

• • • • • • • • • • • • • • •

How To...

Make the Best of Your Interview

To be considered for a position, a potential employer will want to interview you. This is your opportunity to make the best impression possible and to convince the employer to hire you for the position.

Research the Employer Find out as much as you can about the employer. Ask people who work at the business why they like to work there. Check the company Web site for background information and details about the company. Know directions to the company ahead of time so you do not get lost, or make arrangements for transportation.

Make a Good Impression Choose appropriate clothing for the interview. Make sure it is clean and pressed. Keep jewelry to a minimum. Make sure you are clean, your hair is clean, your breath is fresh, and you have clean fingernails. If you do not appear professional, the employer will not take you seriously.

Prepare for the Interview Arrive at least 10 minutes early for the interview. Have some questions prepared to ask the interviewer about the job. For example, you may want to know what days and hours you would be expected to work, and what kind of training is offered. Bring your résumé and any other materials that were requested, such as your portfolio, or a list of references if you have not already provided them.

Be Professional During the Interview Turn off your cell phone or other electronic devices. Think before you answer each question. Smile, speak clearly, and be friendly and enthusiastic. Make eye contact. Practice good posture and good manners. Do not chew gum.

Follow Up after the Interview Send a thank-you letter after the interview. Tell the employer that you appreciate his or her consideration. Ask for feedback on how you did during the interview for future growth and development. If you decide that you do not want the job, it is still important to send a thank-you letter to thank the employer for his or her time.

© Chris Ryan/age fotostock

166   Unit 3   Make Your Career Plan

Job Offers

When you receive a job offer, you have three options:

- **Accept the offer.** The employer will usually set up an **orientation** ('or-ən-'tā-shən) during which you will be given details about pay, benefits, and job expectations. You may be given a tour as well.
- **Ask for time to consider the offer.** This is the time to bring up any unanswered questions that might affect your decision. With the employer, agree on when you will notify him or her of your decision. Do not put off responding to the employer.
- **Turn down the job offer.** You may decide the job is not right for you. Say, "Thank you for considering me, but I am no longer interested in the job."

The Interview An interview gives you a chance to convince the employer that you are right for the job. *Why should you send a thank-you letter to the employer after the interview?*

Section **8.1** After You Read

Review What You Have Learned

1. **Name** the steps for the SQ3R reading comprehension technique.
2. **Describe** how you use math and science skills everyday.
3. **Identify** ways to improve your listening skills.

Practice Academic Skills

English Language Arts

4. Think of three questions you expect a job interviewer to ask. Respond to those questions with answers that will persuade the employer to offer you the job.

Social Studies

5. Interview someone you know about how he or she prepared for a job. Ask: How did your family influence your choice? How did your family react to your job? What experience did you have? What is important to you in your job? Summarize their answers, and explain how he or she may influence your ideas about work.

✈ **Check Your Answers** Check Your Answers at **connectED.mcgraw-hill.com**.

Section 8.2 On the Job

Reading Guide

Before You Read

Prior Knowledge Look over the Key Concepts at the beginning of the section. Write down what you already know about each concept and what you want to find out by reading the lesson. As you read, find examples for both categories.

Read to Learn

Key Concepts

✓ **List** the responsibilities that you have as an employee.

✓ **Recognize** the importance of leaving a job on a positive note.

Main Idea

A successful interview helps you get a job, and being responsible on the job helps you keep your job.

Content Vocabulary

○ discrimination   ○ work ethic
○ harassment   ○ promotion
○ flexibility   ○ resign

Academic Vocabulary

■ accommodation   ■ notice

Graphic Organizer

As you read, identify four keys to being a responsible employee. Use a graphic organizer like the one shown to help you organize your information.

Being a Responsible Employee

✈ **Graphic Organizer** Go to connectED. mcgraw-hill.com to download this graphic organizer.

How you perform on a job can determine whether you keep or lose the job. It can also affect whether or not you move into a job with more responsibility. Your habits at work determine what you can achieve. Being a responsible and flexible team player can help you succeed on the job. There are several keys to being effective in the workplace.

Be a Responsible Employee

The key to success in any job is to be a responsible employee. Job responsibilities are similar to your responsibilities at school. You need to arrive on time, follow rules, and do your work.

Fulfill Your Responsibilities

Besides general job responsibilities, every job also has specific duties. Your supervisor will explain your specific responsibilities to you. You may be given an employee manual which outlines the rules that employees must follow. In particular, it is important to follow safety rules. These rules help protect employees from workplace hazards and human errors. The key to success is to do your job. This sounds simple, and it is. Arrive on time, ask questions if you do not understand something, and make your job responsibilities your top priority. It is also important to avoid inappropriate conversations at work. For example, Sean ignored customers at the check-out because he was on the phone with his friend. Sean was fired. Conversations at work should be professional and work-related.

As You Read

Connect How can your strengths and weaknesses at school affect the way you may perform on a job?

▷ Vocabulary

You can find definitions in the glossary at the back of this book.

⬤ Show Responsibility Working as a team shows responsibility. *How else can you demonstrate that you are responsible?*

Radius/SuperStock

Accept Diversity

Each workplace is made up of people from diverse cultures and with varying abilities. The Equal Employment Opportunities Act requires businesses to keep discrimination from occurring. **Discrimination** (dis-ˈkri-mə-ˈnā-shən) is the unfair treatment of people based on age, gender, race, or religion. The Americans with Disabilities Act (ADA) ensures that all employees are treated equally, regardless of any disability they may have. The law requires reasonable accommodations, or adjustments, be made for people with disabilities, whether they are employees or customers. Working with people who are culturally diverse and who have different abilities makes the workplace more interesting. Together, people can help each other get the job done.

Avoid Harassment

Teasing, intimidation, and threats are all forms of **harassment**. Workplace harassment is offensive and violates people's rights. Any kind of harassment in the workplace is unacceptable. Sexual harassment involves unwelcome behavior of a sexual nature, whether physical or verbal. If you experience or observe any type of harassment, tell the harasser to stop. Report the situation to your supervisor.

Evaluate Yourself

At the end of each workday, you should evaluate your performance on the job. Did you fulfill your responsibilities? How could you have done your job better? Conditions on the job often change, so most work situations require flexibility. **Flexibility** is the ability to adjust to new conditions. For example, technology is constantly changing. Workers must adapt their skills to accomplish tasks.

Teamwork

Relationships are an important part of every job. You have to learn to get along with your employer, supervisor, and coworkers, and perhaps customers or clients. The better your relationships are with the people around you, the more you will enjoy work and experience success.

Character Counts

Teamwork

Sam is a member of a team at work. They are doing a research project together. He has a good idea about how he thinks the project should be done. There are several meetings planned for the team to make decisions before they begin. Sam thinks that his time could be used for more important things, but his supervisor has directed him and the rest of the team to work together.

You Make the Call

How can Sam be a successful part of the team? Write a paragraph to explain what Sam should do and why.

Hands-On LAB

Teamwork

In this activity, you will work in a team to complete a project of your choice. Before you begin, read through the entire Hands-On Lab assignment. Write down any questions that you have about the assignment. Reread the text or ask your teacher for help if you need it.

Supplies
✓ White board, chalk board, or newspaper print
✓ Paper or pen

Develop Your Plan

■ Make a timeline for what needs to be accomplished by the team.

■ Write down the topics you will talk about at your meetings.

■ Decide how decisions will be made, such as by majority vote, or when everyone agrees.

■ Decide who will lead the group.

■ Pick one person to remind other group members of meeting times and places, and to take notes when you meet.

Implement Your Plan

■ As a team, choose a project to complete during class.

■ Set goals for your team meeting and a time limit for the meeting. Make sure all team members understand the goals.

■ Make everyone comfortable by giving each team member a chance to share his or her ideas. When a team member is silent, the leader should ask for his or her input.

■ Write down what each person is responsible for along with any special instructions.

■ Set a deadline for the project, and work as a team to complete it.

Evaluate Your Results

What did you accomplish at your team meeting? What would you change if you could do it over again? How did team members interact while working on the project? Write one or more paragraphs to explain your answer.

 **Projects and Activities** Go to **connectED.mcgraw-hill.com**.

Blend Images/Getty Images

At work, you become part of a team. A team can be any group of two or more people who work toward a common goal. As a team member, you work with and listen to others and have a helpful attitude. You build teamwork while working together to reach a goal. When coworkers cooperate with one another and share feelings of pride in their work, they get along better and can reach their goals more effectively.

Work Ethic

A positive work ethic can lead to job success. **Work ethic** is a personal commitment to doing your very best. You can develop a positive work ethic by being responsible, flexible, and a team player. Avoid such poor habits such as being tardy, uncooperative, or unreliable. These traits do not contribute to a positive work ethic. In fact, they could cause you to lose a job.

If you apply for a job with a different company, that employer will probably check with your former employer to see how you worked. Work hard and fulfill your responsibilities. This will help you keep a job, and it can help you when it is time to move on to other jobs.

Reading Check *Describe*
How can you develop a positive work ethic that leads to job success?

Changing Jobs

Employees who use their employability skills to do a good job are likely to be promoted. A **promotion** is a move into a job with more responsibility. For example, you might be promoted from stock clerk to assistant manager. A promotion usually includes a raise in salary. Another way to advance, or move ahead, is to accept a job with more responsibilities and higher pay with another company.

Leaving Your Job

The decision to **resign** from a job should be made very carefully. When you decide to leave a job, try to leave on good terms with the employer. Show courtesy, respect, and appreciation to your employer. The following tips can help you leave on a positive note:

Spending Your Salary

Monica works 12 hours a week, 3 weeks a month, at a part-time job after school, where she makes $8 an hour. Each month she has expenses of $75 for gas and $100 for food, and she has also set aside $50 a month for clothes and $25 a month toward paying off a new set of skis. How much money does she have left to spend on entertainment?

Math Concept **Net Cash Flow** Your net cash flow, which equals income minus expenses for a given period of time, is one part of your financial health.

Starting Hint Determine Monica's total income for the month (12 hours per week x $8 per hour x 3 weeks), and then subtract her total monthly expenses.

 For math help, go to the Math Appendix at the back of the book.

D.Hurst/Alamy

- **Give Notice.** Notice, or an announcement, should be given soon enough for the employer to find a replacement by the time you leave the job. A two-week notice is what most workplaces consider appropriate.
- **Submit a Letter of Resignation.** The letter should be given to your direct supervisor. The letter should state the exact date you expect to be your last day of employment. It should also thank the employer for his or her help during your time with the company. Be sure to give a brief explanation of why you are leaving.

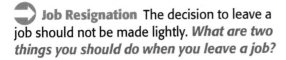 **Job Resignation** The decision to leave a job should not be made lightly. *What are two things you should do when you leave a job?*

Section 8.2 After You Read

Review What You Have Learned
1. **Explain** what to do if you experience or observe harassment.
2. **Summarize** what a letter of resignation should include.

Practice Academic Skills

English Language Arts

3. Imagine that you have decided to quit your job. Write a letter of resignation that includes the information recommended in the chapter.

Social Studies

4. Research current guidelines for giving references to former employees. What can a supervisor legally say about a former employee? What are your rights as an employee regarding your personal work record? Share your findings with the class.

Check Your Answers Check Your Answers at connectED.mcgraw-hill.com.

Discovering Careers

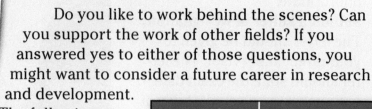

Do you like to work behind the scenes? Can you support the work of other fields? If you answered yes to either of those questions, you might want to consider a future career in research and development. The following chart explores several careers in the research and development industry.

Job Title	Job Description
Press-Service Reader	Reads newspapers, magazines, and other articles on specific subjects. Marks items to be clipped for each customer.
Mathematician	Conducts research for science, management, and other fields. Tests hypotheses. Develops ideas for use in a variety of fields.
Scientific Linguist	Studies structure and relationships of languages. Helps develop methods of translation. Prepares teaching materials and handbooks.
Computer Software Engineer	Installs and tests computer software and hardware. Writes computer programs to meet company or client needs.
Quality Assurance Tester	Designs methods, tests, and procedures for use by the development team to ensure company standards are met.

Career Activities ▼

At School

1 Select three of the careers listed. Research the education, training, and work experience required for each career. Write a summary of your results.

At Home

2 Virtually every product in your home required work from a team of research and development experts. Choose a product in your home, such as shampoo, a frozen dinner, or a kitchen appliance, and write a paragraph about what kind of research was needed to develop the product.

At Work

3 On a sheet of paper, create one column for each of the seven employability skills discussed in this chapter. Under each heading, list all of the ways you can think of to use these skills in the workplace.

In the Community

4 Contact and interview someone in your community who works in the research and development industry. Ask this person to describe what his or her typical work day is like. Share what you learned with your class.

nullplus/Getty Images

Chapter Summary

Section 8.1 Your Job Search

The key to your success is developing basic employability skills in reading, writing, math, science, speaking, listening, and technology. When you find a job that interests you, fill out a job application with information about your education, skills, activities, work experience, and references. If the employer thinks that you are suitable, you will be asked for an interview.

Section 8.2 On the Job

An important part of any job is to be a responsible employee. You have to learn to get along with your employer, supervisor, and coworkers, and perhaps customers or clients. At work, you become part of a team working toward a common goal. A positive work ethic can lead to job success. Employees who use their employability skills to do a good job are likely to be promoted.

Words You Learned

1. Write your own definition for each of these content and academic vocabulary words.

Content Vocabulary
- employability skill (p. 159)
- comprehend (p. 160)
- reference (p. 164)
- résumé (p. 164)
- orientation (p. 167)
- discrimination (p. 170)
- harassment (p. 170)
- flexibility (p. 170)
- work ethic (p. 172)
- promotion (p. 172)
- resign (p. 172)

Academic Vocabulary
- persuade (p. 160)
- essential (p. 163)
- accommodation (p. 170)
- notice (p. 173)

Review Key Concepts

2. **Examine** the importance of developing basic employability skills.

3. **Identify** the paperwork you need before you begin a job search.

4. **Describe** what to do to apply for a job.

5. **List** the responsibilities that you have as an employee.

6. **Recognize** the importance of leaving a job on a positive note.

Critical Thinking

7. **Predict** how your positive work ethic will affect coworkers and supervisors.

8. **Explain** why you should send a thank-you letter when you decide not to accept a job.

9. **Analyze** how you can play up your strengths and abilities in a job interview without sounding like you are bragging.

Real-World Skills and Applications

Problem-Solving

10. **Organize Information** Use the résumé on page 165 as a model for writing a résumé. Gather your own employment history, skills, and information so that you can create your résumé. If you do not have any work history or job experience yet, ask a parent or family member for help. Together, come up with a fictional background to help you create a résumé. Organize the information for reference.

Interpersonal and Collaborative

11. **Teen Jobs** Follow your teacher's directions to form teams. Research jobs available in your area that would be suitable for teens. Consider the hours, type of work, skills required, and other factors to present a list of jobs you would recommend for teens. As a team, rank the jobs in order of preference based on your research.

Financial Literacy

12. **Overtime Pay** Casey, a senior in high school, is planning to go to junior college next year before transferring to a 4-year university. He plans to major in veterinary medicine, so he just accepted a summer job as a tour guide at the zoo. He makes $8.50 per hour at the zoo job, and he hopes to get as much overtime as he can to save for college expenses. His employer pays time-and-a-half overtime for any hours worked over 8 per day. Casey's first week on the job was a busy one, and as a result, he was able to get some overtime hours right away. During that first week, he worked 9 hours on Monday, 10 hours on Wednesday, and 8 hours on Friday. How much money did he make during his first week?

13. **Teamwork Poster** Conduct research to find information about how to successfully work in teams. Come up with at least five tips. Create a poster with photos, illustrations, or computer graphics to communicate this information. Display the poster in your classroom.

14. **Research Job Changes** Jobs have changed throughout history based on economic and technological changes. Fifty years ago, there were few jobs in genetic engineering or environmental engineering. Research a job that is growing in demand that did not exist fifty years ago. Include information about the job and its requirements. What happened to create a need for this job? Share what you learned with the class.

15. **Job Search** With permission from your parents or teachers, go online to search for three jobs that you would be interested in. For each position, research the company's background, and note the qualifications, salaries, benefits, and job requirements. Use this information to create a spreadsheet. Then, using what you learned in the chapter, include information about how you would prepare for each job. Include this information in your Life Skills Binder.

D.Hurst/Alamy

Academic Skills

English Language Arts

16. Speak Up You can use several basic employability skills by preparing a speech. Write a one-minute speech on the importance of employability skills. Make note cards for reference during your speech. Practice your speech in front of the mirror. Present the speech to your classmates. Ask them what they learned from it and how you could make it better.

Social Studies

17. The ADA The Americans with Disabilities Act is a law that ensures that all employees are treated equally, regardless of any disability they may have. The law requires that reasonable accommodations be made for people with disabilities. Imagine that you visit a place of business and observe that a person in a wheelchair is having difficulty accessing certain areas. Write a letter to the owner or manager of the business. Express your concern, and offer suggestions to help.

Mathematics

18. Prepare a Résumé Tanya would like to send her résumé out to local employers with the hope of finding a summer job. Tanya wants to make a good impression on potential employers so she thinks it would be a good idea to have her résumé printed on high-quality paper. After printing a copy of the résumé, she heads to her local copy shop. Tanya has budgeted $6 for making copies of her résumé. If she selects a paper stock that costs 5 cents a copy, how many can she make? What if she selects one that costs 6 cents per copy?

Math Concept **Dividing Decimals** When dividing a number by a decimal, multiply the decimal by a power of ten to make it a whole number. Multiply the other number by the same power of ten.

Starting Hint You will need to divide $6.00 by $0.05, and also divide $6.00 by $0.06. To remove the decimals, multiply all numbers by 100, which you can do by moving each decimal point two places to the right.

Standardized Test Practice

Multiple-Choice

Read the sentence. Then read the question below the sentence. Read the answer choices and choose the best answer to fill in the blank.

Test-Taking Tip With multiple choice questions that rely on information given, read the paragraph very carefully to make sure you understand what it is about. Read the answer choices. Then read the paragraph again before choosing the answer.

19. Mark and Grace started their new jobs at the restaurant on the same day. Their supervisor took them on a tour of the kitchen and the dining area during a 1-hour *orientation,* which also included a review of the New Hire Handbook. In this sentence, the word *orientation* means _____ .

a. direction **b.** arrangement
c. introduction **d.** position

UNIT 3 Life Skills Project

You in Ten Years

What you choose to do for a living is important. Investigating jobs that parents and other adults are doing can help you decide what would be suitable for you. Classified Ads show different skills that employers look for. This project can help you explore your job opportunities.

My Journal Complete the journal entry from page 135, and refer to it to complete your list of skills and talents.

Project Assignment ▼

In this project, you will:

- Write an outline of your skills and talents.
- Research jobs that are interesting to you.
- Create a PowerPoint presentation about your chosen career.
- Interview someone with a profession you want to learn more about.
- Present your findings to your class.
- Include this project in the third section of your personal Life Skills binder.

Step 1 List Your Skills, Talents, and Abilities

What you do for a living will be more satisfying if it is something you are good at. List your qualifications, and then open the classified section of the newspaper. Circle job listings that match your skills, and make a list of the skills you still need to learn.

Step 2 Choose a Job or Career to Investigate

Choose a job you can imagine doing in ten years. Write down your ideas for a PowerPoint presentation that outlines the education, training, and experience you will need to be qualified for that job. Answer these questions in your PowerPoint:

✔ Does this job require some talents that you already have?
✔ How many years of education or training will you need?
✔ What will you need to wear to work each day?
✔ What rewards do you imagine this job will bring you?

Step 3 Interview Someone with an Appealing Job

Interview someone in your community with the job that you have chosen. Ask these questions:

✔ Why did you choose to do this for a living?
✔ What is the most important skill for this job?
✔ Where did you get your training and education?

Use these interviewing skills when conducting your interview and these writing skills when writing the summary of notes from your interview.

Interviewing Skills
- Record interview responses and take notes.
- Listen attentively.

Writing Skills
- Use complete sentences.
- Use correct spelling and grammar.

Step 4 Create and Present Your PowerPoint Presentation

Use the Life Skills Project Checklist on the right to plan and complete your PowerPoint presentation and give an oral report on it. Present your information as if it were ten years in the future. Imagine you are already working in this job and describing it to students on Career Day.

Use these speaking skills when presenting your final report.

Speaking Skills
- Speak clearly and concisely.
- Be sensitive to the needs of your audience.
- Use standard English to communicate.

Step 5 Evaluate Your Presentation

Your project will be evaluated based on:

- ✔ Completeness and organization of your outline of skills and talents.
- ✔ Your PowerPoint presentation of the steps to qualify for your job.
- ✔ The presentation as if you are doing the job in ten years.
- ✔ The summary written from interview notes.
- ✔ Grammar and sentence structure.
- ✔ Presentation to the class.
- ✔ Creativity and neatness.

⚓ **Evaluation Rubric** Go to connectED. mcgraw-hill.com for a rubric you can use to evaluate your final project.

Amos Morgan/Getty Images

Life Skills Project Checklist

Research Job Skills and Training

- ✅ List your skills and talents.
- ✅ Circle classified ads of jobs that might suit you.
- ✅ Create a PowerPoint presentation of the steps to qualify for your job.
- ✅ Interview someone who currently holds that job.

Writing Skills

- ✅ Write about skills you need to achieve.
- ✅ Write the presentation as if you are doing the job you chose in ten years.
- ✅ Write a summary from your interview with a person who does that job.

Present Your Findings

- ✅ Prepare a short presentation about what you will be doing in ten years. Wear a uniform or appropriate clothing of your job.
- ✅ Invite the students of the class to ask any questions they may have. Answer these questions with responses that respect their perspectives.
- ✅ Add this project to your Life Skills binder.

Academic Skills

- ✅ Conduct research to gather information.
- ✅ Communicate effectively.
- ✅ Organize your presentation so the audience can follow along easily.
- ✅ Thoroughly express your ideas.

Chapter 9
Caring for Children

Chapter 10
Child Care Basics

Unit Preview

This unit is about child development and caring for children. In this unit, you will learn about:

- Being a successful parent.
- The different stages of childhood.
- Keeping children safe.
- The benefits of being a babysitter.

Explore the Photo

Being a babysitter can help you to develop important skills that can be useful later in life. *What are some skills that babysitting might help you learn?*

© OJO Images Ltd/Alamy

Your Relationship with Children

When you are done studying this unit, you will complete a project in which you will:

✓ Observe and analyze how children play with toys.

✓ Interview someone who cares for young children.

✓ Design a game or toy and share it with the class.

The prewriting activity below will help you get started.

My Journal

**Prewriting Activity
Make a List**

Make a list of your five favorite toys or games from when you were young. After each toy or game, write a description that answers these questions:

● What age group was the toy or game designed for?

● Why was the toy or game fun?

● How did the toy or game help you learn?

Chapter 9

Caring for Children

Section 9.1

Responsible Parenting

■ **Main Idea** Strong parenting skills can help you protect children and meet their needs.

Section 9.2

Child Development

■ **Main Idea** Children develop in stages and learn through play and interaction at every stage.

Paragraph

Your Parents Write a paragraph about a parental quality, such as strict, compassionate, or supportive, that you experienced growing up. Include examples and details that demonstrate the quality. You can get ideas from vacation memories, attendance at your school functions, or how discipline is handled.

Writing Tips Follow these steps to write a unified paragraph:

1. Write a topic sentence about the parental quality you chose.
2. Write about examples that demonstrate this quality.
3. Use details to connect the topic sentence with your examples.

Potapova Valeryia/Getty Images

183

Reading Guide

Before You Read

Pace Yourself Short blocks of concentrated reading repeated frequently are more effective than one long session. Focus on reading for 10 minutes. Take a short break. Then read for another 10 minutes.

Read to Learn

Key Concepts

✓ **Recognize** that parenting is a lifelong commitment to help children grow and learn.

✓ **Explain** the causes of child abuse and neglect and how it can be prevented.

Main Idea

Strong parenting skills can help you protect children and meet their needs.

Content Vocabulary

○ parenting
○ guidance
○ discipline
○ child abuse
○ child neglect

Academic Vocabulary

■ commitment
■ consistent

Graphic Organizer

As you read, list examples for each of the three basic needs that must be met for children to develop in healthy ways. Use a graphic organizer like the one shown to help you organize your information.

Children's Basic Needs		
Physical	Intellectual	Emotional/Social

Graphic Organizer Go to **connectED.mcgraw-hill.com** to download this graphic organizer.

Do you remember who taught you to ride a bike, tie your shoes, or tell time? Was it your mother, father, grandmother, grandfather, or another adult? You can probably think of many people who have taught you what you know today. These caregivers have had a major influence on your life.

Parenthood

As You Read

Connect In what ways will you still need your parents after you enter adulthood?

Parents and other caregivers need to use good parenting skills. **Parenting** is the process of caring for children and helping them to grow and learn. This process can be very rewarding, but it also takes a lot of hard work.

Babysitting for younger siblings or other young children can introduce you to the basic skills necessary for good parenting. You can also learn parenting skills from watching your parents and by taking a child development or parenting course. The more you know about children, the more comfortable you will be with them. You will find that the way you handle children affects the way they behave toward you.

◆ Vocabulary

You can find definitions in the glossary at the back of this book.

Lifelong Commitment

Imagine coming across this job description:

- Work or be on-call 24 hours a day.
- Accept full responsibility for everything that happens.
- Give up a good deal of sleep, personal time, and freedom.
- Promise that you will do this job for a lifetime.
- Benefits may include unconditional love, joy, and a deep feeling of satisfaction.
- Do it all for no paycheck. In fact, this job will cost you money!

Would you apply for this job? These are just a few of the many things that might appear in a job description for parenthood. Parenthood is a major decision and a lifelong **commitment**, or promise. Effective parents must provide love, patience, guidance, and financial resources.

⟲ Parenthood Lasts Forever Choosing to be a mother or a father is a lifelong commitment. *What skills do you have that might make you a good parent?*

Words for "Mom"

What do you call your mother? Is it Mom, mommy, or mama? People who study linguistics know that there are many names for "mother" around the world, and it is interesting to see how much the names are alike. For example, *ma* and *mama* are used in parts of the Middle East and Latin America. In much of North America, she is *mom* or *mommy*. In some parts of the United Kingdom, children call their mothers *mum* or *mummy*, and in other parts she is called *mam* or *mammy*. She may be called *maman* in France, or *maadar* in the Farsi-speaking world.

linguistics |lin-ˌgwis-tiks| the study of human language, including the nature, structure, and modification of language. Linguists study the words, the sounds, and the written representations of languages around the world.

Parents are primary caregivers. They are responsible for providing a safe, loving, and educational environment for their children. They must fulfill a child's physical needs as well as provide emotional support.

Many new parents are surprised to find how demanding parenthood can be in terms of time, energy, and money. Parents often have to make adjustments or give up their personal desires in order to provide for their children.

Parenthood can also bring many joys, however. The special relationship that develops between a parent and child is a fulfilling experience. All over the world parents claim that parenthood brings them happiness, love, and pride.

Intellectual Needs Interacting with children helps improve their intellectual skills. *What are some other ways you can meet a child's intellectual needs?*

(t)©Anita van Zyl/age fotostock; (b)©Hero/age fotostock

Children's Needs

Young children have physical, emotional, social, and intellectual needs that must be met. While you care for, play with, and teach children, it is up to you to fulfill these needs.

- **Physical Needs** All children have basic physical needs. They need healthful food, appropriate clothing, rest and sleep, and a safe environment. Infants express their needs by crying. Crying is their way of telling you they are hungry, wet, tired, frightened, ill, or unhappy. As children get older, they are better able to use words and sentences to express their needs.

- **Intellectual Needs** Children have intellectual needs, too. They need a stimulating, or interesting and exciting, environment and opportunities to explore. Read books out loud to children. Help a child play with puzzles and blocks. Offer toys or other safe objects, such as a wooden spoon and a plastic bowl, to experiment with. All of these activities can help children develop intellectual abilities.

- **Emotional and Social Needs** Children need to be held, cuddled, and comforted. Sometimes a kiss, a hug, or a gentle pat is all children need to be reassured that someone cares. Children are very sensitive to your feelings about them. Speak kindly to them. They can tell by the way you touch, hold, and talk to them that they are loved. In turn, children learn how to make friends, how to love, and how to interact with other people.

Positive Communication

Children, like adults, respond better to positive statements than to negative ones. For example, say "Let's play outside for awhile," instead of "Do not play in the living room." Emphasize what the children are allowed to do rather than what they should not do. You may also need to explain why. "Try to climb on the jungle gym this way, so you will not fall and get hurt."

Praise is another way of focusing on the positive. You might say to a young child, "I think you did a terrific job finding all those marbles that spilled. You have really sharp eyes."

MATH YOU CAN USE

Distribute Your Time

After dinner, Alice has two hours to spend with her young son before he must be put to bed. She would like to use this time to accomplish several tasks that will help meet a variety of his needs. If she would like to spend an equal amount of time helping him play with his toys, teaching him the alphabet, giving him a bath, getting him ready for bed, and reading him a story, how many minutes should she spend on each activity?

Math Concept **Time Calculations**
When performing calculations with time, remember that there are 60 minutes in one hour. You can convert all numbers to the proper units before performing the calculation. Convert hours to minutes by multiplying by 60; convert minutes to hours by dividing by 60.

Starting Hint The question asks for an amount in minutes, so determine the total minutes Alice has available by multiplying 2 by 60. Count up the number of activities Alice would like to accomplish, and divide the total minutes by the total number of activities.

 For more math help, go to the Math Appendix located at the back of this book.

Encourage Independence

Children want to become independent and be able to perform tasks by themselves. As children try to do new tasks on their own, they will make mistakes and make messes. Be patient with children. It takes practice to learn skills such as using a fork, brushing teeth, or tying a shoe. Just like you, they learn from their mistakes.

As children perform more tasks for themselves, they learn to be more independent. Encourage independence:

- A step stool by the sink lets children wash their hands by themselves.
- Child-size toothbrushes, combs, and towels help children learn to groom and clean themselves.
- If children make mistakes, encourage them to keep trying. Praise their efforts, even when the results are not perfect.
- Allow children to decide which story to read or what game to play to make them feel important.

Provide Guidance

Children need guidance to learn appropriate behavior. **Guidance** is the direction caregivers need to give children so they can learn basic rules for behavior. These rules help children stay safe, learn self-control, and learn to get along with others. Guidance can be direct, such as when you remind a child to put her shoes away, or when you make sure she does not touch the hot stove. Guidance can also be indirect. You can show children the proper ways to behave when you set good examples, such as practicing good habits and manners.

With effective guidance, children start to learn to control their emotions and reactions. Guidance gives children security and positive self-esteem. When children are very young, they only understand being praised or being scolded. As they grow older, the guidance from caregivers will help them learn the difference between right and wrong. Children will gradually learn how to act appropriately in new situations.

Hands-On LAB

Quiet-Play Activities

In this activity you will create an activity box of quiet play activities that you can use with small children. Before you begin, read through the entire Hands-On Lab assignment. Write down any questions that you have about the assignment. Reread the text or ask your teacher for help if you need it.

Supplies
- ✓ Paper
- ✓ Child-safe scissors
- ✓ Nontoxic glue sticks
- ✓ Nontoxic crayons
- ✓ Old magazines
- ✓ Modeling clay
- ✓ Storybooks
- ✓ Music CDs
- ✓ Craft box or plastic tub

Develop Your Plan

- Making up stories, reading books aloud, or listening to music are good activities for infants and toddlers. Drawing with crayons, painting, making collages, and playing with clay are quiet activities for preschoolers.

- Fill a craft box or plastic tub with paper, children's safety scissors, nontoxic glue sticks, old magazines, crayons and markers, and modeling clay. Add your favorite children's books and CDs of children's music.

Implement Your Plan

- Take your quiet-play activity box to a babysitting job. Choose one or more age-appropriate activities to use.

- Watch how the child reacts to each quiet activity. Write down what you learn by watching the child's response to each activity.

- Make a list of how the child used his or her senses during each activity.

Evaluate Your Results

List the ways that quiet activities differed from active play activities. What conclusions can you draw? What other activities could you add to your activity box? Write one or more paragraphs to explain your answers.

Projects and Activities Go to **connectED.mcgraw-hill.com**.

Set an Example You can guide children in the right direction by your own actions and behaviors. *What can you do to set a good example?*

Discipline (ˈdi-sə-ˈplən) is the task of teaching a child which behaviors are acceptable and which are not. It is important to be consistent, or react the same way to a situation each time it occurs. It also means that you follow through and do what you say you will do. For example, 4-year-old Kyle throws his stuffed bear at his sister. If you tell Kyle that you will take the bear away if he does it again, then you must follow through and take away the bear. If you do not follow through, Kyle will not take you seriously and the negative behavior will continue. When you are consistent, children know what to expect.

In addition to being consistent, avoid making false threats. For example, telling a child that you will leave him or her at home alone if he or she misbehaves is a false threat. You know that it would be unsafe to leave a child at home alone without supervision.

Reading Check *Explain* *What are some ways to encourage children to be independent?*

Community Resources
Public Libraries
Librarians in public libraries may be able to help you find online resources. You may be able to access these resources at home or use them in the library.

Child Abuse and Neglect

"Abuse that happens in the home is called domestic violence. Children of all ages, and even adults, can be victims of domestic violence. **Child abuse** means physical, emotional, or sexual injury to children. **Child neglect** is failure to meet a child's physical and emotional needs. People who leave young children alone or do not provide adequate food or medical attention are guilty of neglect. Many abused and neglected children are the victims of their own parents. Some children suffer from both abuse and neglect.

S. Olsson/PhotoAlto

Abuse and neglect occur in families from all income levels and racial and ethnic groups. Many victims suffer silently. They may have been threatened by their abusers with harm if they tell someone. Victims often feel guilty, even though the abuse was not their fault. Unless help is found, abuse and neglect tend to occur again and again.

Causes of Abuse and Neglect

Why would someone injure a child? Adults who lose their tempers can inflict serious, life-threatening injuries on infants and children. The abuser may expect too much of a child. He or she may not be able to cope with personal problems. In some cases, substance abuse is also involved.
In others cases, parents or caregivers may incorrectly think they are helping to teach the child right from wrong. Often times the abusers were abused or neglected as children. The emotional and physical damage that was done to them may cause them to do the same thing to their own children. It is never acceptable to hurt a child, no matter what the reason.

When a child does not receive basic food, clothing, shelter, or health care, he or she is the victim of neglect. Families under financial or emotional stress should seek help from agencies, friends, or extended family members.

Prevent Abuse and Neglect

Abuse is very serious. If you ever suspect a child has been abused or neglected, tell a trusted adult. You can even make an anonymous report to a child protective services agency. If you think a child is in immediate danger, call 9-1-1. State child protective agencies require a social case-worker to investigate each report. In addition, early childhood professionals, health care providers, and teachers are required by law to report child abuse and neglect.

Safety Check

Child Abuse and Neglect

If you suspect that a child is being abused or neglected, you must report the situation. You can help keep the child safe. To report the situation:

- Tell a trusted adult what you suspect.
- Make an anonymous report to a child protective services agency.
- Call 9-1-1 if you think the child is in immediate danger.

Victim Assistance There are many agencies that provide assistance to families and children in abusive situations. *What resources are available in your area that might provide assistance to victims of abuse?*

Community Resources

Tutoring Programs
Some school districts offer free after-school tutoring. Check with your guidance counselor to see if any schools in your area provide tutoring.

To help prevent abuse, a child should never be left with someone who is not reliable. Relatives, neighbors, and friends can often provide help in times of need. Several helpful groups exist to provide parenting support, including parenting courses. Some communities even have crisis nurseries where parents can leave their children while they cool off. One self-help group found in many cities is Parents Anonymous. While the children are occupied with activities, parents support each other as they learn new parenting skills and attitudes.

Child abuse is illegal and should never be hidden. All types of abuse and neglect have lasting effects on children. The longer abuse continues, the more serious the problem becomes. There is no prescribed treatment for child abusers. Counseling and parenting courses can help abusers face their problems. However, a good support system is always necessary. You can get more information about child abuse and its prevention from groups such as the National Committee for the Prevention of Child Abuse. Lists of agencies, organizations, and laws that provide help for victims of child abuse and neglect in your area can be found in telephone directories and online.

Section 9.1 After You Read

Review What You Have Learned

1. **Explain** why it is important to be consistent in discipline.
2. **Summarize** the reasons for child abuse and child neglect.

Practice Academic Skills

English Language Arts

3. Create an informational flyer that offers tips to new parents about how to create a loving environment for children. Be sure to include information about providing for basic needs, independence, guidance, discipline, and setting a good example.

Social Studies

4. Abuse and neglect have long-term effects. Research the long-term mental effects of child abuse or neglect. Prepare a short presentation for your classmates on how being abused as a child can affect a person as an adult.

🖊 **Check Your Answers** Check Your Answers at connectED.mcgraw-hill.com.

Section 9.2 Child Development

Reading Guide

Before You Read

Be Organized A messy environment can be distracting. To lessen distractions, organize an area where you can read this section comfortably.

Read to Learn
Key Concepts
- ✓ **Name** the developmental stages between birth and 5 years.
- ✓ **Analyze** the importance of learning through play.

Main Idea
Children develop in stages and learn through play and interaction at every stage.

Content Vocabulary
- ○ developmental task
- ○ attention span
- ○ independent play
- ○ cooperative play

Academic Vocabulary
- ■ sequence
- ■ coordination

Graphic Organizer
As you read, identify five milestones that usually occur during the preschool years of ages 3 to 5. Use a graphic organizer like the one shown to help you organize your information.

Milestones: The Preschool Years

Graphic Organizer Go to **connectED.mcgraw-hill.com** to download this graphic organizer.

As you grow, you change physically, emotionally, and mentally. These changes begin when you are born and continue through childhood. Much growth and development occurs during infancy, the toddler years, and the preschooler years. Play and positive interaction with parents and other caregivers are the major ways that children learn and develop during these rapidly changing years.

Expectations for Children

There are general patterns to how children develop, but each child is unique and will develop in his or her own special way. It is important to treat each child as an individual. Even children who have the same parents experience different growth rates and patterns. After you spend time with children and get to know them, you will have an idea of what you can expect from each child.

As You Read

Connect What did you learn from playing with toys when you were a young child?

The concept of developmental tasks is important to understand when caring for children. A **developmental task** is an achievement, such as walking or talking, that can be expected at specific ages and stages of growth.

The *sequence*, or order, of developmental tasks follows a pattern. For example, infants crawl before they walk. Some children achieve these milestones faster than others. Janie learned to walk by the age of 12 months, but Marta did not take her first step until 15 months.

Developmental tasks are useful for explaining what the typical child can do by certain ages. Toddlers babble sounds before they learn to say words. They say individual words before they speak in complete sentences. However, each child is a unique individual. Just as children do not grow at the same rate physically, they do not all perform developmental tasks at the same time.

◆ **Vocabulary**

You can find definitions in the glossary at the back of this book.

① Growth Milestones Children reach different milestones as they grow and develop. *What can you do to encourage development?*

© Fabrice Lerouge/SuperStock

Infants

Katrina, a newborn baby, eats every few hours. She sleeps 16 to 20 hours each day. As she gets older, she will stay awake longer and eat less often. In the first few months, her parents will develop a schedule so that Katrina can learn to have regular times for eating, bathing, sleeping, and playing.

Katrina will have many developmental tasks to learn, such as how to eat, sit alone, pick up objects, and crawl. She will learn how to play with toys and be comfortable with different people and places. Katrina will also need a great deal of love and attention. See **Figure 9.1** for a summary of developmental principles, or milestones, that Katrina and all children will experience.

Everything Is New You have been looking at the world for a long time, but everything is brand new to infants and toddlers. *What are some important things to remember when caring for adventurous toddlers?*

Infant Milestones (Birth to 1 year of age)

- Coos and laughs (Birth to 6 months)
- Grasps at rattle (2 months)
- Smiles (2 months)
- Puts objects in mouth (2 months)
- Rolls over (3 to 6 months)
- Sits up alone (4 to 6 months)
- Says single words (6 to 12 months)
- Crawls (7 to 9 months)
- Pulls self up (9 to 12 months)
- Plays peek-a-boo (10 to 12 months)

Toddlers

Toddlers are children who are one to three years old. The name comes from the unsteady way they walk, or toddle. Toddlers are full of energy and ideas. At birth, a child's brain is about 25 percent of its approximate adult weight. By age three, a child's brain has reached almost 90 percent of its size.

They are learning to be more independent by doing tasks for themselves and by being less dependent on the people who care for them. As a part of this new independence, they often use the word "no." Toddlers can come to the table for meals when called, eat food without being encouraged, and follow safety rules such as not touching something hot.

Figure (9.1) Child Development

Growing in Stages Children develop physically, intellectually, emotionally, socially, and morally. *Other than parents, who plays a role in the development of children?*

Physical Development During the first 12 months of life, a child puts on weight, grows longer, and gains the muscle control to hold her head up, sit up, and crawl.

Intellectual Development During the first few years of life, a child develops the ability to think, reason, and solve simple problems. She learns to recognize familiar faces and places, and she learns to talk.

Social Development During the first weeks of life, a child has begun to learn how to relate to others. As a toddler, he learned to play with other children, make friends, and share toys.

Moral Development Parents teach their child a system of rules to guide his behavior. They teach him right from wrong, and they help him learn about the world around him.

Emotional Development As an infant, a child's needs were met as soon as she cried. A child learns to trust her caregivers, which is the first stage of emotional development.

Toddler Milestones (1 to 3 years of age)

- Walks
- Learns the meaning of "No"
- Follows simple instructions
- Feeds self with spoon
- Identifies pictures
- Climbs stairs
- Undresses self
- Plays beside others
- Puts words into sentences
- Begins toilet learning

Preschoolers

Preschoolers are children who are three to five years old. Preschoolers interact more with their playmates and like to play with children of all ages. They like to talk. Preschool children may carry on a conversation with make-believe playmates. They might imitate their heroes or pretend to be superhuman.

Preschooler Milestones (3 to 5 years of age)

- Opens doors
- Dresses self
- Recognizes colors
- Rides a tricycle
- Repeats rhymes and songs
- Brushes teeth
- Speaks in sentences
- Begins cooperative play

Special Needs Children with special needs learn from caregivers who encourage independence. *How can children with special needs benefit from being independent?*

Children with Special Needs

Some children have special needs. Jake walks with a leg brace. Peter wears a hearing aid. Joanna has emotional problems. Each of these children has a particular special need, yet what they need most is to learn how to develop their abilities and enjoy life. For example, they need to learn to be as independent as possible, and they need encouragement to develop a positive self-concept. The attitudes of people around them are important in making this possible.

Reading Check *Define What is a developmental task?*

COMMUNITY CONNECTIONS

Child Care There are many opportunities to help parents and children. Find out what organizations in your community could use help providing childcare. Volunteer to provide childcare for the organization during meetings or other events.

UpperCut Images/SuperStock

Age-Appropriate Toys

In this activity you will learn to choose age-appropriate toys. Before you begin, read through the entire Hands-On Lab assignment. Write down any questions that you have about the activity. Reread the text or ask your teacher for help if you need it.

Supplies
✓ Toy catalogs
✓ Computer with Internet access (optional)

Develop Your Plan

■ Look through toy catalogs or visit Web sites that sell toys, or go to a store with a large selection of toys.

■ Read the descriptions of several toys for different ages. If possible, visit an actual toy store so you can examine the toys.

■ Toy packages are labeled for the appropriate age, usually 0-6 months, 6-12 months, 1-3 years, and 3 years and up. Choose at least two toys from each age group.

■ For each toy, write what you think the child would learn. For example, does the toy teach about shapes and colors, or letters and numbers?

■ Note any dangers, such as choking hazards, that each toy might have if given to a child who is not the appropriate age.

Implement Your Plan

■ Choose a toy to give to a sibling, family friend, or neighbor's child, based on his or her age.

■ Watch how the child plays with the toy. Make a list of all the things he or she learns by using the toy.

■ Compare the list with the one you made while developing your plan, and see how many matches you have.

Evaluate Your Results

What types of toys do you think are the favorites among infants, toddlers, or preschoolers? What did you learn about choosing toys for children? Write one or more paragraphs to explain your answer.

Projects and Activities Go to **connectED.mcgraw-hill.com**.

How Children Learn

Young children learn from exploring their environment through the five senses of sight, sound, taste, touch, and smell. Children learn something from everyone and everything around them, including toys. Their first toys help develop their coordination, or movement. Other toys help children learn shapes, colors, letters, and numbers. As children grow, activities and toys can help them improve their intellectual abilities.

Young children also learn when they practice tasks over and over again. They learn when they observe and imitate others, and explore their environment. Everywhere a child is taken is a learning opportunity. Whether it is an aquarium, zoo, museum, garden, the neighbor's house, or a music festival, all of the senses are affected.

Learning Through Play

Although every child is unique, most children go through a similar pattern of growth and development. As an older brother or sister, or as a babysitter, you can help children learn and discover new things by interacting with them. Show children that you are interested in them and that what they say and do matters to you. Children at every stage of development can benefit from playing with parents, caregivers, siblings, and other children. Playtime helps them develop motor skills, which is the development of their muscles, as well as their emotional, social, and intellectual skills.

Community Resources
Summer Programs
Some schools and communities offer summer programs that help students improve their academic skills. Check your local newspaper or school bulletin board, or go online to find out what services are available in your area.

The Five Senses Young children learn by using all five senses. *How can you provide hands-on learning experiences?*

The George F. Landegger Collection of Connecticut, Photographs in the Carol M. Highsmith's America, Library of Congress, Prints & Photographs Division [LC-DIG-highsm-19178]

Observe Child Behavior

To complete a scientific investigation or experiment, you collect data. Scientists collect data as numbers and descriptions, and then organize the data in different ways. Use your science skills to research the way different children react to the same activity.

Procedure Go to a park or children's play area to observe children at play. Select three individual children of the same age to observe. Record your observations in a chart like the one below. Examples are filled in for you.

Activity	Child 1	Child 2	Child 3
Slide	afraid to use it	used slide over and over	got to the top and changed her mind
Sandbox	played with pail and shovel	not interested	only wanted to use it when he was alone

Analysis What patterns do you notice in the data? What conclusions can you draw about the way children play?

Infant Playtime

Four-month-old Nicholas is happy waving his arms and kicking his legs. He likes when someone plays with him. He enjoys being moved from place to place so he can look at new sights. A walk outside or to the grocery store is very interesting to him. Nicholas does not stay with one toy for very long. He, like other infants, has a short **attention span**. This means that toys and other objects hold his interest for only a short amount of time.

When infants discover their hands and can hold a toy, play becomes more important to them. They gradually learn to pick up a toy and hold it. It is natural for infants to play happily, first picking up one toy, then another. Playing with toys is one way babies learn about the world around them.

Infants who play alone and show little interest in interacting with other children are engaging in **independent play**. Infants play with their hands, toes, toys, or other objects. Toys that are easy to pick up and hold with tiny fingers are best for first toys. Infants like toys that are pleasant to touch, see, and chew on. Musical toys, squeeze toys, and stacking and nesting blocks are good toys for infants. Even small kitchen items, such as plastic measuring cups and spoons, or pots and pans, can be entertaining toys.

Toddler Playtime

Toddlers need to play to develop their minds, bodies, and social skills. Toddlers are curious about everything and spend much of their time exploring. They pull out various toys, look them over, and go on to something else. Most toddlers play alone or watch others play. They engage in parallel play, which is play that occurs next to another child instead of with another child. They are just beginning to learn to share toys with others.

Toddlers need toys for both active and quiet play. Their toys should help them develop socially and physically. The toys you choose for toddlers should also help them think and use their imagination. Toddlers like toys that move.

However, save the jack-in-the-box for older children. Toys with too much noise or movement can frighten a toddler. Riding toys and balls help toddlers develop skill and coordination. Toy cars, bulldozers, and airplanes stimulate their imagination.

Preschooler Playtime

Preschoolers play together with one or two other children and share toys. This is called **cooperative play**. As they get older, they enjoy playing with other children, especially those their own age. The benefits of playtime for preschoolers include learning how to take turns, share with others, and get along with a group. These skills will become more important and necessary as children get older.

As children develop, their interests slowly start to change. New toys help keep pace with their natural development. Preschoolers are increasing their motor skills and using their imaginations. Preschoolers enjoy action toys that encourage physical exercise, such as tricycles and climbing equipment. Toys for pretend play include briefcases, dress-up clothes, and nontoxic art materials.

Section 9.2 After You Read

Review What You Have Learned

1. **Explain** why children from the same family have different growth and development patterns.
2. **Describe** ways that children learn.

Practice Academic Skills

English Language Arts

3. Write a one-page "How To" guide for playing and interacting with infants. Include information about activities or toys that support and encourage infant development. Use illustrations to make your guide more interesting.

Social Studies

4. Abraham Maslow developed a list of the basic human needs (see Chapter 1, page 14). Review Maslow's list of five human needs. Explain how these needs relate to child development. Summarize your findings in a one-page report.

Check Your Answers Check Your Answers at connectED.mcgraw-hill.com.

Discovering Careers

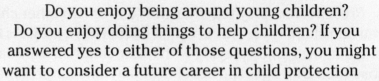

Do you enjoy being around young children? Do you enjoy doing things to help children? If you answered yes to either of those questions, you might want to consider a future career in child protection and development. The following chart explores several careers in the field of child protection and development.

Career Activities ▼

At School

1 Select three of the careers listed. Research the education, training, and work experience required for each career. Write a summary of your results.

At Home

2 Work with your parents to put together a list of toys you played with as an infant, toddler, and preschooler.

At Work

3 Make a list of subject areas you would need to study in school in order to find a job in the field of child development.

In the Community

4 Contact and interview someone in your community who works in the field of child protection and development. Ask this person to describe what his or her typical work day is like. Share what you learned with your class.

Job Title	Job Description
School Nurse	Provides health care services to students. Plans school health program. Evaluates health of students and establishes policies for health emergencies.
Pediatrician	Plans medical care program for children. Examines patients to determine presence of disease and to establish preventive health. Prescribes medicine.
Clinical Social Worker	Provides mental health services and counseling to children and families in crisis. May work in hospitals, child welfare agencies, schools, or community organizations.
Child Advocate	Works to represent the best interests of neglected, abused, or abandoned children. Provides suggestions in court cases for resolutions that benefit children in custody battles.
Preschool Teacher	Plans age-appropriate curriculum and activities. Interacts positively with children. Provides safe environment for children to learn and develop.

Blend Images/Alamy

Chapter Summary

Section 9.1 Responsible Parenting
Parenting is the process of caring for children and helping them to grow and learn. Effective parents must provide love, patience, guidance, and financial resources. Children want to become independent and be able to perform tasks by themselves. Caregivers need to give children guidance, or direction. That is how children learn basic rules for behavior.

Section 9.2 Child Development
Developmental tasks are achievements, such as walking and talking, that can be expected at various ages and stages of growth. Developmental tasks are useful for explaining what the typical child can do by certain ages. It is important to treat each child as an individual. Young children learn from exploring their environment. Children learn something from everyone and everything around them.

Words You Learned

1. Use each of these content vocabulary words and academic vocabulary words in a sentence.

Content Vocabulary
○ parenting (p. 185)
○ guidance (p. 188)
○ discipline (p. 190)
○ child abuse (p. 190)
○ child neglect (p. 190)
○ developmental task (p. 194)
○ attention span (p. 200)
○ independent play (p. 200)
○ cooperative play (p. 201)

Academic Vocabulary
■ commitment (p. 185)
■ consistent (p. 190)
■ sequence (p. 194)
■ coordination (p. 199)

Review Key Concepts

2. **Recognize** that parenting is a lifelong commitment to help children grow and learn.

3. **Explain** the causes of child abuse and neglect and how it can be prevented.

4. **Name** the developmental stages between birth and 5 years.

5. **Analyze** the importance of learning through play.

Critical Thinking

6. **Predict** how parents can raise children to feel good about themselves without making them feel self-centered.

7. **Evaluate** how a family who eats meals together can help encourage the physical, intellectual, social, and emotional growth of the child or children in the family.

8. **Analyze** the ways empty threats can result in developmental problems.

9. **Compare and contrast** independent play and cooperative play.

Real-World Skills and Applications

Problem-Solving

10. Communication Skills Dan thinks his wife, Kelly, is too strict with their daughter, Teri. Dan puts up with some of Teri's behaviors that Kelly will not accept. Dan rarely disciplines or punishes Teri. Kelly thinks Dan is making her look like a mean parent. What should Dan and Kelly do? Create a list of suggestions.

Interpersonal and Collaborative

11. Family Dinner Follow your teacher's directions to form groups. In groups, create an imaginary scene in which several children have dinner with their parents, siblings, and extended family members. Demonstrate ways for family members to interact positively with the children. When your group is finished, ask others to explain what was successful about the dinner, and what could be improved.

Financial Literacy

12. Planning for College Paying for a private college can be expensive. Most experts predict that college tuition will increase by 7% a year for the foreseeable future. A child born today would head off to college in about 18 years. If tuition continues to rise at the same rate until then, tuition will cost about 340% more in 18 years than it does today. Research the current annual tuition costs of three different types of schools near you: a four-year private university, a four-year public school, and a two-year public school. How much will it cost to send a child to each of those schools in 18 years? Remember to multiply the annual cost by 4 for the four-year schools and by 2 for the two-year school.

13. Sensory Learning Create musical shakers for children. You will need two sturdy paper plates to make each shaker. Use colored markers to decorate the backside of each paper plate. Fill one plate with dried beans or rice. Use masking tape to attach the two plates together so the food is completely sealed between the two plates. If possible, give your shaker to a child and encourage him or her to use it to keep pace with their favorite music.

14. Kid Show Analysis Watch two different television programs made for young children. What do the programs teach? How does the program deliver its message? Would you want your child to watch these shows? Why or why not? Write an analysis of each program to explain your answers.

15. Research Toys Choose one development stage to focus on: infant, toddler, or preschool. Then, with permission from your teacher or parents, go online to research a variety of children's toys and games. Put together a list of the ten best educational toys and games for the age group you chose. Write a short description of each toy or game. Describe why it is good for learning. Include the list and descriptions in your Life Skills Binder.

D.Hurst/Alamy

Academic Skills

English Language Arts

16. Interpret Read an article in a parenting magazine about a problem or challenge in raising children. Summarize the problem or challenge in your own words. What advice does the article give? Do you think the advice is realistic? Ask your own parents or guardians what they think about the article. Write one or more paragraphs to explain your answers.

Science

17. Video Games Learn about the effects of video game playing on early childhood development.

Procedure Research what can happen to children who spend too much time playing video games.

Analysis Write a paragraph to summarize the results of your research. Using this information, decide how much time you think is acceptable for a child to play video games. How do video games compare with active play?

Mathematics

18. Make Estimates Rosalind has just given birth to a son, Peter, who weighs 6 pounds, 14 ounces. On average, babies weigh twice their birth weight at 5 months, triple their birth weight at 12 months, and quadruple their birth weight at 2 years. Estimate how much Peter will weigh at 5 months, 12 months, and 2 years.

Math Concept **Using Compatible Numbers** When asked to make an estimate, you can perform calculations quickly without using a calculator by replacing any decimals, fractions, or other difficult numbers with their closest compatible numbers. The compatible number should be easy to work with in your head.

Starting Hint Since Peter's birth weight of 6 pounds, 14 ounces is close to 7 pounds, use 7 pounds as the compatible number. Calculate 7×2, 7×3, and 7×4 to estimate his weight for the different time periods.

Standardized Test Practice

True/False

Read each of the statements and determine whether they are true or false.

> **Test-Taking Tip** In a true/false test, be sure to budget your time. Go through the questions and statements. Answer the ones you know first. As time allows, reread the ones you are unsure of and try to answer them. Many times your first guess is the correct answer.

19. Parenting ends when children turn 18.

20. Learning about children before becoming a parent does not help when you have your own children.

21. Most preschoolers are ready to use tricycles and climbing equipment.

Chapter 10

Child Care Basics

Section 10.1

Child Safety

■ **Main Idea** Keep children safe by childproofing, preventing accidents, and always being aware of where children are.

Section 10.2

Babysitting

■ **Main Idea** Caring for children is a serious and important job. Good babysitters are responsible, reliable, and help children grow and learn.

Fabrice Lerouge/SuperStock

Coherent Paragraph

Child Care Tasks Made Easy
Coherent means logical. Write a coherent paragraph about how to perform a child care task such as changing a diaper, bottle feeding, or putting a child down for a nap. Reread your paragraph to see if it will make sense to the reader.

Writing Tips Follow these steps to write a coherent paragraph.

1. Use a natural or recognized order.
2. Use transition words, such as "first," "the next step," and "finally."
3. Repeat key words throughout the paragraph.

Potapova Valeriya/Getty Images

Section 10.1 Child Safety

Reading Guide

Before You Read

Adjust Reading Speed Improve your comprehension by adjusting reading speed to match the difficulty of the text. Slow down and, when needed, reread each paragraph. Reading slower may take longer, but you will understand and remember more.

Read to Learn

Key Concepts

✓ **Identify** ways to childproof a home.

✓ **Explain** the purpose of learning first aid.

Main Idea

Keep children safe by childproofing, preventing accidents, and always being aware of where children are.

Content Vocabulary

○ childproof
○ monitor
○ intruder

Academic Vocabulary

■ precaution
■ restrict

Graphic Organizer

As you read, identify what you know, what you want to learn, what you learned, and how you can learn more about keeping children safe. Use a graphic organizer like the one shown to help you organize your information.

What I Know	What I Want to Learn	What I Learned	How I Can Learn More

Graphic Organizer Go to connectED. mcgraw-hill.com to download this graphic organizer.

Caring for children is a big responsibility. The more often you care for children, the more you learn about protecting them and caring for their basic needs. Training and taking safety measures can prepare you to care for children in a variety of situations.

Keep Children Safe

Safety should be a top priority for every person who cares for a child. Accidents and injuries can have tragic results. However, most can be avoided by paying attention and by taking some simple steps to avoid common hazards. Young children do not understand the dangers that surround them. In their eagerness to explore, they can easily hurt themselves by playing with a dangerous object or substance. Families with a child or children need to make their homes childproof. A **childproof** home is a safe environment where children can play and explore. A good way to identify hazards is to explore on your hands and knees. At that level, which is the level of a young child, it is easier to see potential dangers that you might not spot otherwise. **Figure 10.1** lists some precautions, or safety measures, caregivers can take to help keep children from getting hurt.

Even if a home has been childproofed, you still need to watch children carefully to make sure that they are safe. Infants will put just about anything in their mouths. It is extremely important that you make sure anything small enough to be swallowed is kept out of reach. If an object can fit in or through a roll that holds paper towels, it is too small for children under four years old.

It is very important to monitor young children at all times. **Monitor** means to watch carefully over someone or something. You may be surprised by how quickly toddlers can get themselves into new and sometimes dangerous situations. Toddlers are adventurous. They do not know yet what it means to be careful. It is up to caregivers to keep busy toddlers out of danger. Preschoolers are just starting to learn what it means to be careful. However, they are just as likely as toddlers to get into dangerous situations. Preschoolers need constant reminders to be careful.

As You Read

Connect What can you do in your home to keep visiting children safe?

◆ Vocabulary

You can find definitions in the glossary at the back of this book.

Figure 10.1 Childproofing

Eager to Explore Babies and young children love to explore, which very often includes putting things in their mouths and grasping anything that might look interesting. *What dangers are in your home that would need to be fixed to keep a child safe?*

Steven Puetzer/Getty Images

- Put safety latches on cabinet doors and drawers.
- Use safety gates at the top and bottom of stairs.
- Put safety covers on electrical outlets.
- Move cleaning supplies and other dangerous items out of children's reach.
- Remove poisonous plants.
- Check all toys to be sure they are nontoxic and do not have any small or broken parts.

SUCCEED IN SCHOOL!

Study Skills
Avoid Distractions
Study in a quiet place. Turn off the television. If you have a cell phone, let voicemail answer your calls until you are done studying.

· · · · · · · · · · · · ·

Intruders

Keeping children safe involves more than childproofing the child's living areas. It also means protecting children, and yourself, from intruders. An **intruder** is someone who uses force to get into a home. Caregivers need to take the following precautions:

- Make sure that all doors and windows are locked.
- Do not open the door for strangers.
- Do not let callers know that you are alone with the children.
- Call a neighbor, another trusted adult, or dial 9-1-1 if a stranger does not go away.

Reading Check   *Predict* *Why is it necessary to watch infants and children who are in childproof areas?*

Prevent Accidents

When caring for young children, you need to take precautions to prevent accidents. Some common accidents are falls, injuries, fires, and poisoning. It is a very good idea to take a first-aid course. Some parents will only hire caregivers and babysitters who know basic first aid. Small cuts, scrapes, contact with common poisonous plants, and nosebleeds are minor injuries that can be treated with first aid.

➥ **Safe Toys** Infants explore by putting things in their mouths. *How can you help keep an infant from choking?*

©JGI/Jamie Grill/Blend Images LLC

If a child gets hurt and requires emergency care, stay calm and call for help. A broken bone, serious bleeding, and burns require emergency care. Insect stings and animal bites can be very dangerous, too. Call the child's parents, a neighbor, or dial 9-1-1 for help.

Falls and Injuries

Falls are the leading cause of accidental deaths in the home in the United States. When caring for children, follow these guidelines to help prevent falls and other common injuries:

- Never leave an infant alone on a changing table, sofa, or bed. The infant may roll over and fall off.
- Make sure all stairways are blocked with safety gates.
- Restrict, or limit, crawling infants and toddlers only to places they can explore safely.
- Never leave a child alone in or near a bathtub or pool.
- Keep children away from electrical wires and outlets.
- Remove all breakable or dangerous objects.
- Make sure that toys are age-appropriate and free of loose parts.
- Do not allow plastic bags near children. Plastic bags can cover their mouths or noses and lead to suffocation.
- Keep knives and other sharp objects away from children.
- Always watch children to keep them from running into the street.
- Children should always ride in a properly installed child car seat.
- Never leave children alone in a car or a home.

Fires

Fires are the second leading cause of accidental death in the United States. Follow these guidelines to help prevent fires in the home:

- Be sure that there are smoke alarms on every floor of the home.
- Keep all matches and lighters away from children.

SCIENCE YOU CAN USE

Disposable vs. Cloth Diapers

Though most parents use disposable diapers for infants, there is also the option of using cloth diapers. Compare the environmental effects of disposable diapers versus cloth diapers and laundering them.

Procedure Interview parents and conduct research to find out how many diapers an infant goes through in his or her first year of life.

Analysis Use this information to determine the environmental effects of both disposable and cloth diapers. Which choice has the least impact on our environment?

Learn First Aid Basic first aid is a must for caregivers. *What are some minor injuries that do not require emergency care?*

- When cooking, avoid wearing clothing with long, full sleeves.
- Turn pot and pan handles away from the edge of the stove, and keep the oven door closed.
- Never allow a child to be alone in the cooking area.

If you smell smoke or see a fire while you are caring for children, get the children out safely first. Then call the fire department (9-1-1) after you are safely away from the fire. Use a cell phone if you have one. If not, ask a neighbor to call. Do not try to put out the fire yourself.

Try not to panic if you are trapped by smoke or fire. Stay close to the floor. If you can, put a wet cloth over your nose and mouth and crawl to safety. If you cannot get out, close the door to the room and stuff wet towels around the cracks in the door. Call for help immediately.

Poisonings

Common sense is the best way to keep children away from dangerous household substances. All poisonous items should be kept in locked cabinets. If that is not possible, keep the items on a high shelf, out of the reach of children.

House Fires

According to the National Fire Protection Association (NFPA), it takes less than five minutes for a fire to spread through a house. Follow these tips when you are babysitting:

- Ask the parents for their emergency evacuation plan.
- Be aware of stoves and ovens if you cook while babysitting.
- Supervise children's activities at all times.

The first step to take if you suspect a child has been poisoned is to call 9-1-1 or the poison control center. Get this number before you start any babysitting job, and keep it near the phone. You can find the number of the nearest poison control center in the telephone book or by calling directory assistance.

Dangerous Products Many common household items are dangerous and even deadly. Keep them out of a child's reach. *What can you do to help children stay safe while you are babysitting?*

Section 10.1 After You Read

Review What You Have Learned

1. **Explain** what precautions a caregiver can take to protect against an intruder.
2. **Name** the two leading causes of accidental deaths in the United States.

Practice Academic Skills

English Language Arts

3. Write a guide to parents-to-be or new parents to explain how they can childproof their home for an infant. Conduct research to find out what equipment or supplies they might need. You may want to ask your own parents for ideas. If possible, illustrate your guide with graphics or drawings.

Social Studies

4. Interview a person who was raised in a culture different from yours. Name and describe three values about children in his or her culture. Explain how these values affect childcare. Present your findings to the class in an oral report.

Check Your Answers Check Your Answers at connectED.mcgraw-hill.com

Andersen Ross/Getty Images

Before You Read

Stay Engaged One way to stay engaged when reading is to turn each of the headings into a question, then read the section to find the answers.

Read to Learn

Key Concepts

✓ **List** the information you should find out before accepting a babysitting job.

✓ **Name** four needs that require attention when caring for infants.

✓ **Describe** how to distract a toddler after his or her parents leave.

✓ **Plan** what you should have when caring for preschoolers.

Main Idea

Caring for children is a serious and important job. Good babysitters are responsible, reliable, and help children grow and learn.

Content Vocabulary

○ reliable
○ redirect

Academic Vocabulary

■ appreciate
■ imitate

Graphic Organizer

As you read, identify five ways you can show that you are a reliable babysitter. Use a graphic organizer like the one shown to help you organize your information. The first one is filled in for you.

How I Can Show That I Am Reliable
1. Keep a constant, careful eye on the children.
2.
3.
4.
5.

⬈ **Graphic Organizer** Go to connectED. mcgraw-hill.com to download this graphic organizer.

Babysitting is often the easiest kind of job for young people to find. It provides good experience. It gives teens an opportunity to interact with children. It also gives teens a chance to learn about responsibility and discipline. The best babysitter is a person parents can rely on to care about their children.

Babysitting Responsibilities

When you babysit, you are totally responsible for the safety and well-being of the children in your care. If you do your job well, you will gain valuable experience and earn money. You will also have an opportunity to play with children and teach them new things.

Before you begin looking for a babysitting job, you should take a course in first aid through a local hospital, a community center, or the American Red Cross. You could also volunteer as a parent's helper. This is someone who cares for an infant or a young child under a parent's supervision. Parents looking for babysitters will **appreciate**, or be thankful for, someone who has taken steps to prepare for the serious job of babysitter.

When parents ask you to babysit, find out the following information before you accept the job:

- the number of children and their ages
- the time you should arrive
- how long the parents plan to be gone
- the rate of pay you will receive

If everything about the job sounds good to you, check with your parents to make sure that the job meets with their approval. After you accept the job, write down the date, time, and place. Give your parents the telephone number at the home where you will be babysitting. If possible, you should also give your parents the cell phone numbers of the parents for whom you are babysitting.

As You Read

Connect Think about your favorite babysitter. Why was he or she your favorite?

Study Skills

Be Comfortable Find a good table and chair or desk for studying. If you are comfortable, you are more likely to focus and study longer.

• • • • • • • • • • • • •

Parent's Helper Volunteer to be a parent's helper to gain childcare experience. *How can this prepare you for babysitting jobs?*

Babysitting Resource Binder

In this activity you will create a resource binder for babysitting. Before you begin, read through the entire Hands-On Lab assignment. Write down any questions that you have about the activity. Reread the text or ask your teacher for help if you need it.

Supplies
✓ 3-ring binder
✓ 3 section dividers
✓ Paper and pens

Develop Your Plan

■ Divide your binder into three sections: Families, Emergencies, and Entertainment.

■ Gather information on burns, CPR, choking, poisons, drowning, insect bites, and other injuries.

■ Gather meal and entertainment ideas.

Implement Your Plan

■ In the Families section, write down the names of all the adults for whom you babysit. Include addresses, home, work, and cell phone numbers, e-mail addresses, and children's names.

■ In the Emergencies section, write down telephone numbers for the local fire, police, and rescue units, poison control center, and local hospitals. Include the name and number of each child's doctor.

■ In the Entertainment section, write your ideas for games, toys, and activities. You may also want to include fun meal ideas, such as pancakes with faces made of fruit and yogurt.

■ Take your binder with you on each babysitting job and use it as a reference.

Evaluate Your Results

What other information could you add to your binder? How can having the information in the binder help you on babysitting jobs? Write one or more paragraphs to explain your answer.

Projects and Activities Go to connectED.mcgraw-hill.com.

Babysitting Job Tips

The first time you babysit for a family, ask the parents if you can arrive a little early. That way, you have a chance to get to know the children while the parents are still at home. It is a good idea to ask the parents to go over a few of the family rules in front of the children. Be sure to ask about:

- television viewing
- homework
- telephone use
- visits from friends
- snacks
- bedtime

Discuss any rules or limits that might cause problems later. Meet the family pets. Find out if the family has a swimming pool. Take a walk through the house with the parents to become familiar with the layout and emergency exits. Find out if there are any rooms that the children should not enter, such as a room that has not been childproofed.

If you are friendly and caring with children, it can help them feel comfortable with you in charge. Show the children that you enjoy being with them. Let them know you are interested in what they want to do or say. Try to get them involved in something enjoyable so they stay happy and busy. Take time to put the children you are babysitting at ease. **Figure 10.2** on page 218 lists some suggestions you can follow to help children feel comfortable with you.

If the children are comfortable with you, the parents will seek you out again. **Reliable** babysitters can be counted on. Parents need babysitters they can trust with the safety and care of their children. Reliable, trustworthy babysitters are likely to be asked to babysit in the future. They establish good relationships with the parents and children. Parents who are happy with your work may recommend you to their friends who have young children. To show that you are a reliable babysitter:

- Keep a constant, careful eye on the children.
- Ask questions to show you are serious about the job.
- Leave the home as neat as you found it.

Financial Literacy

Babysitting Income

Miya currently makes $7.00 per hour working as a babysitter for her neighbors. She is trying to work extra hours during the summer to save money for school expenses. The family gave her two options. The first option is for her to babysit for 20 hours a week with a 15% raise beginning immediately. The second option is for her to receive a $200 cash bonus at the end of the summer. If the summer is ten weeks long, which option will provide Miya with more pay?

Math Concept **Percent Increase** When a number is increased by a certain percentage, you can determine the amount of increase by multiplying the percent times the original number. Add this amount of increase to the original number to find the new increased number.

Starting Hint Determine Miya's pay rate if she takes the raise by multiplying $7.00 by 0.15, and then adding that amount to $7.00. Multiply this new pay rate by the number of hours per week (20) and by the number of weeks (10) to find her total pay for the summer. For the bonus option, you will need to use her current pay rate ($7.00) and multiply $7.00 × 20 × 10. Add the bonus amount to that total to find her total pay for the summer.

 For math help, go to the Math Appendix at the back of the book.

D.Hurst/Alamy

Figure (10.2) Help Children Feel at Ease

Join in the Fun Like you, children are more comfortable when the people around them are enjoying themselves. *What can you do to show a child that you are ready to play?*

- When talking children, sit or kneel so that you are at eye level.
- Ask children how you can join in their play. For example, "Those farm animals look like fun! Can I help you feed the cows?"
- Smile and speak kindly.
- Some children do not like people outside of their family to give them hugs and kisses. Let the parents decide if and when affection is appropriate.
- Be patient. Listen to what they say without correcting them or trying to finish their sentences.

- Do not allow your friends to visit.
- Do not open the door for strangers.

Being responsible for children is a serious and important task. It can also be a lot of fun. Children of different ages have different needs and require different types of care. Learning how to take care of infants, toddlers, and preschoolers will help you meet their needs and enjoy your time with them.

Reading Check *Predict What is likely to happen if you are a reliable babysitter?*

Infant Care

Infants are cute, fun to cuddle, and easy to entertain. Infants cannot do things for themselves. They rely entirely on their caregivers for all of their physical, emotional, and social needs. Infants communicate their needs for sleep, food, comfort, and attention by crying.

When an infant cries, check to see if she has dirty diapers. Offer a bottle to see if she is hungry. She may be too hot or too cold. Maybe something on her clothing is irritating her skin. She may need to be burped. If none of these things calm her, try rocking with her or walking her around the room. Some babies are comforted by riding in their strollers.

Ingram Publishing

If possible, secure the infant in her stroller and take her for a walk. If you cannot go outside, walk her around the house. The movement of going back and forth down a hallway can soothe a cranky baby.

Holding Infants

Infants cannot hold their heads up without help. To support an infant's head, place one hand under his head and the other hand and arm under the lower part of his back. Then you can lift him safely to your shoulder or cradle him in the bend of your arm and elbow area.

Diaper Changes

Ask the parent to show you the diaper changing area and where to put dirty diapers. When you change a diaper, gather everything you need before you begin. Infants can roll off changing tables and beds. Never leave an infant alone or even turn your back to the infant while changing a diaper.

Feeding Time

A young infant drinks mother's milk or formula. Cradle the infant in your arm when you give a bottle. After he stops drinking, hold him over your shoulder, and lightly pat his back until you hear a burp. It may take a few moments for the burp to come. Be patient. Some infants do not always burp.

Character Counts

Reliability

Joann is babysitting for a new family. When she first arrived, the parents made it clear that they did not want any other teens in their home while they were gone. After the children went to bed, Joann's friend, Brenda, dropped by with a movie that just came out on DVD that Joann really wanted to see. There is plenty of time to watch the movie before the parents return.

You Make the Call

Is there really anything wrong with watching a movie while the children sleep? Write a paragraph that explains what you think Joann should do.

More Than Nutrition
Babies rely entirely on their caregivers for all of their physical, emotional, and social needs. *What benefits do infants receive from being fed besides nutrition?*

Diaper a Baby

An infant needs several diapers a day. The most important thing to remember when changing a baby's diaper is safety. Never leave an infant unattended at any time during the process. It takes practice, but by following some basic guidelines, changing a diaper can be a fairly smooth process.

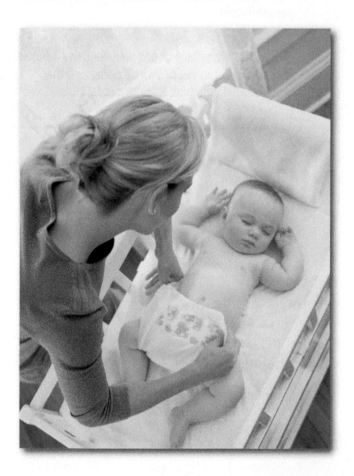

Step 1. Gather the supplies. You will need a diaper, baby wipes or washcloth, and diaper rash ointment (optional). Make sure all your supplies are within reach before setting the baby on the changing surface.

Step 2. Find a safe place for the baby. Most likely, there will be a changing table in the baby's room. If not, you can set a towel or blanket on a bed or even on the floor. Wherever you choose to change the baby, make sure the surface is secure and free of any hazards.

Step 3. Remove the dirty diaper. Lay the baby on his or her back. Unfasten the diaper tabs. Raise the child's bottom off the dirty diaper by gently grasping the ankles and lifting. Use baby wipes or a wet washcloth to clean the baby's bottom, wiping front to back. Remove the diaper from the baby's reach.

Step 4. Put on the clean diaper. Apply diaper rash ointment if needed. Pull the front of the new diaper between the baby's legs. While holding the front of the diaper over the baby's belly, open one side tab and pull it across to the front placement mark. Open the other side tab and pull it into place so the diaper is snug, but not too tight. Redress the baby, then place him or her in a safe place, such as a crib or playpen.

Step 5. Clean up. Dispose of the dirty diaper by wrapping the tabs all the way around it to form a ball. Clean up the changing area and thoroughly wash your hands.

Safe Sleeping

To put an infant to sleep, place her on the side or back, never on the stomach. Be sure to pull up the side of the crib and fasten it securely. When the infant is sleeping, check her often to make sure that everything is all right. Keep toys and other objects out of the crib, and make sure she is not too hot or too cold. Many experts agree that it is best to avoid blankets and pillows in cribs.

Reading Check *List* *What can you check when an infant is crying?*

Toddler Care

Toddlers require a lot of attention. They need help and understanding as they grow and make new discoveries. They also demand a lot of attention because they are busy moving from one thing to another. Toddlers are starting to enjoy the company of others. They will want you to play with them and keep them entertained. However, they may not stay interested in the same activity for very long!

Meal Time

Children between one and three years old are able to eat many of the foods that adults enjoy. However, they are still learning the proper way to eat, chew, and swallow. Make sure you only feed the child food that his parents approve. Foods should be soft and cut into small pieces to avoid choking. Never leave a toddler unattended while she is eating. Be patient. Some young children eat very slowly, and they tend to be messy.

Activities and Skills

Coordination and understanding improve a great deal during the toddler years. While toddlers enjoy showing off their growing independence, most will need extra comfort when their parents leave. Ask the parents for a selection of their favorite toys or a beloved blanket. You may need to redirect them with a toy, puzzle, or game. When you **redirect** children, you turn their attention to something else. They will usually get over missing their parents in a few minutes.

Interaction
Toddlers enjoy showing their new discoveries to the people around them. *What can you do to encourage a toddler to explore his or her world?*

Children at this age like to **imitate**, or copy, what their caregivers do. Fun activities for toddlers include playing with a toy vacuum cleaner, lawn mower, or telephone. They might also enjoy plastic dishes and food, plastic or wooden tools, or a bucket and shovel.

If the toddler has learned to use the toilet, you may have to help him or her in the bathroom. Depending on the child's level of skill, help him or her unfasten clothes and get onto the toilet or potty seat. Afterwards, help the child wash his or her hands. Clean up any accidents, and replace the diaper or underpants if needed.

Reading Check *Explain* *How can you help a toddler use the toilet?*

Preschooler Care

Preschoolers are curious and often look forward to being with caregivers they like. They like to be kept busy, and they want others to interact with them.

Creative Playtime Involve children in activities while you babysit. *What creative ideas do you have for playtime?*

Meal Time

Preschoolers are often picky eaters. Be sure to follow their parent's list of acceptable foods and snacks. Preschoolers have all of their teeth and are much more experienced with eating. However, they can still be messy. As with toddlers, be patient and keep an eye on the child while he or she is eating.

Activities

Babysitting preschoolers can be exhausting, but it can be a good experience if you plan well. During this period, children's motor skills and imagination improve. Their creativity and curiosity seem endless. Plan to have a list of back-up activities to help keep them entertained. Fun activities for most preschoolers include play dough, puzzles, dolls, construction sets, coloring with crayons, and using paints. Ask the child to tell you to draw something, such as a favorite animal or a familiar character. The child will enjoy watching what you create. Then have the child do the same thing. If you can manage to keep an active preschooler busy, you can help him or her be more willing to go to sleep at bedtime.

Section 10.2 After You Read

Review What You Have Learned

1. **Identify** which family rules you should discuss with parents before they leave.
2. **Recall** the instructions for properly holding an infant.
3. **Explain** why it is important to stay with a toddler who is eating a meal.
4. **Describe** what you can do to prepare a busy preschooler for bedtime.

Practice Academic Skills

English Language Arts

5. Create a flyer to advertise the babysitting services of a teen who has had a good deal of babysitting practice. Include his or her experience, special skills, contact information, and the fee charged. Use graphics to make the flyer colorful and interesting.

Social Studies

6. Write a short essay about the impact of daycare on society. How is daycare used and provided in today's society? How are children affected by daycare?

Check Your Answers Check Your Answers at connectED.mcgraw-hill.com.

Discovering Careers

A
Alligator
Airplane
Acorn
Arrow

Do you enjoy caring for children? Do you seek out opportunities where you can teach or be a role model for children? If you answered yes to either of those questions, you might want to consider a future career in child care. The following chart explores several careers in the child care industry.

Job Title	Job Description
Pediatric Speech Therapist	Develops programs for children with speech and language disorders, hearing disorders, and oral motor disorders.
Child Care Instructor	Organizes and leads activities of preschool children in nursery schools and daycares. Directs snack time, nap time, and toileting.
Special Needs Aide	Attends to personal needs of disabled children. Secures children in medically-required equipment. Helps children perform physical activities.
School Music Director	Plans and develops music education program. Coordinates vocal and instrumental music activities.
T-Ball Coach	Organizes and teaches preschool-age children how to play baseball. Helps develop basic throwing, running, and catching skills for young children.

Career Activities ▼

At School

1 Select three of the careers listed. Research the education, training, and work experience required for each career. Write a summary of your results.

At Home

2 With your parent, put together a list of the regular tasks he or she did for you when you were an infant or toddler. Use the list to come up with the job description of "Parent."

At Work

3 Make a list of five or more jobs aside from those listed on this page for people who want to work with children. Compare your list with those of your classmates.

In the Community

4 Contact and interview someone in your community who works in the child care industry. Ask this person to describe what his or her typical work day is like. Share what you learned with your class.

Juan Silva/Getty Images

Chapter Summary

Section 10.1 Child Safety

Children do not understand the dangers that surround them. Families can child-proof their homes to create a safe environment for children to play and explore. Even if a home has been childproofed, children must be watched carefully to make sure they are safe. To keep children safe, protect them from intruders, take precautions to prevent accidents, learn how to handle emergencies, and keep children away from dangerous household products.

Section 10.2 Babysitting

When you babysit, you are totally responsible for the safety and well-being of the children in your care. Prepare for babysitting by learning first aid and volunteering as a parent's helper. Being responsible for children is a serious and important task. Infants rely on their caregivers for all their needs. Toddlers need help and understanding as they grow and make new discoveries. Preschoolers are curious and often look forward to being with caregivers they like.

Words You Learned

1. Use each of these content vocabulary words and academic vocabulary words in a sentence.

Content Vocabulary
- childproof (p. 209)
- monitor (p. 210)
- intruder (p. 210)
- reliable (p. 217)
- redirect (p. 221)

Academic Vocabulary
- precaution (p. 209)
- restrict (p. 211)
- appreciate (p. 215)
- imitate (p. 222)

Review Key Concepts

2. **Identify** ways to childproof a home.

3. **Explain** the purpose of learning first aid.

4. **List** the information you should find out before accepting a babysitting job.

5. **Name** four needs that require attention when caring for infants.

6. **Describe** how to distract a toddler after his or her parents leave.

7. **Plan** what you should have when caring for preschoolers.

Critical Thinking

8. **Evaluate** whether or not you should allow a well-coordinated 18-month-old child to play with a toy that is designed for a 3-year-old child.

9. **Predict** what you would do if a child in your care was exposed to poison ivy.

Real-World Skills and Applications

Problem-Solving

10. Learn What to Expect You have been recommended as a great babysitter. A new family has called you to find out if you are able to babysit this weekend. List five questions to ask the family about what you can expect on your first night of babysitting.

Technology Applications

11. Write an Evaluation Using word processing software, create an evaluation to give to parents after you have completed a babysitting job for them. Choose areas for the parents to evaluate that would be helpful for your growth and development in caring for children. Have parents rate each area with a number, for example:
1 = poor, 2 = needs improvement, 3 = fair, 4 = good, and 5 = excellent. Leave space for them to add their own comments.

Financial Literacy

12. Plan Ahead Your school's formal Winter Dance is coming up in just three months, but you are worried about the costs of attending the event. Your parents have agreed to help you by paying half of your expenses, but you still need to come up with your share. You estimate that a new outfit and shoes will cost $350, tickets to the dance will cost $89, and transportation will be another $65. To cover your half of the expenses, you would like to take a babysitting job. If the job pays $7.00 per hour, how many hours will you have to work each week to raise enough money to pay for your share of expenses? Assume there are four weeks in a month.

13. Puppet Play Children love to use their imaginations. A favorite activity for young children is to use puppets for storytelling. Make puppets from socks, yarn, ribbon, buttons, markers, and pieces of scrap fabric. You could also use lunch-size paper bags. Take your puppets to your next babysitting job and let the kids tell stories and play with the puppets. Bring extra supplies to let the children make their own puppets.

14. Babysitting History In the 1900s on the American plains, the care of children was the responsibility of all family members and they were not paid for it. Children were expected to care for themselves and siblings much earlier than they are today. Choose a time in history and find out how children were cared for during that period. Did they call it "babysitting?" Did sitters get paid? If so, how much? Present your findings to the class.

15. Babysitting Training With permission from your parents or teacher, go online to find what kind of training is offered to prepare babysitters for their work. Find out about training for CPR, first-aid techniques, child development, and activities for children. Include this information in your Life Skills Binder.

Academic Skills

English Language Arts

16. Seeking Babysitters Imagine that you are a parent seeking a babysitter for your two children. Use the information from this chapter as well as any personal experience you may have to write an advertisement that would attract qualified babysitters. The ad would appear at local high schools and colleges. Describe the duties you expect to be performed, and list the qualifications you expect from the babysitter.

Social Studies

17. Car Seats Find information about child safety seats for use in vehicles. How have they changed since they were invented in the 1920s? What are the current standards for car seats? What is the proper use and position of the car seat? How do they help children stay safe? Are there laws in place about using car seats? Explain your answers in a short report.

Mathematics

18. Comparing Numbers During the summer, LaTisha has been working many evenings as a babysitter for families in her neighborhood. Last week, she worked two nights at the Aquino house, and four nights for the Brooks family. What is the ratio of nights worked at the Aquino house to nights worked at the Brooks house? For the week, what was LaTisha's ratio of nights that she did not work to nights that she did work?

Math Concept **Ratios** A ratio is a comparison of two numbers that can be represented in different forms: as a fraction (for example, ½), with a colon (1:2), or as a phrase ("1 to 2"). Whichever form is used, the ratio should be reduced to the lowest terms.

Starting Hint For each question, write a ratio as a fraction in the lowest terms. Make sure that the two numbers in your ratios are in the same order given by the question.

Standardized Test Practice

Multiple-Choice
Read the questions, then choose the appropriate answer.

> **Test-Taking Tip** Look for negative words such as *not* and *no* in multiple choice questions. These words can be easily missed but can change the entire meaning of a sentence.

19. Which is not a characteristic of a good babysitter?
  a. Reliable
  b. Social
  c. Caring
  d. Prompt

UNIT Life Skills Project

Your Relationship with Children

Understanding how to take care of children can help you become a good caregiver. Watch a younger relative or friend to see how they play and learn. This project can help you to understand how young children learn through play.

My Journal Complete the journal entry from page 181, and refer to it to complete your list of favorite toys.

Project Assignment ▼

In this project you will:

■ Create a list of your favorite toys or games from when you were young.

■ Choose an age group and research its development.

■ Design a toy or game for a young child.

■ Interview someone who cares for children.

■ Present your design to your class.

■ Include this project in the fourth section of your personal Life Skills binder.

Step 1 Make a List of Your Favorite Toys and Games

Understanding what children enjoy can be easier if you remember the toys and games you liked when you were younger. Choose your favorite toy, and describe it. Write about why you loved it and what made it fun to play with.

Step 2 Choose a Toy for an Infant, Toddler, or Preschooler

Review Section 9.2 to remind yourself of the developmental milestones of the three age groups. Think about a toy you could design that would help a child develop or practice these skills. Then write two or more paragraphs that answer these questions:

✔ What age group are you designing a toy for?
✔ Which milestones will your toy help develop or practice?
✔ Why do you think children will enjoy your toy?
✔ How can you ensure that your toy will be safe?

Step 3 Interview Someone Who is Responsible for Children

Interview someone in your community who takes care of young children. Ask these questions:

✔ How old are the children you take care of?
✔ What are the children's favorite toys?
✔ What skills have they learned from playing with each one?

Use these interviewing skills when conducting your interview and these writing skills when writing the summary of notes from your interview.

Interviewing Skills
• Record interview responses and take notes.
• Listen attentively.

Writing Skills
• Use complete sentences.
• Use correct spelling and grammar.

Step 4 Create and Present Your Toy or Game

Use the Life Skills Project Checklist on the right to plan and design a toy or game. Draw your design in a diagram or build it out of craft materials to show how it works, and give an oral presentation to the class.

Use these speaking skills when presenting your final report.

Speaking Skills

- Speak clearly and concisely.
- Be sensitive to the needs of your audience.
- Use standard English to communicate.

Step 5 Evaluate Your Presentation

Your project will be evaluated based on:

- ✔ Completeness and organization of your list of favorite toys and games.
- ✔ The design of the toy or game for a young child.
- ✔ The description of how your toy or game is safe and appropriate for its age group.
- ✔ The summary written from interview notes.
- ✔ Grammar and sentence structure.
- ✔ Presentation to the class.
- ✔ Creativity and neatness.

🖈 **Evaluation Rubric** Go to connectED. mcgraw-hill.com for a rubric you can use to evaluate your final project.

Life Skills Project Checklist

Research Toys and Games

- ✅ Create a list of toys and games you enjoyed when you were a child.
- ✅ Check the developmental milestones of infants, toddlers, and preschoolers.
- ✅ Interview someone in your community who takes care of children.
- ✅ Design or build a toy or game.

Writing Skills

- ✅ Describe your favorite toy or game from your childhood.
- ✅ Explain how your design will be age-appropriate.
- ✅ Write a summary from your interview with someone who takes care of children.

Present Your Findings

- ✅ Prepare a short presentation to share and describe your toy or game design and explain how it is age-appropriate, safe, and fun.
- ✅ Invite the students of the class to ask any questions they may have. Answer these questions with responses that respect their perspectives.
- ✅ Add this project to your Life Skills binder.

Academic Skills

- ✅ Conduct research to gather information.
- ✅ Communicate effectively.
- ✅ Organize your presentation so the audience can follow along easily.
- ✅ Thoroughly express your ideas.

Amos Morgan/Getty Images

Management Skills

Chapter 11
Manage Your Money

Chapter 12
Manage Resources, Time, and Stress

Unit Preview

This unit is about learning how to manage your time, money, and other resources. In this unit, you will learn about:

- Evaluating the purchases you make.
- The importance of managing your money.
- The resources that are available to you and how to manage them.
- Different methods of dealing with stress.

Explore the Photo

It is very important for you to learn how to manage your resources, including money. *What are some things you should consider when you want to buy something?*

Manage Your Grocery Budget

When you are done studying this unit, you will complete a project in which you will:

✓ Make a list and shop for groceries.

✓ Interview a grocery store worker.

✓ Demonstrate the results of your shopping experience to your class.

The prewriting activity below will help you get started.

My Journal

Prewriting Activity
Create a Chart

Ask the primary shopper in your family for a receipt from the last time he or she went grocery shopping. Create a chart with two columns. In the first column, list the items your family must have, such as nutritious foods, and label it "Needed Items." In the second column, list the items your family wants but does not necessarily need, such as magazines and snack food, and label it "Wanted Items."

● How much money could your family have saved if the "Wanted Items" had not been purchased?

● How can your family save money on the "Needed Items?"

Chapter 11

Manage Your Money

Be a Smart Consumer

■ **Main Idea** Evaluate advertisements and carefully consider what you want and need from the products you purchase.

Spending and Saving Basics

■ **Main Idea** Shopping skills, consumer rights and responsibilities, and money management help you spend and save wisely.

Blend Images/SuperStock

Explore the Photo

When you shop, it is important to know how to manage your money. *What are some ways you can keep track of how you spend your money?*

Write an Essay

Resourcefulness Being resourceful means using what you already have to get something you want or need. Sometimes this requires creativity. Money is a resource, but so are your skills and talents. Write a 3-paragraph essay with an introduction, body, and conclusion to explain a way you can be resourceful.

Writing Tips Follow these steps to write an essay:

1. Introduce the topic by writing what the essay will be about.
2. Use details and examples in the body to support the introduction.
3. Write a conclusion that restates and emphasizes the introduction.

Section 11.1 Be a Smart Consumer

Reading Guide

Before You Read

What You Want to Know Write a list of what you want to know about being a smart shopper. As you read, write down the heads that provide that information.

Read to Learn
Key Concepts

✓ **Evaluate** how you can be a smart shopper.

✓ **Explain** how your habits affect the way you decide what to buy.

✓ **Identify** the purpose of advertising.

Main Idea

Evaluate advertisements and carefully consider what you want and need from the products you purchase.

Content Vocabulary

○ consumer
○ advertisement
○ trend
○ media

Academic Vocabulary

■ service
■ endorse

Graphic Organizer

As you read, compare and contrast information advertisements and image advertisements. Use a graphic organizer like the one shown to help you organize your information.

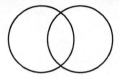

Information Ads   Image Ads

⬆ **Graphic Organizer** Graphic Organizer
Go to **connectED.mcgraw-hill.com** to download this graphic organizer.

Do you ever think about how you spend your money? Do you spend all of your money as soon as you receive it, or do you put some away for later? Maybe you want to save money for a friend's birthday gift. At the same time, you may be hoping to buy a new video game. The way people manage their money can depend on their needs and wants. How do your needs and wants influence your spending?

Teens as Consumers

Teens spend their money to buy goods and services. Goods are products made for sale, such as MP3 players, computer games, or jeans. A service, or work performed for others, is also something people purchase. Services include the work done to repair your bike, or the time your instructor spends teaching you how to play an instrument.

Even if you do not spend a great deal of money, you can be a smart shopper if you know what factors influence your buying decisions. A **consumer** is a person who buys goods and services.

As a consumer, you have many decisions to make. You must decide what to buy, where to buy, and when to buy. You have to decide how to get the best value for your money. By making wise purchases, you will be a satisfied consumer.

As You Read

Connect Think about the last product you bought. What did you consider before you bought it?

> **Reading Check**　　*Define* What is a consumer?

◆ Vocabulary

You can find definitions in the glossary at the back of this book.

Spend Wisely As a consumer, you have many choices when it comes to spending your money. *How can you make wise spending choices?*

Mazer Creative Services

Buying Decisions

When you bought your last pair of athletic shoes, what influenced your decision? Did your friends convince you that you needed the shoes? Maybe your decision was based on price. Perhaps you saw an athlete you admire endorse, or recommend, the shoes in a television advertisement. An **advertisement** is a message that persuades consumers to buy a product or service.

Have you ever tried out a new shampoo because your friend recommended it? Have you ever decided to buy a new backpack because your friend has one? Your friends can have an influence on your buying decisions.

A **trend** is a temporary fashion or product. Can you think of any recent movies that inspired a line of products in toy stores? What celebrities can you think of who start trends with their personal styles? These items may become status symbols, or signs of popularity and importance.

Before you make a purchase, evaluate the product. Give it some thought. Ask yourself, "Do I really need these jeans for $80.00?" or "Is it really necessary for me to wear sunglasses by this designer?" Trends come and go. You may decide that you do not really need the product at all. Do what is best for you, and be proud of your individuality.

Buying Habits

As you have probably discovered, many of your buying decisions are influenced by your habits. If you always shop at the same store, you may be passing up good prices offered at another store. Perhaps you feel loyal to certain brands. Loyalty is good, but if you do not take notice of other options, you may be missing out on good products and good deals. Sometimes you need to evaluate your habits to make sure that you are being a careful shopper.

MATH YOU CAN USE

Saving Money

When you put money in a savings account, the bank can use that money for other purposes until you withdraw it. The bank pays you a fee, known as interest, for this privilege of being able to use your money. Interest is usually paid at a rate based on an annual percentage of the money you have deposited, known as the principal. The interest is added to your savings account along with the principal. Imagine that Andrew has $550 in his savings account on January 1st. If the account pays 5% simple interest, how much money will be in Andrew's account at the end of the year?

Math Concept **Simple Interest** Calculate simple interest by multiplying the interest rate by the principal.

Starting Hint To calculate the interest Andrew will receive for the year, multiply $550 by 5%, which is the same as multiplying $550 x 0.05. Add this interest amount to the principal (the amount already in the account at the beginning of the year).

 Math *For math help, go to the Math Appendix at the back of the book.*

Reading Check *Assess Why should you evaluate a product before you buy it?*

Trends Before you buy something trendy, think about why you want to make the purchase. *Who or what has an influence on what you buy?*

Advertising

Advertising is a major influence on people's buying decisions. Advertising is everywhere you look. **Figure 11.1** on page 238 shows several types of media. **Media** are various forms of communication that advertisers use.

Advertisements, or ads, are designed to catch the attention of consumers and convince them to buy a product or service. Ads influence consumers by presenting goods or services in an attractive way.

Ads introduce new products and point out their benefits. In addition, they let you know about sales. Looking at the weekly advertising circulars you find in newspapers or in your mail is a great way to compare prices.

Some ads deliver a public-service message. They may warn people about the dangers of tobacco, alcohol, and other drugs. Other advertisements ask people to conserve resources or donate money to charitable organizations.

There are some disadvantages to advertising. Some ads persuade people to buy items they may not need, especially if the product is endorsed by an admired celebrity. Ads can also be misleading or make exaggerated or unrealistic claims. If something sounds too good to be true, it probably is not.

Figure 11.1 Types of Advertising

Media Advertisers use different media to tell consumers about their products or services. *Why do you think some are more effective than others?*

Electronic Media

The Internet, radio, and television are examples of electronic media. Internet advertising appears on the computer screen when users are online. The ads that you hear on the radio and see on television are called commercials.

Print Media

Newspapers and magazines are examples of print media. Food and clothing stores often place ads in newspapers to reach their local customers.

Signs and Displays

Signs and displays are two other types of media that you have seen many times. Advertising signs can appear on billboards, buses, taxis, and storefronts. Stores attract buyers with window displays and product displays.

Direct Mail

Mail-order catalogs and coupons are examples of direct mail. Catalog retailers and wholesalers use direct mail. Some companies use only direct mail to advertise their products.

Telemarketing

Telemarketing means calling a person directly to discuss a product or service. Telemarketers use this means to reach people they think will respond to telephone offers.

Types of Advertisements

Advertisements generally fall into one of two categories: information ads and image ads. Both are used to grab your attention and sell a product or service, but each type of ad sends a different kind of message.

Information Ads

These ads describe the features of a product or service and give facts about its price and quality. Information ads send the message that an item is a good buy for the price or because of its high quality.

Image Ad

These ads connect a product or service to a lifestyle that consumers would like to have. Image ads often use celebrities

Class Attendance
Get Notes If you know that you are going to be absent, arrange with a classmate to take notes and make a copy for you.

Andreas Pollok/Getty Images

to endorse a product. They send the message that consumers will be more attractive or popular, or perhaps smarter or healthier, if they use the product or service. Image ads are often used to promote fashions, cosmetics, and other items that a person may want but does not necessarily need.

Evaluate Advertising

Before you decide to buy a service or product, be sure to analyze the advertising claims. **Figure 11.2** describes common techniques that advertisers use to get your attention and your business. Ask yourself questions like these to help you make wise choices:

- Does the ad suggest that the product will make me healthier, more attractive, or even happier than is realistic?
- Is the celebrity in the commercial an expert in nutrition, medicine, or fashion?
- Does the catchy slogan really mean something, or is it just to make me remember the product's name?

Figure 11.2 Getting Your Attention

Advertising Techniques Advertisers use different techniques to get you to buy their products or services. *Name some ads you have seen on television or online, heard on the radio, or seen in print that use some of these techniques.*

Slogans
Advertisers use slogans and jingles, or catchy songs, to remind people of their products.

Endorsements
Advertisers use famous people, including movie and television celebrities, politicians, athletes, and musicians, to promote their products.

Cartoon Characters
A popular technique is to use animated characters to advertise products.

Emotional Appeals
With this technique, advertisers tell you that you will be happier, healthier, or more popular if you use their products.

Get More Information

Although the federal government requires advertisers to make truthful claims, there are some companies that will exaggerate how good their products are. Product advertisements, whether in print, online, on the radio, or on television, can be misleading. You do not have to depend on advertisements for all of your information about a product or service, however. Other sources of useful information are also available to you.

One of the most reliable sources of information is the people you know. Ask your family and friends what brand of a product they use, whether it works well, and if the item was worth the money they paid. The Consumer Product Safety Commission is a government agency that provides safety information about various products. You can check the Better Business Bureau (BBB) for reputable, or trustworthy, businesses. Another good way to obtain information is from consumer resources in print or online. Consumer organizations test products, survey the customers, and then report their findings. They are independent and are not paid by the advertisers, so they have no reason to make false claims.

Section 11.1 After You Read

Review What You Have Learned

1. **Identify** the decisions that you make as a consumer.
2. **Recognize** the influences on your buying decisions.
3. **Name** two types of advertisements.

Practice Academic Skills

English Language Arts

4. Choose a common product or service such as window cleaner or car insurance. Compare and contrast two types of ads, such as a television commercial and a magazine ad, that promote that type of product or service. Write a short report to present your analysis.

Social Studies

5. Evaluate how Internet advertising affects consumers. How is it different from traditional advertising? Explain your answer in a short oral report.

✈ **Check Your Answers** Check Your Answers at connectED.mcgraw-hill.com.

Section 11.2 Spending and Saving Basics

Reading Guide

Before You Read

Preview A cause is an action that makes something happen. An effect is a result of a cause. Ask yourself, "Why does this happen?" to help you recognize cause-and-effect relationships.

Read to Learn

Key Concepts

✓ **List** the different types of stores where you can shop.

✓ **Explain** why consumers need rights and how you can be a responsible consumer.

✓ **Understand** how to manage your money wisely.

Main Idea

Shopping skills, consumer rights and responsibilities, and money management help you spend and save wisely.

Content Vocabulary

- ○ impulse buying
- ○ comparison shopping
- ○ guarantee
- ○ shoplifting
- ○ income
- ○ expenses
- ○ budget
- ○ credit

Academic Vocabulary

- ■ merchandise
- ■ expire

Graphic Organizer

As you read, list four guidelines for exchanging merchandise or asking for a refund. Use a graphic organizer like the one shown to help you organize your information.

Refunds and Exchanges

✈ **Graphic Organizer** Graphic Organizer Go to connectED.mcgraw-hill.com to download this graphic organizer.

It is easier to spend money than to save it, but managing money so you can do both is important for your long-term financial goals. Shopping for the best buys and knowing your rights and responsibilities as consumers can contribute to successful money management.

Shopping Skills

Skillful shoppers get the best value for their money. As you develop your shopping skills, you will learn how to spot a good value and how to spot an overpriced product. This ability can help you save a great deal of money over the years.

As You Read

Connect How can reading the care instructions on a clothing label help you to decide whether or not to buy it?

◆ Vocabulary

You can find definitions in the glossary at the back of this book.

Be an informed shopper. Read labels and compare prices at different stores and among different brands. Look closely at merchandise to judge its quality. Check to see whether the manufacturer will replace or repair the item if it breaks. It is possible to find out some of this information before you even walk into a store. Conduct research, ask friends and family, and read consumer publications to get as much information as possible in order to guide your spending.

Impulse buying means making a sudden decision to buy something you did not plan to purchase. Did you ever decide to buy candy or a magazine while you were standing in the checkout line? Stores place items in these locations just for that reason. If you buy something on impulse, you may end up with something you do not need or that is not worth the money. You risk wasting your money and hurting your budget.

Collect information about products from friends and family members and advertisements. Word of mouth is a great way to find out about products and services. Information obtained from people you know and who are not paid to sell products is generally reliable. Ask friends and family such questions as:

- Are you satisfied with the product?
- What do you like or dislike about it?
- Would you buy the product again?

➡ **Impulse Buying** Store managers often stock impulse-buy items, such as magazines and candy, near the checkout counter. *How can you avoid impulse buying?*

neal and molly jansen/Alamy

Where Should I Shop?

What types of stores are familiar to you? Different kinds of stores carry different selections of merchandise, or products available to buy. The best stores for you depend on the particular items you want to buy, the prices you are willing to pay, and the kinds of services you need.

- **Department Stores** Most department stores sell clothing, shoes, household items, and electronic equipment. Prices for the same item often vary among stores. Department stores usually offer many services, such as gift-wrapping and delivery.
- **Specialty Stores** A store that carries only a specific type of merchandise is a specialty store. The prices may be higher than in a department store.
- **Chain Stores** Stores in separate locations that have the same name and carry the same merchandise are called chain stores.
- **Factory Outlets** A factory outlet generally carries only one manufacturer's products. Outlets stock items that are left over from other stores. Some of the products may have slight defects but are still useable. Shopping at factory outlets can be a great way to save money on brand name products.
- **Discount Stores** Discount stores carry a selection of items at low prices. Some discount stores specialize in a particular kind of merchandise. Other stores that sell merchandise at discounted prices include membership warehouses and thrift shops.

Catalogs and the Internet

Besides going to actual stores, you can also buy products from catalogs. Some catalogs are associated with stores and carry merchandise that the stores cannot keep in stock. Other catalog companies do business only by telephone and mail.

Electronic shopping is available on the Internet. Consumers can view pictures and descriptions of the merchandise offered by many different stores and manufacturers. While online, you can place an order that will be processed instantly, then shipped directly to you.

Catalog and online shopping are fast and convenient ways to shop. However, keep in mind that you cannot inspect merchandise before buying. Before you commit to an online or catalog purchase, find out about their return policy. This information should be provided in the catalog or on the Web site.

Safety Check

Credit Card Safety
You may not have a credit card yet, but debit cards and credit cards are virtually unavoidable for today's purchases, especially online. Credit card numbers are personal. Do not share them with anyone. Make sure you are aware of where your credit card is at all times.

- When using a Web site, make sure it is a secure site.
- When paying in a store, watch the clerk as he or she runs your card to make sure that the card is only used for your purchase.
- Keep receipts in a safe place, or destroy them when you are sure you no longer need them.

Comparison Shopping

After you decide where to shop, you need to consider certain factors before making your purchase. **Comparison shopping** is evaluating similar items to check quality and price. Which one is the better value? Also, compare labels and guarantees to help you get the best value for your money.

Some people think that price is a sign of how good a product is. They think that a more expensive product must be superior. That is not always the case. Items that are on sale may be less expensive than regular-priced items, but may not be of the same quality. Stores sometimes sell products that they have bought at special, lower prices. The quality of these items may also be lower than that of their regular merchandise. You need to look carefully at products on sale to see if they really are bargains. Sometimes it is worth extra money to get higher quality.

Higher-priced items may be of good quality, but they may also contain features that you do not need. For example, you may not want to spend the extra money on an MP3 player that holds 20,000 songs when one that holds 500 is all you need. Be practical, especially when deciding on expensive items.

You can often save money by using generic products. Generic products do not have a famous brand name. However, generic products are often made from the same or similar ingredients or materials as the brand-name products. The difference is the amount of money spent on packaging and advertising. The extra cost of brand-name products is passed on to consumers.

Shopping Options Choosing where to shop can be challenging. *What should you consider when deciding where to shop?*

Purestock/SuperStock

Guatemalan Quetzal

The quetzal is the currency, or money, of Guatemala. It is named after the national bird of Guatemala, the "Resplendent Quetzal." It is divided into 100 centavos, much like a United States dollar is divided into 100 cents. The Mayans, who are the native people of Guatemala, used the long tail feathers of the male quetzal bird as currency in ancient times. Today, both the United States dollar and the Guatemalan quetzal carry value for making purchases in Guatemala. The image of the quetzal bird appears on Guatemalan paper currency and on some coins, and it carries historical importance for the people of Guatemala.

quetzal |ket-|säl 1. a Central American bird with brilliant green and red feathers. The male quetzal has very long, streaming tail feathers. 2. the main unit of Guatemalan currency.

Guarantees

Many items come with a guarantee, sometimes called a warranty. A **guarantee** ('gär-ən-tē) is the manufacturer's written promise to repair or replace a product if it does not work as claimed. Service providers also offer guarantees that they will perform their services as promised. Be sure to read the guarantee or warranty so that you know what is promised. Some warranties apply only to certain parts of the product or only under specific conditions. For example, a product may be guaranteed to work properly for a specific length of time unless it is misused by the consumer.

No matter how you pay for an item, remember to keep the receipt and tags as proof of your purchase. Keep the receipt and the guarantee or warranty in a safe place. If you decide to return the item, you will need the receipt.

Reading Check   *Identify* What are the risks of impulse buying?

Your Consumer Rights and Responsibilities

Do you consider yourself a responsible consumer? Be courteous, count your change, handle merchandise carefully, and get the information you need. This is all part of being a responsible consumer.

Consumers have rights that protect them from false advertising and unsafe products. The law requires manufacturers to put labels on food and clothing and to make products that are safe to use. Your rights make it possible for you to make a complaint if you are not satisfied with a product or service. Your consumer rights may have helped you already. If you returned a shirt that did not fit, you exercised some of your rights. **Figure 11.3** explains the rights you have as a consumer.

Be Courteous

When you have to return an item to the store, you should do so in a polite way. Calmly explain what the problem is and how you would like to resolve it. For example, do you want your money back, or do you want to trade the item for another size or color? Remember to bring your receipt with you.

Figure 11.3 Consumer Rights

Exercise Your Rights As a consumer, you have the right to return items that do not fit your needs. Return policies vary by store. *What should you have available if you need to return a product?*

- **The Right to Safety** Products must be well designed and, if used properly, must not cause harm or injury.
- **The Right to Be Informed** Labels give you information about products. Laws protect you from false or misleading advertisements.
- **The Right to Choose** Consumers are entitled to choose from a variety of products. They have the right to select the items that fit their needs.

- **The Right to Be Heard** Consumers can speak out about a product if they are not satisfied with it.
- **The Right to Redress** Action taken to correct a wrong is called redress. Consumers can seek redress if they have a problem with a product.
- **The Right to Consumer Education** Consumers are entitled to learn about their rights. Consumer rights protect you and help you get the best product for your money. However, along with those rights you also have responsibilities.

Digital Vision/Getty Images

Behave Responsibly

The manufacturer also has responsibilities. Manufacturers must produce products that are functional, safe, and reasonably priced. As a responsible consumer, you need to read and follow the instructions. Experts who understand the product prepare instructions that provide for your safety and satisfaction. It is important to follow them.

Another way to behave responsibly is to handle merchandise with care. This applies to more than breakable items. Clothing can be damaged while you are trying it on. Remove your shoes before trying on pants. Make sure any jewelry you wear does not snag on fabric. Leave the dressing room neat.

If you get a warranty card with a product, fill it out and send it to the manufacturer. The date on the card lets the manufacturer know when the warranty will **expire**, or come to an end. Keep your warranties together in one place.

Be Honest

When paying cash for your purchases, pay attention to the change you receive. If you receive too much change, return it to the clerk. Otherwise the clerk may be responsible for replacing the money.

Some people do not realize the seriousness of shoplifting. **Shoplifting** is taking items from a store without paying for them. It is stealing and it is punishable by law. Some people look at shoplifting as a prank. Their friends may dare them to do it. Shoplifting is a serious crime for which a person may go to jail and pay a fine. It is a crime that remains on that person's record. All customers have to pay higher prices to make up for the money that stores lose because of shoplifting.

Refunds and Exchanges

Like most people, you have probably purchased a product that did not work properly, did not fit, or was not what you expected. What did you do? Did you ask to exchange the unwanted product for something else? Did you ask for a refund, or return, of your money? Perhaps you accepted store credit.

Before you return a product, follow these guidelines:

- **Know the store's policy.** Every store sets its own return-and-exchange policy. The policy is usually posted where you pay for the item. Read the policy. If you do not understand it, ask the clerk before paying for the purchase. Never assume that you can return an item.
- **Keep proof of your purchase.** The store receipt is proof of the price, date of purchase, and store where you bought an item. Most stores require you to show your receipt in order to receive a refund.
- **Determine whether you are entitled to a refund.** Defective, or broken or flawed, merchandise may be sold "as is." Sale items may be marked "All Sales Final." In these cases you are not entitled to a refund. Certain products such as bathing suits, underwear, and pierced earrings are usually not returnable because of health codes.
- **Be ready to process your claim.** Take your merchandise and sales receipt to the store if you are entitled to a refund. You may be asked to complete a form giving a reason for returning the item. When the item is defective, be sure to provide this information so that the store can notify the manufacturer.

Take Responsibility
As a consumer, it is your responsibility to follow the manufacturer's instructions. *What else can you do to be a responsible consumer?*

Reading Check *Connect* What are the long-term consequences of shoplifting for the consumer?

Money Management

You will be earning, spending, and saving money all of your life. The key to managing your money is to remember that the amount you have to spend is less important than how you spend it. Even if you have only a small amount to spend, you can stretch your buying power by learning to buy and save wisely.

To manage your money wisely you will need to:

- Know the source of your income.
- Determine how much money you will have.
- Look at how much money you are spending.
- Evaluate what you are buying.

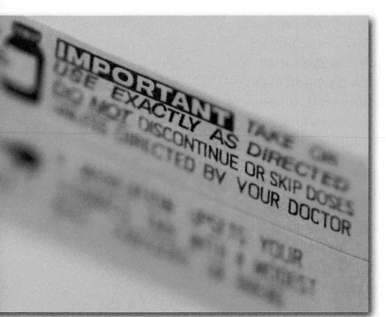

Thinkstock/Jupiterimages

Create a Budget

In this activity you will create a budget to plan and track your expenses. Before you begin, read through the entire Hands-On Lab assignment. Write down any questions that you have about the activity. Reread the text or ask your teacher for help if you need it.

Supplies

✓ Notebook and pen
✓ Spreadsheet software (optional)

Develop Your Plan

■ Figure how much money you make every month from work or allowance. This is your monthly income. If you do not have a monthly income, use imaginary but realistic numbers.

■ Create categories for your regular expenses, such as Food, Entertainment, and School Expenses.

■ Add another category for miscellaneous expenses, such as unexpected purchases or items that do not fit your other categories.

■ Add a final category to your chart so you can label each item as a need or a want. For example, you need food, but you want a new wallet.

Implement Your Plan

■ Create a budget for the next month. If available, use spreadsheet software.

■ Estimate how much of your monthly income you will spend on each category.

■ Write the amounts down, or enter the amounts into your spreadsheet.

■ Record your income and expenses for one month.

■ At the end of the month, add the total spent on needs and the total spent on wants.

Evaluate Your Results

What surprised you about your spending habits? Did you spend more or less that you thought you would? Where did you spend the most? The least? How can you better spend your money next month? Write one or more paragraphs to explain your answer.

🧭 **Projects and Activities** Go to connectED.mcgraw-hill.com.

Comstock/Getty Images

Your **income** is the amount of money you earn or receive regularly. Your **expenses** are the goods and services on which you spend your money. If you manage your money well, you will not spend more on expenses than you receive as income. What are your sources of income? What are your expenses?

Plan and Budget

A **budget** is a plan for using your money. You need to examine your goals before you set up a budget. Do you want to save enough money for a new skateboard? Do you want to pay for singing lessons so that you can try out for the musical at school? Are you saving money to buy your parents an anniversary gift?

Your budget should include a savings plan. A savings plan helps you put money aside for unexpected needs and for future use. Many people find it easier to save when they set goals, such as having money for holiday activities. Some teens begin saving for a car or a college education. Unless you plan ahead and save regularly, it will be difficult to achieve your financial goals.

Planning a budget requires an income, a record of your expenses, and a goal. Begin by setting aside enough money to cover your expenses. When your income does not cover your expenses, you will need to make some adjustments. You may choose to cut back on some of your expenses. Another option is to look for new ways to add money to your income, such as babysitting or taking on extra chores for an allowance.

Paying for Purchases

Most people pay for their purchases with cash until they are ready to open a checking account or apply for a credit card. There are a variety of payment options besides cash:

- **Check** A check is a written order directing a bank to pay the person or business named on the check. In order to pay by check, you must open a checking account and deposit enough money to cover the checks you write. A checking account is a convenient way of handling money without keeping cash on hand.
- **Layaway Plan** A layaway plan is a scheduled payment plan in which you put a small amount of money down and make regular payments until you have paid for the item. When the item has been paid for in full, you can take it home.
- **Debit Card** A debit card is used to electronically withdraw money directly from a person's checking account.

Debit cards are considered the same as cash. There must be a balance, or a certain amount of money, in the account in order to use the card. Debit card transactions are an option at most retail establishments.

- **Credit Cards** You can buy now and pay later using a method of payment called **credit**. The seller or a bank issues credit to the buyer. That means that the buyer can use credit to make an immediate purchase. Then he or she must make regular payments to the seller or bank until the item is paid for in full. Credit is often used to buy expensive items such as furniture or large appliances. Be very careful when you use credit cards. It is easy to get caught in the credit trap. Credit cards are easily available, but you will pay a high price if you do not use them wisely. Your unpaid balance rolls over each month and extra fees called finance charges are added. If you only pay the minimum amount due, you will get further into debt because of the finance charges. This can damage your credit rating. A bad credit rating will make it difficult to get an apartment or a loan for a car or home. Do not take on the responsibility of credit card payments until you are fully prepared to pay what you owe.

Section 11.2 After You Read

Review What You Have Learned
1. **Describe** how you can become an informed shopper.
2. **Explain** how to return an item in a courteous way.
3. **Evaluate** how a savings plan can help you meet financial goals.

Practice Academic Skills

English Language Arts
4. Create a pamphlet that encourages teens to save money for financial goals. Use graphics to make your pamphlet colorful and easy to read. Include steps for how to save, and the benefits of saving money.

Social Studies
5. Research laws about consumer protection and consumer rights in your state. Choose a specific law that you find interesting, and present the information to the class in a short report.

Check Your Answers Check Your Answers at connectED.mcgraw-hill.com.

Discovering Careers

Do you plan carefully before you spend your money? Have you offered advice to others about their finances? If you answered yes to either of those questions, you might want to consider a future career in finance. The following chart explores several careers in the finance field.

Job Title	Job Description
Accountant	Prepares financial reports. Documents business transactions. Prepares balance sheets and profit-and-loss statements.
Bank Teller	Receive, process, deposit, and distribute money for bank and financial institution customers. Cash payroll checks, exchange foreign currency, receive loan payments, issue traveler's checks.
Debt Collector	Collects debts by phone, mail, and in person. Contacts people to set up payment arrangements. Reports delinquent accounts.
Tax Preparer	Prepares federal, state, or local tax returns for individuals, businesses, or organizations. Computes taxes owed according to laws and regulations.
Credit Counselor	Counsels people who have difficulty managing money. Sets up spending plans. Arranges pay plans between creditors and debtors for debt repayment.

Career Activities ▼

At School

1 Select three of the careers listed. Research the education, training, and work experience required for each career. Write a summary of your results.

At Home

2 With help from family members, keep a record of all purchases made by your family in one week. List expenses by category. Other than rent and house payments, where does your family spend the most money?

At Work

3 Make a list of buying decisions that might need to be made in a business office. Compare lists with your classmates.

In the Community

4 Contact and interview someone in your community who works in the finance field. Ask this person to describe what his or her typical work day is like. Share what you learned with your class.

Chapter Summary

Section 11.1 Be a Smart Consumer

Teens spend their money to buy goods and services. As a consumer, you must decide what to buy, where to buy, and when to buy. An advertisement is a message that persuades consumers to buy a product or service. Family, friends, and the media influence your buying decisions. Before you decide to buy a service or product, analyze the advertising claims and get as much information as possible.

Section 11.2 Spending and Saving Basics

Skillful shoppers get the best value for their money. Today's consumers have many shopping options. Consumers have rights and responsibilities. Be courteous, follow instructions, and get the information you need to be a responsible consumer. The key to managing your money is to save more than you spend. Set up a budget that includes a savings plan.

Words You Learned

1. Write your own definition for each content and academic vocabulary term.

Content Vocabulary

- ○ consumer (p. 235)
- ○ advertisement (p. 236)
- ○ trend (p. 236)
- ○ media (p. 237)
- ○ impulse buying (p. 242)
- ○ comparison shopping (p. 244)
- ○ guarantee (p. 245)
- ○ shoplifting (p. 247)
- ○ income (p. 250)
- ○ expenses (p. 250)
- ○ budget (p. 250)
- ○ credit (p. 251)

Academic Vocabulary

- ■ service (p. 235)
- ■ endorse (p. 236)
- ■ merchandise (p. 243)
- ■ expire (p. 247)

Review Key Concepts

2. **Evaluate** how you can be a smart shopper.

3. **Explain** how your habits affect the way you decide what to buy.

4. **Identify** the purpose of advertising.

5. **List** the different types of stores where you can shop.

6. **Explain** why consumers need rights and how you can be a responsible consumer.

7. **Understand** how to manage your money wisely.

Critical Thinking

8. **Predict** what can happen if you fall into the credit card trap.

9. **Analyze** the way advertising works in your age group. What do advertisers do to appeal to you as a member of the teen audience? In what media forms are you likely to find ads for your age group?

Real-World Skills and Applications

Problem-Solving

10. Shop Around You need a new radio alarm clock to use in your room. You arrive at the electronics department and find that the store carries a large variety of radio alarm clocks, with a wide price range and several brands. What should you do before you make your decision?

Interpersonal and Collaborative

11. The Power of Influence Follow your teacher's directions to form groups. Make a list of at least five items that you purchased recently. Next to each item, identify what influenced your buying decision the most. Was it friends, family, habit, the media, or advertising? Compare your lists, and determine which influence has the most power in your group. What conclusions can you draw from this activity?

Financial Literacy

12. The Rule of 72 In finance, the "Rule of 72" works as a rule of thumb for quickly estimating the number of years it will take for your money to double at a given interest rate. Simply divide 72 by the interest rate percentage to find the number of years until your money doubles. For example, Shannon is a first-year college student who will have loans to pay off when she graduates. She wants to start saving now. If she chooses an account that pays 9% interest, it will take approximately $72 \div 9 = 8$ years to double her money. How many years would it take to double her money at a rate of 4%? If she wanted to double her money in 2 years, what rate would she need?

13. Savings Plans Conduct research to learn about saving money at a bank. Choose three banks. For each bank, create an information card with the bank name and the type or name of the savings account on the front. On the back of each card, list the details of the plan. For example, how much money do you need to open an account? What is the interest rate? When can you access your money? Highlight any unfamiliar terms on your cards to discuss in your class.

14. Advertising Analysis Find five advertisements for products geared toward teen buyers. Using Figure 11.2 on page 239 as a guide, identify the advertising techniques used. Which do you think is the most effective? Which is the least effective? After reading this chapter, do you think you will react to ads in different ways? Why or why not? Explain your answer in a presentation to your class.

15. Start Saving Now You may think it is difficult to save money when you do not make much money in the first place. However, with creative planning you can start your money management strategies now. With permission from your teacher or parents, go online to find information that can help teens save money. Write down or print out the tips and suggestions you find and include them in your Life Skills Binder.

D.Hurst/Alamy

Academic Skills

English Language Arts

16. Create a Brochure Conduct research to learn more about how to manage credit. Use the information to write a brochure that will help teens manage their credit when they are on their own. Provide useful tips from the chapter and other resources. If possible, illustrate your brochure to add color and interest.

Science

17. Research Ingredients To complete a scientific investigation, you collect data. Use this science skill to research the ingredients in brand-name and generic products.

Procedure Record the ingredients of brand-name and generic condiments. Choose your five favorite condiments, and create a chart to collect your data.

Analysis Using your chart, determine whether or not generic products are the same as brand-name products. What conclusions can you draw from the information you found?

Mathematics

18. Calculating Insurance Decreases John pays $500 for car insurance a year. When he turns 21, his payments will decrease by 10%. After that, if he takes a safe driving course, he will receive another 2% discount. How much will he pay each year after receiving both reductions?

Math Concept **Calculating Discounted Prices** To calculate a discounted price when you know the percentage of discount, subtract the discount percentage from 100%, and multiply the resulting percentage by the original price. For example, if you receive a 25% discount, then the new price will be 100% - 25% = 75% of the original price.

Starting Hint Subtract the first discount (10%) from 100%. Multiply the new percent by the insurance payment ($500). The result is the price after the 21-and-over discount. Multiply that price by 100% minus 2% to find the price after the safe driving course discount is also added.

Standardized Test Practice

Essay

Write a half-page response to the writing prompt.

> **Test-Taking Tip** When writing an essay test response, it is important to take a few moments to plan. Read the question several times and underline key words or phrases, such as explain, support, details, and examples. Key words or phrases tell you what you have to do.

19. Advertising and other influences bombard students on every front. It can be difficult to know how to make choices about spending and saving money. Write an essay about how to make the best choice when making a major purchase. Explain how you make your choice, the events or people who influence your choice, and the effects of your purchase on your finances. Support your explanation with details and examples.

Chapter **12**

Manage Resources, Time, and Stress

Section 12.1

Manage Resources

■ **Main Idea** Learn how to use personal resources and how to apply management skills to all areas of your life.

Section 12.2

Manage Time and Handle Stress

■ **Main Idea** Learn and use time-management skills to have more time for things you want to do, and to help you reduce the stress that can happen when you try to do too much.

Moodboard/SuperStock

Dialogue

Make Conversation A dialogue is a conversation between two or more people. Write a dialogue between a teen and a parent about how to find time throughout the week for studying, meeting deadlines, and being with friends and family.

Writing Tips Follow these steps to write a dialogue:

1. Use real but appropriate language that you would hear between a parent and teen.

2. Give each person his or her own speech characteristics.

3. Read the dialogue aloud to see if it sounds sincere, or realistic.

Reading Guide

Before You Read

Use Diagrams As you are reading through this section, write down the main idea. Write down any facts, explanations, or examples you find in the text. Start at the main idea and draw arrows to the information that directly supports it. Then draw arrows from these examples to any information that supports them.

Read to Learn

Key Concepts

✓ **Describe** each of the four steps you can take to be a good manager.

✓ **Identify** resources that can help you manage your life.

Main Idea

Learn how to use personal resources and how to apply management skills to all areas of your life.

Content Vocabulary

○ management   ○ energy
○ resource

Academic Vocabulary

■ potent   ■ material

Graphic Organizer

As you read, list the four steps you can take to be a good manager. Use a graphic organizer like the one shown to help you organize your information.

Steps to be a Good Manager	
Step 1	
Step 2	
Step 3	
Step 4	

➔ **Graphic Organizer** Go to connectED. mcgraw-hill.com to download this graphic organizer.

You probably have a friend who is your opposite. She always has her homework done on time, while you are often working on yours until the last minute, or maybe it is the other way around. Perhaps you have another friend with a schedule full of activities, but he still has time to spend with you. Being organized and planning ahead can help you manage your resources.

The Management Process

People who manage well accomplish more with greater ease. They use their time and energy wisely. You may hear the word management and think of the workplace. However, you can apply management skills to all areas of your life.

Management is the skillful use of resources to accomplish a task. Katie and Hassan are good managers. For example, Katie uses the time in her mom's car on the way to school to study. Hassan catches an early bus so he can get to school in time to spend 30 minutes in the computer lab.

You can be a good manager if you learn to follow the steps in the How To feature on page 260. These steps work whether you are writing a report or organizing a fundraiser for the school band. Tasks, assignments, goals, and even unexpected events can be more manageable when you make a plan. Writing out your plan is useful for several reasons. Having a written list gives you a visual reminder of what you need to do. It helps you organize your ideas. The physical act of writing something down can help you remember it better than just thinking about it. What goals do you have for which the four-step management plan would be helpful?

Reading Check   *Explain*   *How can management skills help you get more accomplished?*

As You Read

Connect Name a goal you achieved recently. What did you do to meet that goal?

Vocabulary

You can find definitions in the glossary at the back of this book.

Westend61/Glow Images

Write It Down
The key to management, whether in class, at home, or at work, is planning. *Why does writing down goals make planning easier?*

Make a Management Plan

It may seem like more work to take the time to write down a plan for your goals. However, if you take that extra time in the beginning, you can save time later. Creating a plan can help you focus and organize your thoughts. Use these four steps to help you map out the path to whatever you want to achieve.

Step 1
Decide on Your Goal Do you need to finish your science project by a certain date? Write down your goal to help you commit to it.

What is Your Goal?
Write it down in a notebook or keep a file in your computer.

Step 2
Make a Plan Decide how you want to achieve the goal. Maybe the goal can be broken into smaller, short-term goals that are easier to reach. For example, if you want to finish the project in two weeks, you could work on research this week and a rough draft next week.

Break It Down
Break your goal down into smaller, easy-to-manage goals.

Step 3
Put the Plan into Action Begin working on your plan. If you are going to try out for the soccer team, do not just talk about it. Start practicing now!

Just Do It Do not put it off. Get started on your plan today.

Step 4
Evaluate the Results When you evaluate the outcome of your plan, you determine the value of what you accomplished. Are you satisfied with the way your plan worked? If not, what would you do differently the next time?

Evaluate Your Plan Think about what you accomplished and what you would do differently next time.

Resource Management

Management is a word often applied to supervisors and their tasks in a work environment. While this is true, management also applies to just about any task you do. For example, did you know that when you organize your school papers or arrange music on a portable music player, you are using management skills? To be a good manager you must make full use of your resources. A **resource** is something or someone that is a source of help or information. Learn how to manage personal resources, material resources, and community resources to help you reach goals and get things accomplished.

Personal Resources

Personal resources are time, energy, knowledge and education, skills and talents, and people. How well you use your personal resources can make a difference in how much you accomplish.

Time

Everyone has 24 hours each day. Much of this time is spent sleeping, eating, grooming, studying, working, and socializing. Learn to use your time wisely. Section 12.2 will provide more information to help you manage your time effectively.

Energy

Energy is the power or ability to be active. It has to do with the strength of the body and mind to work and to enjoy your free time. You can keep your energy level up when you get enough sleep, eat nutritious foods, and participate in physical activities. Keep a positive attitude toward what has to be done to help improve your energy level.

Knowledge and Education

Knowledge is information and understanding. Education does not stop when you finish school. There will always be something new to learn. Keep yourself open to new ideas and other opinions. Knowledge and education are potent, or powerful, personal resources. You can continue to strengthen them for the rest of your life.

Financial Literacy

Pay Yourself First

When you receive your paycheck or allowance, pay yourself first. That means that you should set aside some money for savings before you spend any of it. Imagine that you have a job that pays $860 per month. If you save 2% of each monthly paycheck for one year, how much would you have at the end of the year? What if you saved 5%?

Math Concept **Find the Percent of a Number**
A percent is a ratio of a number to 100. For example, 27% is the same thing as 27/100, or 27 divided by 100. To find a percent of a number, multiply the number by the percent. Change the percent to a decimal by removing the percent sign and moving the decimal point two places to the left. Multiply this decimal by the number.

Starting Hint At the end of one month, you will have $860 x 2%, or $860 x 0.02 in your savings account. Multiply that monthly amount by 12 to find out your total savings for the full year. Then, do the same calculations using 5% instead of 2%. How much more do you have at the 5% rate?

 For math help, go to the Math Appendix at the back of the book.

Character Counts

Commitment

Raquel was just offered a big part in the school's yearly musical production. If she accepts the part, rehearsals will be every Tuesday and Wednesday from 4:00 until 8:30 for the next three months. On Mondays she has her French club meetings after school, and on Thursday evenings she takes a dance class at the recreation center. Every other Friday after school, she works in her dad's office to help him file papers. Raquel decided to start a weekly planner to keep track of her busy schedule. She quickly realized that with the addition of the musical rehearsals, she would not have any free evenings for homework or studying. She also realized that her only free time would be on weekends, and that is when she does her chores and spends time with her friends.

You Make the Call

Raquel has over-committed herself. She wants to do it all, but there just is not enough time. Write a paragraph explaining what you think Raquel should do and why.

Skills and Talents

A skill is an ability that comes from training or practice. You have reading, writing, and computer skills. You may also have other skills, such as the ability to play tennis, which you learned by taking lessons. Talents are different from skills. A talent is a natural ability, such as being able to draw, sing, or dance. Both skills and talents can be improved. What are your talents and skills? It is important to explore these areas to find out what you like to do. Making time for fun activities is important for relieving stress and enjoying life.

People

People are valuable resources. Strong relationships with family and friends can provide support all your life. The encouragement of family and friends can help you gain confidence and strengthen your self-concept. Take advantage of opportunities to meet new people. Even if you never see someone again, a brief conversation with a person can inspire you or give you an idea. For example, you might go to an art festival and meet someone from another country or culture. Perhaps her artwork inspires you to redecorate your room.

Material Resources

Material resources are possessions, objects, and money. Material things are not necessary for survival like food, shelter, and water, but they can make life easier and more enjoyable. Your personal possessions might include a bike, a stereo, or books. Objects might include a refrigerator, a table, or a microwave oven. How do these possessions and objects help you do what you want to do? What role does money play in reaching your goals?

Personal possessions give you enjoyment and satisfaction. Riding your bike and listening to your stereo are two ways that you gain enjoyment from your possessions. Objects make life easier. For example, using a washing machine to wash clothes is easier than washing them by hand. Buying a cake is quicker and easier than baking your own cake.

Community Resources

Every community provides a variety of resources for its citizens to use. These include schools, hospitals, and police and fire departments. Many communities have interesting places to visit, such as museums or important historic buildings. Among other community resources are youth programs, libraries, parks, and recreational facilities.

Communities also provide resources for people who have special kinds of problems. Most communities offer programs for the homeless, the elderly, people with low income, and people who have problems with alcohol and other drugs. There are also programs to protect battered spouses and abused children.

Local Activities Community parks allow you to enjoy many outdoor activities. *What resources are provided by your community?*

Section 12.1 After You Read

Review What You Have Learned

1. **Define** management.
2. **Identify** what you can gain from material resources.

Practice Academic Skills

English Language Arts

3. Apply the four-step management plan to a goal that you recently achieved. What was the goal? How did you break it into smaller steps? What was your action plan? What were the results? What would you do differently next time? Share an outline of your achievement and evaluation with your class.

Social Studies

4. People can be a valuable resource. Write a scenario in which you meet a teen from another culture who inspires you to do or to think about something new. Explain how this encounter can be beneficial to both of you.

· ·

Check Your Answers Check Your Answers at **connectED.mcgraw-hill.com**.

Reading Guide

Before You Read

Be Organized A messy environment can be distracting. To lesson distractions, organize an area where you can read this section comfortably.

Read to Learn

Key Concepts

✓ **Explain** the benefits of having good time-management skills.

✓ **Understand** techniques you can use to handle stress.

Main Idea

Learn and use time-management skills to have more time for things you want to do, and to help you reduce the stress that can happen when you try to do too much.

Content Vocabulary

○ time management   ○ procrastinate
○ multi-tasking   ○ stress

Academic Vocabulary

■ alternate   ■ cope

Graphic Organizer

As you read, list five things you can do to make the best use of your study time. Add your own ideas to the list. Use a graphic organizer like the one shown to help you organize your information.

Study Skills
1.
2.
3.
4.
5.
My own ideas:

 **Graphic Organizer** Go to connectED. mcgraw-hill.com to download this graphic organizer.

Do you sometimes feel that with school responsibilities, homework, extracurricular activities, and family commitments, you do not have time left over for yourself? It is easy to get involved in so many things that you feel like you cannot get anything done. Learn how to manage your time so that you can make the best use of the 24 hours you get every day.

Time Management

Use good time-management skills to help you in all areas of your life. **Time management** is the development of practices and skills that increase how quickly and effectively you can do something. Learn and use these skills so that you will have more time for the things you want to do. You can finish your homework and studying and still have time left for basketball, dance lessons, or for relaxing with a good book. Good time-management skills can help you meet deadlines and stay on schedule. Here are some ways to save time:

- Divide big jobs into small tasks.
- Do more than one task at the same time. This is called **multi-tasking**.
- Try to avoid interruptions.
- Tell your family members about your plans so they know when you are available, and when you need time for yourself.
- Stick with a task until it is done.
- Establish routines for daily tasks.
- Evaluate your activities on a regular basis so that you do not over-commit yourself.

To-Do List Making a to-do list can help you organize and prioritize your goals. *How can you prioritize your study time to make it count?*

As You Read

Connect What can lead to a feeling of not having enough time in the day to finish what you need to do?

⬦ Vocabulary

You can find definitions in the glossary at the back of this book.

Time Management
Update Your Schedule Look at your schedule each morning. Add any tasks you did not complete the day before, and add new tasks.

• • • • • • • • • • • • •

Time management also includes dealing with problems that may arise. You may find that two activities occur at the same time. You may have to make a choice between two things you really want to do. Try making a list of pros and cons. Pros are the good things about an activity or event. Cons are the negative things. For example, one of your choices may be going to the movies with your friend. A "pro" would be spending time with your friend. A "con" might be that it will take away from the time you need to practice for your piano recital. When you have a pros and cons list written down for each option, it will probably become clear which choice to make.

Sometimes you have several things you want to accomplish during a day. It may be difficult to know where to begin. When you prioritize, you rank tasks in order of importance. For example, if you use a to-do list, put a *1, 2, 3* and so on next to each task. As you complete each task, cross it off the list. It can motivate you to continue when you see how much you have accomplished.

Another challenge is dealing with unexpected changes. Sometimes schedules and plans do not work out exactly as planned. You may need to rearrange your priority list. A friend may have to cancel a shopping trip to the mall. The rain may prevent you from raking leaves. Whatever the case, stay flexible. Make the most of your time by having ideas for alternate, or different, activities.

Organize Supplies Organizing the tools or supplies you need before beginning a task helps you save time. *What are some other ways to save time?*

Make Time Count

Have you ever turned on the television to watch one 30-minute show, and then several hours later you were still watching television? Perhaps you spent a lot of time looking for your math book, only to find that it was on your desk all along, hidden under a pile of papers. Here are some ways to help you avoid wasting time:

- **Do not put things off for later.** If you **procrastinate** (prō-ˈkras-tə-nāt,) by waiting until the last minute to do something, you can waste a lot of time thinking and worrying about the task. Often you will find that the task itself does not take as long as the time you spent worrying about it.

- **Get organized.** Almost any task goes faster when you are organized. Before you begin the task, gather the tools or equipment you need and find out how to do the task. When you are finished, clean up or put things away. It may seem like it takes too much time to tidy up. However, think about the math book example above. Neatness and organization will save you time when you can find your book right away next time you need it.

- **Get Your Sleep.** You may think that you can give yourself more time by sleeping less. It does not work that way. You will accomplish less instead of more, because you are tired and unfocused.

- **Schedule Breaks.** Another mistake people can make is working nonstop on a task. You may think a job will be finished quicker if you plow through it. However, it is better to allow yourself a break or two while you work. A break, even if it is only for 5 or 10 minutes to get a snack or play with a pet, can help refresh your mind and body before getting back to your task.

Study Skills

As a student, you will find that much of your time is spent studying. Effective study skills include reading, note-taking, test-taking, listening, computer skills, and time-management skills. Make sure your study time is well spent by organizing and prioritizing your homework assignments, projects, and test preparation time.

SCIENCE YOU CAN USE

The Buddy System

Studies show that having a support system in place can help ease the stress of certain situations. Support from others can help take the stress out of a situation and have a calming effect on the person or people experiencing stress.

Procedure Study your classmates during a stressful time, such as waiting to be chosen for a team, or during the last few minutes of a ball game. Record the reactions of those who have support from peers and those who do not.

Analysis Using your results, determine whether or not the Buddy System relieves stress.

SUCCEED IN SCHOOL!

Time Management
Make a Checklist
Write down all of your assignments and tasks for the next week. Draw a small box next to each item. As you finish each task, put a check in the box. You can see your progress and feel a sense of accomplishment with each check.

● ● ● ● ● ● ● ● ● ● ● ● ● ●

Keep track of the areas where you need to improve your study skills. Ask for help when you need it. Parents, teachers, siblings, and friends are resources you can use for help. Ask a parent to quiz you before a test, or ask your brother to help you with your vocabulary assignment. Teachers can suggest extra resources such as tutoring if you need it. It is important that you continue to improve your study skills. You will use them at home, at school, on the job, and in the community. See **Figure 12.1** for some more suggestions to help improve your study skills.

Reading Check   *Evaluate How can you decide between doing two things that you really want to do?*

The Stress Connection

When you try to do too much, you may experience stress. **Stress** is the body's reaction to feeling overwhelmed by responsibilities, demands, or events. Both pleasant and unpleasant events can cause stress. For example, performing a solo in a school concert may be stressful even though you enjoy singing. A fight with your parents causes a different kind of stress. Whatever the situation, remember that stress is a natural part of life. You have the power to learn how to control the way you handle stress.

Figure 12.1 Improve Your Study Skills

Organize and Prioritize Create a plan to organize and arrange your tasks to make the most of your study time. *How do you plan for your study time?*

- **Make a to-do list.** Write down what you want to accomplish.
- **Set the time.** Decide how much time you are going to spend studying. Prioritize your tasks to fit that block of time. Try to study at the same time every day.
- **Set the atmosphere.** Choose a quiet place to study. Make sure the space has enough light, and enough space to spread out. If it helps to have music, keep the volume low.
- **Remove distractions.** Turn off the television, and do not use the telephone while you study. If you have a cell phone, let your calls go to voicemail. When using a computer, disable instant messaging. Keep your e-mail closed until you are finished studying.
- **Gather supplies.** Collect all of your pens, pencils, papers, and books before you begin.

How much stress you feel depends on how much is going on in your life and how you react to events. For example, adjusting to a new class and making new friends can be stressful. If you are experiencing another major life change at the same time, such as starting a new job or attending a new school, the stress may be even greater.

Stress and Your Health

Stress can motivate and challenge you. It can help you accomplish your goals. The stress of wanting to make the soccer team, for example, can motivate you to exercise and practice. However, too much stress, especially when it is not managed well, can have a negative impact on your health. Symptoms of too much stress can include headaches, stomachaches, loss of appetite, fatigue, depression, and anxiety. People who are unable to cope, or adjust to difficult and stressful situations, may become seriously ill. Sometimes they try to run away from their problems by turning to alcohol or other drugs. When you manage your time and other resources in your life, you will be better equipped to handle stress when it occurs.

Stress and Nutrition

When you get busy with homework, studying, friends, hobbies, sports, and other activities, it is easy to forget about having a balanced diet. You may be tempted to skip meals or eat unhealthful foods out of convenience.

SUCCEED IN SCHOOL!

Time Management
Time for Tasks
Estimate how much time each of your assignments will take. Make a daily schedule. Write down due dates and the time you think each assignment will take. This can help you meet deadlines.

Fancy Collection/Superstock

Relax Take the time to unwind, relax, and enjoy a few moments alone. *What are some other ways you can cope with stress?*

Manage Stress

Stress can affect your life in many ways. Symptoms may include changes in appetite, headaches, stomachaches, mood swings, and the inability to concentrate. Use these techniques to help you manage activities and events that can cause stress.

Get Away from the Routine Remove yourself from stressful situations, even if it is just a short break. Take a walk, spend time with a pet, or listen to some music. Do something you enjoy. Deep-breathing exercises can slow a racing heart and help clear your mind.

Set Priorities Decide what tasks or activities are the most important and prioritize them. Make sure your goals are realistic. Plan ahead for events that you know will happen.

Seek Out Your Support System Go to the people in your life who can provide support, encouragement, and advice. Friends and family who care about you can help in times of stress.

Do Something for Others Volunteer to help someone else. When you do something that benefits another person, it can help you feel proud and satisfied, and it can give you a greater sense of self-worth. These feelings can go a long way toward decreasing your own stress level.

Take Care of Yourself Do not let your health suffer when you are feeling stressed. Participate in a physical activity to release endorphins (en-ˈdȯr-fənz), your body's natural stress and pain reliever. Also, get plenty of sleep, eat balanced and nutritious meals, drink water, and take time to relax.

Adjust Your Attitude Be positive about your situation. Remind yourself that stress is a part of life and you can work through it. Do your best to maintain a positive and flexible attitude.

When your body does not get the nutrients it needs, you may end up trying to do more with less energy. This can lead to poor health and add even more stress to your busy life. Here are some easy ways to eat healthfully, even when you think you do not have the time:

Eat breakfast. When you skip breakfast, it is more difficult for your body to maintain stable blood sugar levels and energy during your busy morning. You can easily grab a hard-boiled egg and container of orange juice on your way out the door.

Carry a snack. Keep some protein-rich, healthful snacks in your backpack to help you avoid dips in your blood sugar levels and the mood swings and tiredness that can result. Trail mix, granola bars, and some energy bars all contain good nutrition.

Drink water. You should always have water handy. It is vital to health and proper physical functioning.

Get your family involved. It is easier to avoid sugary, fatty, and otherwise unhealthful foods if they are not in your home. Ask family members to stock the house with healthful foods and snacks, and to keep unhealthful foods to a minimum.

Section 12.2 After You Read

Review What You Have Learned

1. **Explain** how you can prioritize tasks you need to accomplish.
2. **Identify** five tips for managing stress.

Practice Academic Skills

English Language Arts

3. Write an e-mail to a friend who feels stressed because she cannot seem to find time to do her homework, rehearse for the play, prepare for exams, practice for softball tryouts, and hang out with her friends. Suggest things she can do to manage her time and help reduce her stress.

Social Studies

5. Interview family members about how they manage their time. How is the way you manage time similar or different? What influences do you see on your own time-management skills? Write a paragraph that describes your findings about how you and your family manage time.

Check Your Answers Check Your Answers at connectED.mcgraw-hill.com.

Discovering Careers

Are you a detail-oriented person? Do you like to be in charge of organizing people or events? If you answered yes to either of those questions, you might want to consider a future career in management. The following chart explores several careers in the management field.

Job Title	Job Description
Librarian	Maintains collections of books, magazines, documents, and other materials. Assists individuals in locating and obtaining materials.
Transportation Scheduler	Prepares schedules for transportation. Determines number of vehicles and trips. Arranges stops, length of routes, and runs per shift.
Production Manager	Trains and supervises employees in production of radio or television programs. Makes sure the program follows station policies and regulations.
Hotel Manager	Coordinates reservations and room assignments. Trains and directs hotel's front desk staff. Greets guests, resolves complaints and problems, handles special requests from guests.
School Principal	Works with administrators, students, parents, and local representatives to set school policies and goals and to raise funds. Prepares budgets and attendance reports.

Career Activities ▼

At School

❶ Select three of the careers listed. Research the education, training, and work experience required for each career. Write a summary of your results.

At Home

❷ Develop a master schedule for your family for a week. Use all the activities your family is involved in at home, as well as commitments at work or in the community.

At Work

❸ Make a list of your computer skills and the software you know how to use. How will these skills help you on the job?

In the Community

❹ Contact and interview someone in your community who works in a management position. Ask this person to describe what his or her typical work day is like. Share what you learned with your class.

Blend Images/SuperStock

Chapter Summary

Section 12.1 Manage Resources
Management skills are not just for the workplace. Follow a plan for your goals, and make full use of your resources. Learn how to manage personal resources, material resources, and community resources to help you reach goals and get things accomplished. Personal resources are time, energy, knowledge, skills, and people. Material resources are possessions, objects, and money. Every community provides a variety of resources for its citizens to use.

Section 12.2 Manage Time and Handle Stress
Time management is the development of practices and skills that increase how quickly and effectively you can do something. Learn to organize and prioritize your time. When you try to do too much, you can experience stress. Stress can motivate and challenge you, but too much stress can have a negative effect on you. When you manage your time and other resources in your life, you will be better equipped to handle stress.

Words You Learned

1. Create a fill-in-the-blank sentence for each of these vocabulary words. The sentence should contain enough information to help determine the missing word.

Content Vocabulary
- management (p. 259)
- resource (p. 261)
- energy (p. 261)
- time management (p. 265)
- multi-tasking (p. 265)
- procrastinate (p. 267)
- stress (p. 268)

Academic Vocabulary
- potent (p. 261)
- material (p. 262)
- alternate (p. 266)
- cope (p. 269)

Review Key Concepts

2. **Describe** each of the four steps you can take to be a good manager.

3. **Identify** resources that can help you manage your life.

4. **Explain** the benefits of having good time-management skills.

5. **Understand** techniques you can use to handle stress.

Critical Thinking

6. **Evaluate** how your family manages the tasks and activities of everyday life.

7. **Compare and contrast** material resources and personal resources.

8. **Predict** what could happen if you allow day-to-day stress, such as studying for tests or getting to class on time, to upset you.

9. **Recognize** that stress can be a positive factor in your life.

Real-World Skills and Applications

Problem-Solving

10. Action Plan Your brother needs help managing his busy schedule. He has to find time for homework, studying, hockey practice, family obligations, and his scout troop. Write a list of suggestions to help him manage his time and resources.

Technology Applications

11. Weekly Planner Create a weekly planner using spreadsheet, word processing, or design software. Customize it to your personal schedule. Include school activities, assignments, tests, family activities, chores, special events, and personal time. What do you notice about your week's activities? Are they manageable, or can you make adjustments to better organize your time and resources?

Financial Literacy

12. Financial Document Organization Andre's financial records are out of control. His receipts and bills are scattered all over his room. He does not know what is due, what is late, or how much he has spent. Andre also tends to forget about keeping track of his bank balance, so he never knows how much money he has available. Not only does this lack of organization cause Andre unneeded stress, but he also wastes about 15 minutes a week looking for his bills and paperwork. If Andre spent 20 minutes a month carefully organizing all of his financial documents to eliminate this stress and wasted time, how much time would he save over the course of a 52-week year?

13. Organize Your Study Area Collect an assortment of boxes, cartons, and jars in a variety of sizes. Use your imagination to decorate the containers. For example, cut the top off of a small milk carton and cover it with construction paper or left over gift wrap. Glue beads to the outside of a recycled pickle jar. Use the finished containers as pencil holders, paper trays, and storage for items like paperclips to organize your study area at home.

14. Successful Stress Management Interview someone you know, such as a teacher, a family member, or friend, about how they handle stress at work, at home, or in other areas of their lives. Ask such questions as, "What situations make you feel stressed?" and "What stress relief techniques work for you?" Ask him or her for tips and suggestions that you might be able to apply when you feel stressed. Prepare a list of tips and present them to your class.

15. Learn How to Study With permission from your parents or teacher, go online to search for tips on how to study. It may seem like something you already know how to do, but there are different methods for studying. You may find a method or idea that will help you improve the way you study. Make a list of at least five study tips. Explain how you can apply them to your homework and test preparation. Include the list in your Life Skills Binder.

D.J-Hurst/Alamy

Academic Skills

English Language Arts

16. Design a Workspace What does your ideal workspace look like? Create a sketch of a workspace that would help you organize your personal resources and study tools. Look for ideas in magazines, furniture catalogs, interior decorating books, or online resources. Next to the sketch, list all of the supplies you would like to have in your ideal workspace. Present your sketch and list to the class and explain how your design and supplies will help you manage time and reduce stress.

Science

17. Long-Term Stress Chronic, or long-term, stress can affect physical health. **Procedure** Conduct research to find out what people can do to help prevent long-term stress. What recommendations can you find for managing stress? **Analysis** Prepare a short presentation to share with the class.

Mathematics

18. Evaluate Your Time Chiyoko has decided to evaluate how he uses his time so he can make adjustments that would allow for more study time. When he realized that he spends 3 hours a day watching television, and 45 minutes a day playing video games, he knew it was time for some changes. Figure out what percentage of the day Chiyoko spent watching television. What percentage of the day did he spend playing video games?

Math Concept **Time Calculations** When performing multiplication or division with time, make sure all numbers are in the same units. Since there are 60 minutes in an hour, you can convert hours to minutes by multiplying by 60. Similarly, convert days to hours by multiplying by 24.

Starting Hint To find the TV percentage, divide 3 hours by 24 hours, then write the result as a percentage (multiply by 100 and add the "%" symbol). To find the videogame percentage, first you will need to convert 24 hours into minutes by multiplying 24 by 60.

Standardized Test Practice

Analogies

Select the pair of words that best expresses a relationship similar to that expressed in the capitalized pair.

Test-Taking Tip Analogies are relationships between two words or concepts. Common relationships in analogy questions include cause and effect, part-to-whole, general classification and specific example, and synonym/antonym.

19. NUTRIENTS:HEALTH
  a. safety:injury
  b. stress:deep breathing
  c. sleep:alertness
  d. emergency:rescue breathing

Life Skills Project

Manage Your Grocery Budget

Knowing how to shop is a key life skill. Observing the choices your parents make at the grocery story can be useful. Clip coupons, compare prices in newspapers, buy in bulk, and read labels to help you save money and become a better consumer.

My Journal Complete the journal entry from page 231, and refer to it to complete your grocery list.

Project Assignment ▼

In this project, you will:

- Analyze the groceries your family usually buys.
- Make a grocery list and shop for your family.
- Describe your shopping experience.
- Interview someone who works in a grocery store.
- Create a chart to demonstrate cost-saving techniques.
- Present your findings to your class.
- Include this project in the fifth section of your personal Life Skills binder.

Step 1 Research the Best Buys and Make a List

Creating a shopping list is easier if you know what your family usually buys. While making your list, check newspapers for prices, sales, and coupons. Write a summary of your research, explaining how you plan to save money at the grocery store.

Step 2 Go Shopping

Finalize your grocery list. Go to a grocery store with a parent or trusted adult. Compare products before you buy, use coupons, and search for the best deals. Then write two or more paragraphs that answer these questions:

- ✔ Did you decide to cross any items off of your list?

- ✔ What coupons did you use?
- ✔ What generic items did you buy instead of brand-name products?
- ✔ Did you find items you could buy in bulk?
- ✔ What other ways did you find to save money?
- ✔ How much money did you save?

Step 3 Interview a Grocery Store Worker

Interview a person who works in a store where groceries are sold. Ask these questions:

- ✔ What tips or tricks can you share that would help families save money on groceries?
- ✔ Is there a time of day or week that is better for getting good deals?
- ✔ What are your own strategies for saving money at the market?

Use these interviewing skills when conducting your interview and these writing skills when writing the summary of notes from your interview.

Interviewing Skills
- Record interview responses and take notes.
- Listen attentively.

Writing Skills
- Use complete sentences.
- Use correct spelling and grammar.

Step 4 Create and Present Your Chart

Use the Life Skills Project Checklist on the right to plan and complete your chart. Use information from your observations, your personal shopping experience, and your interview with the grocery store worker to complete your chart and give an oral report on it.

Use these speaking skills when presenting your final report.

Speaking Skills
- Speak clearly and concisely.
- Be sensitive to the needs of your audience.
- Use standard English to communicate.

Step 5 Evaluate Your Presentation

Your project will be evaluated based on:

- ✔ Completeness and organization of your shopping list.
- ✔ Your chart of cost-saving techniques.
- ✔ The description of your shopping experience.
- ✔ The summary written from interview notes.
- ✔ Grammar and sentence structure.
- ✔ Presentation to the class.
- ✔ Creativity and neatness.

Evaluation Rubric Go to connectED. mcgraw-hill.com for a rubric you can use to evaluate your final project.

Amos Morgan/Getty Images

Life Skills Project Checklist

Research Cost-Saving Techniques

- ✅ Study your family's grocery receipts for ways to save money.
- ✅ Collect coupons for products your family would buy.
- ✅ Read newspapers to search for bargains.
- ✅ Read labels on products at the market.
- ✅ Interview a grocery store worker.
- ✅ Include your cost-saving techniques in a chart.

Writing Skills

- ✅ Describe some of the groceries your family typically buys.
- ✅ Describe your shopping experience.
- ✅ Write a summary from your interview with a grocery store worker.

Present Your Findings

- ✅ Prepare a short presentation to explain what you did to save money.
- ✅ Invite the students of the class to ask any questions they may have. Answer these questions with responses that respect their perspectives.
- ✅ Add this project to your Life Skills binder.

Academic Skills

- ✅ Conduct research to gather information.
- ✅ Communicate effectively.
- ✅ Organize your presentation so the audience can follow along easily.
- ✅ Thoroughly express your ideas.

Chapter 13
Your Living Space

Chapter 14
Your Environment

Unit Preview

This unit is about the world you live in, both inside and outside of your home. In this unit, you will learn about:

● Making your home safe and comfortable.

● Adding your personal style to your living space.

● The different types of natural resources and how to conserve them.

● What you can do as an individual to protect the environment.

Explore the Photo

Spending time exploring nature can be enjoyable and relaxing. *What are some of the activities you enjoy doing in nature?*

Improve Your Home

When you are done studying this unit, you will complete a project in which you will:

✓ Evaluate your living space.

✓ Interview a home design or construction professional.

✓ Create and share floor plans to demonstrate your improved arrangements.

The prewriting activity below will help you get started.

My Journal

Prewriting Activity
Freewrite

Visit three rooms or areas in your home or someone else's home. Describe how each room or area looks and how it is meant to be used.

● Which rooms or areas seem to work well for their purpose?

● Which rooms or areas need to be rearranged to better suit their purpose?

Chapter  13

Your Living Space

Ariel Skelley/Blend Images LLC

Explore the Photo

To design your living space, you will need to work with your roommates. *How can you work with others to create a comfortable home for all involved?*

Descriptive Paragraph

Describe What would your perfect room be like? Write a paragraph that describes your perfect room and the mood or feel you want it to have. For example, you might want a room that makes you feel like you are in a log cabin. Choose furniture, colors, decorations, and accessories to create the mood or feel you want in your room.

Writing Tips Follow these steps to write a descriptive paragraph:

1. Choose a few words to describe the mood or feel you want and include them in your topic sentence.

2. Describe the furniture, colors, decorations, and accessories that create the mood or feel.

3. Use details and descriptive words to help the reader's imagination.

Section 13.1 Home Organization and Safety

Reading Guide

Before You Read

How Can You Improve? Before starting the section, think about the last exam you took on material you had to read. What reading strategies helped you on the test? Make a list of ways to improve your strategies in order to succeed on your next exam.

Read to Learn

Key Concepts

✓ **Describe** how a home is more than shelter.

✓ **Explain** the functions of furniture and storage space.

✓ **Identify** reasons for keeping your home clean and neat.

✓ **List** ways to stay safe in and around your home.

Main Idea

Make your home appealing, functional, and safe by organizing your space.

Content Vocabulary

○ shelter
○ floor plan
○ traffic pattern
○ functional

Academic Vocabulary

■ convenient   ■ routine

Graphic Organizer

As you read, write down four things you should consider when organizing your living space. Use a graphic organizer like the one shown to help you organize your information.

Living Space Organization

⬏ **Graphic Organizer** Go to connectED. mcgraw-hill.com to download this graphic organizer.

People live in many types of homes. Apartments, manufactured homes, mobile homes, duplexes, town homes, single-family houses, and condominiums all serve the basic human need for shelter. All of these dwellings have one common feature. To the people living inside, each place is called "home." Everyone deserves to live in a comfortable and safe home.

Your Home

Homes satisfy the basic need for shelter. A **shelter** is a structure built to protect people from the weather and extreme temperatures. Homes also provide a place for you to take care of your personal needs. In your home you can bathe, prepare meals, and sleep comfortably. You also have a place to keep your clothes and personal possessions.

You get a sense of well-being and a feeling of security in your home. It is a place to relax and be yourself. Home is a place where you can enjoy listening to music, playing video games, or reading. It is a great place to spend time with family members and friends.

Living Areas

Most homes are divided into living areas in order to meet people's needs and interests. Some areas, such as bedrooms, are designed for sleep and privacy. Other areas, such as family rooms, are used for gathering with family members and entertaining friends. Bathrooms are for bathing and taking care of grooming and personal needs. Dividing space into specific areas makes a home more **convenient**, or easier to manage.

Some areas serve more than one function. When you organize rooms for more than one function, you can make the best use of space, equipment, and furniture. For example, you probably use your bedroom not only for sleeping but also for studying, reading, and listening to music.

Reading Check *Understand* *What is the benefit of organizing rooms for more than one function?*

Organize Your Space

To organize the space within your home, begin by thinking of the various activities of all your family members. What area would be best for each activity? For example, would exercise equipment be better located in a bedroom, the basement, or the family room? Should the computer be set up in a bedroom or in the den?

As You Read

Connect What are your favorite memories of being home with your family?

◆ **Vocabulary**

You can find definitions in the glossary at the back of this book.

Fancy Collection/SuperStock

↶ **More than Shelter**
Your home is a place to relax with your family and friends. *What does your home provide other than shelter?*

How do you and your family use the living space now? Are there improvements that could be made? If a shelving unit or different lighting were added, could the space be expanded to serve an additional function? A **floor plan** is a drawing of a room and how its furniture is arranged. It allows you to see how furniture fits together without actually moving any furniture.

The way you organize your living space depends on the activities in which you and your family participate. Think about the following concepts when arranging your space:

- **Traffic Pattern** Consider the traffic pattern in the room. The **traffic pattern** is the path people take to move around within a room as well as enter and exit the room. Furniture should be placed so it does not get in the way. If you find that you have to constantly walk around a chair, you should try a different arrangement.
- **Space Around Furniture** Leave space around furniture so it can be used comfortably. Drawers and doors require extra space for opening and closing.
- **Functional Arrangements** Place furniture and other items in **functional** groupings so that the arrangement is useful and convenient. Place a small table next to a sofa to keep eyeglasses, the telephone, and remote controls within easy reach.
- **Related Groups** Group related items together. For example, by storing DVDs near the DVD player, your movies are organized and ready to use.

Select Furniture

Furniture is necessary for comfort and convenience, but it is also decorative. Furniture style is a matter of personal taste. You may like furniture with sleek, modern lines. Your sister may prefer country-style furniture. Look in magazines and books to find the furniture styles you like best. Some furniture can serve more than one purpose. A desk that has a large surface area may be used as a computer station or a drawing table. An infant's diaper changing table may be designed to turn into a dresser when the child gets older.

Storage Space

Having enough storage space is important for a room to be functional. Decide what objects should be stored in a given space. For example, paper, pens and pencils, and a dictionary should be stored in a study area. Items that would not be used in this area, such as cleaning supplies, should be stored in another place. Sometimes your storage space might be limited.

When you run out of room, get rid of things you no longer need. See if anyone else in your family could use the items you no longer want. Have a yard sale or donate useable items to charity, and recycle or throw away things that are broken or unusable. Storage containers and crates are available to fit all kinds of spaces, such as your closet floor, under your bed, or in the garage. **Figure 13.1** on page 286 lists several suggestions for how to best use the space in your closet. Shelves can be used for both storing items and for decoration.

 **A Place for Everything** Putting dishes away after washing creates a clean kitchen space. *What can you do when storage space is limited?*

Reading Check *Categorize How can you decide what to store in certain places in your room?*

A Clean and Neat Home

Do you feel proud of your home or your room when it is clean and neat? Do you feel good knowing that your home is safe and secure? Caring for a home means more than just keeping things tidy. It also means keeping things clean and taking safety measures to prevent accidents. Keeping your home clean, neat, safe, and secure is so important because:

A neat home saves time and energy. You waste time and energy when you have to search for items that you need.

Clothes and other possessions last longer. If you take good care of your belongings, they will last longer.

Family members stay healthier in a clean home. A clean home helps family members avoid disease-causing germs.

Most home accidents can be prevented. When everyone in the home takes safety measures, many home accidents and injuries can be avoided.

Security measures can keep a home safe. If a home has good locks, it will be more difficult for intruders to break in.

Organize Cleaning Tasks

Routine, or regular, cleaning tasks are those that must be done every day or every week. These chores include washing dishes, making beds, keeping rooms picked up, and hanging up clothes. Routine tasks keep the home clean and neat so that heavy cleaning is needed less often.

Figure 13.1 Organize Your Closet

Take Advantage of Space Your closet is probably the main storage area in your room. *What can you do to improve the way you use the space in your closet?*

- **Double Your Hanging Space** Add extra rods to the closet for hanging clothes. Double up rods for shirts, vests, and shorter items. Leave one space open to hang longer items such as dresses and dress pants.

- **Add Shelves** Add a shelf along the top of the closet for items you do not use very often. If space allows, build shelves for shoes, accessories, and storage containers.
- **Make Use of Boxes and Baskets** Store loose items like socks and baseball hats in plastic storage boxes, shoeboxes, and baskets.
- **Use Floor Space** Place boots and shoes on the floor of the closet, along with any storage boxes that do not fit on the shelves.
- **Doors** Use the back side of the closet door to hang a mirror or a shoe holder.
- **Install Hooks** You can purchase inexpensive hooks in a variety of sizes to hang belts, ties, and other small accessories.

A cleaning plan can help families manage their cleaning tasks. A cleaning plan is a list of daily, weekly, and occasional household jobs, with the name of the person responsible for each job. To make a cleaning plan, decide what jobs need to be done and who will perform each task. Change responsibilities on a regular basis so the work is divided fairly.

Cleaning Shared Space

When each person takes responsibility for keeping his or her personal space in order, much of the housekeeping gets done automatically. To get your share done with ease, you need to establish a routine. For example, hang up your clothes or put them in a hamper. It may seem like tossing them on the floor will take less time, but you will only have to pick them up later.

Bathrooms and the kitchen are used by all family members, so every person in the home must help keep them in order. Rinse the bathtub and sink after each use. Hang towels neatly after each use. Return personal grooming items to their proper place. In the kitchen, wash and dry the dishes, or put them in the dishwasher. Clean up spills right away.

Cleaning Your Room

It will be easier to keep your room clean if you take a little time each day to put it in order. All the tasks do not have to be done at the same time. For instance, make your bed every morning after you brush your teeth. Empty the wastebasket after you finish your homework. Hang up your clothes and straighten your dresser and desk before you go to bed. Throughout the day, put away your belongings as soon as you finish using them. When you do a little bit every day, it makes it easier and quicker to finish your bigger cleaning jobs.

Reading Check   *Plan*   *What can you do to make heavy cleaning an easier task to handle?*

Safety at Home and in Your Community

Many of the accidents that happen in homes can be prevented or avoided with a little care. Do not let someone in your home get hurt by carelessness. Read the following guidelines and then take the time to make your home safe.

Fire Safety

Protect your home from fire by following these safety rules:

- Have an exit route planned and practice using the exit route on a regular basis.
- Make sure that smoke alarms are installed in the home. Alarms should be installed near the kitchen, outside the bedrooms, and at the top of the stairs. Check smoke alarms once a month to be sure that they are working properly. Change the batteries routinely.
- Keep a fire extinguisher in the home. Learn how to use it properly. Keep the extinguisher properly serviced.
- Make sure that all electrical cords are in good condition. A damaged cord can cause surrounding material to catch fire.

Home Care
When you take care of your home, you also take care of yourself and others , including pets, who live in the home. *What are some typical cleaning jobs that help keep a home safe?*

CDC/Cade Martin

Smoke Alarms

Properly installed and maintained smoke alarms provide an early warning and give people inside the home a chance to escape. *What else can you do to prevent fire-related injuries?*

Safety Check

Kitchen Fires

According to the U.S. Fire Administration, cooking is the leading cause of home fires and home fire injuries. To help prevent cooking fires:

- Never leave the stove unattended when cooking.
- Make sure all towels or paper are away from where you are cooking.

- Do not let curtains, towels, or potholders get too close to the stove. If you are cooking, avoid wearing a shirt with loose sleeves that might easily catch fire.
- Keep the area around the stove free of grease. Grease burns easily and can spread a fire.
- If you have a fireplace in your home, make sure that it is used properly. Keep flammable objects away from the fireplace. Use a fireplace screen.

Fall Safety

Protect people from falls in your home by following these safety rules.

- If something is spilled, wipe it up immediately.
- Place nonskid pads under rugs so that they will not slide.
- Be sure to use nonskid strips or mats in bathtubs and showers.
- Make sure that stairs are in good repair, well lit, and free from clutter. Stairs should also have handrails.
- Keep walkways free of clutter.
- Secure windows so children do not climb out.

Hands-On LAB

Plan an Escape Route

In this activity you will plan an escape route for your family. In case of an emergency, it is important for your family to know what to do. Before you begin, read through the entire Hands-On Lab assignment. Write down any questions that you have about the assignment. Reread the text or ask your teacher for help if you need it.

Supplies
✓ Paper and pencil or pen

Develop Your Plan

■ Sit down with all your family members.

■ Make sure everyone in the family knows ways to get out of every room in your home.

■ Teach younger children to crawl on their hands and knees and stay low under smoke.

■ Teach younger children to shout their names out if they are trapped in a smoke-filled room.

■ Plan your escape routes. Choose a place where everyone will meet outside in the event of a fire.

■ Make sure everyone knows that they should never go back into the building after leaving.

■ Use a buddy system to assure everyone gets out safely.

■ Assign someone to call 9-1-1 or the fire department.

■ Assign an adult the responsibility for getting any pets out of the building.

Implement Your Plan

■ Make a drawing of the layout of each floor of your home. Indicate where the windows and doors are. Mark the escape routes from each room.

■ Hold a fire drill once a month.

Evaluate Your Results

How did your family react to creating the escape plan? After your family held a fire drill, did you find anything in the procedure that you wanted to change? If so, what? How will you change it? Write one or more paragraphs to explain your answer.

➤ **Projects and Activities** Go to connectED.mcgraw-hill.com.

Other Safety Precautions

In addition to fires and falls, there are many other types of accidents that can happen in homes. If there are small children in the home, poisoning is a serious danger. Make sure that all cleaning products and chemicals are kept out of the reach of children. Read the label on every chemical or cleaning product before using it so that you will know how to handle it correctly. If anyone in your family accidentally swallows a poisonous substance, immediately call 9-1-1, a poison control center, or a hospital.

Power tools and sharp knives can also cause injuries if they are not used with care. Knives and other dangerous objects should be kept out of children's reach.

Improper use of electrical appliances is another common cause of accidents. Be sure to connect and disconnect an electrical appliance with dry hands. Do not use any appliance that has a damaged cord. Do not use a hair dryer while in the bathtub or while standing in water.

Community Safety

Have you ever been startled by a loud noise while walking in your neighborhood? Have you ever felt uneasy when you walked home from a friend's house at dusk?

Compromise

Yanett and Deenie are twins. Each sister has her own bedroom, and they share a bathroom. Both girls are neat and take care of their rooms, but they have different ideas about how to clean and organize the bathroom. Yanett thinks it is faster and easier to clean when the supplies are kept on the counter. If she does not see them, she forgets that she needs to clean. Deenie thinks it looks messy to have the supplies out in the open. To her, leaving supplies out is the same as not making a bed. Though Yanett and Deenie get along most of the time, the bathroom cleaning situation is bothering them, and it is bothering other members of the family who have to listen to them argue.

You Make the Call

Who is right? Who is wrong? Is there only one efficient way to clean a shared space? Write a paragraph explaining what Yanett and Deenie should do before their situation gets worse.

Everyone wants to feel safe in his or her own neighborhood. There are steps you can take to protect yourself. Make sure your home is well lit on the outside. Keep a porch light or yard light on. Solar lights can be placed around the outside of the home and do not require electrical wiring. They absorb light during the day and then glow at night, providing light.

Your family can join or help set up a Neighborhood Watch group. Members of such groups are trained by the police to identify and report suspicious activities. When you walk down the street, keep alert, especially at night. Pay attention to the people around you and to what they are doing. Stay away from dangerous areas and poorly lighted streets. Avoid taking any unnecessary risks.

Get to know your neighbors. If you know who belongs in your neighborhood, it will be easier to spot suspicious activity by strangers. If there is ever an emergency, you will know which neighbors you can call for help. Communities can work together to look after each other.

Safety Check

Social Networking

Most people who join social networking Web sites do not want to hurt anyone. However, just as in the real world, there are people who try to cause harm. Use these tips to help you stay safe online:

- Never reveal personal information.
- Only allow access to people you know in person.
- Never respond to suggestive or threatening messages.
- Never arrange a meeting with a stranger.

Section 13.1 — After You Read

Review What You Have Learned

1. **Explain** how to make an area functional.
2. **Define** floor plan and explain how it can help you organize your living space.
3. **List** routine cleaning tasks that should be done every day.
4. **Predict** how knowing your neighbors can help keep you safe.

Practice Academic Skills

English Language Arts

5. Create a poster to show how to prevent accidents at home. Use guidelines from your text as well as other print or online resources. Use colorful illustrations and large letters to make the information easy to read and understand.

Social Studies

6. Many "smart" houses have convenient features such as automatic lights and appliances. What do you expect to see in homes of the future? Create a futuristic "home for sale" ad and list the technological features you think it will have.

Check Your Answers Check Your Answers at **connectED.mcgraw-hill.com.**

Section 13.2 Home Design

Reading Guide

Before You Read

Check for Understanding If you have questions as you read, that means you are checking to see if you understand the material. Try to answer those questions as you read.

Read to Learn
Key Concepts

✓ **Name** the elements and principles of design.

✓ **Understand** how to use decorations and accessories to create your own style.

Main Idea
Use the elements and principles of design to create a living space that reflects your personality and style.

Content Vocabulary
○ design
○ color scheme
○ design principle
○ emphasis
○ proportion
○ accessory

Academic Vocabulary
■ element
■ outline

Graphic Organizer
As you read, identify and describe five design principles that guide how design elements are organized. Use a graphic organizer like the one shown to help you organize your information.

Five Design Principles	Description
1. Balance	items provide equal visual weight or stability
2.	
3.	
4.	
5.	

✈ **Graphic Organizer** Go to connectED. mcgraw-hill.com to download this graphic organizer.

You want your home to reflect not only who you are, but also to reflect good design and style. How can you go beyond just organizing? Combine good design with your personal style to help give you the look you want and a place to entertain friends.

Your Room Design

Why do some rooms look more inviting than others? How can a room seem large, even though it is actually small? Different elements, or parts, can be combined to create a variety of looks. The way a room appears depends a great deal on how design is used, or not used, to create an overall effect. **Design** is the art of combining elements in a pleasing way. You can use design to create the type of look you want in a room.

Design Elements

The elements of design are space, shape, line, texture, and color. These elements can work alone, or in a variety of combinations. Each contributes its own effect to the final design.

Space Space helps draw attention to objects. For example, a vase on a shelf will stand out and be seen if some space is left on either side of it. On the other hand, too much space between objects can result in a bare, empty look. You can create many looks just by dividing space in various ways.

Shape Shape refers to the outline, or form, of solid objects. A bed has a rectangular shape. A table may be rectangular, square, oval, or round. Attractive designs use shape effectively. Too many different shapes in one room can be distracting.

Line Lines are very important to design. Look around a room, and you can see them in the legs of a table, the frame of a door, or the stripes on a curtain. Straight lines make objects seem strong and dignified. Curved lines make objects seem softer and more graceful. Vertical lines go straight up and down and give the appearance of height. They can make objects look taller. Horizontal lines move straight across and make objects appear wider. Lines that are set at a diagonal, or on an angle, suggest action or movement.

As You Read

Connect Think about the last time you visited someone's home. How did the person's personal style show in his or her home?

 **Vocabulary**

You can find definitions in the glossary at the back of this book.

Eric Audras/Getty Images

Set the Mood By using different design elements, you can affect the mood of a room. *How do the design elements in this room contribute to the mood?*

Have Fun

Look for Ideas Check your local newspaper's special events section. You may find inexpensive or free activities to enjoy instead of the usual movie or television show.

Texture Texture is the way something feels or looks as if it would feel. Texture provides visual interest in a room, and you can add more interest by using a variety of textures. A rug might feel soft and fuzzy. A polished table feels hard and smooth. Textures can also affect the mood of a room. Soft and rounded surfaces make a room look cozy. Angled, hard surfaces create a clean, cool effect.

Color Color probably has the greatest effect on the appearance of a room. Color schemes are used to create style and appeal. A **color scheme** is a system of arranging colors in a pleasing manner. A change of color can make a room look completely different. For example, white or light colors on the walls make a room look larger. Darker colors make a room seem smaller. **Figure 13.2** illustrates cool and warm colors.

Design Principles

A **design principle** is a rule that directs how the elements of design are organized. There are five design principles you can use when creating your personal living space.

Balance Use two similar items to provide equal visual weight to keep a room or area from looking lopsided. You can balance a room when you place several small items on one side of a fireplace, and a larger object on the other side.

Figure 13.2 The Color Wheel

Warm or Cool? The color wheel shows the relationships among colors. *If you want your living area to be warm, comfortable, and welcoming, what colors would you choose?*

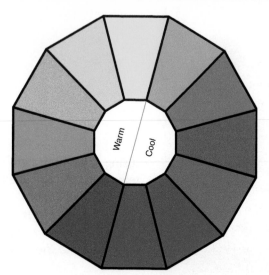

Colors are often described as warm or cool. Pick a few colors from the wheel and imagine how your room would feel if decorated using these colors.

■ **Warm Colors**

Red, yellow, and orange are warm colors. If a room does not get much sunlight or is cold in the winter, warm colors can make the room seem more comfortable.

■ **Cool Colors**

Blue, green, and violet are cool, restful colors. A cool color is a good choice for a room that gets a lot of sunlight. Cool colors are used to set a relaxing mood.

Emphasis Place **emphasis** on an item of special importance if you want it to be noticed. Select one item to serve as the focus of the room. Having a focal point draws the eye directly to the object. For example, a red pillow on a white sofa provides emphasis.

Proportion How one part relates to another is called **proportion**. It is important to keep in mind the sizes of objects in the room as they relate to each other, and to the room as a whole. A large painting with a dark, heavy wood frame would not look well-proportioned in a small room with delicate white furniture.

Rhythm Create a visual path through a room by placing elements carefully. Hang a series of posters on a wall to create a pattern of visual movement, or rhythm.

Unity Combining similar elements brings unity, or harmony, to a room. Arrange several framed photos in an attractive grouping to create unity, or use shades of the same color throughout a room.

Reading Check *Identify* the elements of design.

Your Own Style

Before you start redesigning your room, you need to think about the look you want for your space. It depends on what you have to work with, but it also depends on your personal taste. Of course, if you share a room you will also need to consider what the other person likes. The elements of design and the design principles can be used in many ways with pleasing results, but not all of them will appeal to you.

First, consider what kind of mood you want to create. What are your interests? Do you want your space to be restful or lively? Are you looking for ways to make the room seem larger? Keep in mind that you will probably have to live with your changes for a long time. Your friend's neon pink and black bedroom might seem like a fun idea, but do you really want to live with those colors for several years? Be sure of your decisions before starting any work on a new look.

MATH YOU CAN USE

Calculate Square Footage

House, apartment, and room sizes are typically listed in "square feet." One square foot is the area of a rectangle that measures 1 foot by 1 foot. Square feet measurements tell you the area of the living space available inside a home. Derek has measured the inside of his bedroom and determined that it is 12 feet long and 9 feet wide. How many square feet of floor space does Derek have in his room?

Math Concept **Area of a Rectangle**
The area of a geometric shape measures the total size of its surface. For a rectangle, area (A) is given by the formula $A = l \times w$, where l and w are the length and width of the rectangle. If l and w are measured in inches, the area will be in square inches.

Starting Hint Read the problem to determine what numbers to use for l and w, and then use the area formula to determine the area of Derek's room in square feet.

 For math help, go to the Math Appendix at the back of the book.

SUCCEED IN SCHOOL!

Have Fun

Fun Is Important Fun is an important part of living a balanced life. Fun activities can help relieve stress so you can be your best in other areas of your life.

Create a Look

Once you have decided on the mood and style, you can plan how to achieve that look in your room. Make a plan before you start to help your project go smoothly.

Perhaps you would like a new color scheme. What parts of the room will be easiest to change? Walls can be repainted, and you can hang new pictures. Carpet, on the other hand, is difficult and expensive to replace. There a lots of ways to change the look of your room or space. Even small changes can make a big difference.

Accessorize

No room is complete without accessories. An **accessory** is an interesting item added to make a space more personal. You can make your own accessories, such as storage organizers, or buy accessories like lamps and plants. Use accessories to personalize your room. You can add your personal touch with any of these items:

- Curtains
- Handmade items
- Quilts
- Pillows
- Posters and pictures

- Collections and mementos
- Trophies and awards
- Baskets
- Rugs

Decorate

Decorating your room or a personal space in your home is a great way to show off your style and creativity. Get permission from your parents or guardians before putting your creativity to work. Here are some ideas:

Discover International...
Design

Feng Shui

According to Chinese philosophy, all things are composed of five basic elements. Those elements are earth, water, fire, metal, and wood. Many objects in and around a home symbolize these elements. *Feng* means wind and *shui* means water. Feng shui aims to balance and simplify all five of the basic elements in a harmonious design. A design created with the principles of feng shui is meant to provide peace, comfort, balance, and harmony with nature. Feng shui principles can be applied to gardens, homes, and work environments.

feng shui |ˈfən-shwā| the Chinese art of designing gardens, buildings, and interiors to promote harmony between humans and nature.

- **Walls** Paint can quickly and dramatically change the look of a room. Draw and paint a scene or a geometric pattern on a wall. You can also use an accent color to draw attention to one wall. Hang posters, banners, and bulletin boards to add interest to bare walls.
- **Books** Books are more than just reading material. Put some of your favorites on display in a bookcase or on a shelf.
- **Lampshades** Jazz up an old lampshade. Use hot glue to attach trim or fringe to the upper and lower edges.
- **Pillows** Make or purchase toss pillows for your bed. Choose fabrics that go with your room colors and stitch them using a pattern that you can find at your local fabric store.
- **Picture Frames** Decorate plain, inexpensive picture frames. Use hot glue to attach buttons, bows, shells, small polished rocks, team pins, or felt or foam shapes in a random pattern around the frame. Showcase your favorite photos inside.

Express Yourself Your living space, whether it is your bedroom or your own apartment, says a lot about you. *What does your room reveal about you?*

Section **13.2** After You Read

Review What You Have Learned

1. **Describe** how color can affect the mood or feel of a room.
2. **Plan** what you need to do before starting a room design change.

Practice Academic Skills

English Language Arts

3. Design your ideal living space. Use magazines, photos, and your own drawings to create a collage of furniture, colors, accessories, and fabrics. Sketch a floor plan. Present your collage to the class, and explain how you would put your plan into action.

Social Studies

4. Conduct research to learn how school designs are planned. What factors do designers and builders have to consider? What do you think they considered when your own school was designed? Write a summary of your findings.

Check Your Answers Check Your Answers at **connectED.mcgraw-hill.com.**

© Paul Bradbury/age fotostock

Discovering Careers

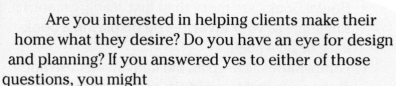

Focus on Careers in Home Design ▼

Are you interested in helping clients make their home what they desire? Do you have an eye for design and planning? If you answered yes to either of those questions, you might want to consider a future career in home design. The following chart explores several careers in the home design industry.

Career Activities ▼

At School

1 Select three of the careers listed. Research the education, training, and work experience required for each career. Write a summary of your results.

At Home

2 What projects in your home could be done by a contractor or design professional?

At Work

3 Describe how the elements and principles of design can be used in an office setting. Share your list with your classmates.

In the Community

4 Contact and interview someone in your community who works in interior or exterior home design. Ask this person to describe what his or her typical work day is like. Share what you learned with your class.

Job Title	Job Description
Architect	Plans and designs buildings for clients. Uses knowledge of design, construction, zoning and building codes, and building materials. Prepares scale drawings.
Interior Designer	Plans, designs, and furnishes interiors of residential, commercial, and industrial buildings. Determines preferences, purpose, and function of living spaces with client.
Carpet Layer	Lays carpet and rugs. Measures and cuts carpeting to size. Steams sections of carpeting together at seams. Secures carpeting to floor.
Upholstery Cleaner	Cleans upholstered furniture using vacuum cleaner or dry-cleaning fluids. Rubs surfaces with oil and buffs with cloth or hand buffer.
Contractor	Contracts with clients to build new homes or home improvement projects. Works to meet client specifications about projects.

Chapter Summary

Section 13.1 Home Organization and Safety
Homes satisfy the basic need for shelter. You get a sense of well-being, a feeling of security, and self-expression. Most homes are divided into living areas in order to meet people's needs and interests. Keep your home clean, neat, safe, and secure. When each person keeps his or her personal space in order, most housekeeping gets done automatically. Many accidents that happen in homes can be prevented with a little care.

Section 13.2 Home Design
Design is the art of combining elements in a pleasing way. Design elements are space, shape, line, texture, and color. Before you start planning a room makeover, think about the look you want for your space. Be sure of your decisions before starting any work on a new look. Once you have decided, you can plan how to achieve that look in your room. Making a plan before you start will help your project go smoothly.

Words You Learned

1. Create a fill-in-the-blank sentence for each of these vocabulary terms. The sentence should contain enough information to help determine the missing word.

Content Vocabulary
- shelter (p. 283)
- floor plan (p. 284)
- traffic pattern (p. 284)
- functional (p. 284)
- design (p. 293)
- color scheme (p. 294)
- design principle (p. 294)
- emphasis (p. 295)
- proportion (p. 295)
- accessory (p. 296)

Academic Vocabulary
- convenient (p. 283)
- routine (p. 285)
- element (p. 293)
- outline (p. 293)

Review Key Concepts

2. **Describe** how a home is more than shelter.
3. **Explain** the functions of furniture and storage space.
4. **Identify** reasons for keeping your home clean and neat.
5. **List** ways to stay safe in and around your home.
6. **Name** the elements and principles of design.
7. **Understand** how to use decorations and accessories to create your own style.

Critical Thinking

8. **Predict** what might happen if you try to redecorate your room without knowing the principles and elements of design.
9. **Plan** what you can do at home to prepare for a weather or geographical emergency, such as tornadoes or earthquakes, in your area.

Real-World Skills and Applications

Problem-Solving

10. Buying Furniture Imagine that you are moving into your first apartment. You have a limited budget and must decide between buying used furniture and buying inexpensive new furniture. Make a list of pros and cons for each, then decide which would be the best option for your budget and needs.

Interpersonal and Collaborative

11. Share Living Space Follow your teacher's directions to form groups. In your group, discuss problems that might arise when people share a living space. For example, who will clean the bathroom? Who will take care of the plants? Write a list of 5 problems, and then come up with solutions for each.

Financial Literacy

12. Comparison Shopping Choose three accessories, such as a lamp, a collector's item, and a painting, that you would like to have in your room at home. Research the prices for each item from various sources. Consider retail stores, discount stores, garage sales, and online auctions. Determine the best deal for each of the three items. Are there any drawbacks to the least expensive options? Write a brief summary of your findings, including a description or listing of the various shopping locations and their range of prices. Also, determine if the less expensive sources are truly your best options.

13. Herb Garden Create an herb garden display. Choose an attractive assortment of boxes or pots, or make your own. Research which kinds of herbs are suitable for the amount of sunlight that reaches your window. Find out what kind of care is needed for your herb selections. Write a paragraph that explains how an herb garden is both decorative and functional.

14. Caring Communities Neighborhood Watch programs depend on citizens to organize themselves and work with law enforcement to keep an eye and ear on their communities. Neighbors watch out for each other by being alert, observant, and caring. They report suspicious activity or crimes immediately to the police. Research Neighborhood Watch programs to find out what neighbors can do to help each other. Make a list of 5 actions that would benefit your neighborhood.

15. Decorating Styles With permission from your teacher or parents, go online to research decorating styles, such as traditional, modern, or country. Choose your favorite and imagine your room redecorated in that style. How would the room look and feel? How would the style mix with your personal accessories? How do you think visitors would respond? Write one or more paragraphs to answer these questions. Include the information in your Life Skills Binder.

D. Hurst/Alamy

Academic Skills

English Language Arts

16. Internet Safety Pledge Create a list of promises to your family that you will keep to help you stay safe online. For example, your first promise could be "I will ask permission from my parents before downloading anything from the Internet." Show the list to your parents and discuss with them what changes might need to be made. Write your final list in the form of an Internet Safety Pledge and sign it.

Science

17. Mold Molds are part of the natural environment. Outdoors, molds break down dead organic matter such as fallen leaves. Indoors, mold can cause health problems.
Procedure Conduct research to learn how mold can contribute to health problems, and how you can prevent mold from growing inside your home.
Analysis Present a report that summarizes your findings

Mathematics

18. Painting a Room Amanda wants to paint her bedroom. Her bedroom is 12 feet long and 9 feet wide, and the walls are 10 feet high. If one gallon of paint covers approximately 350 square feet, will one gallon be enough to cover all four of Amanda's walls? If not, how much will she need?

Math Concept **Perimeter** Perimeter is the distance around the edge of a geometric shape. You can calculate perimeter by adding up the lengths of every side, but for some shapes, you can use a shortcut formula. The perimeter (P) of a rectangle is given by the formula $P = 2l + 2w$, where l and w are the length and width of the rectangle.

Starting Hint To find the surface area of all walls in a rectangular room, you can use another shortcut: multiply the perimeter of the room by the height of the walls. Determine the perimeter of Amanda's room, and multiply it by 10 feet. Is the result less than 350?

Standardized Test Practice

Multiple-Choice

Read the scenario. Determine the meaning of neutral within the context of the scenario, and choose the best answer.

Test-Taking Tip In a multiple-choice test, the answers should be specific and precise. Read the questions first, then read all the answer choices. Eliminate answers that you know are incorrect.

19. Julia's bedroom had not been redecorated since she was a little girl. She decided to change the pink walls to a neutral shade of beige. That way, she could change the look of her room often by simply changing the colors of her pillows, rugs, and other accessories.
In this scenario, the meaning of neutral is
a. not taking sides
b. blends easily with other colors
c. powerful
d. unable to decide

Chapter 14

Your Environment

Section 14.1

Resources and Conservation

■ **Main Idea** It is essential to conserve the natural resources that animals, plants, and humans need for survival.

Section 14.2

Protect the Environment

■ **Main Idea** Individual efforts make a difference when it comes to protecting the environment. Do your part by limiting waste, and use air, water, land, and energy wisely.

Purestock/SuperStock

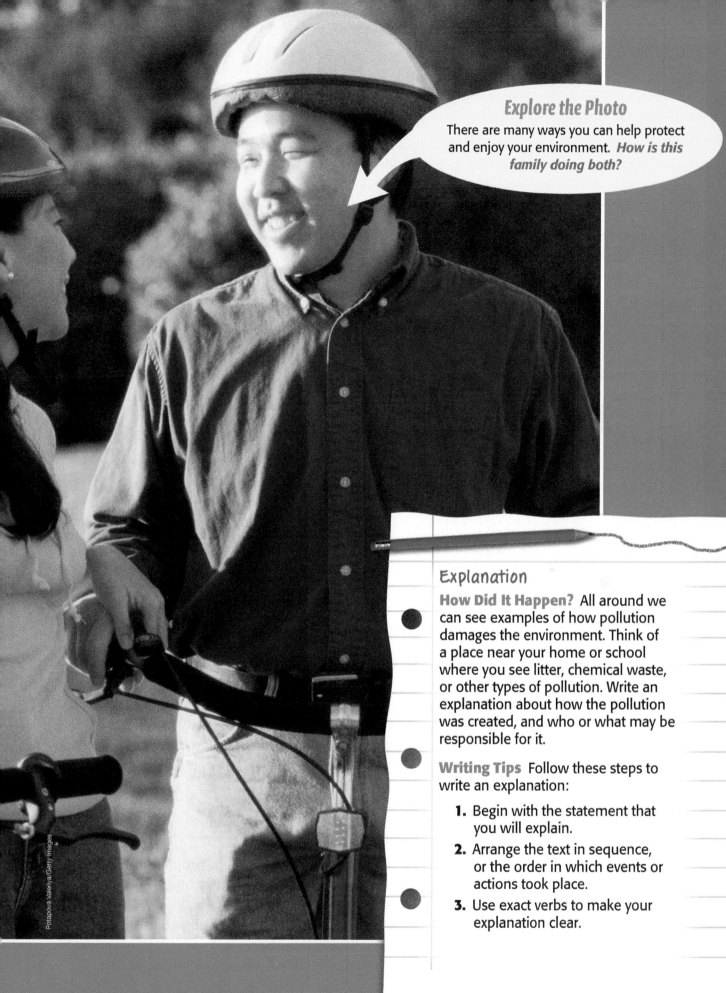

Explore the Photo

There are many ways you can help protect and enjoy your environment. *How is this family doing both?*

Explanation

How Did It Happen? All around we can see examples of how pollution damages the environment. Think of a place near your home or school where you see litter, chemical waste, or other types of pollution. Write an explanation about how the pollution was created, and who or what may be responsible for it.

Writing Tips Follow these steps to write an explanation:

1. Begin with the statement that you will explain.
2. Arrange the text in sequence, or the order in which events or actions took place.
3. Use exact verbs to make your explanation clear.

303

Reading Guide

Before You Read

Use Notes When you are reading, keep a notebook handy. When you read a phrase or term that you do not understand, write it down in the form of a question in your notebook. After you have finished the section, look up the terms and try to answer your questions based on what you have read.

Read to Learn

Key Concepts

✓ **Identify** the four key natural resources and why we need to protect them.

✓ **Explain** how you can do your part to conserve water and energy.

Main Idea

It is essential to conserve the natural resources that animals, plants, and humans need for survival.

Content Vocabulary

○ natural resource
○ pollution
○ soil
○ fossil fuel
○ conservation

Academic Vocabulary

■ key
■ efficient

Graphic Organizer

As you read, identify the four main natural resources. Use a graphic organizer like the one shown to help you organize your information.

Graphic Organizer Go to connectED. mcgraw-hill.com to download this graphic organizer.

Do you like to spend time at the beach or in the mountains? Have you ever gone swimming or fishing in a lake or an ocean? Enjoying outdoor activities is one of the greatest pleasures of life. In addition, you could not survive without the elements that nature provides. Taking care of the environment is essential to our survival. This responsiblity belongs to everyone.

Natural Resources

A **natural resource** is a material that is supplied by nature. You might not think about them very often, and you may even take them for granted. For example, you probably take a shower every day without even thinking about where the water comes from, or whether or not it will be there the next day. The health of every human, animal, and plant depends on several **key**, or necessary, natural resources. These include air, water, soil, and the energy that comes from coal, oil, and gas. We must protect these resources for our health and our survival.

At one time it seemed like these resources would last forever. Some, however, are nonrenewable. If they are used up or permanently damaged, they will no longer be available. This damage is often caused by pollution. **Pollution** is the changing of air, water, and land from clean and safe to dirty and unsafe.

Air

Your body uses the oxygen in air to produce energy. Plants use the carbon dioxide in air to produce food and oxygen. Unfortunately, the air you breathe is not completely clean. It may contain dust, smoke, chemical particles, and smog. These substances, which are all forms of air pollution, can be harmful to your health. Some causes of air pollution are:

- **Poisonous gases** such as car exhaust fumes that combine with the atmosphere to create smog when fuels are burned to provide energy.
- **Smoke** from sources such as fireplaces, barbecues, and burning leaves.
- **Chemicals**, including those that kill insects and those used as cooling substances in air conditioners and refrigerators.

Water

Water, like air, is necessary to all living things. In fact, water is your body's most essential nutrient. It is needed for every bodily function. Humans can only survive for a few days without water.

You may think that there is plenty of water. After all, about 70 percent of the earth's surface is covered by water. Most of it, however, is salt water. Many plants and animals cannot use salt water. Humans cannot drink salt water. Animals and humans need clean, fresh water to survive.

Much of the earth's water is polluted by wastes. Common sources of water pollution are human wastes, detergents, and the chemicals used to kill insects or to fertilize crops. This can cause damage to animals and plants

As You Read

Connect Imagine enjoying an ice cold glass of water or tea on a hot day. Besides drinking, what do you do every day that requires water?

◆ **Vocabulary**

You can find definitions in the glossary at the back of this book.

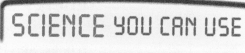

Alternative Energy

Natural resources can provide alternative sources of energy. Alternative energy sources can be used instead of fossil fuels, coal, wood, and uranium. Alternative energy sources must be renewable, nonpolluting, easy to get, and affordable.

Procedure Collect data about alternative power sources. Create a chart that includes the alternative sources of energy and how they are used.

Analysis What alternative energy sources are used most? What do you think could be used more?

Clean Food and Water Animals, plants, and humans all depend on water for survival. *What can happen when animals drink or live in polluted water?*

that use the polluted water. Polluted water can cause people and animals to become sick or die.

Soil

The earth's land is made up of soil. **Soil** is the loose material in which plants can grow. Soil is made up of a mixture of rocks, decayed material, minerals, water, and air. Plants get the nutrients and water they need from the soil. People, in turn, need the nutrients that plants provide in order to live.

Energy

What would happen if we ran out of gasoline for cars, trucks, and buses? How would we heat homes, schools, and office buildings if we ran out of oil and other kinds of fuel? You may think that this could never happen. However, many sources of energy are in limited supply. When oil, natural gas, and coal are used up, they cannot be replaced.

Another form of energy is nuclear energy. Nuclear energy boils water, creates steam, and turns generators to create electricity. Nuclear energy is made partly from uranium, a dense metal found in most rocks. Uranium is more plentiful than **fossil fuels**, which come from the remains of prehistoric plants and animals. Coal, natural gas, and petroleum are examples of fossil fuels.

Reading Skills
Read for Fun Reading is not just for school. Make it a habit to read for pleasure every day. Spend time with an entertaining novel, comic books, magazines, or a graphic novel.

● ● ● ● ● ● ● ● ● ● ● ● ●

Reading Check *Identify* What can cause air pollution?

Purestock/SuperStock

Conserve Resources

You may think that pollution and the shrinking supply of natural resources are beyond your control. There are many ways, however, that you can make a difference. One important way is to practice **conservation**, or the saving of resources. The best way to conserve a resource is to use less of it. When you take initiative, you take the first steps toward solving a particular problem. You and your family can work together to conserve natural resources. Some families add more insulation to their homes to save fuel. Insulation is a material installed in a building to keep it cooler in summer and warmer in winter. Families also can help by using extra sweaters and blankets in the winter so the heater does not get overused.

Water

Water is a resource you may often take for granted. All you do is turn on the faucet, and the supply seems limitless. But there is a limit, and you need to conserve the water you have so that there is enough for everyone and for the future. Here are some ways you can conserve water:

- Turn off the water when brushing your teeth.
- Take showers instead of baths.
- Install water-saving showerheads and toilets.
- Repair leaky faucets.
- Run the washing machine only with a full load. Change the level of water in the washing machine according to the amount and type of clothing being washed.

Energy

The **efficient**, or non-wasteful, use of energy is an important way to conserve resources. You can learn to use energy wisely. Look for appliances that are energy-efficient, or made to use less energy. By using energy efficiently, you not only conserve resources, but you can also save money and help reduce pollution.

Active Conservation This teen is conserving water by turning off the faucet while she brushes her teeth. *What can you do to conserve natural resources?*

Purestock/SuperStock

Reading Skills

Skimming Before you read, skim the section or chapter. This means to quickly look through the pages for headlines, bold or italicized words, highlighted words, and captions. This will give you the main idea before you go back to read closely.

You can save energy at home in many ways. Most of the energy used at home is for heating and cooling, running appliances, and lighting. When your family members buy new appliances, they can look for the most energy-efficient ones by comparing guides that list energy costs per year. Here are some ways to conserve energy at home:

- Use only the amount of hot water you actually need.
- Keep doors to closets and unused rooms closed. There is no need to heat or cool those spaces.
- Whenever possible, use a microwave oven.
- When you use a conventional oven, cook several items at the same time, and avoid opening the oven door while foods are cooking.
- Run the dishwasher only with a full load.
- Avoid leaving the refrigerator door open for too long.
- Use lined drapes to keep the cold out in the winter and the heat out in the summer.
- Seal cracks or gaps around the doors and windows.
- Use energy-saving light bulbs. Many types are available that use less energy and burn longer than standard bulbs.
- Turn the thermostat up in the summer and down in the winter.

Section **14.1** After You Read

Review What You Have Learned

1. **Identify** common sources of water pollution.
2. **Recognize** energy-efficient appliances.

Practice Academic Skills

English Language Arts

3. Find out how your family uses water and electricity. Then, evaluate the efficiency of your family's use of resources. Record what needs to be improved. Write a plan for your family to improve resource conservation in your home.

Social Studies

4. Research environmental organizations that focus on ending pollution or conserving natural resources. Write a list of five different issues the organizations address. Next to each issue, suggest an idea for how you can do your part.

↗ Check Your Answers Check Your Answers at connectED.mcgraw-hill.com.

Reading Guide

Before You Read

Pace Yourself It can be more effective to focus on reading short sections in 10-minute blocks than trying to read a long section all at once. Read for 10 minutes. Take a short break. Then read for another 10 minutes.

Read to Learn

Key Concepts

✓ **Define** what is meant by "throwaway" society.

✓ **Identify** the negative effects of incineration and landfills.

✓ **Name** the "three Rs."

Main Idea

Individual efforts make a difference when it comes to protecting the environment. Do your part by limiting waste, and use air, water, land, and energy wisely.

Content Vocabulary

○ recycling
○ landfill
○ decompose
○ incineration
○ biodegradable

Academic Vocabulary

■ dispose
■ permanent

Graphic Organizer

As you read, identify and define the "three Rs" for how to limit waste. Use a graphic organizer like the one shown to help you organize your information.

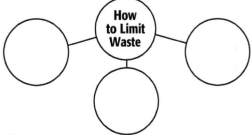

Graphic Organizer Go to connectED. mcgraw-hill.com to download this graphic organizer.

How much do you add to the waste that is piling up? Do you know how to limit your use of resources and the amount of waste you create? By following the "three Rs," you, your family, and your friends can contribute to waste reduction and environmental protection.

Do Your Part

As You Read

Connect Why do many people think that they cannot make a difference in their environment?

You may think that as long as you do not litter, you are doing your part to keep your community clean. However, there is much more you can do. Since the middle of the 20th century, Americans have lived in a "throwaway" society. Many items are used only once and then thrown away. Think about the bags you use to carry groceries, or the containers used for leftover restaurant meals. As a result, a serious problem exists because there is too much waste. Currently, there are not enough safe ways to remove waste.

Protection of natural resources and the environment begins with people like you. There are many ways for you to make a difference:

- You can use air, water, land, and energy wisely.
- You can make an effort to be energy-efficient at home.
- You can be a concerned citizen who cares about the environment and works with others to keep it clean.

Reading Check *Describe* *What problems are created for the environment in a "throwaway" society?*

Waste Removal

Billions of tons of waste are created every year in the United States. Where does it all go? Where should it all go? These questions are urgent because the waste continues to grow.

You can work to change the situation. Even though the waste problem is a national issue, the solution depends on individual actions. Your actions can help to make a difference. One way that individuals can help is by recycling. **Recycling** is turning waste items into products that can be used. You will read more about recycling later in this section.

Reading Skills
What You Know
Before you read, write down what you already know about the subject. You may know more about the subject than you think you do!

• • • • • • • • • • • •

Paper or Plastic?
Neither! Using a cloth grocery bag over and over again is one way an individual can help protect resources and the environment. *What other everyday items can you use over again?*

Annabelle Breakey/Getty Images

Composting

In this activity you will learn how to make your own compost for fertilizer. Before you begin, read through the entire Hands-On Lab assignment. Write down any questions that you have about the activity. Reread the text or ask your teacher for help if you need it.

Supplies
- ✓ Kitchen scraps
- ✓ Garden clippings
- ✓ Water
- ✓ Small shovel
- ✓ Garden soil

Develop Your Plan

- Compost is a mixture of decayed plants and other organic matter used for enriching soil. Use compost to recycle materials that may otherwise end up in a landfill.

- Find a 3-foot by 3-foot spot outdoors where you can create your compost pile. If this is not possible where you live, ask your teacher for other options.

- Plan a carbon to nitrogen ratio of 20 to 1. For carbon, collect vegetable scraps, fresh lawn and garden clippings, and weeds. For nitrogen, collect dry leaves, sawdust, paper, straw, dry grass, and wood ashes.

Implement Your Plan

- Pile your nitrogen and carbon materials into the 3-foot by 3-foot spot to decompose.

- With your shovel, turn the materials every two weeks for 10–12 weeks. Add more materials if they become available, keeping the 20 to 1 carbon to nitrogen ratio.

- Add water regularly so that there is about a 50% moisture content.

- After 10–12 weeks, mix the compost with garden soil.

Evaluate Your Results

How much waste did you save by composting? Where can you use the compost? What was the most difficult part of the process? What would you change if you did this project again? Write one or more paragraphs to explain your answer.

Projects and Activities Go to connectED.mcgraw-hill.com.

Vocabulary

You can find definitions in the glossary at the back of this book.

Landfills

About 80 percent of the waste in the United States is sent to landfills. A **landfill** is a huge pit where waste is buried between layers of earth. Most large communities have landfills somewhere on their outskirts, away from homes. These landfills are carefully designed to control the odors, germs, and other unhealthy situations that are created by piles of waste.

Landfills do cause problems, however. Waste buried in landfills is supposed to **decompose** so that it breaks down and becomes part of the soil. However, recent studies have shown that certain kinds of waste, such as plastic foam, do not break down for many years. Landfills take up huge amounts of space, and no one wants to live near a landfill.

Incineration

Another common way to dispose, or get rid, of waste in the United States is by incineration. **Incineration** is disposing of waste by burning it. About 10 percent of the waste in the United States is incinerated. When poisonous waste is burned, its smoke is especially dangerous. The air pollution created by burning waste can be so hazardous that it is illegal in many communities to burn waste.

Reading Check *Decide Why is it important to have a carefully designed landfill in a community?*

Landfill Pollution There are thousands of landfills in the United States. *Why do you think landfills will not be a waste-removal option in the future?*

Corbis Premium RF/Alamy

How To...

Reduce Waste

Every day, Americans throw away thousands of pounds of trash that ends up in landfills. You can make a difference in reducing waste at home, at your school, and in your community.

Home Separate plastic, glass, paper, and cardboard from the garbage you collect at home. Manufacturers can process all of these items and use them for new products or packaging.

School If your school participates in a recycling program, you can recycle the paper plates and plastic utensils you use for your lunch. Recycled paper is used to make newspaper and other everyday paper products. If your school does not have a recycling program, ask your teachers to help start one.

Community You can contribute to a recycling program, such as aluminum cans. Recycled aluminum is used every day by manufacturers around the world.

Limit Waste

Burying waste in landfills and incinerating it both have serious drawbacks. They are both unsafe, and neither choice is a permanent, or long-term, solution. What should be done about the problem? The key is to reduce the amount of waste we create. All Americans can do their part by following the "three Rs," which are Reduce, Reuse, and Recycle.

Reduce

The first step is to reduce, or lessen, the amount of waste created. To start reducing the amount of waste you create, you can reduce the amount of paper you throw away by using both sides of notebook and printer paper, using only washable cups and plates, and using cloth napkins. Avoid buying disposable products, and pre-cycle, or buy products that use less packaging material than others so there is less to throw away. Use cloth grocery bags instead of paper or plastic ones. Buy products that can be broken down and absorbed by the environment. These types of products are called **biodegradable**.

Reuse

The second of the "three Rs" is reuse. You can limit the amount of waste you create by reusing items you might otherwise throw away. If you use your imagination, you can probably think of many ways to reuse items. Buy products packed in containers that can be refilled or used for something else. Keep boxes, bottles, and cans to use as storage containers. Save and use old towels and clothes as cleaning rags. Think twice before throwing something away. Ask yourself, "What else can I do with this?"

Recycle

Many of the materials we throw away can be easily recycled. Recycling can greatly reduce the amount of waste in our country. For example, newspapers can be turned into pulp to make new paper. Aluminum cans can be melted down and turned into new cans and other products. Plastic can also be recycled. Over half of the waste we create is recyclable.

D. Hurst/Alamy

Recycling also means donating clothes, books, and other items to charities. You also recycle when you give or receive secondhand clothes or exchange magazines with a friend after reading them. These actions may seem small, but each one helps to limit the amount of waste. Imagine how much can be accomplished if every individual makes an effort to use the suggestions in this chapter. By applying the "three Rs," you will do your share to preserve the environment.

Use Your Imagination Find creative ways to reuse items instead of throwing them away. *How can an art project also be a recycling project?*

Section 14.2 After You Read

Review What You Have Learned

1. **Identify** three ways you can do your part to protect the environment.
2. **Explain** why incineration is not a safe way to remove waste.
3. **Suggest** three ways for people to reduce waste.

Practice Academic Skills

English Language Arts

4. Imagine that you have a friend who thinks one person cannot make a difference when it comes to protecting the environment. Write a letter to your friend to convince him or her that individuals really can make a difference.

Social Studies

5. Conduct research to find out about your school's recycling policy. Does your school have a recycling program? Does your school make it easy to recycle? Prepare a short presentation for your class that explains the school's policy, and add your own suggestions for improvement.

Check Your Answers Check Your Answers at connectED.mcgraw-hill.com.

Purestock/SuperStock

Discovering Careers

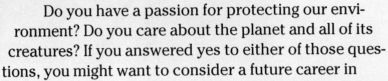

Do you have a passion for protecting our environment? Do you care about the planet and all of its creatures? If you answered yes to either of those questions, you might want to consider a future career in environmental studies. The following chart explores several careers in the environmental studies field.

Career Activities ▼

At School

 Select three of the careers listed. Research the education, training, and work experience required for each career. Write a summary of your results.

At Home

2 Go through your trash at home, and pull out items that can be reused or recycled. Create a reference list for your family.

At Work

3 List five careers for people who want to protect animals.

In the Community

4 Contact and interview someone in your community who works in environmental studies. Ask this person to describe what his or her typical work day is like. Share what you learned with your class.

Job Title	Job Description
Environmental Analyst	Conducts research studies to develop methods of controlling pollutants. Analyzes sources of pollution to determine their effects.
Ecologist	Researches environmental concerns. Makes studies to determine in what conditions varieties of plants grow and how species resist disease and insects.
Pollution Control Engineer	Plans and conducts engineering studies. Evaluates methods of pollution control to determine contaminants. Performs calculations to determine pollution emissions.
Forester	Manages forests for economic and recreational purposes. Maps forest areas. Estimates the number of trees and future growth. Plans cutting programs.
Wildlife Biologist	Studies habitat, development, growth and influences on wildlife habitat. Make plans for survival and population control of wildlife.

NPS Photo

Chapter Summary

Section 14.1 Resources and Conservation
Natural resources are materials that are supplied by nature. Some are nonrenewable and can be damaged by pollution. The air you breathe may contain dust, smoke, chemical particles, and smog. Much of the earth's water is polluted. Energy is in limited supply. You may think that pollution and the shrinking supply of natural resources are beyond your control. However, you can make a difference by conserving resources.

Section 14.2 Protect the Environment
Protection of natural resources and the environment begins with you. Even though the waste problem is a national issue, the solution depends on individual actions. The key is to reduce the amount of waste we create. Do your part by following the "three Rs," which are reduce, reuse, and recycle. Reduce the amount of waste created. Reuse items you might otherwise throw away. Recycle waste items into products that can be used.

Words You Learned

1. Write a sentence using two or more of these content and vocabulary words. The sentence should clearly show how the words are related.

Content Vocabulary
- natural resource (p. 305)
- pollution (p. 305)
- soil (p. 306)
- fossil fuel (p. 306)
- conservation (p. 307)
- recycling (p. 312)
- landfill (p. 312)
- decompose (p. 312)
- incineration (p. 312)
- biodegradable (p. 314)

Academic Vocabulary
- key (p. 305)
- efficient (p. 307)
- dispose (p. 312)
- permanent (p. 314)

Review Key Concepts

2. **Identify** the four key natural resources and why we need to protect them.

3. **Explain** how you can do your part to conserve water and energy.

4. **Define** what is meant by "throwaway" society.

5. **Describe** the negative effects of landfills and incineration.

6. **Name** the "three Rs".

Critical Thinking

7. **Predict** how recycling can make a difference to you personally.

8. **Evaluate** how waste created in the kitchen can be reduced, reused, or recycled.

9. **Compare and contrast** these options for drinking beverages: wash a ceramic cup over and over, and use a new foam cup for every drink. Which do you think is better for the environment?

Real-World Skills and Applications

Problem-Solving

10. Adopt a Mile Many communities provide ways for individuals, organizations, or businesses to help maintain sections of roadside by "adopting" a section of road. Conduct research to find out what these programs do for the environment, and how you can volunteer.

Technology Applications

11. Deforestation Conduct research to find out about deforestation. What does deforestation mean? What causes deforestation? What are the effects of deforestation? Use presentation software to share your findings. Include graphics, photographs, and descriptive text.

Financial Literacy

12. Recycling Pays Research the law in your state to see how much money you can receive for recycling beverage containers. You can usually find this amount printed on the side of bottles and cans. If you recycled all of the glass and aluminum drink containers you use in a week, how much money would you have at the end of a week? A 4-week month? A 52-week year? If your state does not pay for recycling, calculate the numbers using a fee of 5 cents per container.

13. Pressed-Flower Bookmarks Create bookmarks using pressed flowers. Gather small flower blossoms in several colors, paper towels or tissue paper (if you can find tissue paper left over from a gift-wrapping project, reuse it!), a few heavy books, scissors, and clear contact paper. Place the flowers between paper towels or tissue paper and set the heavy books on them overnight. Place the pressed flowers between two sheets of contact paper and gently push out any air bubbles. Cut the bookmarks into strips, about 4 inches long and 1½ inches wide. In what other ways can you used pressed flowers?

14. Research Nuclear Energy Nuclear energy is stored in the nucleus (center) of an atom. Atoms are tiny particles that make up every object in the universe. Conduct research to find out how this energy is released to produce electricity. Why is nuclear energy considered cleaner than traditional forms of energy? Prepare a brief presentation about your findings.

15. Household Hazardous Waste The Environmental Protection Agency (EPA) has given the name "household hazardous waste" to leftover household products that contain poisonous, flammable, or reactive ingredients. With permission from your parents or teacher, go online to learn about the dangers of household hazardous wastes. Create a list of hazardous products that might be found in the typical home. Then write a list of tips to safely store and dispose of household hazardous waste. Keep a copy of the tips in your Life Skills Binder.

D.Hurst/Alamy

Academic Skills

English Language Arts

16. Write a News Story A technique used by journalists when writing a news story is to ask and answer these six questions: Who? What? When? Where? Why? How? Choose a topic from this chapter, such as pollution, energy use, or wildlife protection. Using the six questions, write an article for your school newspaper that inspires other students to do something positive for the environment.

Social Studies

17. Identify Influences Interview your parents, grandparents, or other older relatives about how and why attitudes toward the environment have changed since they were your age. Ask questions about the three Rs, nuclear energy, waste disposal concerns, and other environmental issues. Summarize your findings in a short essay.

Mathematics

18. Save Water Vanessa's kitchen faucet has been dripping for three days at a steady rate of one drip every two seconds (or 30 drips per minute). If it takes 8,000 drips to fill up a two-liter soda bottle, how many two-liter soda bottles could Vanessa fill with all of the water that dripped in three full days?

Math Concept **Multi-Step Problems** When solving problems with more than one step, think through the steps before you start.

Starting Hint Since there are 60 minutes in one hour, and 24 hours in one day, determine the total minutes in three days by multiplying 3 x 24 x 60. Since there are 30 drips per minute, multiply the total minutes by 30 to find the total number of drips. Divide that number by 8,000 to determine how many soda bottles could be filled with those drips.

Standardized Test Practice

Open-Ended Response

An open-ended response requires more than a simple yes or no answer. It can usually be answered with one or two sentences.

> **Test-Taking Tip** Open-ended test questions most often require a specific response rather than an opinion. They may include definitions, comparisons, or examples.

Write one or two sentences to answer the questions.

19. Why should you practice conservation?
20. What are biodegradable products?
21. How is an energy-efficient appliance beneficial?

Improve Your Home

You probably spend a lot of time at home, so why not make your living space as attractive and functional as possible? Magazines, home stores, and the homes of your friends can give you ideas. This project can help you learn how to improve the space you live in.

My Journal Complete the journal entry from page 279, and refer to it to complete your evaluation of the place you live.

Project Assignment ▼

In this project, you will:

- Evaluate your living space for ways it can be improved.
- Draw two floor plans for a room showing how you can change it.
- Describe how you would make the room better.
- Interview someone who designs or builds homes or furnishings for a living.
- Present your findings to your class.
- Include this project in the sixth section of your personal Life Skills binder.

 Step 1 **Observe How Rooms are Used**

Spend a few hours observing the way people use rooms and living spaces. Write a summary of your observations that identifies problems in how the room looks or functions.

Step 2 **Draw Two Floor Plans**

Choose the room or area you want to redesign and measure it. Create two scale-model floor plans. On the first, draw in the furniture of the room the way it looks now. On the second, lay out your new arrangement. Then write two or more paragraphs that answer these questions:

✔What problems are you trying to solve?
✔How does the new plan improve functionality?
✔Describe the new look of your room.
✔Does your new room plan allow for wiser energy use and less waste?

Step 3 **Interview Someone Who Works in Design or Construction**

Interview someone in your community who is a professional builder or designer. Ask these questions:

✔How would you fix the problems in this room?
✔What are the most common safety issues you encounter in your work?
✔What ways do you keep your work environmentally friendly?

Use these interviewing skills when conducting your interview and these writing skills when writing the summary of notes from your interview.

Interviewing Skills
- Record interview responses and take notes.
- Listen attentively.

Writing Skills
- Use complete sentences.
- Use correct spelling and grammar.

Step 4 Create and Present Your Room Improvement Design

Use the Life Skills Project Checklist on the right to plan and complete your floor plans and give an oral report comparing the two plans.

Use these speaking skills when presenting your final report.

Speaking Skills
- Speak clearly and concisely.
- Be sensitive to the needs of your audience.
- Use standard English to communicate.

Step 5 Evaluate Your Presentation

Your project will be evaluated based on:

- ✔ Organization and attention to detail of your room evaluation.
- ✔ The accuracy and creativity of your floor plans.
- ✔ The description of improvements to your room.
- ✔ The summary written from interview notes.
- ✔ Grammar and sentence structure.
- ✔ Presentation to the class.
- ✔ Creativity and neatness.

Evaluation Rubric Go to **connectED. mcgraw-hill.com** for a rubric you can use to evaluate your final project.

Amos Morgan/Getty Images

Life Skills Project Checklist

Research How Rooms Are Used

- ✓ Evaluate rooms that could be improved.
- ✓ Measure and draw an accurate floor plan of the current room layout.
- ✓ Draw a floor plan that shows how you would improve the layout.
- ✓ Interview an architect, construction worker, or interior designer in your community.

Writing Skills

- ✓ Describe the design problems in the room.
- ✓ Describe how your changes improve that room.
- ✓ Write a summary from your interview with a person who works in construction or design.

Present Your Findings

- ✓ Prepare a short presentation to share your two floor plans and compare the problems in the first to the solutions in the second.
- ✓ Invite the students of the class to ask any questions they may have. Answer these questions with responses that respect their perspectives.
- ✓ Add this project to your Life Skills binder.

Academic Skills

- ✓ Conduct research to gather information.
- ✓ Communicate effectively.
- ✓ Organize your presentation so the audience can follow along easily.
- ✓ Thoroughly express your ideas.

Chapter 15
Your Fashion Statement

Chapter 16
Clothing Basics

Unit Preview

This unit is about selecting and caring for clothes. In this unit, you will learn about:

- Your personal style and ways to creatively express it.
- Color, line, and texture in clothing.
- Selecting comfortable and high-quality clothing.
- Clothing care basics.

Explore the Photo

Today's clothing choices are virtually endless. *What are some ways that you can make smart clothing choices to reflect your personal style?*

© Fancy Collection/SuperStock

Your Personal Style

When you are done studying this unit, you will complete a project in which you will:

✓ Discover your own personal style.

✓ Interview someone whose style you admire.

✓ Share with your class what your project says about you.

The prewriting activity below will help you get started.

My Journal

Prewriting Activity
Make a Chart

Choose ten items of clothing from your closet. Write each item in one of two columns. Label the first column "Wear a Lot" and label the second column "Wear Rarely".

● What does the clothing in your "Wear a Lot" column have in common?

● What does the clothing in your "Wear Rarely" column have in common?

Chapter 15

Your Fashion Statement

Section 15.1

Selecting Your Clothes

◼ **Main Idea** People wear clothes out of necessity and to make a personal statement. You can expand your wardrobe when you add accessories and evaluate what you already have.

Section 15.2

Color, Lines, and Texture

◼ **Main Idea** Learn how color, line, and texture can be used to make your wardrobe flattering and flexible.

Hongqi Zhang/Getty Images

Explore the Photo
Clothes can say a lot about who you are. *When you choose your clothes, do you look for comfort, durability, low cost, easy care, or the latest style?*

Step-by-Step Guide

A Special Event A step-by step guide helps you break a task into smaller parts so that you can accomplish the larger goal. Imagine a special event that you might attend, such as a school dance, a wedding, or a job interview. Write out the steps that you would follow to get dressed and ready for the event.

Writing Tips Follow these steps to write a step-by-step guide:

1. Choose a beginning and ending point to your task.
2. Brainstorm the steps required to meet your goal.
3. Describe what you need to do for each step.

Section 15.1 Selecting Your Clothes

Reading Guide

Before You Read

Prior Knowledge Look over the Key Concepts at the beginning of the section. Write down what you already know about each concept and what you want to find out by reading the lesson. As you read, find examples for both categories.

Read to Learn

Key Concepts

✓ **Recognize** the factors that influence your clothing choices.

✓ **Explain** how you can make the most of your wardrobe.

Main Idea

People wear clothes out of necessity and to make a personal statement. You can expand your wardrobe when you add accessories and evaluate what you already have.

Content Vocabulary

- ○ modesty
- ○ style
- ○ fashion
- ○ alteration
- ○ fad

Academic Vocabulary

- ■ status
- ■ inventory

Graphic Organizer

As you read, identify five reasons for why people wear clothing. Use a graphic organizer like the one shown to help you organize your information.

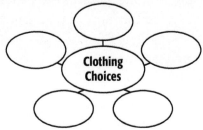

🖱 **Graphic Organizer** Go to connectED.mcgraw-hill.com to download this graphic organizer.

How do you decide what to wear? Everyone has likes and dislikes. This is why clothes come in so many styles, colors, and fabrics. The clothes you wear are your fashion statement. They send a message about how you see yourself. Clothes and accessories can reflect your individuality. They can also identify you as part of a group.

Clothing Choices

People first wore clothing to protect themselves against the wind, snow, rain, cold, and heat. That first clothing was made from animal skins. As time went on, people decorated their clothes with natural materials, such as earth and clay. Seeds, stones, and shell beads were sometimes added to clothing to show a person's status, or position in society.

Today, clothing choices are much more varied, but the purpose of clothing has not changed. Your clothing choices may be influenced by your personal preferences, your family, your friends, and the media. Here are some reasons people wear clothing:

- **Protection** Clothes protect you from the weather and climate. Some occupations require special clothing, such as police uniforms and firefighting gear. Workers in restaurants and hospitals often wear hair coverings and gloves to help protect others.

- **Adornment** Scarves, ties, hats, and vests can be used as adornment, or decoration. People use such decorations to express creativity and individuality.

- **Identification** You do not always need to announce who you are. Sometimes your clothing can do it for you. For example, uniforms show others that you work at a particular restaurant, play in a school band, or are part of an athletic team.

- **Modesty** The way you wear your clothes and the type of clothing you wear suggest your personal sense of modesty. **Modesty** is a belief about the proper way to cover the body with clothes. The level of modesty can vary with the occasion. For example, it is acceptable to wear a bathing suit to the beach, but not to the office.

As You Read

Connect What does your clothing reveal about your personality?

Vocabulary

You can find definitions in the glossary at the back of this book.

Mary–Ella Keith/Alamy

Uniformity The teens in this photo share a common interest. *How can you tell?*

- **Status** Some clothes or accessories are worn to show a person's status. Designer labels, logos, and other recognized names and symbols can set certain individuals apart from the group.

Learning what influences your clothing decisions can help you choose clothes that are best for you. Making good clothing choices can help you present the image you want others to see. Your clothing choices say a lot about who you are and what is important to you.

Fashions, Fads, and Styles

The occasion or activity that you are dressing for helps to determine your clothing choices. For instance, you would wear different clothes to a basketball game than to a formal dance. It is important to choose the right outfit for the occasion. When choosing clothes based on your wants instead of your needs, it is important to reflect your personality. Danielle and Brianna shop for clothes together, but they choose different styles. A **style** is the design of a garment. A bomber jacket, a straight skirt, and baggy pants are all types of styles.

Not all styles of clothing are considered fashions. A **fashion** is a style of clothing that is popular at a particular time. Fashions change frequently. Just a slight **alteration** can be made to change the style and give a fashion a fresh, new look. For example, think about how a minor change in skirt length can change the whole look of an outfit. The same can be said for jacket length, collar shape, or the width of pant legs. At any one time, there will be some new fashions coming in, some going out, and other styles that remain popular season after season.

Many fashions become popular very quickly and then lose their appeal. A fashion that is very popular for a short time is called a **fad**. Fad clothing is fun to wear, but often goes out of style as quickly as it came in. Usually, it is not a good idea to spend a lot of money on fad items. It is better to spend most of your clothing budget on classic styles, which are styles that remain in fashion for a long time. Classics include a blazer, crew neck shirt, and cardigan sweater. You can change the look of styles and fashions with accessories such as belts, hats, and jewelry.

Reading Check *Explain Why is it better to spend most of your clothing budget on classic styles?*

Combine Separates

A good way to expand your wardrobe is by combining separates, or single pieces of clothing that can be mixed and matched. Try these ideas for making the most out of your wardrobe.

© Paul Bradbury/age fotostock

Mix and Match Lay out all of your clothing pieces and combine them in different ways. When you see everything together instead of hanging in your closet, you may notice possible combinations you might have missed.

Variety Keep your wardrobe versatile, or flexible, with many different colors and styles. Variety can make your outfits more fun and interesting.

Keep it Simple Styles without trim, such as beads and sequins, are more versatile. If you like prints, select prints that include a basic color, such as black or white, so they will go with your more basic items.

Flatter Yourself Make sure you choose styles that flatter your shape, your skin tone, and your personality. Do not waste money on clothes that do not fit or make you look your best.

Quality Invest in good quality. It is better to spend your money on clothes that will last. Choose clothes that are not only classic, but durable as well.

Resist Fads There is nothing wrong with an occasional trendy item just for fun. However, do not waste your money on something that may go out of style in a matter of weeks.

Evaluate Once you have looked over all of your clothing, accessories, and shoes, make a list of other items you can use to add to what you have. As your budget allows, add these items to your wardrobe for even more options.

Make the Most of Your Wardrobe

The first step in deciding what kind of clothes you need is to think about what kind of clothes you wear. Think about your various activities. You need clothes for school, casual clothes for spending time with friends, dressier clothes for special occasions, and clothes for activities such as sports or dance class.

You also need to evaluate your personal style, or the kind of clothes you like best. For example, do you wear a lot of tailored, buttoned shirts, or do you feel more comfortable in T-shirts? The best planning involves thinking about all of your clothes, not just about individual outfits. Keep in mind that shoes and accessories, such as belts, scarves, hats, socks, and jewelry, are part of your clothing wardrobe.

To take a clothing **inventory**, or list, sort your clothing into the following four categories:

- **Clothes that you wear often.**
  Use these clothes to help you evaluate your personal clothing style. What do you like about these clothes? Is it the style, color, or texture?

➡ **Take Inventory** Before you go on your next shopping trip for clothes, take a look in your closet. *What can you do to help you decide what you really need to buy?*

© Pascal Broze/SuperStock

A New Look Imagine this boy's outfit without the tie. *What does the tie add to the look of his outfit?*

- **Clothes that do not fit.** There is no point in keeping these clothes in your closet. Before you set them aside, however, think about how they might still be used. If the sleeves on a shirt are too short, could they be cut off and hemmed to make a short-sleeved shirt instead? Clothes that are still in good condition but that you are sure you do not want can be donated to charity or given to a younger sibling.
- **Clothes that you never wear.** You may be able to add items to your wardrobe that will make these clothes more useful. Perhaps you bought a great pair of pants, but you do not have a shirt to go with them. If you like the pants, invest in a shirt so you can wear the pants. If not, give them away. As with clothes that do not fit, there is no reason to keep clothes you will never wear in your closet.
- **Clothes in need of repair.** Set these aside and see if they can be fixed. Repair the items you like.

Character Counts

Confidence

Debra loves clothes and likes to keep up with the latest fashions. However, she does not have a lot of money to spend on clothes. Next week, she has a special occasion to attend with her friends, and she will have to wear something from her closet. She is afraid that she will not feel good about herself in something that her friends have already seen her wear.

You Make the Call

How can Debra feel confident in an outfit that is not brand new? Write a paragraph explaining what she should do.

Add Accessories

If you are bored with a piece of clothing you have had for a long time, try adding a new accessory before discarding the item. A new belt, scarf, tie, or piece of jewelry can create a new look. You can also try changing buttons or adding trim to make a casual garment look dressier. Before you throw away a worn-out garment, check to see if you can save the buttons. Well-chosen accessories can stretch your wardrobe by giving the same outfit an entirely different look.

You can also use accessories to draw attention to your best features and away from features you do not want emphasized, or noticed. For instance, a wide belt can draw attention to a slim waistline. A watchband or bracelet can show off graceful hands. Scarves and neckties can be used to add color or emphasis.

When using accessories, it is best to choose one center of interest, or focal point. Choose a wide belt with a big buckle, for example. Any other accessories should be less noticeable and blend in with the outfit. Too many accessories can create a cluttered look.

Section 15.1 After You Read

Review What You Have Learned

1. **Contrast** style and fashion.
2. **Describe** the four categories you can use to take a clothing inventory.

Practice Academic Skills

English Language Arts

3. Read this statement: It is not important for teens to be concerned about style and fashion. Do you agree or disagree? Prepare a brief oral presentation in which you clearly state your position. Include details to support your statement.

Social Studies

4. Choose a fashion fad that is popular now or was popular in the past. Where did it begin? How did people find out about it? Who was most influenced by the fad? Create a small poster with images or drawings of the fad, and include the information you found in your research.

Check Your Answers Check Your Answers at **connectED.mcgraw-hill.com**.

Reading Guide

Before You Read

Two-Column Notes Divide a piece of paper into two columns. In the left column, write down main ideas as you read. In the right column, list supporting details.

Read to Learn

Key Concepts

✓ **Summarize** how color can affect you.

✓ **Describe** how the lines of your clothing can change the way you look.

✓ **Define** texture and list examples.

Main Idea

Learn how color, line, and texture can be used to make your wardrobe flattering and flexible.

Content Vocabulary

○ hue
○ tint
○ shade
○ intensity
○ monochromatic
○ complementary
○ analogous
○ texture

Academic Vocabulary

■ primary   ■ value

Graphic Organizer

As you read, identify what you know, what you want to learn, what you learned, and how you can learn more about color, lines, and texture. Use a graphic organizer like the one shown to help you organize your information.

What I Know	What I Want to Learn	What I Learned	How I Can Learn More

⬈ **Graphic Organizer** Go to connectED. mcgraw-hill.com to download this graphic organizer.

Colors, texture, and lines all add to the way you appear to others. Colors can reflect your moods and also affect your clothing choices. When you are feeling happy, you may choose to wear bright colors. On days when you are feeling thoughtful and quiet, you may select pale or dark colors. You can use clothes to help change your mood or your look.

Color

What is the first thing you notice when you see a display of clothing in a store? Like most people, you probably notice the color. As one of several elements of design, color is often noticed first. As you learned in Chapter 13, the other

As You Read

Connect What is your favorite color to wear? How do you feel when you wear that color?

Vocabulary

You can find definitions in the glossary at the back of this book.

Presentation Skills

Rehearse Practice your speech before you present it to the class. Practice in front a mirror, or with a friend who will give you constructive feedback.

• • • • • • • • • • • • • •

elements of design are line, shape, space, and texture. These are important, but usually do not have as much impact as color.

Learning about color is useful in many ways, especially when making the clothing decisions that build your wardrobe. Why do some colors look better on you than other colors look? If you become familiar with the relationships among colors, you will understand how colors affect your appearance and the way clothes look on you.

Color matters. Colors can affect your mood, energy level, and appetite. For example, red is a powerful color that is full of energy. It stimulates the appetite. Yellow catches the eye better than all other colors. It lifts your mood and brightens rooms. Blue is a soothing color. It can lull you to sleep and suppress the appetite. Green has a calming effect. It is a common color in hospitals, schools, and offices.

When you put clothes together, you can create either single-color outfits or outfits that combine colors. You can learn to combine colors successfully using the color wheel in **Figure 15.1**. A color wheel shows the relationships of colors to each other.

Primary and Secondary Colors

To understand the basic principles of color, you need to know the names of the hues. The three basic **hues** are red, yellow, and blue. These three main colors are called primary colors because all other colors can be made from them. Combining equal amounts of red and yellow makes orange. Equal amounts of blue and yellow make green, and combining red and blue makes violet. These are called secondary colors. Intermediate colors are a blend of a primary and secondary color.

Color Values

Another basic element to consider is the value, or the lightness and darkness of color. For instance, blue can vary in value from very light blue to navy blue. A light value of a hue is called a **tint**. A dark value of a hue is called a **shade**. The brightness or dullness of a color is called its **intensity**. Bright red is a high-intensity color. Pale pink is a low-intensity color.

Figure 15.1 Color Relationships

The Color Wheel This color wheel shows how colors are related to one another. *How can you tell which colors are intermediate colors?*

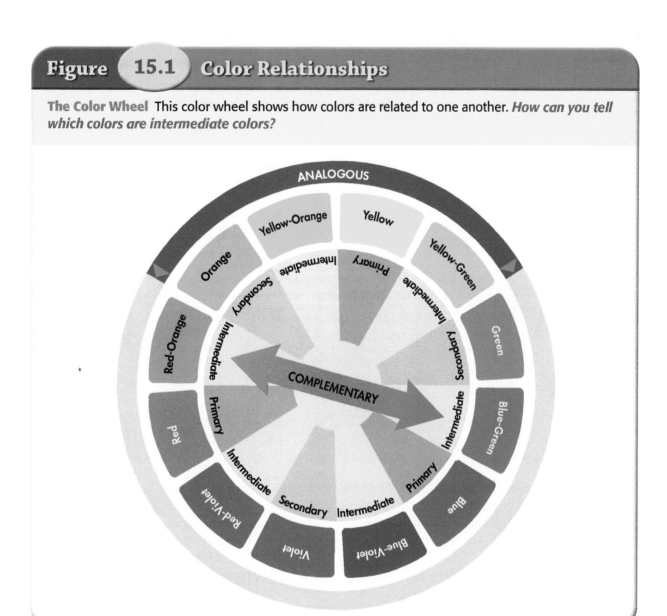

Colors as Symbols

Not only can colors reveal moods, they can provide information. Imagine a driver coming up on a traffic light and not knowing the meanings of the colors. Anyone who does not understand that green means go and red means stop can get into some serious trouble! Colors can represent groups and countries. The combination of red, white, and blue has very special meaning to Americans. Those same colors are also the colors of France. Think of the flags of Canada and Japan. They are both red and white. What are your school's colors? What are the colors of your favorite athletic team? What are the colors in the flags that represent your heritage? These colors probably mean something to you because you associate them with something that makes you feel proud.

Figure **15.2** **Color Schemes**

A Plan for Using Color You can use color to decorate a room and to put together an outfit. *Name a color from each color scheme that could be worn with a yellow shirt.*

Monochromatic Color Scheme An outfit made up of one hue, and the tints and shades of that hue, is a monochromatic color scheme.

Complementary Color Scheme This type of color scheme gives great contrast because it combines colors that are opposite each other on the color wheel. Orange and blue used together form a complementary color scheme.

Analogous Color Scheme The colors in an analogous color scheme have one common hue. A combination of yellow and green is an analogous color scheme.

Accented Neutral Color Scheme Wearing a neutral color, such as beige, gray, black, or white, with another color as the accent is an accented neutral color scheme. A combination of black and yellow is an example of this color scheme.

Color Warmth and Coolness

Colors are considered either warm or cool. Red, yellow, and orange are warm colors. They are bright and cheerful. Blue, green, and violet are cool colors. They can give you a sense of tranquility, or peacefulness.

Selecting Colors

When you try different color combinations, you will discover that some look better on you than others. Flattering colors can make your complexion look healthier and draw attention to your hair and eyes.

Colors affect your appearance in other ways, too. They can highlight certain areas of your body. Light, warm, and bright colors can make you look larger. Dark, cool, and dull colors can make you look smaller. Carl wears one-color **monochromatic** ('mä-nə-krō-'ma-tik) outfits so that he will look taller. Ronda, on the other hand, likes complementary colors. **Complementary** ('käm-plə-'men-t(ə-)rē) means contrasting or opposite, such as purple and yellow, and the effect makes her appear shorter than she is. Joaquin tends to wear **analogous** (ə-'na-lə-gəs) colors, which means he likes colors that are next to each other on the color wheel, like green and yellow. Experiment with colors and combinations to see what looks best on you. See **Figure 15.2** for ideas.

SUCCEED IN SCHOOL!

Presentation Skills
Learn from Others
You can learn a lot from watching and listening to others when they speak. Pay attention to how speakers use their hands, make eye contact, and vary their speech patterns. All of these things can help make your speech more interesting.

Reading Check   *Contrast* **What is the difference between monochromatic colors and complementary colors?**

Discover International...
Styles

Kente Cloth
Kente cloth, a hand-woven cloth from Africa, is worn today by people from every social class. In the past, certain designs were meant to be worn only by royalty. In the United States in the 1960s, traditional African garments and home fashions made of kente cloth became popular again in the African-American community. African-Americans began using kente cloth as a symbol of their cultural heritage and as a mark of pride and inspiration.

kente cloth |'ken-,tā| a colorful, patterned, hand-woven cloth from Ghana. The designs in the fabric may reflect cultural beliefs, historical events, social relationships, or political organizations.

Ken Karp/McGraw-Hill Education

Lines and Appearance

The way a garment looks on you is also affected by its lines. Lines form the outer shape, or outline, of a garment. For example, compare straight-leg, tapered, and flared pants. Sometimes lines are formed by the seams and waistlines of a garment. Other lines can be part of the fabric's design, such as stripes or plaids.

Lines can be either straight or curved. Curved lines soften a garment's appearance. Straight lines look strong. When you shop for clothes, learn to look for lines. Try to see vertical, or up-and-down, lines instead of just a row of buttons or a zipper down the front. Look for horizontal lines, or lines that go straight across, instead of seeing only belts, waistlines, or hemlines. See diagonal or curved lines instead of necklines and collars.

You can change the way you look by changing the lines of your clothes:

- Vertical lines can make you look taller and thinner.
- Horizontal lines can make you look shorter and wider.
- Diagonal lines can make you look taller and thinner or shorter and wider, depending on the length and angle of the lines.

Reading Check *List What are four types of lines you should look for when selecting clothes?*

COMMUNITY CONNECTIONS

Dress for Success
There are charitable organizations that specialize in collecting donated business suits to help men and women dress for job interviews. Ask family members if they have such items to donate.

🔊 **Look at Lines** When choosing an outfit, look at the direction of the lines. *If you want a soft appearance, what should you look for?*

Clothing Texture

When you choose clothing, you need to consider its texture. **Texture** is the feel and appearance of the fabric's surface. Just as colors and lines create different looks, textures can create different impressions, too. Texture is created by using different yarns and weaves in making fabric. For instance, a wool sweater has a coarse texture that is created in the knitting process. A fabric may be dull like denim or shiny like silk and satin. Nubby fabrics like corduroy and tweed are often used for heavy suit coats. Smooth fabrics like flannel are used for pajamas.

You can use textures to change the way you look. Dull textures can make you look smaller. Nubby or shiny textures add bulk. A tall person can wear a coarse texture, but the same fabric may overpower a small person. To see which textures look best on you, try on clothing with different types of textures.

It All Comes Together Several design elements come together to create a look. Experiment until you find what works best for you. *Discuss this boy's outfit in terms of color, line, and texture.*

Section 15.2 After You Read

Review What You Have Learned

1. **List** the primary and secondary colors.
2. **Describe** how lines are formed in clothing.
3. **Explain** how texture is created.

Practice Academic Skills

English Language Arts

4. Write a description of an outfit that would make a good first impression at a job interview. Use what you have learned about color, lines, and texture to choose the right outfit.

Social Studies

5. When you think of a traditional wedding dress worn by a bride in the United States, white is the color that most likely comes to your mind. Conduct research to learn about a culture in which white is not the traditional color choice for weddings. Write a brief paragraph to describe the color scheme and the significance of the color.

Check Your Answers Check Your Answers at connectED.mcgraw-hill.com.

Discovering Careers

Do you always seem to notice what other people are wearing? Do you think about how you would design a piece of clothing differently? If you answered yes to either of those questions, you might want to consider a future career in fashion. The following chart explores several careers in the fashion industry.

Job Title	Job Description
Fashion Coordinator	Selects garments and accessories for fashion shows. Provides information on current fashions, style trends, and use of accessories.
Fashion Designer	Designs men's, women's, and children's clothing or accessories. Analyzes fashion trends. Uses knowledge to create new styles.
Fabric Designer	Specifies weave patterns, colors, and threads to make new fabrics. Sketches designs and writes instructions to specify fabric details.
Costume Historian	Researches documents and archives of museums, libraries, and historical societies. Describes how the garments people wore reflect history.
Movie Wardrobe Designer	Researches clothing based on movie scripts. Creates authentic designs to fit the period of the movie.

Career Activities ▼

At School

1 Select three of the careers listed. Research the education, training, and work experience required for each career. Write a summary of your results.

At Home

2 Interview a family about the clothing and accessories he or she wears to accomplish tasks in and around the home.

At Work

3 Choose three jobs that you might consider in the future. List the type of clothing that would be appropriate for each job.

In the Community

4 Contact and interview someone in your community who works in the fashion industry. Ask this person to describe what his or her typical work day is like. Share what you learned with your class.

Chapter Summary

Section 15.1 Selecting Your Clothes
Clothing can help you present who you are and what is important to you. The occasion or activity that you are dressing for helps to determine your clothing choices. Think about what kind of clothes you wear. Evaluate your personal style and the clothes you like best.

Section 15.2 Color, Lines, and Texture
Your clothing tells a lot about your personality. Colors can affect your mood, energy level, and appetite. Colors can be either warm or cool. When you try different color combinations, you will discover that some colors look better on you than other colors. The way a garment looks on you is also affected by its lines and texture.

Words You Learned

1. Create a true-false quiz based on the content and academic vocabulary words. Exchange quizzes with a classmate and complete.

Content Vocabulary
- modesty (p. 327)
- style (p. 328)
- fashion (p. 328)
- alteration (p. 328)
- fad (p. 328)
- hue (p. 334)
- tint (p. 334)
- shade (p. 334)
- intensity (p. 334)
- monochromatic (p. 337)
- complementary (p. 337)
- analogous (p. 337)
- texture (p. 339)

Academic Vocabulary
- status (p. 327)
- inventory (p. 330)
- primary (p. 334)
- value (p. 334)

Review Key Concepts

2. **Recognize** the factors that influence your clothing choices.
3. **Explain** how you can make the most of your wardrobe.
4. **Summarize** how color can affect you.
5. **Describe** how the lines of your clothing can change the way you look.
6. **Define** texture and list examples.

Critical Thinking

7. **Decide** whether or not you would follow the fashion example set by a celebrity. Explain your answer.
8. **Explain** why some people feel offended when they dress up for dinner at a nice restaurant, and they see that other diners are dressed casually.
9. **Analyze** why neon pink clothes may be "in" one year and "out" the next. Why do you think such color trends occur?

Real-World Skills and Applications

Problem-Solving

10. Fashion Mistakes Imagine that you are invited to the fifteenth birthday of your friend's cousin. You have been to many birthday parties for your friends, and you have always dressed casually. When you arrive at the party in your jeans and casual shirt, you see that the girls are wearing formal dresses and the boys are wearing tuxedos! What should you do? How can you avoid this kind of mistake next time?

Interpersonal and Collaborative

11. Fashion Inspiration Follow your teacher's directions to form small groups. Work with your group to identify how celebrities, athletes, movies, and television shows inspire current fashion. Collect photos and write descriptive captions to create a poster that illustrates this inspiration.

Financial Literacy

12. Investigate Clothing Stocks A share of stock represents partial ownership in a corporation. That means when you own a stock, you actually own part of a company. These shares can be bought and sold through what is called a central exchange, such as the New York Stock Exchange. The share prices of each corporation go up and down during each day based on news reports, trends, and other events. Pick three large, clothing-related corporations, such as companies that own the clothing stores where you shop, or that make some of the clothes you own. Research today's stock price for each company. Find a chart that shows the change in each company's stock price over time. Is the current price higher or lower than it was a year ago?

13. Costume Design Many countries have a national costume or typical style of dress that is instantly recognizable to others. For example, when you see a woman in a kimono, you know that she is wearing clothing from Japan. If you see a man wearing a plaid-patterned kilt, he is likely representing Scotland. The United States has long been called a "melting pot." This means that the people who live in the U.S. come from all over the world to live together in one country. Considering this diversity, design a national costume for America. Share your design with the class, and explain your creation.

14. Color Schemes Identify a color scheme in a room you are familiar with, such as a room in your home, a restaurant, or a classroom. Determine if the room's color scheme is monochromatic, analogous, complementary, or accented neutral. What minor changes could you make to the room to change the color scheme? Present your ideas to the class.

15. Designers Today With permission from your parents or teacher, go online to find information on a current fashion designer of your choice. How did he or she get started in fashion design? What or who were his or her inspirations? What types of designs does he or she create? Who wears the clothes? Summarize your findings and include images. Add the information to your Life Skills Binder.

D.Hurst/Alamy

Academic Skills

English Language Arts

16. Identify Influences List ten different clothing items, outfits, or accessories in your wardrobe. For each item, write down who or what influenced you to buy or wear that item. Are there any items you wish that you had not bought? If so, explain why.

Social Studies

17. Cultural Values How can clothing reflect a society's values? Conduct research on historical and modern clothing in various cultures. Select three styles or outfits that interest you. For each one, write one or two sentences to describe what you can tell about the culture's values.

Mathematics

18. Calculate Payments Andrea bought some clothing on a department store credit card. Her total came to $250. She qualified for interest-free financing. She made a first payment of $35 and agreed to pay $25 twice a month until the $250 balance was paid. How long will it take for Andrea to pay off her bill?

Math Concept **Operations** To determine the number of payments, subtract the down payment, divide the principal by payment, and divide the number of payments by the frequency of the payment.

Starting Hint Take $35 from $250 and then divide the result by her payments of $25 to see how many payments. Then divide this number by two to figure out how many months it will take.

Standardized Test Practice

Multiple-Choice

Read the sentence. Determine which underlined word contains a spelling error.

> **Test-Taking Tip** As you read, you will often "see" a missing word or letter because you expect to see it. When checking for spelling, slow down your reading speed and carefully look at each letter in the word.

19. Using a monchromatic color scheme, Danetta carefully matched the outfit that she planned to wear for the award ceremony at her school.
   a. monchromatic
   b. carefully
   c. wear
   d. award

Chapter  16

Clothing Basics

Section 16.1

Quality Clothing

■ **Main Idea** Learn about fabric, quality, comfort, and planning to help you make smart clothing purchases.

Section 16.2

Clothing Care Basics

■ **Main Idea** You can stretch your clothing budget and keep your wardrobe looking good when you know how to properly care for and store your clothes.

Blend Images/KidStock/Getty Images

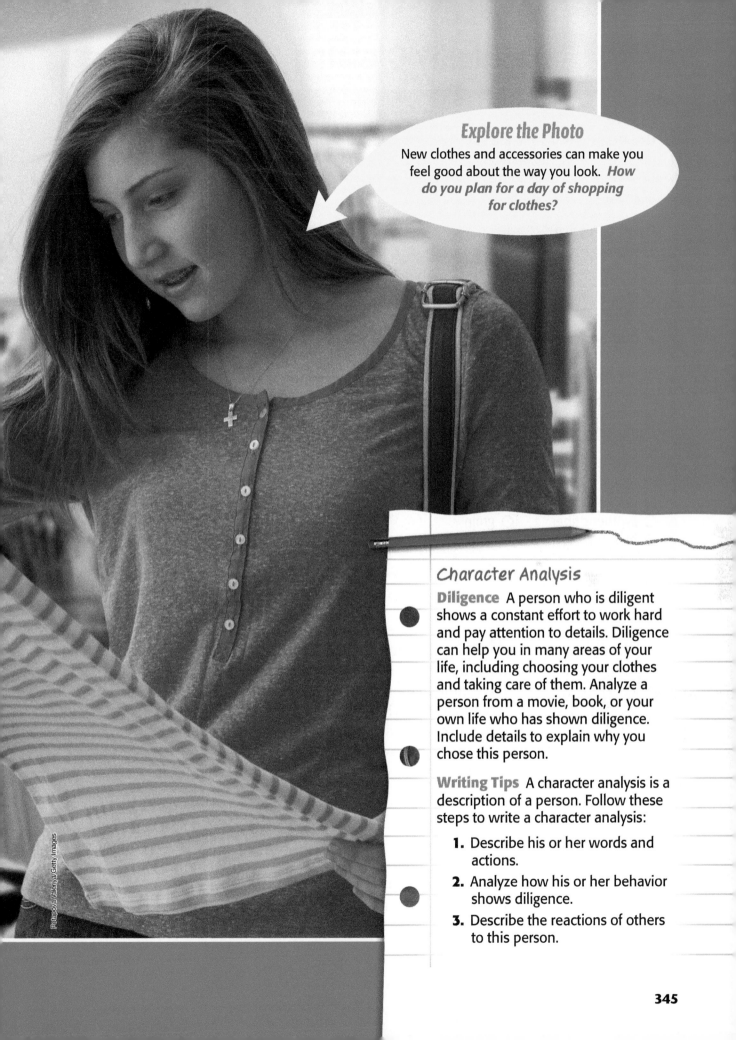

Explore the Photo

New clothes and accessories can make you feel good about the way you look. *How do you plan for a day of shopping for clothes?*

Character Analysis

Diligence A person who is diligent shows a constant effort to work hard and pay attention to details. Diligence can help you in many areas of your life, including choosing your clothes and taking care of them. Analyze a person from a movie, book, or your own life who has shown diligence. Include details to explain why you chose this person.

Writing Tips A character analysis is a description of a person. Follow these steps to write a character analysis:

1. Describe his or her words and actions.
2. Analyze how his or her behavior shows diligence.
3. Describe the reactions of others to this person.

345

Section 16.1 Quality Clothing

Visiting clothing stores is a way to discover new styles. Maybe you love to shop, but sometimes you think you do not have enough money for what you want. It is important to know what to look for. It is also important to consider your clothing budget. You can save both time and money by looking for the best values, following care label directions, and storing your clothes properly.

Recognize Quality Fabrics

The best way to learn about fabrics is to take a trip to a fabric store. Check the label on the end of the fabric bolt to see the fiber content. Compare fabrics in different price ranges. Feel various fabrics to see how they handle when stretched or crushed. Quality fabric will spring back. A basic understanding of fabrics can help you make better clothing choices.

Fibers and Fabrics

Most fabrics are made from tiny strands called **fibers**. Fibers can be made from natural or synthetic (sin-ˌthe-tik) materials. **Natural fibers** are made from plant and animal products. Cotton comes from the seedpod of the cotton plant. It is the most widely used fiber in the world. Linen comes from the flax plant. Linen is very absorbent, but wrinkles easily. Silk is generated by silkworms as they spin their cocoons. Silk is strong and resists wrinkling, but it has to be dry-cleaned or hand-washed. Wool is made from the fleece of sheep. It is a durable fiber that traps air, preventing the loss of body heat. Wool is worn in cold weather.

Synthetic fibers are manufactured from substances such as wood pulp and petroleum. Rayon and nylon are both synthetic fibers. Polyester, the most widely used synthetic fiber, is often combined with cotton. When two or more fibers are combined to create a fabric, it is referred to as a **blend**. The clothing label lists the percentage of each type of fiber. For example, a shirt might be a blend of 60% cotton and 40% polyester. Fabrics are made by weaving or knitting fibers together.

Woven Fabrics

When you were a young child, you may have woven strips of paper together to create an art project. This same basic process is used to create **woven fabrics**. They are made by interlacing lengthwise and crosswise yarns, which are several fibers twisted together, on a loom. **Figure 16.1** on the next page illustrates the most common types of woven fabrics.

As You Read

Connect What do you look for when shopping for clothes?

Vocabulary

You can find definitions in the glossary at the back of this book.

Learn about Fabrics Fiber content can be found on the fabric bolt. *What else can you learn from a visit to a fabric store?*

Knit Fabrics

Like woven fabrics, **knit fabrics** are made by looping threads together. There are many ways to loop the threads for a variety of textures and patterns. Knit fabrics are made to be stretchy. Knit fabrics move well with the body and are comfortable to wear. Not all knits are heavy like sweaters. Cotton T-shirts are also made of knit fabric.

Fabric Grain

Grain is the direction the threads run in a fabric. Both knit and woven fabrics have a grain, as you can see in Figure 16.1. Well-constructed clothes are cut on grain, with the threads running straight up and down and straight across.

Threads can be pulled off grain when the fabric goes through the finishing process. This makes the grain slant, or set at the wrong angle. If the fabric is off-grain, the garment will appear to pull to one side, especially after a few washings.

Figure 16.1 Common Fabric Weaves

Different Weaves Create Different Effects Plain, twill, and satin are the most common weaves. *Can you name something in your wardrobe or home from each of the weave categories?*

Plain Weave The plain weave is the simplest weave. The yarns form an even, balanced weave. Plain weaves are used for shirts, handkerchiefs, and sheets.

Twill Weave Twill weaves create diagonal lines on fabric. Twill weaves are firmer, heavier, and stronger than plain weaves. Denim, used for jeans and jackets, is an example of a twill weave.

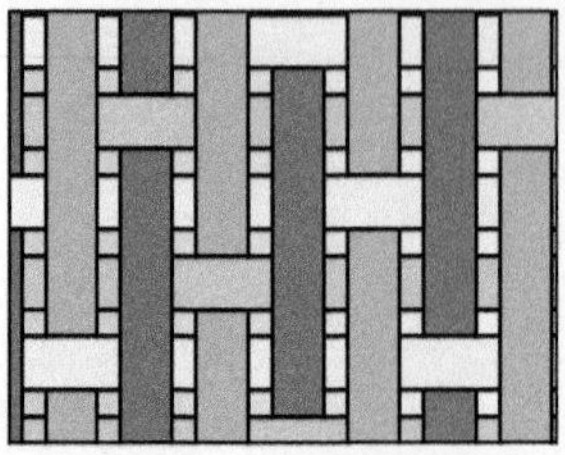

Satin Weave The satin weave creates a smooth, shiny surface. Satin fabrics are often used for blouses and formal evening wear.

You can test the fabric grain of a shirt by making sure that the grain runs straight across the back from one underarm seam to the other. Test pants and skirts at the back of the hipline. The grain should be the same on both sides.

Fabric Finishes

Manufacturers often add various finishes to improve the durability of fabrics. Some finishes add body or bulk. Some hold the threads in place so that the fabric will wear well and will not pull out at the seams. Other finishes add softness, luster, strength, or shrinkage control. Finishes can also make caring for fabrics easier.

Clothing labels often tell you what finishes have been added. For instance, a fabric may be treated to be stain-resistant or water-resistant. Washable clothes may have a drip-dry or permanent-press finish, which means that the garment requires little or no ironing.

Reading Check *Explain* *How can you test the fabric grain of a shirt?*

Clothing Comfort and Fit

To enjoy wearing your clothes, you must be comfortable in them. Your clothes need to fit correctly. The fabric that a garment is made from and the style of the garment also affect comfort. Knowing how to evaluate these factors can help you select clothes that you will feel comfortable wearing. **Figure 16.2** on page 350 shows what to look for when checking the fit and comfort of clothing.

Selecting Size

Clothing may be sized simply as small, medium, large, or extra-large. Examples of this type of clothing include sweat-shirts, T-shirts, and sweaters. Try on and compare the fit of various styles until you find one that feels comfortable to you. Look in a full-length mirror at the front and back. Sit, bend, walk, and reach while wearing the garment to make sure it feels comfortable as you move around. Since you are still growing, it is a good idea to try clothes on before you buy them, even if you think you are a certain size. Also keep in mind that one manufacturer's "small" may be the same size as another manufacturer's "medium."

Note-Taking Skills
Main Points Your teacher will write the most important information, or the main points, on the board or on transparencies for the overhead projector. Include this information in your notebook, and then listen for the supporting details.

Sizes for Girls and Women Female clothing is sold in girls', juniors', misses', women's, and plus sizes. Girls' sizes go up to 14 and are roughly equal to the age of the wearer. Juniors' sizes are designed for a developing figure, but are smaller and shorter-waisted than misses' sizes. Petite sizes are shorter in length, while tall sizes are longer.

Sizes for Boys and Men For males there are three basic size groups: boys', teen boys', and men's. Boys' sizes are designed for small, undeveloped bodies. Teen boys' sizes are for slim teens and young men. Men's sizes are designed for adult bodies. Men's pants are sized by the waist measurement and the inside leg measurement, or inseam. For example, jeans with a 28-inch waist and a 30-inch inseam would be labeled "size 28/30." Dress shirts list two measurements, the collar size and the sleeve length, such as 15/34. Jackets are sold by chest measurement and length, such as 38 short or 38 long.

Figure 16.2 Does It Feel as Good as It Looks?

Comfort Check these features for a comfortable fit. *What can happen if you buy an outfit or garment without trying it on first?*

Neck Opening Is the neck opening comfortable? If it is too large, the front of the garment falls forward and sags. If it is too small, the neck binds and the front rides up.

Shoulder Seams Do the shoulder seams hit you at the shoulder? They should not go over your shoulder unless the garment is designed that way.

Sleeves Do long sleeves cover your wristbone? Can you lift your arms over your head with ease?

Waistband and Hips Does the waistband feel comfortable and fasten easily? Can you sit comfortably in pants or jeans?

Fasteners Do buttonholes, zippers, and other closures lie smoothly?

Hemline Is the hemline even around the bottom? Is the length right for you?

Ken Karp/McGraw-Hill Education

Natural Dyes

In this activity you will experiment with natural dyes. Dyes are used to add color to fabric. Before you begin, read through the entire Hands-On Lab assignment. Write down any questions that you have about the activity. Reread the text or ask your teacher for help if you need it.

Supplies
✓ Four 4-inch squares of undyed muslin fabric
✓ 2 types of fruit, such as blackberries, blueberries, or raspberries.
✓ Carrot juice
✓ Tea bag
✓ 4 small bowls

Develop Your Plan
■ Choose 2 fruits to use as natural dyes.
■ Gather the supplies.

Implement Your Plan
■ Place a fabric square in each bowl.
■ Rub the juice of each fruit on two of the fabric squares.
■ Brew a bag of tea. Pour the tea into a bowl with a third fabric square.

■ In the last bowl, pour carrot juice over the fabric square.
■ Make notes of how the fabric reacted to each natural dye.
■ After several minutes, rinse the fabric samples and allow them to dry.

Evaluate Your Results
Which natural dye was the easiest to use? Which made the brightest color? Which dye kept the most color after rinsing and drying? Make a list of items you could dye naturally. Do you think using natural dyes could help the environment? Write one or more paragraphs to explain your answer.

Projects and Activities Go to connectED.mcgraw-hill.com.

Comfort and Style

The fabric that a garment is made from can affect its comfort in many ways. Which fabrics do you think feel pleasant to the touch? Some people dislike the feel of slippery or clingy fabrics. Others find woolen knits rough and scratchy. You will want to buy clothes that suit your own preferences. When you buy clothes, be sure to check the feel of the fabric carefully.

Clothing style also affects its comfort. For example, a full skirt or pants with pleats may provide more room for you to move freely. A scoop neckline or an open collar may feel less restrictive than a turtleneck sweater.

Some styles may also suit your body shape better than others. Trying on a garment is the best way to decide whether a particular style is comfortable and looks good on you.

Comfortable, durable shoes will complete your wardrobe. When shopping for shoes, shop early in the day to get a more accurate fit. Feet tend to get slightly swollen after a day of walking. Try on shoes with the type of socks or hosiery that you would normally wear. Look for shoes that are not too tight or too loose. Be sure that you have room to wiggle your toes. Try on both left and right shoes, and walk around in them. When shopping for shoes to match a certain outfit, wear the outfit or take a sample of the fabric with you.

Evaluate Fit
Learning how to choose the right fit can help you make wise clothing choices. *Why is it so important to choose clothes according to fit?*

Reading Check *Explain* Why should you try on clothes even if you know your size?

Make a Shopping Plan

A shopping plan is a strategy, or way to prepare, for spending the money you have available to buy the clothing you need or want. Before you develop a shopping plan, discuss your ideas with your parents or guardians. They can help you determine how much money should be used to buy the clothes you need, as well as how much money you can spend for items you want.

In addition to your list of clothing needs, your shopping plan should consider these three factors:

- **Clothing Budget** It is a good idea to set up a monthly spending plan. Go over your spending plan with your parents to decide how to make your money go further.
- **Purchase Plan** You learned about several payment methods, including cash, check, credit card, and debit card, in Chapter 11. Can you recall some of the advantages and disadvantages of each payment method?

- **Shopping Options** In most areas, there are several stores to choose from. Specialty stores, discount stores, and department stores are some options. Another choice is to shop for clothes by mail order or on the Internet.

Quality and Cost

It is easy to assume that more expensive clothes are better quality than less expensive clothes. This may be true sometimes, but not always. In addition to looking for details that indicate a well-made garment, you need to evaluate the cost. Consider not only the price tag, but also the cost per wearing. Before you buy a garment, ask yourself these questions:

- How often am I likely to wear it?
- How long is it likely to fit and stay looking nice?
- Is the price appropriate for the level of quality?
- Could I save money by waiting for a sale or buying it somewhere else?
- Could I make it myself for less?
- Is the item worth spending this much of my clothing budget?

SUCCEED IN SCHOOL!

Note-Taking Skills
Three-Ring Binder
A three-ring binder with tabs is a great way to keep and organize your notes and handouts. You can add, remove, or rearrange your notes as you need to.

Section 16.1 After You Read

Review What You Have Learned

1. **Name** the three most common types of woven fabrics.
2. **Describe** ways to check for fit and comfort while trying clothes on.
3. **Explain** why talking with your parents can help you with shopping.

Practice Academic Skills

English Language Arts

4. Create an illustration that represents one of your favorite outfits, including shoes. Label each part of the outfit with a suggestion for how to check for fit and comfort.

Social Studies

5. Federal law requires flame-retardant fabrics for children's sleepwear. Conduct research to learn about other kinds of fabric finishes that make life safer or easier. Share your findings with the class.

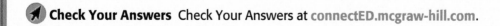

Check Your Answers Check Your Answers at connectED.mcgraw-hill.com.

Section 16.2 Clothing Care Basics

Reading Guide

Before You Read

Preview A cause is an event or action that makes something happen. An effect is the result of a cause. Ask yourself, "Why does this happen?" to help you recognize cause-and-effect relationships as you read.

Read to Learn
Key Concepts

✓ **Describe** the information provided on clothing labels.

✓ **Name** six guidelines for stretching your clothing budget.

✓ **List** six steps you can take to properly clean your clothes.

Main Idea
You can stretch your clothing budget and keep your wardrobe looking good when you know how to properly care for and store your clothes.

Content Vocabulary
○ colorfast
○ brand name
○ static cling

Academic Vocabulary
■ coordinate
■ pressed

Graphic Organizer
As you read, create step-by-step instructions for hand washing a garment. Use a graphic organizer like the one shown to organize your information.

How to Hand Wash a Garment	
Step 1:	Step 4:
Step 2:	Step 5:
Step 3:	Step 6:

⬆ **Graphic Organizer** Go to connectED. mcgraw-hill.com to download this graphic organizer.

Clothing can be a significant expense, so you want your clothes to last as long as possible. Imagine that the ketchup stain did not come out of your shirt. Maybe the pants you want to wear have a ripped seam. What if you cannot find your favorite sweater? If any of this sounds familiar, this section can help.

Clothing Labels

You can find a great deal of helpful information by reading clothing labels. Take the time to check the care label before you buy to help you determine the quality, durability, and care of garments. Checking the care labels before you buy clothing can save you time and money. Not following care labels can cause clothing items to shrink, fade, or lose shape.

Every item of clothing must carry a care label that describes its fiber content, where it was made, and how to care for it. This information may be on the same label or on two different labels. Look for this information on labels inside the garment:

- The fiber content is listed on the care label. It also gives the name of the manufacturer and tells where the garment was made.
- The care label will tell you the correct way to clean the garment. Some items must be dry cleaned only.
- A "no bleach" warning on the label means all types of bleach will damage the fabric.
- If the label tells you not to iron the garment, it is because the fabric will be damaged by the heat of the iron.
- If the fabric is colorfast, that fact may be included on the label. A **colorfast** fabric will keep its original color through many washings.

As You Read

Connect How can you benefit from making clothing care a part of your daily routine?

◼◇ **Vocabulary**

You can find definitions in the glossary at the back of this book.

🔲 **Shop Wisely and Read Labels** Manufacturers print fiber content and care instructions on clothing labels. *How can reading care labels help you as a consumer?*

Corbis/SuperStock

Character Counts

Self-Discipline

Avery is at the mall to buy some clothes for the new school year that will start in just a few weeks. His dad gave him $250.00 to spend, with the instructions that he should not spend it all on one outfit. Avery is excited about the new school year, and he wants to make a good impression. He thinks brand names are important. He goes to a very popular retail store in the mall where a lot of his friends shop, and he finds a really great jacket with the name of the store brand printed across the back. The jacket is $235.00. Avery has a jacket he bought last year, but he thinks his dad will understand if he spends almost all of the money on the brand-name jacket.

You Make the Call

Should Avery buy the jacket and tell his dad how important it is to him that he wears the brand name? Write a paragraph that explains what you think Avery should do.

Brand Name Labels

A **brand name** is a trademark used by a manufacturer to identify its products. Sometimes stores have their own brand names. In addition, clothing labels may identify the designer, which is another kind of brand name. Some people use brand names as a guide in selecting clothing. Brand name items are usually more expensive than those with less well-known names. However, brand names and designer labels are not always signs of quality. Experience will help you decide if brand-name clothing is worth the extra cost.

Reading Check *Distinguish Why is it important to judge clothing on more than just the brand name?*

Your Clothing Budget

When you made your shopping plan, you calculated your clothing budget, or how much money you had to spend. You can make that money go further by understanding and following some simple guidelines:

- **Start with two or three basic outfits.** Choose a few basic colors and classic styles to start your wardrobe. Then you can coordinate, or mix and match, additional pieces to go with what you already have.
- **Make the best use of what you have.** Try different combinations and accessories with clothes you own.
- **Take good care of your clothes.** Follow the directions on the care labels to make clothes last longer. Hang up or fold clothes after wearing and washing. Treat stains and wash clothes before putting them away.
- **Compare cost and quality.** No matter what type of fabric your clothing is made from, a quality garment requires good construction. For example, well-made clothes will have straight and smooth seams.
- **Take advantage of sales.** Plan ahead and shop during seasonal sales to get more for your money.
- **Learn to sew.** Save money and express your personality. Knowing how to make simple repairs can help your clothes last longer.

Clothing Care and Saving Money

You can save money when you keep your clothes in good condition. Follow these simple guidelines to take proper care of your clothes:

- Wear clothing that is suitable for the activity. When doing yard work or cleaning out the garage, for example, wear old clothes so that it does not matter if they get dirty.
- Dress and undress carefully to avoid snagging, ripping, or stretching your garments.
- Inspect your clothes carefully after each wearing. Repair any tears or holes before they get worse. If you find stains, treat them immediately and wash the garment as soon as possible.

Note-Taking Skills
Reading Assignments
It is important to finish your assigned reading before class starts. When you know what topics will be discussed in class, you can focus on taking notes about new information.

• • • • • • • • • • • • • • •

Reading Check *Predict How can simple sewing skills help you save money?*

©DreamPictures/Blend Images LLC

Special Care Learn how to take care of special clothing, such as team uniforms and formal wear. *What special care might be necessary for these types of clothing?*

Doing the Laundry

Cleaning clothes properly requires a basic knowledge of fabrics and simple cleaning techniques. Cleaning is just the beginning. You also need to know how to properly dry and iron your clothes. However, these tasks are not difficult if you follow the instructions on clothing care labels and on laundry products and appliances.

Learning the right way to launder, or wash, clothes will help you keep your clothes looking newer longer. Follow these guidelines when washing your clothes:

- **Pretreat stains.** Pretreat means to apply a stain remover before laundering. Besides stains, sleeve cuffs and the fold line on collars often need to be pretreated.
- **Sort clothes.** Check care labels on clothes carefully. Then separate clothes into piles by color: light-colored fabrics, medium-colored fabrics, and dark fabrics.
- **Select the correct water temperature.** Wash your clothes in the water temperature recommended on the care label. Unless otherwise specified, most clothing can be washed in warm water and rinsed in cold.
- **Choose the correct load size.** If you are washing only a few clothes, choose a small-load setting to save water and energy. Never overload the washing machine. Clothes will not get clean if they are packed in too tightly.
- **Use the correct amount of detergent.** Check the detergent label for the correct amount to use. Remember to adjust for the load setting you selected.
- **Use a fabric softener.** If static cling is a problem, liquid fabric softeners can be added to the washer, or dryer sheets can be used in the dryer. **Static cling** happens when electricity builds up in the dryer and causes clothing to stick to itself or to your body. Read product labels carefully to determine which type of softener you are using, and how and when it should be added.

Drying Your Clothes

Generally, clothes can be either line-dried or machine-dried. Line-drying saves energy and money but takes longer. Machine-drying is quick and convenient, but it uses energy and therefore costs more. If you use a dryer, remove clothing as soon as the dryer shuts off. Hang up items such as shirts, pants, and dresses as soon as you take them out of the dryer. This will help reduce wrinkling and make ironing easier. Sort and fold the other items.

Ironing Your Clothes

Some fabrics require that they be **pressed**, or ironed, after each wash. Other items may require some light pressing with a steam iron. The care label gives the proper temperature setting for the fabric. Always match the temperature setting on the iron with the fiber listed on the label. Synthetic fabrics may melt if the iron is too hot. Start by ironing or pressing small areas of the garment, such as the collar, yoke, and sleeves. Then press the larger areas. This way, you can avoid accidentally wrinkling areas you have already ironed.

Laundry Basics Doing laundry includes cleaning, drying, and ironing clothes. *Why is it important to read all instructions before washing, drying, or pressing your clothes?*

i love images/families/Alamy

Financial Literacy

Clothing Costs

Daniel went shopping for new clothes for his upcoming job interview. He found the following on sale: a $140 suit at $35 off, a $52 briefcase at 25% off, and two pairs of socks that are $8.00 each. How much did Daniel spend?

Math Concept **Order of Operations** To solve an equation, you must use the correct order of operations. First, simplify within the parentheses. Multiply and divide from left to right, then add and subtract from left to right.

Starting Hint Before solving this problem, write an expression using the correct symbols (remember that 25% off means that he paid 75% (0.75) of the price: $(\$140 - \$35) + (\$52 \times 0.75) + (2 \times \$8)$. Solve using the correct order of operations.

 For math help, go to the Math Appendix at the back of the book.

Hand Washing Your Clothes

Some delicate garments are labeled "hand wash" because machine washing and drying will cause damage to the garment. You might also want to hand wash when you only have one or two garments to wash. To hand wash, start by soaking the item in sudsy water. Then gently squeeze the suds through the garment. Avoid twisting or wringing the garment. Drain the sink or basin and refill it with fresh water to rinse the garment. Repeat the rinse step until there are no more suds in the water. After rinsing, roll the garment in a towel to remove excess water. Then, hang the garment or lay it flat to dry.

Dry Cleaning

Some clothes cannot be washed by a machine or by hand. Rather, they may need to be dry cleaned. The dry cleaning process uses special chemicals instead of water and detergent to get clothes clean. Dry cleaning can be expensive, so choose your clothes wisely to avoid extra costs. You might consider alternatives to taking clothes to a commercial dry cleaner. Some coin-operated laundry facilities have machines for dry cleaning.

Clothing Storage Store your clothes properly so they will last longer. *What are the advantages of storing your clothes properly?*

(t)D.Hurst/Alamy; (b)Eclipse Studios/McGraw-Hill Education

You can also buy dry cleaning kits to be used with a dryer. The kits contain specially-treated cloths to place in a bag with your garments. After the garments tumble in the dryer, they must be removed right away. This process works best with wool, rayon, silk, linen, and cotton knits. As with all laundry products, it is important to follow directions carefully.

Storing Your Clothes

Another important part of caring for clothes is storing them properly. When you hang up your clothes, take the time to close zippers and fasten buttons so that the garment will hang straight. Do not overcrowd closets and drawers, or your clothes may wrinkle. Check to be sure that pockets are empty and that garments are clean and repaired before putting them away. Seasonal clothes such as coats, heavy sweaters, and bathing suits, should be washed and dried before storing for the year. Clothes that are worn only for special occasions should be given extra attention, such as covering them with plastic bags to prevent damage and dust build-up. All clothing should be stored in dry areas to prevent mildew damage.

SUCCEED IN SCHOOL!

Note-Taking Skills
Use Colored Pens
Try using different colored pens or pencils when taking notes. For example, use red for new words, blue for the main ideas, and green for supporting details.
• • • • • • • • • • • • • • •

Section 16.2 After You Read

Review What You Have Learned

1. **Explain** why you should take time to read labels before you buy your clothes.
2. **Name** three things you can do to keep your clothing in good condition.
3. **Compare and contrast** line-drying and machine-drying.

Practice Academic Skills

English Language Arts

4. Choose two washable items from your wardrobe, each with different care instructions. For each item, write down the label information. Then describe in detail how you would launder and care for each item. Begin with sorting and end with storage.

Social Studies

5. Would you rather wear used clothes, hand-me-downs, or vintage clothing? Is there a difference? Why do you think society's attitudes toward wearing used clothing are changing? How do you feel about wearing used clothing? Write one or more paragraphs to express your opinion.

• •

🡕 **Check Your Answers** Check Your Answers at connectED.mcgraw-hill.com.

Discovering Careers

Do you like to shop for clothing? Are you interested in the different kinds of fabric? If you answered yes to either of those questions, you might want to consider a future career in the clothing and fabric industry. The following chart explores several careers in the clothing and fabric industry.

Job Title	Job Description
Dry Cleaner	Operates various dry-cleaning machines to clean garments, draperies, and other items as specified by customers.
Fabric Inspector	Inspects fabrics for defective weaving, stitching errors, color variations, and damaged or dirty fabrics. Pulls defective fabrics off the line.
Fabric Store Manager	Supervises and trains staff in customer service, fabric and notion selection, and fabric cutting. Orders supplies and equipment. Builds a team that is enthusiastic about fabric and sewing.
Fabric Designer	Predicts what fibers, textures, and colors will be popular. Designs fabrics.
Fashion Consultant	Helps clients understand their wardrobe needs. Shows customers ways to maximize their purchases by selecting garments that can be worn in a combination of ways.

Career Activities ▼

At School

1 Select three of the careers listed. Research the education, training, and work experience required for each career. Write a summary of your results.

At Home

2 Sort your family's laundry into piles according to the care instructions. How many piles did you create? What are the different types of cleaning that will need to be done?

At Work

3 Imagine that you work in a juice and smoothie shop. What kinds of stains are you likely to get on your uniform? How can you remove the stains?

In the Community

4 Contact and interview someone in your community who works in the clothing or fabric industry. Ask this person to describe what his or her typical work day is like. Share what you learned with your class.

Ron Chapple Stock/Alamy

Chapter Summary

Section 16.1 Quality Clothing

A basic understanding of fabrics can help you make better clothing choices. Fabrics are made from natural or synthetic materials. Fabrics are made by weaving or knitting fibers together. Manufacturers may add finishes to improve the durability and feel of fabrics. When you buy clothes, check the feel of the fabric and check for the correct fit. Use a shopping plan to spend your clothing budget wisely.

Section 16.2 Clothing Care Basics

All clothing must have a care label with fiber content and care instructions. Read labels before you buy to help you determine the quality, durability, and care of garments. Keep clothes in good condition to help save money. Cleaning clothes properly requires a basic knowledge of fabrics and simple cleaning techniques. Your wardrobe will look newer longer when you learn the correct ways to launder and store your clothes.

Words You Learned

1. Arrange the vocabulary words below into groups of related words. Explain why you put the words together.

Content Vocabulary

- fiber (p. 347)
- natural fiber (p. 347)
- synthetic fiber (p. 347)
- blend (p. 347)
- woven fabric (p. 347)
- knit fabric (p. 348)
- grain (p. 348)
- colorfast (p. 355)
- brand name (p. 356)
- static cling (p. 358)

Academic Vocabulary

- slant (p. 348)
- strategy (p. 352)
- coordinate (p. 356)
- pressed (p. 359)

Review Key Concepts

2. **Explain** three features of quality fabric.

3. **Identify** three factors that affect clothing comfort.

4. **Outline** a shopping plan for clothes.

5. **Describe** the information provided on clothing labels.

6. **Name** six guidelines for stretching your clothing budget.

7. **List** six steps you can take to properly clean your clothes.

Critical Thinking

8. **Predict** what you would do if you needed to clean a garment without a care label.

9. **Analyze** what assumptions consumers might make about high-priced clothing with designer logos.

Real-World Skills and Applications

Problem-Solving

10. Ask Questions The eighth-grade graduation party is coming up, and your friend wants to buy a new outfit for the occasion. She found a shirt with a designer logo at a popular mall store. The pants she wants are also in the mall, but at a different store. She found a pair of shoes that cost more than the pants, but she says she can wear them with many different outfits. What questions can you ask your friend to help her decide if buying the outfit is a good idea?

Technology Applications

11. Clothing Information for Teens Using presentation software, create a slide show called "A Teen's Guide to Shopping for Clothes." Include tips for choosing fabric, making smart purchases, and caring for clothes. Use illustrations to make your presentation attractive and interesting.

Financial Literacy

12. Be a Smart Shopper There are many ways to get more clothes for your money. If you want to shop at brand-name stores at the mall or other locations, it is a good idea to wait for sales. For example, by shopping at the end of a season, you can often find brand names for lower prices. However, brand-name clothing stores are not your only shopping option, and better bargains can often be found elsewhere. Identify five options for buying clothes. Make a table listing the five options, and identify the pros and cons of each one. How many of these options have you already tried? Which options are you likely to choose in the future?

13. Expand Your Wardrobe Create a collage with photos of clothing, shoes, and accessories that express your personal style. Look through magazines and cut out pictures of clothing and accessories that you like. Add captions to explain how each item could be used with something you already have in your wardrobe

14. Synthetic Fibers There are more than 25 different kinds of synthetic, or man-made, fibers. Find information about five types of synthetic fibers used for clothing. Create a chart that includes what kinds of clothing each type of fiber is suitable for, and what special characteristics the fiber has, such as water resistance or insulation. Also include any drawbacks each fiber may have.

15. Fabric Development With permission from your parents or teacher, go online to find information about new types of fabrics. For example, look for fabrics that increase the speed of an athlete, protect against allergies, or fight stains. Create a list of at least five new fabrics. Then choose one that you find especially interesting and write a paragraph about how people can benefit from the new fabric. Include the information in your Life Skills Binder.

Academic Skills

English Language Arts

16. Write a Catalog Description Imagine you are writer for a sportswear company. Describe an outfit for the catalog. Who will wear this outfit? What fabrics and fibers are used? What sizes and colors are available? What are the care instructions? What are the selling points of the outfit? How much do you think this outfit should cost? Use this information to write a catalog ad.

Science

17. Environmental Impact As a consumer, it is important to know what you can do to help the environment.

Procedure Locate a detergent designed to be environmentally safe. Look for "green" or "environmentally friendly" on the label. Make a list of the ingredients. Conduct an experiment to compare the cleaning ability of this detergent with a standard brand.

Analysis Is there a difference in cleaning ability, fragrance, or in the feel of the fabric after washing? Summarize your findings.

Mathematics

18. Buy on Layaway Victoria needs a new heavy coat for the winter, but the one she wants is $320, and she has not yet saved up enough money to buy it. The store offers a layaway plan requiring a 25% initial deposit and additional 25% deposits every 30 days until the item is paid in full after 90 days. There is also a $5 service charge per payment after the initial deposit. How much will each payment cost Victoria?

Math Concept **Changing Percents to Fractions.** One way to find the percent of a number is to first convert the percent to a fraction. Since a percent is simply a ratio of a number to 100, write the percent as a fraction with 100 as the denominator, and reduce to lowest terms. Multiply this fraction by the number.

Starting Hint Convert 25% to a fraction by rewriting it as 25/100, and reducing it to lowest terms. Multiply this fraction by $320. Do not forget to add the service charge to the last three payments.

Standardized Test Practice

True/False

Read the statements and determine if they are true or false.

> **Test-Taking Tip** When answering true/false questions, pay close attention to the wording as you read the questions. Look for words such as *not, nor, any,* or *all.* These words are important in determining the correct answer.

19. Synthetic fibers are not made with plants or animal fleece.

20. All clothing can be hand washed.

21. Creating a shopping plan can help you get the most out of your clothing purchases.

UNIT 7 Life Skills Project

Your Personal Style

Looking your best and showing your own style is important. Magazines may offer ideas on how to be creative with clothes. Craft books may also offer jewelry and other projects that help you express yourself. This project will help you explore your personal style.

My Journal Complete the journal entry from page 323, and refer to it to complete your design concept.

Project Assignment ▼

In this project, you will:

- Create a list of all the clothes you already own.
- Find examples of clothing that reflect your personal style.
- Describe your personal style.
- Create an illustrated pamphlet to display your personal style.
- Interview someone whose style you admire.
- Present your findings to your class.
- Include this project in the seventh section of your personal Life Skills binder.

 Step 1 Create a Clothing Inventory Chart

Analyzing your own personal style is easier if you know what clothing accessories you already have. Create a clothing inventory chart to list and describe the clothing and accessories you own.

Step 2 Find Examples of Clothing That Reflect Your Style

Look through several magazines geared toward teens and preteens. Collect clipped photos to use in a pamphlet that reflects your personal style. Then write two or more paragraphs that answer these questions:

✔What do these outfits have in common?

✔How would you describe the colors and styles?

✔How does your collection of photos reflect your personal style?

✔How would you describe your personal style?

Step 3 Interview Someone Whose Style You Admire

Interview someone in your community whose fashion style you admire. Ask these questions:

✔How would you describe your personal style?

✔Who or what influences your style the most?

✔How has your style changed over the years?

Use these interviewing skills when conducting your interview and these writing skills when writing the summary of notes from your interview.

Interviewing Skills
- Record interview responses and take notes.
- Listen attentively.

Writing Skills
- Use complete sentences.
- Use correct spelling and grammar.

Life Skills Project Checklist

Research Personal Clothing Styles

- ✅ Create your clothing inventory chart.
- ✅ Collect photos from magazines that show clothing styles you like.
- ✅ Interview someone in your community whose style you admire.
- ✅ Include your inventory chart, photos, and descriptions in a pamphlet that displays your personal style.

Writing Skills

- ✅ Describe the clothing represented in your pamphlet.
- ✅ Describe your own personal style.
- ✅ Write a summary from your interview with someone whose style you admire.

Present Your Findings

- ✅ Prepare a short presentation to share and describe your pamphlet and explain how it reflects your personal style.
- ✅ Invite the students of the class to ask any questions they may have. Answer these questions with responses that respect their perspectives.
- ✅ Add this project to your Life Skills binder.

Academic Skills

- ✅ Conduct research to gather information.
- ✅ Communicate effectively.
- ✅ Organize your presentation so the audience can follow along easily.
- ✅ Thoroughly express your ideas.

Step 4 Create and Present Your Personal Style Pamphlet

Use the Life Skills Project Checklist on the right to plan and complete your pamphlet and give an oral report on it.

Use these speaking skills when presenting your final report.

Speaking Skills
- Speak clearly and concisely.
- Be sensitive to the needs of your audience.
- Use standard English to communicate.

Step 5 Evaluate Your Presentation

Your project will be evaluated based on:

- ✔ Completeness and organization of your clothing inventory chart.
- ✔ The collection of photographs that represent your personal style.
- ✔ The description of your personal style.
- ✔ Thoroughness of your personal style pamphlet.
- ✔ The summary written from interview notes.
- ✔ Grammar and sentence structure.
- ✔ Presentation to the class.
- ✔ Creativity and neatness.

🧭 **Evaluation Rubric** Go to connectED.mcgraw-hill.com for a rubric you can use to evaluate your final project.

Chapter 17
Plan Sewing Projects

Chapter 18
Learn How To Sew

Unit Preview

This unit is about the sewing basics. In this unit, you will learn about:

- Using a sewing machine for basic stitches.
- Preparing and planning for sewing projects.
- Selecting and preparing fabrics and patterns.
- Basic sewing and serging skills.

Explore the Photo

Knowing how to sew can be a very valuable skill. *What are some useful things you can do if you know how to sew?*

© Hero/Corbis/Glow Images

Design Your Own Clothing

When you are done studying this unit, you will complete a project in which you will:

✓ Create a pattern for an article of clothing.

✓ Interview someone who sews as part of his or her job.

✓ Share with your class what your project says about you.

The prewriting activity below will help you get started.

My Journal

Prewriting Activity
Sketch Ideas

Think of ideas for simple sewing projects that you could wear. Sketch several designs. Below each sketch, describe what fabrics, supplies, tools, and notions you might need to complete it.

● What elements of your designs make them practical, or useful, in regular life?

● What elements of your sketches make your designs stylish?

Chapter  17

Plan Sewing Projects

Section 17.1

Sewing Machine Basics

■ **Main Idea** All sewing machines operate in the same basic way. Use the machine's operating manual to learn the functions of individual machines so you can start learning basic stitches.

Section 17.2

Patterns, Fabrics, and Notions

■ **Main Idea** Before beginning a sewing project, learn about the basics of pattern selection, fabric selection, and choosing notions.

Hero/agefotostock

Explore the Photo
You can learn basic sewing skills at school. *What do you want to make as your first sewing project?*

"How To" Paper

Sewing Repairs Choose a common clothing repair, such as fixing a seam, adjusting a hem, or sewing on a button. Write a "how to" paper to explain the process of making the repair. Remember to include an introduction and a conclusion.

Writing Tips In order to write an effective "how to" paper, follow these steps:

1. List all of the materials you will need.
2. List detailed steps in the order they should be completed.
3. Use transitional words and phrases, such as "first," "next," "and then."

Section 17.1 Sewing Machine Basics

Reading Guide

Before You Read

Look It Up As you read, use a dictionary in addition to the glossary at the back of the book. If you read a word that you do not know, look it up in the glossary or the dictionary. Before long, this practice will become a habit.

Read to Learn

Key Concepts

✓ **Describe** the main function all sewing machines have in common.

✓ **Explain** how a hem is created.

Main Idea

All sewing machines operate in the same basic way. Use the machine's operating manual to learn the functions of individual machines so you can start learning basic stitches.

Content Vocabulary

○ interlock
○ hem

Academic Vocabulary

■ operate   ■ raw

Graphic Organizer

As you read, list and describe the four basic sewing machine stitches a beginning student can practice. The first one is done for you. Use a graphic organizer like the one shown to help you organize your information.

Sewing Machine Stitch	Description
regular stitch	a medium-length stitch used for sewing most projects

Graphic Organizer Go to connected.mcgraw-hill.com to download this graphic organizer.

Sewing is a great way to show off your personal style in your wardrobe and in your living space. You can make gifts, personalize your garments, and adjust patterns to make clothes exactly the way you want them. This section introduces you to the sewing machine.

Sewing Machines

Most sewing machines have the same basic parts. Before you use any sewing machine, read the operating manual. You can use it to find the parts on your sewing machine and learn how to use its special features and any accessories. All sewing machines operate, or work, in the same basic way. A needle moves up and down through the fabric, and two sets of threads **interlock** to form closely fitted stitches.

Although sewing machines work the same way, there is a wide range in the number and complexity of functions they can perform. A very basic machine is useful for general sewing projects. Modern sewing machines are computerized and can create detailed embroidery designs for special projects. The more a machine can do, the more it costs. Be sure to use sewing machines carefully and according to the instructions to keep them in good working order. See **Figure 17.1** to familiarize yourself with the parts of a basic sewing machine.

As You Read

Connect What, if any, sewing experience have you had?

◆ Vocabulary

You can find definitions in the glossary at the back of this book.

Figure 17.1 The Sewing Machine

Standard Parts All sewing machines have the same basic parts and functions. *Why do you think sewing machines include different stitch patterns to choose from?*

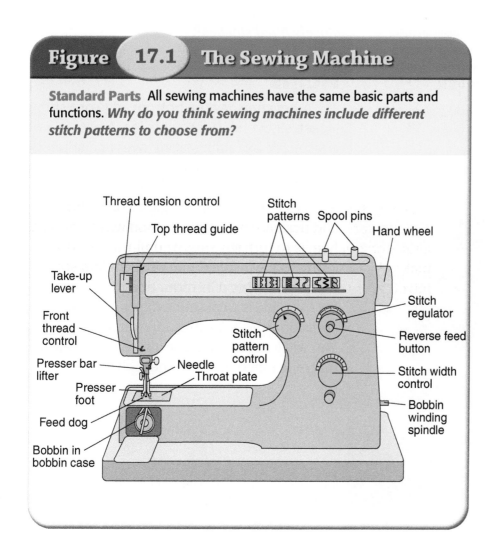

Converting Measurements

While on vacation in Europe, Grace went into a store that sold sewing patterns. However, when looking for patterns in her size, Grace realized that all of the measurements provided on the envelopes are in the metric system. Grace's measurements are 33 inches (chest), 25 inches (waist), 34 inches (hip), and 16 inches (back-waist). What are her measurements in centimeters? The package tells her that she needs 1.9 meters of fabric. How many yards will she need?

Math Concept **Length Conversions** While the U.S. generally uses the customary system of measurement, most other countries use the metric system. To convert inches to centimeters, multiply by 2.54. To convert yards to meters, multiply by 0.914.

Starting Hint Multiply each inch measurement by 2.54 to convert to centimeters, and round to the nearest centimeter. To convert meters into yards, you will need to divide by 0.914.

 For more math help, go to the Math Appendix located at the back of this book.

Sewing Lab

Your sewing lab is a great place to learn and practice basic sewing skills. Equipment and supplies are important to understand. However, it is just as important to work cooperatively with others in your sewing class and manage your time wisely. The keys to making the most of your time in the sewing lab are:

- **Organization** Keep your supplies neat and organized so they will be ready to use when you need them.
- **Preparation** Bring in or gather the required supplies. Before you start to sew, read any instructions carefully.
- **Consideration** When you finish using an item, return it to where it belongs.

Reading Check *Identify* What is the term for two sets of threads that form closely fitted stitches?

Hems

A hem finishes the bottom edge of a shirt, jacket, sleeve, skirt, or pants leg. A **hem** is an edge made by folding fabric over and stitching it down. Hems can be sewn by hand or with a sewing machine. Hems are made in ways that depend on the garment's fabric and design. The most common way to make a hem is to turn the raw, or unfinished, edge of fabric to the inside of the garment and stitch it in place. A good introduction to using a sewing machine is to practice making hems. The steps on page 376 explain how to make a hem. You will learn much more about other sewing machine functions in the next chapter.

Sewing in Class When you are in your sewing class, you need to share equipment and supplies. *Why is it so important to be organized?*

Blend Images/Alamy

Basic Sewing Machine Stitches

In this activity you will learn to use a sewing machine for four basic stitches. Before you begin, read through the entire Hands-On Lab assignment. Write down any questions that you have about the activity. Reread the text or ask your teacher for help if you need it.

Supplies

✓ Sewing machine
✓ Operating manual
✓ Thread
✓ Scissors
✓ Fabric scraps

Develop Your Plan

- Review the sewing machine operating manual.
- Practice making four basic stitches.

Implement Your Plan

- Follow the instructions in the operating manual to wind your thread from your spool onto the bobbin.
- After you thread the bobbin, insert it in the bobbin case.
- Follow the instructions in the operating manual to thread the machine.

Projects and Activities Go to connected.mcgraw-hill.com.

- Use a separate fabric scrap to make each of the four basic stitches:

Regular Stitch A medium-length stitch used for sewing most projects.

Basting Stitch A very long stitch used for holding layers of fabric together temporarily.

Reinforcement Stitch A short stitch used to strengthen a corner or a point.

Zigzag Stitch A sideways stitch used to make buttonholes, finish seam edges, and sew special seams.

Evaluate Your Results

Did you have trouble with any of the stitches? Review the operating manual to find out what you can do to correct any problems you had. Compare your stitch samples with your classmates. How are they the same or different? Write one or more paragraphs to describe your experience.

Step 1 Use a seam ripper to remove the thread in the old hem. Press out the hem crease.

Step 2 Put on the garment to determine the new hem length. Place pins every 2 to 4 inches (5–10 cm) around the hemline.

Step 3 Fold the hem to the new length, and pin it in place. Double-check the length to make sure that it is even.

Step 4 Take off the garment. Using a sewing gauge or a ruler, mark the proper length of the finished hem with pins or chalk.

Step 5 Trim away the excess fabric along the markings. Lightly press the fold of the hem.

Step 6 The raw edge can be pinked, zigzag stitched, edge-stitched, or overlapped with hem tape to prevent raveling.

Step 7 Stitch the edge of the hem, making sure the stitches do not show on the outside. Keep the stitches loose so the hemline does not pucker.

Step 8 Carefully press the hem.

Section 17.1 After You Read

Review What You Have Learned

1. **Name** three keys to making the most of the time in your sewing class.
2. **Explain** why you should use loose stitches when sewing a hem.

Practice Academic Skills

English Language Arts

3. Go to a library or a fabric store, or get permission to go online to find instructions for sewing projects. Find a project designed for beginners and a project designed for people with advanced sewing experience. What conclusions can you draw by comparing instructions from the two projects?

Social Studies

4. Research the typical clothes of a group of people in American history before 1950, such as a Native American population or an immigrant population. How did families obtain clothing during that time? What materials and techniques were used? Write a summary of your findings in a brief report.

Check Your Answers Check Your Answers at connected.mcgraw-hill.com.

Section 17.2 Patterns, Fabrics, and Notions

Reading Guide

Before You Read

Prepare with a Partner Work with a partner. Read the heads and ask each other questions about the topics that will be discussed. Write down the questions you both have about each section. As you read, help each other answer those questions.

Read to Learn

Key Concepts

- ✓ **List** the factors you need to consider before choosing a pattern.
- ✓ **Explain** how to determine the kind of fabric you need.
- ✓ **Identify** commonly used notions.

Main Idea

Before beginning a sewing project, learn about the basics of pattern selection, fabric selection, and choosing notions.

Content Vocabulary

- ○ pattern
- ○ notions
- ○ ravel
- ○ nap
- ○ interfacing

Academic Vocabulary

- ■ dart
- ■ reinforce

Graphic Organizer

As you read, compare and contrast the ways to take measurement for male and female clothing styles. Use a graphic organizer like the one shown to help you organize your information.

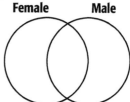

Female   Male

🖋 **Graphic Organizer** Go to connected. mcgraw-hill.com to download this graphic organizer.

Wouldn't it be nice to just be able to sit down at the sewing machine and start sewing? Unfortunately, it is not quite that easy. As with almost every project you want to complete, there are steps that need to be taken to get you to the finished product. In addition to learning basic sewing skills, you need to choose the right pattern, the right fabric, and the right tools.

Connect Like any
project, you need the
right tools to get the
job done. Other than a
sewing machine, what
tools do you think you
will need to start a
sewing project?

 **Vocabulary**

You can find
definitions in the
glossary at the back
of this book.

Pattern Selection

Most sewing projects call for a pattern. A **pattern** is a plan
for making a garment or project. It contains paper shapes of
the various pieces and gives the instructions for sewing. Your
success in completing your project depends in part on the
pattern you choose.

When you choose a pattern, you will want one that
matches your abilities and the time you have to complete the
project. Before you choose a pattern, consider the following:

- **Purpose** Do you want to make clothing for yourself,
  something for your room, or a specialty item, such as
  a backpack or a purse?
- **Sewing Skills and Experience** If you have never
  worked on a project before, choose a simple pattern.
  Many patterns are designed especially for beginners.
- **Time** Do you have enough time to complete the
  project? This is especially important if you are sewing
  at school and sharing a sewing machine.
- **Cost** How much money are you willing to spend?

These factors can help you choose the best pattern for
your needs. When you find a pattern that you like in the fabric
store catalog or display, make a note of the brand name and
pattern number. Then you can find and read the pattern
envelope for more information.

Pattern Selection Choose a pattern that matches your skill level, time
frame, and budget. *Why is it so important to choose a pattern carefully?*

The Pattern Envelope

The pattern envelope provides you with the information you need to plan a sewing project. The front of the envelope shows a picture of the completed project. Sometimes more than one view is shown. For example, a shirt pattern may show one view with short sleeves and another with long sleeves. On the back of the envelope, you will find the following:

- A drawing showing the pattern pieces and construction features, such as design details, seams, and darts. A **dart** is a tapered, V-shaped seam used to give shape to the garment.
- A chart that tells you how much fabric to buy for the view and size pattern you are using.
- Recommendations for which fabrics to use.
- Additional materials you will need, such as thread and buttons. These are called **notions**.

Pattern Choice

How can you find an appropriate pattern for your first project? Pattern books indicate which patterns are simple to sew and even have special sections for quick and easy projects. In addition, look for these features to help you choose an easy-to-make pattern:

- **Number of Pattern Pieces** Fewer pattern pieces mean fewer pieces of fabric to cut out and stitch.
- **Number of Seams** Seams join two pieces of fabric together. The fewer seams involved, the easier it will be to complete the pattern.
- **Garment Fit** Loose-fitting styles are easier to sew than close-fitting styles.
- **Closures** Elastic waists require less advanced sewing skills than do zippers and buttonholes.

Pattern Size

Patterns, like ready-to-wear clothing, come in different sizes. Pattern sizes are based on five measurements. For females, measure the sleeve, bust, back waist length, waist, and hips.

For males, measure the sleeve, neck, chest, waist, and hips. See **Figure 17.2** to learn how to take these measurements. When taking measurements, be sure that the measuring tape is held parallel to the floor. Never stretch the measuring tape.

Compare your measurements to the measurements on the pattern envelope. Choose the size that has the closest measurements. Use the following guidelines to decide which measurement is most important for a particular type of garment:

- For blouses and tops, fit the bust measurement.
- For shirts, fit the chest and neck measurements.
- For full skirts, fit the waist measurement.
- For pants and semi-fitted skirts, fit the hip measurement.

Reading Check   *Recall*   *What information can you find on the back of a pattern envelope?*

Figure 17.2   Taking Your Measurements

Accuracy is the Key Choose your pattern size by your actual measurements, not by the size you wear when you buy clothes. *What should you do if your measurements fall between two sizes on the pattern envelope?*

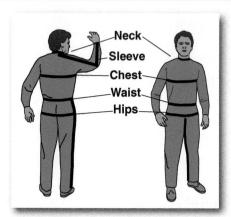

Measurements for Males

Sleeve Bend the arm up, then measure from the base of the neck to the elbow and up over the wrist bone.

Neck Measure around the base of the neck and add ½ inch (1.3 cm).

Chest Measure around the fullest part of the chest.

Waist Measure around the natural waistline over a shirt, but not over pants.

Hips Measure around the fullest part of the hips.

Measurements for Females

Sleeve Measure from the top of the shoulder over the bent elbow to the wrist.

Bust Measure around the fullest part of the bust, continue under the arms and straight across the back.

Back Waist Length Measure from the base of the neck to the waistline.

Waist Measure around the natural waistline.

Hips Measure around the fullest part of the hips.

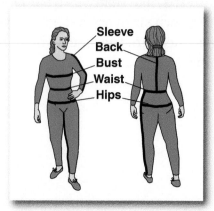

Build a Sewing Kit

To complete any sewing project successfully, you need the right tools. Experience and the types of projects you choose will determine the exact items you need. The items shown on this page represent some basic tools you will probably use for almost every project. These tools are a good start toward building your sewing kit.

Shears, Scissors, and Pinking Shears Shears are large scissors that often have a raised handle for easier cutting. Scissors are used for trimming, clipping, and cutting threads. Pinking shears are scissors that zigzag the edge.

Sewing Gauge A sewing gauge ('gāj) is a 6-inch (16-cm) ruler with an adjustable pointer. It is used to measure short spaces, such as hems and seam widths.

Needles and Thread Needles are used for hand sewing. Select thread color that matches your fabric.

Pins and Pincushion Dressmaker pins are slender, sharp-pointed, and rust proof.

Seam Ripper This pen-shaped tool has a small, hook-like blade at one end for removing stitches.

Tape Measure A flexible tape is used to take body measurements.

Thimble A thimble protects your finger while you are hand sewing. It makes it easier to push the needle through the fabric.

Choosing Fabrics

Fabrics come in many different colors, textures, designs, and finishes. You need to evaluate the fiber content, how the fabric is made, and any finishes that have been added. When choosing a fabric, ask yourself these questions:

How much sewing experience do I have? Select fabrics that are easy to sew for your first few projects.

Who will use the item? When making something for yourself, look for colors that can be mixed and matched with other clothes you own.

When will I use the item? The time of day and the season the item will be used may affect the type of fabric you choose.

How will I use the item? When making a non-clothing item such as a tote bag, a dark-colored fabric that does not show dirt is a good choice.

What type of care is needed? Look for fabrics that are machine washable and that require little or no ironing.

Some fabrics are challenging. Lightweight and extremely soft fabrics can be slippery and hard to sew. Plaids, stripes, and large prints need to be matched at the seams and may require extra fabric. Loosely woven fabrics tend to **ravel**, which is when loose threads pull out of the cut edge. Fabrics such as corduroy have a one-way texture called **nap**. Napped fabrics require special instructions.

Discover International...
Fabric

Indian Textiles

India has a rich and diverse textile tradition. A textile is a cloth or fabric made from raw materials. The origin of Indian textiles can be traced to the people of the Indus valley civilization, where cotton and silk were handwoven for garments. The ancient Indian epic, *Ramayana*, refers to elaborate garments worn by royalty, and simple garments worn by commoners. Indian silk and cotton were traded around the world in ancient times. Fragments of Indian textiles have been found in Rome, Egypt, China, and Indonesia as far back as the 13th century. Muslin, a thin cotton material, and chintz, a shiny cotton cloth often printed with a flower pattern, were especially popular and remain so today.

Muslin |'məz-lən| a thin plain-weave cotton cloth, used to make clothing, curtains, and sheets.

Erica Simone Leeds

Selecting Quality Fabrics

When you shop for fabrics, you will notice that they come in many price categories. How can you tell which ones are high quality? Keep in mind that you do not have to buy the most expensive one to get a good fabric. Quality is not determined by cost alone. Like ready-to-wear clothing, fabrics can be made by brand-name designers and cost more because of the name. When judging quality in fabrics, examine the following:

- **Crosswise Threads** They should be straight and at right angles to the lengthwise threads. This means the fabric is on grain.
- **Pattern** Make sure that a printed pattern runs straight with the grain. If the fabric is not printed properly, the garment will look off-grain.
- **Weave** The weave should be firm and durable.
- **Color** All colors should be consistent.
- **Finish** The finish should feel comfortable and pleasing to the touch.
- **Label** Read the label on the end of the bolt of fabric. It gives facts about fabric width, fiber content, finishes, shrinkage, and care instructions.

Reading Check   *Judge* *Should you buy the most expensive fabric for quality? Why or why not?*

Care Instructions
When choosing fabrics, check the fiber content and care instructions listed on the end of the fabric bolt. *What is the benefit of choosing fabric with easy care instructions?*

©John Lund/Marc Romanelli/Blend Images LLC

Thread Color One of the most essential notions is thread, which comes in many types and colors. *How would you choose a thread color for a print or plaid fabric?*

Notions

After you have chosen a fabric, refer to the back of the pattern envelope for a list of the type of notions you will need. In addition to sewing tools, you will need notions to complete the project. Notions are the small items that become a permanent part of the finished product. Choose notions carefully, making sure the colors look good with the fabric you will use. Also, choose buttons, tapes, trims, and interfacings that require the same care as the fabric. For example, a cotton shirt cannot be machine washed if its trim can only be dry cleaned. Here are some basic notions necessary for many types of sewing projects:

- **Thread** Choose thread to match your fabric color. Thread should be the same color as the fabric or slightly darker because it will appear lighter when stitched. Fabric type determines the thread you need. You can find this information on the pattern envelope. A good quality thread is strong and smooth, has even thickness, and resists tangling.
- **Fasteners** There are many types of fasteners to choose from. They are used to close a garment. Some are designed to be almost invisible, such as snaps, and zippers that are sewn into a seam. Others can be functional as well as decorative, such as buttons, buckles, and hook-and-eye closures.
- **Tapes and Trims** Like fasteners, tapes and trims can be functional or decorative. Tapes and trims cover fabric edges and reinforce, or strengthen seams. They can also be used to create a design on the outside of a garment. They can be woven, knitted, braided, or made of lace. You can match trims to your fabric, or create contrast with a different color or texture.

- **Elastic** Your choice of elastic depends on whether it will be used in a casing, which you will learn about in the next chapter, or stitched directly to the garment. The pattern envelope will describe what kind of elastic may be needed.
- **Linings and Interfacings** Fabrics used on the inside of the garment are linings and interfacings. A lining is fabric used to finish the inside of a jacket, coat, skirt, dress or pants. Linings can be visible, so choose a color to match or contrast with the outside fabric. Fabric **interfacing** is placed between two pieces of fabric to prevent stretching around necklines, closures, and buttonholes. Unlike a lining, it will not be visible in the finished garment. Interfacing adds shape to collars, cuffs, pockets, and hems.

Safety Check

Sewing Equipment
Follow these safety rules when learning how to use the supplies and equipment in the sewing lab:

- Keep your fingers away from the path of the needle.
- Do not attempt to use the machine if it is jammed or making an unusual noise.
- Do not hold pins or needles in your mouth. Use a pin cushion.
- Keep scissors closed when not in use.

Section 17.2 After You Read

Review What You Have Learned

1. **Identify** the features that will help you choose an easy-to-make pattern.
2. **List** the most important qualities to consider when choosing fabric.
3. **Describe** a good quality thread.

Practice Academic Skills

English Language Arts

4. Imagine that you will soon attend a wedding or a family reunion, or go on a vacation. What special outfit would you like to make? Using information from pattern catalogs, pattern envelopes, and this book, make a list of the fabric, equipment, tools, and notions you would need to complete your special outfit. Present your list in the form of a "how to" report.

Social Studies

5. Cultural heritage can be displayed in fabrics. Some fabric designs and weaves are unique to certain cultures, such as Navajo rugs and blankets. Gather three or more samples of cultural fabrics. Use actual fabric if possible. If not, find images you can copy or print. Create a poster with the samples, and include information about the country of origin and the uses for the fabric.

Check Your Answers Check Your Answers at connected.mcgraw-hill.com.

Discovering Careers

Do you like to work with your hands? Do you have an eye for fabric and for creating actual clothes? If you answered yes to either of those questions, you might want to consider a future career in sewing. The following chart explores several careers in the sewing industry.

Job Title	Job Description
Alterations Specialist	Alters clothing to fit individual customers. Repairs garments as requested by customers. Remakes old garments into new styles.
Machine Operator	Creates fibers, yarns, and fabrics by spinning, weaving, knitting, printing, and dyeing. Oversees multiple machines that treat tanks, dye jigs, and vats.
Pattern-maker	Translates sample garments into paper patterns. Increases and decreases the size of all pattern pieces to correspond to garment sizes.
Apparel Stylist	Creates adaptations of designer originals. Produces fashionable, yet affordable clothing. Makes garments that fit the image of a company or clothing line.
Sewing Instructor	Teach basic sewing techniques. Help those who need advanced help with special projects. Motivate students with the possibilities of sewing.

Career Activities ▼

At School

1 Select three of the careers listed. Research the education, training, and work experience required for each career. Write a summary of your results.

At Home

2 Go through your closet to find clothing that needs repairs. Ask your family members if they have clothing that needs repairs. Make a list of the repairs and explain how you would make the repairs.

At Work

3 List five examples of how fabrics are used in a workplace. Compare lists with your classmates.

In the Community

4 Contact and interview someone in your community who works in the sewing industry. Ask this person to describe what his or her typical work day is like. Share what you learned with your class.

Chapter Summary

Section 17.1 Sewing Machine Basics
The keys to making the most of your time in the sewing classroom are organization, preparation, and consideration. Sewing machines all operate in the same way. A needle moves up and down through the fabric, and two sets of threads interlock to form stitches. A good introduction to using a sewing machine is to practice making hems. A hem finishes the bottom edges of sewn projects. Hems can be sewn by hand or with a sewing machine.

Section 17.2 Patterns, Fabrics, and Notions
Patterns, fabrics, and notions are essential for getting started on sewing projects. Choose a pattern to match your abilities and the time you have to complete the project. Quality fabric does not have to be expensive. When selecting fabric, use the information on your pattern envelope to find out what kind and how much fabric you will need. After you have chosen a fabric, refer to the back of the pattern envelope for a list of the type of notions you will need.

Words You Learned

1. Create multiple–choice test questions for each content and academic vocabulary word.

Content Vocabulary
- interlock (p. 373)
- hem (p. 374)
- pattern (p. 378)
- notions (p. 379)
- ravel (p. 382)
- nap (p. 382)
- interfacing (p. 385)

Academic Vocabulary
- operate (p. 373)
- raw (p. 374)
- dart (p. 379)
- reinforce (p. 384)

Review Key Concepts

2. **Describe** the main functions all sewing machines have in common.

3. **Explain** how a hem is created.

4. **List** the factors you need to consider before choosing a pattern.

5. **Explain** how to determine the kind of fabric you need.

6. **Identify** commonly used notions.

Critical Thinking

7. **Analyze** this scenario. Christa says to you, "There is no reason I should learn how to sew." Why do you think she would say this? How would you respond?

8. **Predict** what might happen if a beginning sewing student ignores the recommendation on a pattern envelope to use knit fabric.

9. **Describe** how you could alter a garment in your closet to change its look.

Real-World Skills and Applications

Problem-Solving

10. Help for Beginners Sewing can be an intimidating task for someone who has never sewn before. Look through pattern catalogs and select patterns that beginners might use. Identify which features make patterns easy to follow.

Interpersonal and Collaborative

11. Project Management Follow your teacher's directions to form small groups. Work with your group to write a timeline for a long-term project you might work on in class. When will you work on the project? What tasks can you realistically accomplish each time you meet? Who will be responsible for each task? What will you do if someone misses a class? What supplies and resources will you need? Present your information to the class.

Financial Literacy

12. Estimate Costs Imagine that you are going to make two shirts from the same pattern. Research the prices of the pattern, fabric, notions, and any other supplies and materials you will need to complete the project. Using spreadsheet software or a worksheet, make a table presenting these costs. Label four columns with the names *Item, Price, Quantity,* and *Cost.* List one item per row, such as buttons in the first row, thread in the next row, and so on. Show a grand total of all the costs at the bottom of the table. Compare your results to the cost of buying two similar shirts at a clothing store. Which is the better value for your money? Present your information along with a summary to explain the better value.

13. Fabric Guide Cut out small samples of different types of fabrics. Arrange the fabric samples in a scrapbook or photo album and add descriptive captions. Organize the fabric in a way that is meaningful for you. For example, arrange by texture, color, cultural significance, or type of weave. Add more samples as you discover new fabrics you like to use when sewing.

14. Home Decorating Visit a fabric store and select a pattern for a home furnishings project. Note the recommended fabrics listed on the pattern envelope. Look around the store for fabrics suitable for home decorating. What types of fibers, fabrics, and trims are most common? How are they different from fabrics used for clothing? Summarize your findings in a report to present to your class.

15. Sewing Ideas With permission from your parents or teacher, go online to search for information that can help you learn about different ways to apply sewing techniques, such as how to customize a pattern, how to make stuffed animals, or how to alter something you already own. Choose a project that you find especially interesting. Make a list of the supplies you would need to complete it, and a list of the skills you would need to learn. Include the information in your Life Skills Binder.

Academic Skills

English Language Arts

16. Personal Style When you know how to sew your own clothes, you have freedom to experiment with colors and fabric. Write a one-page journal entry to describe your personal clothing style. Include descriptions of the projects you would like to make that reflect your style.

Science

17. Modern Technology The first sewing machines were operated by a hand-crank. Today, sewing machines are run by computers that do much of the work for you.
Procedure Consider how the modern sewing machine compares to the earliest sewing machines.
Analysis Choose one function of a modern sewing machine, and use these questions to evaluate the function: 1. Is the function necessary? 2. Does it make me less creative? 3. Does it help me make higher quality projects?

Mathematics

18. Estimate Jackson is taking a summer class in clothing construction, and he is planning to make a shirt for his first project. He found a good pattern for $6.98. The project requires 2½ yards of fabric that will cost $10.90. The matching thread costs $2.95, and the buttons he picked out are $8.10. He also needs to add interfacing for $2.60. Use this information to estimate the total amount Jackson needs to make the shirt.

Math Concept **Estimation Using Compatible Numbers** You can perform calculations quickly without using a calculator by replacing decimals with their closest compatible numbers.

Starting Hint Round each dollar amount to the nearest whole dollar by dropping the decimal portion. If the number to the right of the decimal point is 5 or greater, add 1 to the dollar amount.

Standardized Test Practice

Multiple-Choice

Read the sentence. Then read the question below the sentence. Read the answer choices below each question and choose the best answer to fill in the blank.

Test-Taking Tip In a multiple choice test, read the question before you read the answer choices. Try to answer the question before you read the answer choices. This way, the answer choices will not confuse you.

19. By returning the scissors to the teacher's desk, John showed consideration for his classmates. In this sentence, the word consideration means _____.
  a. thoughtfulness
  b. sympathy
  c. disrespect
  d. attention

Chapter 18

Learn How to Sew

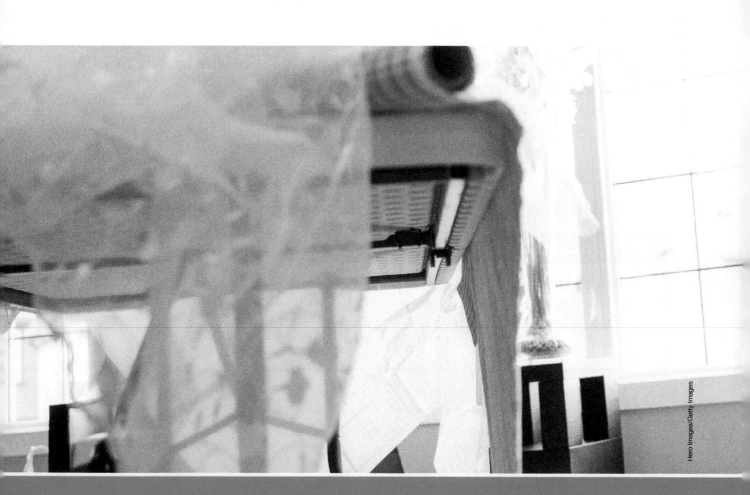

Hero Images/Getty Images

Explore the Photo

Planning is an important step in any successful sewing project. *What actions do you think you should take before you begin sewing?*

Potapova Valerya/Getty Images

Cause and Effect

How Did It Go? A cause is an event or action that makes something happen or not happen. An effect is the result of a cause. Ask, "Why did this happen?" to help you recognize cause-and-effect relationships. Write a paragraph about the results of a recent project or assignment you completed. What caused you to achieve your results?

Writing Tips To write an effective cause-and-effect paragraph, follow these steps:

1. Focus on how the cause created a specific effect.

2. Write a clear thesis statement, and be sure to include an introduction and conclusion.

3. Use transitional words, such as therefore, because, or so, between the cause and the effect.

Section 18.1 Fabric and Pattern Preparation

Reading Guide

Before You Read

Predict Read all of the headings in this section. Think about what the headings mean. Predict what you think the section will be about.

Read to Learn
Key Concepts

✓ **Explain** why fabric preparation is important.

✓ **Outline** the steps in pattern preparation.

Main Idea

A successful sewing project includes planning and preparation.

Content Vocabulary

○ selvage
○ bias
○ guide sheet
○ layout
○ marking
○ ease

Academic Vocabulary

■ determine
■ transfer

Graphic Organizer

As you read, identify five steps you would take in preparing to sew. Use a graphic organizer like the one shown to help you organize your information.

Preparing to Sew
1.
2.
3.
4.
5.

 **Graphic Organizer** Go to connectED. mcgraw-hill.com to download this graphic organizer.

Many people enjoy sewing. Sewing gives you the chance to use patterns and your own creativity to create your own clothing and home fashions. If you have not sewn before, the information in this section can help make your sewing projects successful. You will learn how to prepare your fabric and pattern for sewing. These are important first steps in any sewing project.

Fabric Preparation

It is important to take the time to preshrink your fabric. Some fabrics will not shrink, while others may. Launder the fabric as directed. Cleaning instructions are located on the end of the bolt of fabric. Once the fabric is preshrunk, press it to get rid of wrinkles.

Check the Grain

After you have preshrunk the fabric, you need to check the fabric grain. The fabric grain is the direction that the yarns run in woven fabric. **Figure 18.1** shows where to find the selvages, grains, and bias on a piece of fabric and explains how to check the grain. The **selvage** is the tightly woven edge of the fabric that has no visible loose threads. Raw edges are the unfinished edges of the fabric. You can straighten the fabric by folding it on the true **bias**, or diagonal.

> **Reading Check** *Explain* *Why should you prepare fabric before sewing?*

As You Read

Connect Think about the steps you take before you begin a sewing project. What other things do you do in which you create a plan of action?

◆ Vocabulary

You can find definitions in the glossary at the back of this book.

Figure 18.1 Finding the Grain

Take Time It is important for the lengthwise and crosswise threads in fabrics to meet at right angles when you sew. *What might happen if you forget to align the fabric grain before you sew?*

Labels: Lengthwise grain · True bias · Crosswise grain · Selvage · Selvage

To test the grain, fold the fabric lengthwise so that the selvages are on top of one another. If the raw edges do not line up, do the following:

- For woven fabrics, clip the selvage and pull a crosswise thread. Cut along the line made by the pulled thread.
- For knitted fabrics, cut along one crosswise row of loops to straighten the edges.

Test the grain again by folding your fabric and matching selvages.

- If the crosswise ends match exactly and are at right angles to the selvage, the fabric is straight. The fold will be smooth and unwrinkled.
- If the edges do not match, the fabric is not straight. If cut that way, the finished garment will twist or hang crooked.

Pattern Preparation

Study the guide sheet inside your pattern envelope before you begin sewing. A **guide sheet** is a set of step-by-step instructions for sewing a pattern. The guide sheet, as shown in the photo, contains information on how to use the pattern, a diagram of the pattern pieces, an explanation of the pattern markings, and layouts. **Layouts** are diagrams of how the pattern pieces should be placed on the fabric.

After you have read through the guide sheet, you are ready to prepare the pattern pieces. **Figure 18.2** shows how to prepare pattern pieces and understand markings. **Markings** are symbols located on the pattern pieces.

Pattern Guide Sheets

Follow these steps to use a pattern guide sheet:

- Study the diagram of the pattern pieces.
- Circle the letters of the pieces needed for the garment that you plan to make.
- Circle the layout diagram that you will use for your size and style.
- Read through all of the pattern directions before you start to work.

To prepare your pattern pieces, cut apart the pieces you will use, but do not trim them. You will cut off the margins later, when you cut the fabric. Study each pattern piece, and refer to the guide sheet to find out what each marking means. If the pattern pieces are wrinkled, press them with a warm, dry iron.

Organization Skills
Arrange Your Papers Choose one place to put your papers for each subject. Create color-coded folders for each class. Arrange your papers in time order. Place assignments that are due first on top.

Pattern Guide Sheets Patterns show you how to put your project together. *What might happen if you do not read the entire pattern guide sheet before you sew?*

Vico Collective/Alamy

Figure (**18.2**) **Pattern Markings**

Marked Guides Pattern markings guide you throughout a sewing project. *What might happen if you did not follow the pattern markings?*

Dots are points matched for accuracy. If a shirt pattern shows a dot at the center of the back and a dot at the center of the collar pieces, match these dots to make the collar fit correctly.

Notches are v-shaped markings on cutting lines that show which seams are matched and stitched together to join seams evenly.

Place on folds are thin single lines on straight edges that mean to place the pattern on fabric fold. Do not cut on the fold line.

Adjustment lines are parallel lines that show where patterns can be lengthened or shortened.

Grain lines are double-pointed arrows that show pattern placement on the straight grain of the fabric.

Cutting lines are heavy lines, scissors symbols, or double lines along the pattern edge that show where to cut.

Stitching lines are broken or dotted lines that indicate stitching lines. These are usually 5/8 inches (1.5 cm) inside the cutting lines and are often marked by a presser foot symbol or by arrows. These symbols show the direction to stitch fabric.

Darts are broken lines that indicate stitching lines. Solid lines show where to fold.

Check Pattern Measurements

Before you place the pattern pieces on the fabric, you need to make sure that the pattern you selected fits your body. To do that, compare your measurements with the body measurements listed on the pattern envelope. If you need to make any alterations, or changes to the pattern to make the garment fit, do it before you cut the fabric.

Length Adjustments

Use the two parallel lines labeled lengthen or shorten. Your teacher can show you how to do this. Be sure to make the same changes on both the front and back pieces of the pattern.

Width Adjustments

Determine, or figure out, how much ease is included in the pattern. **Ease** is the amount of fullness added for movement and comfort. The amount of ease depends on the stress that will be put on that part of the garment when it is worn. Your teacher can show you how to adjust the amount of ease.

Reading Check   *Explain*   *Why are pattern changes sometimes needed?*

Pin the Pattern

Look at the layout on the guide sheet to see how to fold your fabric. Most layouts show the right sides of the fabric folded together. Lay the pattern pieces on top of the fabric. The lengthwise grain markings must be parallel to the selvage. Check them with a ruler as you pin. Do not cut out any pieces until they have all been pinned in place. Follow these steps to pin your pattern:

Step 1   Pin the large pattern pieces that belong on the fold.

Step 2   Pin the pattern pieces that have a grain-line arrow. To check the grain line, place a pin at one end of the grain-line arrow. Measure from the arrow to the selvage of the fabric edge. Position the pattern so that the other end of the arrow is exactly the same distance from the edge. Then pin the piece in place.

Step 3   Place the pins diagonally inside the cutting line. This keeps the fabric flat and makes it easier to cut.

Step 4   Place pins about 2 inches (5 cm) apart.

Step 5   Double-check your pinned layout against the layout on the pattern guide sheet.

Cut Out the Pattern

It will be easier to sew straight seams if you cut the edges of the fabric evenly. Follow these steps to cut out your pinned pattern:

Step 1   Place the fabric flat on the table. Use one hand to hold the fabric in place and the other hand to cut.

Step 2   Cut with long, even strokes.

Step 3   Cut in the direction of the arrows printed on the pattern's seamline. In this way, you will be cutting with the fabric grain, and you will not stretch the fabric.

Step 4   Cut around the outside of each notch. Cut double and triple notches together with one long edge across the top.

Step 5   Leave the pattern pieces pinned to the fabric until you are ready to stitch that piece.

JUPITERIMAGES/Creatas/Alamy

Cutting Patterns
Before you cut out your project, practice cutting fabric scraps. *Why are clean edges on the fabric pieces important?*

Transfer Markings

After you cut out your pattern, transfer, or move, the markings from the pattern to the fabric. Markings must be visible as you sew, but they should never show on the outside of a finished garment. The lines and symbols on pattern pieces are important guides during construction. Markings include darts, pleats, tucks, dots, fold lines, and buttonholes. Hemlines need not be marked. Different marking methods may be used for different fabrics and types of marks. These include tailor's chalk, tracing paper, air-soluble pens, and water-soluble marking pens. When transferring markings:

- Always test your marking device on a fabric scrap to make sure the marks come out of the fabric completely.
- When using a tracing wheel and paper, choose a color of tracing paper that will show up on the fabric.
- Mark dots with an X.
- Mark the ends of darts with a short line.
- Mark each seamline so that you will know exactly where to stitch.

Section 18.1 After You Read

Review What You Have Learned

1. **Identify** reasons why pattern preparation is important.
2. **Name** five steps you would take in planning to sew.

Practice Academic Skills

English Language Arts

3. Write a detailed paragraph that discusses why fabric preparation is important.

Social Studies

4. Many fleece and wool garments are made in Peru because of the animals in the region, such as sheep, llamas, and alpacas. Conduct research to find three other types of contemporary or historical fabrics. List the geographic region and the types of garments or objects made from the fabric.

Check Your Answers Check Your Answers at connectED.mcgraw-hill.com.

Section 18.2 Sewing and Serging Basics

Reading Guide

Before You Read

Preview Choose a content or academic vocabulary word that is new to you. When you find it in the text, write down the definition.

Read to Learn

Key Concepts

✓ **List** ten basic sewing techniques.

✓ **Describe** what a serger does.

Main Idea

Sewing and serging skills allow you to achieve a professional quality in your sewing projects.

Content Vocabulary

○ staystitch
○ feed dog
○ casing
○ sew-through button

○ shank button
○ cone
○ looper
○ tail chain

Academic Vocabulary

■ result
■ product

Graphic Organizer

As you read, list the ten basic sewing techniques described in this section. Use a chart like the one shown below to help organize your information.

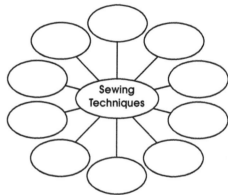

Sewing Techniques

Graphic Organizer Go to connectED. mcgraw-hill.com to download this graphic organizer.

Sewing machines have come a long way since they were first introduced for home use in the late 19th century. Today's sewing machines are computerized. They can do all the traditional stitches, and some models can even embroider your own design onto a garment. This section will introduce you to basic sewing machine techniques, and you will become familiar with the parts and functions of an overlock machine, also called a serger.

Beginning to Sew

When you make a garment, the first step is to staystitch the seams. A **staystitch** is a row of stitching made very near the seamline within the seam allowance. Staystitching, as shown in **Figure 18.3**, prevents stretching and helps in turning under edges of hems and bands.

Stitch Straight Seams

You will sew most projects together by stitching straight seams. To sew a seam, place two pieces of fabric right sides together. Line up the edges so that they are even. Match all markings and notches, and pin the two pieces together. The heads of the pins should be near the outside edges of the fabric. For most sewing, pins should be placed about 2 inches (5 cm) apart. Now look at the throat plate on your sewing machine. The line markings show how far the needle is from the seam edge. Most seams are 5/8 inch (1.5 cm) wide. Find the line on the machine that is 5/8 inch (1.5 cm) from the needle. Keep the fabric edge against this mark as you sew and your seam will be straight. As you stitch, guide the fabric with both hands, but do not push it. The feed dog will move the fabric as you sew. The **feed dogs** are the parts of the machine that position the fabric for the next stitch. Operate the machine at a slow, even speed. Backstitch 2–3 stitches at the beginning and end of the seam.

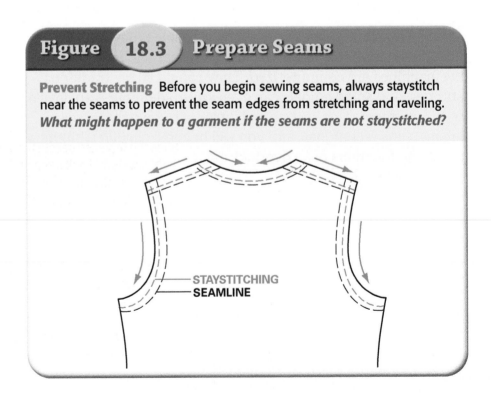

Figure 18.3 Prepare Seams

Prevent Stretching Before you begin sewing seams, always staystitch near the seams to prevent the seam edges from stretching and raveling. *What might happen to a garment if the seams are not staystitched?*

STAYSTITCHING
SEAMLINE

Sew by Hand

Some sewing must be done by hand. Hand sewing gives you more control than you have using a sewing machine or serger. Try these basic stitches.

Basting Stitch The basting stitch is a temporary stitch used to hold fabrics together for fittings and for matching plaids and seams. To baste, pin fabric layers together and use even stitches.

Slipstitch The slipstitch provides an almost invisible finish. Slipstitching is used on patch pockets, hems, linings, and trims. Slide the needle in one folded edge and out, picking up a thread of the under layer.

Hem Stitch This stitch finishes different hems, especially those with seam binding or a folded edge. A hem stitch is made by taking a tiny stitch in the garment, then bringing the needle diagonally through the hem edge.

Blanket Stitch The blanket stitch can be used as a decorative edge finish and as thread loops, eyes, belt carriers, bar tacks, and French tacks. Stick the threaded needle through the right side of the fabric and pull it out at the edge. Keep the thread from the previous stitch under the needle point, pulling the needle and thread through and over the edge.

Backstitch As one of the strongest stitches, backstitches repair machine-stitched seams and fasten thread ends securely. The backstitch is made by carrying the thread back half the length of the preceding stitch. Bring the needle through to the underside of the fabric. Insert the needle back at the beginning of the first stitch, and bring it out again one stitch length in front of the thread.

Stitch Curved Seams

With curved seams, you must guide the fabric with your hands so that the curves are smooth. You also need to keep the stitching an even distance from the edge of the fabric. The best way to learn how to sew curved seams is to practice. Start by stitching curves on a piece of paper. Then practice on scraps of fabric.

Turn Corners

Learning how to turn corners, or pivot, is another skill that takes practice. When turning a corner, follow these steps:

Step 1 Slow down the sewing machine when you come to a corner.

Step 2 Lift the presser foot. Turn the fabric, with the needle still in it. Put the presser foot back down again and stitch the next side. This keeps the sewing line straight and the corner sharp.

Add Seam Finishes

After stitching your project, you may need to add a seam finish. Seam finishes are treatments used on the seam edges to prevent fabric from raveling. The most effective seam finish depends on the type of fabric being used. If the fabric ravels only slightly, pink the edges with pinking shears. For greater protection against raveling, stitch ¼ inch (6 mm) from each edge before pinking. If your fabric ravels easily, use a zigzag finish. Some fabrics do not ravel and do not need seam finishes.

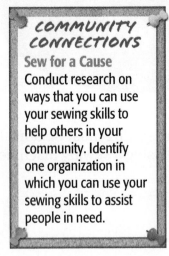

COMMUNITY CONNECTIONS

Sew for a Cause
Conduct research on ways that you can use your sewing skills to help others in your community. Identify one organization in which you can use your sewing skills to assist people in need.

Fabric Placement Keep the fabric edge against the mark on the needle plate as you stitch.
Why should you practice stitches on fabric scraps before you begin sewing?

Tetra Images/Getty Images

Make Darts

Darts are used to help shape fabric to the curves of the body. They are usually found at the bustline, waistline, elbow, or back of the shoulder. For darts to create the right effect, they must have the correct width and shape. Make sure that they are accurately marked, folded, and pinned before you stitch them.

Gather Fabric

When you need to fit a longer piece of fabric to a shorter one, you can gather the longer piece of fabric. For example, you might use gathering at the tops of sleeves or at the waist of a full skirt.

Ease Fabric

When one piece of fabric is only slightly longer than the piece that it will join, easing is used. Easing creates a slight fullness. To ease fabric, you need to pin it before you stitch the seam. Place the fabric right sides together, matching the notches and ends. Pin every ½ inch (1.3 cm). When you stitch, place the longer piece of fabric on top and gently ease in the extra fullness. An eased seam should look smooth, without puckering.

Make Casings

You may need to sew casings if your garment has a pull-on waistband or sleeve band. **Casings** are fabric tunnels made to enclose elastic or drawstrings. When you draw up the elastic or drawstring, a gathered appearance is created.

Types of Casings

When you sew a casing, make sure that it is ¼ to ½ in. (6 mm– 1.3 cm) wider than the elastic or drawstring it will enclose. This will allow the elastic or drawstring to move freely through the fabric tunnel. The two types of casings are fold-down and applied. A fold-down casing is often used for pull-on pants and skirts. An applied casing is often used at the waistline. To make an applied casing, you need to stitch a separate strip of fabric or bias tape to the garment.

Gathering Two pieces of fabric can be fitted by gathering. *Where would you gather fabric in a garment?*

McGraw-Hill Companies

Make Facings

Facings are used to finish the raw edges of a garment. Facings are sewn around the edges of necklines, armholes, and some waistlines. You stitch facings to the right side of the garment and then turn them to the inside. To achieve a smooth appearance, trim and grade the seam allowance to reduce bulk. **Figure 18.4** shows you how to do this.

Figure 18.4 Adjusting Seams

Reducing Bulk There are four ways to reduce bulk in seams. *Can you identify when you would use each of the four ways of reducing bulk in seams?*

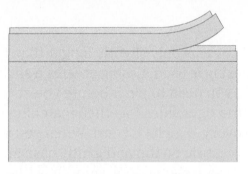

Trimming A seam is trimmed by cutting the seam allowance to 3/8 or ¼ inch (9 or 6 mm). This reduces the bulk of the seam. This is usually done when the seam is enclosed in a collar, cuff, facing, waistband, or set-in sleeve.

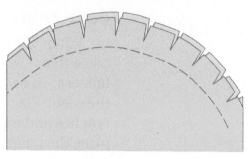

Clipping Curved seams are clipped so that they will lie flat. Slits are cut into the trimmed seam allowance about every ¼ inch to ½ inch (6 mm–1.3 cm). Clip only to within 1/8 inch (3 mm) of the seamline, being careful not to cut through the stitching.

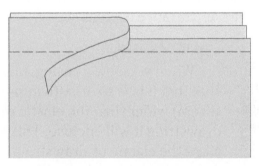

Grading A seam is graded by trimming the seam allowances to different widths. Trim the seam allowance toward the inside of the garment narrower than the outside one. This further reduces the bulk. Grading is often done on seams for facings.

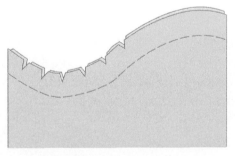

Notching Some curved seams that have too much fabric in the seam allowance may need to be notched. Little Vs or triangles are cut out of the trimmed seam allowance.

Make Drawstring or Pull-On Pants

In this activity you will sew a basic pair of drawstring or pull-on pants using the skills you have learned in this chapter. Before you begin, read through the entire Life Skills Lab assignment. Write down any questions that you may have about the assignment. Reread the text or ask your teacher for help if you need it.

Supplies

✓ Pants pattern of your choice

✓ Cotton fabric such as flannel

✓ Elastic

✓ Thread

Develop Your Plan

■ Choose a basic pants pattern in your size.

■ Acquire the amount of fabric yardage and thread needed.

■ Gather the notions you will need to construct the pants, including scissors, pins, and tape measure.

■ Read through the pattern guide sheet to become familiar with the instructions.

Implement Your Plan

■ Pre-wash, dry, and press your cotton fabric.

■ Circle the correct pattern layout on the pattern guide sheet.

■ Cut out the pattern pieces for your size.

■ Pin the pattern pieces to your fabric according to the pattern layout.

■ Cut out the pattern pieces from your fabric.

■ Transfer markings onto your fabric from the pattern pieces.

■ Wind the bobbin and insert it in the sewing machine. Thread your machine needle.

■ Follow the instructions on the pattern guide sheet to sew your pants.

Evaluate Your Results

What did you learn about pattern layout? Is there anything you would change the next time you make a pair of pants? Write one or more paragraphs to explain your answer.

🖈 **Projects and Activities** Go to connectED.mcgraw-hill.com.

Studiohio/McGraw-Hill Education

Sew on Buttons and Snaps

There are two types of buttons: sew-through and shank. A **sew-through button** has two or four holes through it and no loop on the back. It is used when materials joined need to lie flat. A **shank button** has a stem on the back. Shanks are used with thick fabrics. When you attach a sew-through button, you will need to add a thread shank. **Figure 18.5** shows you how to sew on both types of buttons.

Snaps are used to hold together overlapping edges. The two parts of a snap are the ball half and the socket half. Follow these guidelines when replacing a snap:

- Place the ball half of the snap on the underside of the overlap, far enough from the edge so that it will not show. Sew five or six stitches in each hole. Carry the thread under the snap from hole to hole.
- Mark the position of the socket half. Stitch it in place. Secure the thread and knot it.

Reading Check *Analyze* Why do garments have different types of closures?

Figure 18.5 Sewing on Buttons

Repair Skills Learning to sew on buttons is an essential clothing repair skill. *Where would you use each of the button types on a garment?*

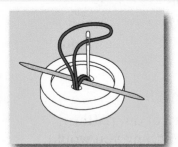

Sew-Through Buttons

Step 1 Start on the underside of the fabric, and bring the needle and thread to the right side.

Step 2 Stick the needle and thread through one hole in the button. Place a toothpick across the top of or underneath the button to allow for a thread shank. Stitch in and out several times through the fabric and buttonholes and over the toothpick. Finish stitching so that your needle and thread are under the button.

Step 3 Remove the toothpick. Pull the button to the top of the thread loop. Wind the thread several times around the stitches under the button to make a thread shank.

Step 4 Bring the needle back to the wrong side of the fabric.

Step 5 Secure the thread by taking several small stitches in the fabric and knot it.

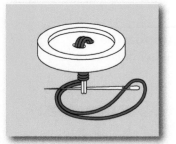

Shank Buttons

Step 1 Sew a shank button in place using five or six small stitches through the shank and into the fabric.

Step 2 Fasten the thread securely.

Step 3 Insert an eye fastener and sew the eye in place first.

Serging Basics

A serger is a machine that sews, trims, and finishes a seam in one step. A serger can save time and handle a variety of fabrics, from slippery silks to stretchy knits. A serger keeps the edges from raveling on all fabrics. On stretchy fabric, serging also allows for movement of the fabric.

How Sergers Work

A serger feeds several strands of thread through guides that are placed above the machine. **Cones** are the large cylinders used to hold large spools of thread. Sergers use cones instead of spools because sergers use more thread than sewing machines do. A cone can hold up to five times more thread than a spool can hold.

Sergers are known as two-thread, three-thread, four-thread, or five-thread, depending on the number of threads used to make the stitch. Each thread passes through its own tension dial. Sergers do not have bobbins. Instead, they have **loopers**, which are rounded parts that hold the thread inside a serger. The looper threads loop around each other and are interlocked with the needle thread or threads. Depending on the model, sergers may have one or two needles. The remaining threads are wrapped by the loopers. **Figure 18.6** on page 408 shows the basic parts of a serger.

Small knife blades are located inside the serger. These knives trim the fabric as it passes through the machine. The result, or outcome, is a seam allowance that is exactly the width of the serger's stitch. As you serge, the entire seam allowance is wrapped inside the serge stitch.

A serger does not replace a sewing machine because it cannot sew a single line of locked stitches, create buttonholes, or insert zippers. It allows you to use a greater variety of fabrics, including stretchy knits and sheers. Sergers are most commonly used to sew knits and stitch stretch fabrics. Sergers can also be used to sew conventional skirt or pant hems or narrow, rolled hems, such as those on scarves safely.

D. Hurst/Alamy

Financial Literacy

Sewing Costs

Katie needs to buy materials for a sewing project, but she does not have a calculator. She has $25.00 to spend. Does she have enough money? Use rounding to determine the total cost of the following items.

Fabric .... $8.99   Thread 2.15
Pattern .... 6.50   Pins .... .99

Math Concept **Cost Estimation** To estimate the sum of a set of numbers, round the amounts to the same place-value position and add. When rounding, look at the first digit to the right of the decimal point. If the first digit to the right of the decimal point is 5 or greater, round up to the nearest dollar. If the digit is less than 5, round down.

Starting Hint: To round $8.99 to the nearest dollar, look at the number to the right of the decimal. Since 9 is more than 5, you would round $8.99 up to $9.00.

 For math help, go to the Math Appendix at the back of the book.

Figure (18.6) Basic Serger Parts

High-Speed Machine A serger has many working parts. *Find the loopers in this diagram and explain their function.*

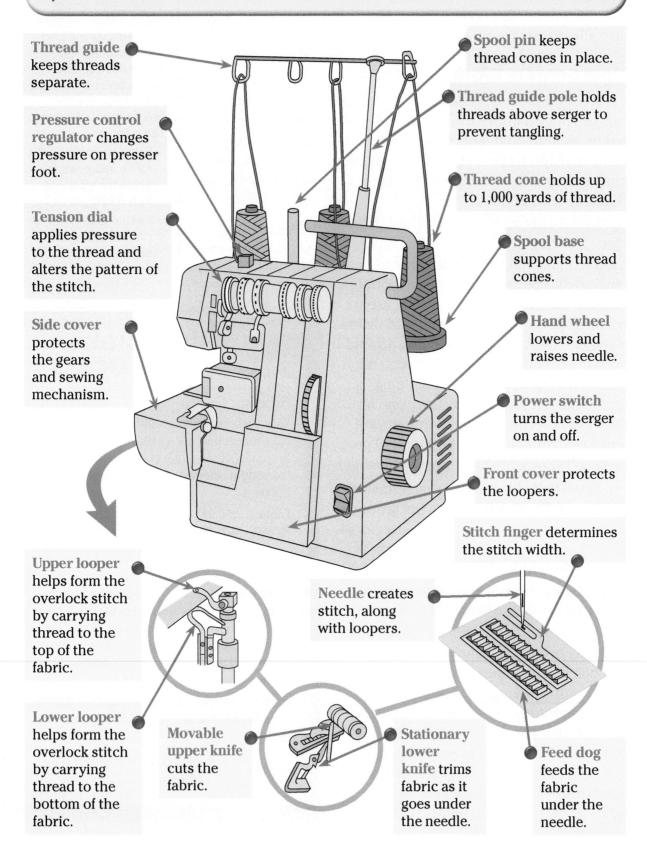

Thread guide keeps threads separate.

Pressure control regulator changes pressure on presser foot.

Tension dial applies pressure to the thread and alters the pattern of the stitch.

Side cover protects the gears and sewing mechanism.

Spool pin keeps thread cones in place.

Thread guide pole holds threads above serger to prevent tangling.

Thread cone holds up to 1,000 yards of thread.

Spool base supports thread cones.

Hand wheel lowers and raises needle.

Power switch turns the serger on and off.

Front cover protects the loopers.

Stitch finger determines the stitch width.

Upper looper helps form the overlock stitch by carrying thread to the top of the fabric.

Needle creates stitch, along with loopers.

Lower looper helps form the overlock stitch by carrying thread to the bottom of the fabric.

Movable upper knife cuts the fabric.

Stationary lower knife trims fabric as it goes under the needle.

Feed dog feeds the fabric under the needle.

Using a Serger

When you are ready to begin a project, set the stitch-length and tension dials on the serger to the desired settings. Use fabric scraps to test how the serged stitch will look on the final product, or result, either with or against the grain. Keep adjusting the stitch length and tension until you achieve the result that you want.

When you have tested the serge stitch on fabric scraps and basted your fabric, you are ready to serge. Position the fabric for feeding through the machine. Unless the fabric is unusually thick, you should not need to lift the presser foot. The fabric is moved along by the feed dogs. You should begin and end each seam with a **tail chain**, a length of thread shaped like a chain. A tail chain is made by pressing on the presser foot without placing fabric under the needle. It keeps the fabric from raveling and eliminates the need to tie off the threads of the seam.

Difficult Fabrics Hard-to-handle fabrics, such as stretchy knits, are easier to handle on a serger than on a regular sewing machine. *Which garments in your wardrobe have "serged" seams?*

Section 18.2 After You Read

Review What You Have Learned

1. **Identify** the two types of casings and how each is used.
2. **Identify** the advantages of using a serger.

Practice Academic Skills

English Language Arts

3. Choose three items of clothing from your closet. Determine if the stitching was done by a sewing machine, a serger, or both. Explain how you can tell.

Social Studies

4. The art of quilt making is experiencing a revival. Quilts are works of art in museums, and can be seen on display at fairs and festivals. Write a paragraph to explain how a quilt can serve as a historical record.

· ·

Check Your Answers Check Your Answers at connectED.mcgraw-hill.com.

Discovering Careers

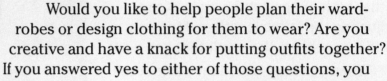

Would you like to help people plan their wardrobes or design clothing for them to wear? Are you creative and have a knack for putting outfits together? If you answered yes to either of those questions, you might want to consider a future career in fashion or design. The following chart explores several careers in the fashion industry.

Job Title	Job Description
Clothier	Designs original garments, sews from existing patterns, and does alterations and repairs.
Clothing Inspector	Checks finished garments for stitching, colors, and sizes. Corrects errors in partially completed garments or returns garments for repairs.
Clothing Clerk	Helps customers find clothing. Checks sizes and makes recommendations to the customer. Organizes and stocks clothing racks.
FACS Teacher	Teaches Family and Consumer Sciences courses in middle or high schools.
Personal Shopper	Assesses clients' styles, needs, wardrobes, and purchases items for clients.
Wardrobe Consultant	Assembles wardrobes to project a desired image. Teaches basic clothes-buying strategies such as mixing, matching, and accessorizing.

Career Activities ▼

At School

1 Select three of the careers listed. Research the education, training, and work experience required for each career. Write a summary of your results.

At Home

2 Role-play with a family member the role of wardrobe consultant. Let your family member be your client. Determine the image he or she wants to project. Compile a wardrobe from magazine photos or online to show your client.

At Work

3 Like all clothing, uniforms require a design and someone to make them. List at least five jobs you can identify by the uniform.

In the Community

4 Contact and interview someone in your community who works in the fashion industry. Ask this person to describe what his or her typical work day is like. Share what you learned with your class.

Nicolas McComber/Getty Images

Chapter Summary

Section 18.1 Fabric and Pattern Preparation
To prepare fabric for sewing, preshrink it and check the grain. Then read the pattern guide sheet. This will allow you to understand the overall project, and will help you avoid making mistakes. Check the pattern pieces and compare the measurements to those on the pattern envelope and make changes as needed.

Section 18.2 Sewing and Serging Basics
Sewing is an enjoyable creative activity that can help you expand your wardrobe by adding new garments and repairing older garments. There are ten basic sewing techniques. A serger sews, trims, and finishes an edge in one step. Serging allows you to use a variety of fabrics and to give your projects a professional look.

Words You Learned

1. Use each of these content vocabulary words and academic vocabulary words in a sentence.

Content Vocabulary
- selvage (p. 393)
- bias (p. 393)
- guide sheet (p. 394)
- layout (p. 394)
- marking (p. 394)
- ease (p. 396)
- staystitch (p. 400)
- feed dog (p. 400)
- casing (p. 403)
- sew-through button (p. 406)
- shank button (p. 406)
- cone (p. 407)
- looper (p. 407)
- tail chain (p. 409)

Academic Vocabulary
- determine (p. 396)
- transfer (p. 398)
- result (p. 407)
- product (p. 409)

Review Key Concepts

2. **Explain** why fabric preparation is important.
3. **Outline** the steps in fabric preparation.
4. **List** ten basic sewing techniques.
5. **Describe** what a serger does.

Critical Thinking

6. **Explain** why various fabrics might need to be prepared for sewing differently.
7. **Describe** problems that might occur if you do not prepare your pattern before beginning
8. **Compare and contrast** the uses of a serger versus the uses of a regular sewing machine.
9. **Analyze** which sewing project would be more challenging: a skirt with a fold-down casing or a round pillow with a ruffle. Explain your answer.

Real-World Skills and Applications

Problem-Solving

10. Making Decisions Evan bought a pattern, some fabric, and notions. He plans to start sewing immediately. Is he leaving out a step? Develop a plan of action for Evan that includes the steps that you recommend he take before he begins sewing.

Interpersonal and Collaborative

11. Sewing Machine Timeline Follow your teacher's instructions to form into teams. Work in teams to research and prepare a timeline display showing the history of the sewing machine. When and where was the first sewing machine developed? Who invented it? Was it first used in private homes or by clothing manufacturers? Present your findings to your class.

Financial Literacy

12. Comparison Shopping Think of two items of clothing you would like to buy. Comparison shop for the items of clothing by locating them in different places. You may find the items of clothing in local stores, magazines, and by searching the Internet. Write down where you found the items and how much they cost. Compare the price of the items to determine which store or other source offers the best buy. If you find the items of clothing on the Internet, be sure to add handling and shipping costs to the total cost of the items. Shipping costs may vary based on the type of shipping you choose and by the location.

13. Sewing Lab Make a personalized pillowcase. Cut a rectangle of fabric 42½ inches × 35½ inches. Serge around the edges ofw the rectangle. Fold the fabric right sides together, and stitch along one long and one short edge. Turn up a 3-inch hem along the remaining short end, facing the wrong side. Stitch in place. Turn the pillowcase right side out.

14. Research Clothing History Clothing styles have changed throughout history. Certain features of clothing, such as colors and fabrics, often represented the status and wealth of the wearer. Choose a historical period and find examples of the clothing worn by both men and women of the period. Did different social groups wear different types of clothing? Prepare a short presentation for your class on what you have found.

15. Clothing Today With permission from your parents or teacher, go online to research teen clothing styles today. How have they changed since a decade ago? One hundred years ago? Find examples of teen clothing styles from past decades and of today's teen styles to include in your Life Skills binder.

Academic Skills

English Language Arts

16. Advertise Imagine that your school is creating a Sewing Club. You have been asked to create a flyer to hand out to your classmates encouraging them to join. Develop a flyer that would encourage both boys and girls to join the club. What information should you include in the flyer? What type of artwork? Describe the advantages of being a member of the club

Science

17. Form a Hypothesis The scientific method is a way to answer questions.
Procedure Collect information, form a hypothesis, study the results, and draw conclusions that can be tested by others. One hypothesis might read: It is more expensive to buy clothes in a store than it is to make them.
Analysis Form your own hypothesis about clothing costs and write a list of facts that support your hypothesis.

Mathematics

18. Calculate Average Project Time Nelly, Shar, and Keisha spend a total of 12 hours working together on an assigned sewing project. Each must keep track of the time he or she spends on the project. What is the average number of minutes each of them spends working on the project?

Math Concept **Use Variables and Operations** Translating words into algebraic expressions requires knowledge of the meaning of the verbal descriptions. In algebra, a variable is a symbol used to represent a number. Arithmetic operations include addition, subtraction, multiplication, and division.

Starting Hint Since you are solving for the answer in minutes, first convert the hours into minutes. If $x =$ the average number of hours each worker spends on the project, the algebraic expression for the problem is $3x = (12 \times 60)$. Solve for x.

Standardized Test Practice

Multiple-Choice

Read the paragraph. Then read the question and the answer choices. Choose the best answer and write it on a separate sheet of paper.

> **Test-Taking Tip** In a multiple-choice test, read the question before you read the answer choices. Try to answer the question before you read the answer choices. This way, the answer choices will not confuse you.

19. Justin is working on a sewing project for his life skills class. He reads the guide sheet included in the pattern he has chosen. The guide sheet says to be sure to check the *bias*. In this sentence, what does the word *bias* mean?

   a. a distortion of a set of statistical data

   b. voltage applied across an electronic device

   c. running diagonally across the weave of a fabric

   d. having a preference

Design Your Own Clothing

Knowing how to sew can help you create unique clothing designs. You can learn about designs from studying pattern booklets in sewing stores. Reading fashion magazines may give you ideas for stylish projects. This project will help you design your own clothing.

My Journal Complete the journal entry from page 369, and refer to it to complete your design concept.

Project Assignment ▼

In this project, you will:

- Sketch ideas for a clothing design.
- Create a sewing pattern for your clothing design.
- Describe your design's practicality and style.
- Interview someone who sews professionally.
- Present your clothing design to your class.
- Include this project in the eighth section of your personal Life Skills binder.

 Step 1 **Develop Your Unique Design Concept**

Pick a sketch that you believe you could successfully design. Color and add detail to the sketch. List the materials someone might need to sew your design and begin to write step-by-step instructions they must follow.

Step 2 **Create a Pattern for Your Design**

Review pattern markings on page 395 (Figure 18.2). Draw a pattern for your clothing design using the proper markings. Use these questions to write step-by-step instructions to go with your pattern:

✔ What supplies must be on hand before starting the project?
✔ Will a sewing machine be necessary, or can it be sewn by hand?
✔ Does the design call for particular types of stitches?
✔ What is the concept for the final project?

Step 3 **Interview Someone Who Uses Sewing in Their Work**

Interview a seamstress, tailor, clothing designer, or anyone who sews professionally. Ask these questions:

✔ Do you think my pattern would work? Why or why not?
✔ What potential problems do you see in my design?
✔ What could I do to improve my design?

Use these interviewing skills when conducting your interview and these writing skills when writing the summary of notes from your interview.

Interviewing Skills
- Record interview responses and take notes.
- Listen attentively.

Writing Skills
- Use complete sentences.
- Use correct spelling and grammar.

Amos Morgan/Getty Images

Step 4 Create and Present Your Pattern

Use the Life Skills Project Checklist on the right to plan and complete your sketch and sewing pattern. Give an oral report on the project.

Use these speaking skills when presenting your final report.

Speaking Skills
- Speak clearly and concisely.
- Be sensitive to the needs of your audience.
- Use standard English to communicate.

Step 5 Evaluate Your Presentation

Your project will be evaluated based on:

- ✔ Your sketched design concepts.
- ✔ The sewing pattern of your clothing design.
- ✔ The step-by-step written instructions.
- ✔ The summary written from interview notes.
- ✔ Grammar and sentence structure.
- ✔ Presentation to the class.
- ✔ Creativity and neatness.

🖱 **Evaluation Rubric** Go to connectED. mcgraw-hill.com for a rubric you can use to evaluate your final project.

Life Skills Project Checklist

Research Clothing Design

- ✅ Sketch designs for a sewing project.
- ✅ Read sewing pattern booklets for ideas.
- ✅ Design a sewing pattern for something to wear.
- ✅ Interview someone who uses sewing skills as part of his or her job.

Writing Skills

- ✅ Write step-by-step instructions explaining how to use your pattern.
- ✅ Describe the style and purpose of your design.
- ✅ Write a summary from your interview with someone who sews professionally.

Present Your Findings

- ✅ Prepare a short presentation to show your clothing pattern, and explain how to sew your design.
- ✅ Invite the students of the class to ask any questions they may have. Answer these questions with responses that respect their perspectives.
- ✅ Add this project to your Life Skills binder.

Academic Skills

- ✅ Conduct research to gather information.
- ✅ Communicate effectively.
- ✅ Organize your presentation so the audience can follow along easily.
- ✅ Thoroughly express your ideas.

UNIT 9

Nutrition and Your Health

Unit Preview

This unit is about how to stay healthy by managing your nutrition and physical activity. In this unit, you will learn about:

- Eating healthful meals that include all the food groups.
- Using the Dietary Guidelines and MyPlate.
- The importance of fitness to your physical and mental health.
- The roles exercise and nutrition play in maintaining a healthy weight.

Explore the Photo

Eating healthful foods is essential if you want to maintain your mental and physical health. *What are some healthful foods that you already eat and enjoy?*

iStockphoto/Getty Images

Play with Your Food!

When you are done studying this unit, you will complete a project in which you will:

✓ Write a play about good nutrition and fitness.

✓ Interview an expert on diet and exercise.

✓ Perform your play in front of your class.

The prewriting activity below will help you get started.

My Journal

Prewriting Activity
Take a Poll

Ask your classmates and friends what they think the most important health topics are for your age group. Suggest topics you may have read about such as junk food, diets, trans fat, and working out.

● What health topics are students interested in learning about?

● What health topics are most important to you? Why?

Chapter  19

Nutrition and Wellness

Section 19.1

Nutrients for Health

■ **Main Idea** Eat healthful and balanced meals with nutrients to help regulate your body functions.

Section 19.2

Healthful Eating

■ **Main Idea** Use the Dietary Guidelines from MyPlate to promote a balanced diet.

Explore the Photo

When you choose to eat nutritious foods and get plenty of physical activity, you can help prevent illness and protect your health. *What good choices have you made to take care of your health?*

Persuasive Paragraph

Eat the Right Food With your busy schedule of homework, classes, family obligations, and other activities, it can be difficult to eat the right foods. It is important, however, to eat a nutritious, balanced diet, even when it seems like you are too busy to think about it. Write a paragraph for teens to persuade them to find time for healthful foods.

Writing Tips Follow these steps to write a persuasive paragraph.

1. State your position clearly.
2. Make sure each sentence in the paragraph includes details to support the main idea.
3. Use facts to back up your position.

Reading Guide

Before You Read

Check for Understanding If you have questions as you are reading, that means you are checking your understanding of the material. To get the most out of the text, try to answer those questions.

Read to Learn

Key Concepts

✓ **Distinguish** the difference between hunger and appetite.

✓ **Describe** the functions of proteins, carbohydrates, and fats in the human body.

Main Idea

Eat healthful and balanced meals with nutrients to help regulate your body functions.

Content Vocabulary

○ wellness
○ nutrient
○ appetite
○ calorie
○ protein
○ amino acid
○ carbohydrate

○ fiber
○ whole grain
○ cholesterol
○ vitamin
○ mineral
○ osteoporosis

Academic Vocabulary

■ adequate   ■ brittle

Graphic Organizer

As you read, write down the six nutrients found in food. Use a graphic organizer like the one shown to help you organize your information.

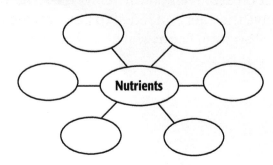

Graphic Organizer Go to connectED. mcgraw-hill.com to download this graphic organizer.

What is your favorite food? Is it pizza, or hamburgers, or maybe yogurt? Perhaps you are a vegetarian and you love vegetable lasagna. Eat a variety of foods to supply your body with the energy you need. Balance your diet by including appropriate foods from all of the food groups.

Look and Feel Good

Your diet affects the way you look and feel. Eating healthful foods can help you look your best. Reaching for your best level of health is called **wellness**. Exercise, adequate rest, and personal hygiene also contribute to your personal health and wellness.

Feeling good and being healthy go hand in hand. Along with exercise and rest, food affects how you feel, no matter what your age. Food is your source of energy for physical and mental activities. You need energy to perform well in school and in all your activities. Without adequate, or enough, nutrients, you may tire easily and feel less alert. A **nutrient** ('nōō-trē-ənt) is a substance in food that is important for the body's growth and maintenance. Proper nutrition has a direct effect on achievement. When you eat right, you are more likely to have the energy needed to perform mental and physical activities well. Eating right can help you look, feel, think, and act your best.

As You Read

Connect Food tastes good, and eating the right foods can keep you healthy. What healthful foods have you eaten today?

◇ Vocabulary

You can find definitions in the glossary at the back of this book.

©Terry Vine/Blend Images LLC

❶ **Nutrition Value** Getting the right nutrients from the foods you eat is very important to your health. *What are some of the body processes which are affected by the nutrients you eat?*

Physical Health
Eat Nutritious Foods
Eating well-balanced meals can help you function at your best in school. When you have the right nutrients in your meals, it can help you focus on your school work and provide energy for other activities.

• • • • • • • • • • • • • •

A healthful eating style helps protect you from illness. When you get the nutrients you need, your body is better able to fight infections, heal wounds, and recover quickly when you do get sick.

Satisfying Your Hunger

When your stomach growls, you are experiencing a sign of hunger. Hunger is the physical need to eat. Hunger tells you that your body needs food, but it does not tell you what to eat. It is up to you to learn to select healthful foods and decide how much to eat.

Appetite is different from hunger. **Appetite** is the desire to eat. When you smell fresh strawberries or a chocolate cake, you might experience an appetite for those foods without necessarily being hungry.

When your hunger is satisfied, it is time to stop eating. Some people still have an appetite, however, so they continue to eat. If people eat too much food, or food that is too high in calories, they may gain weight. A **calorie** is a unit that measures the energy used by the body and the energy that food supplies to the body. However, that energy is stored as fat if you eat food that has more calories than your body uses.

Reading Check   *Explain*   *How can proper nutrition benefit achievement?*

Figure 19.1   What Do Nutrients Do?

Meet the Nutrients There are six kinds of nutrients and each one has an important function. *How do nutrients help the functions of the body?*

- **Proteins** help the body to build, repair, and maintain cells and tissue.
- **Carbohydrates** provide energy and fiber.
- **Fats** provide energy and supply essential fatty acids for normal growth and healthy skin.
- **Vitamins** help your body use other nutrients, store and use energy, and fight infection.
- **Minerals** help build sturdy bones and teeth, maintain healthy blood, and aid in the regular elimination of body wastes.
- **Water** carries nutrients to body cells, aids in digestion, removes wastes, and helps control your body temperature.

Nutrient Functions

Nutrients in food keep you healthy, help you grow, and give you energy. Nutrition is the study of nutrients and how the body uses them. Nutrients are released from food during digestion. Digestion is the process of breaking down food into a form the body can use. Nutrients are then absorbed into the bloodstream and carried to cells where they perform different, important functions. **Figure 19.1** describes the functions of the six kinds of nutrients.

Nutrients affect body processes such as your heartbeat, blood flow, and breathing. These processes, in turn, affect the way you feel and how much energy you have. They also affect the quality of your skin, hair, and nails. To keep your body functioning properly, you must choose foods that supply enough of each nutrient. Lack of nutrients can cause health problems.

Proteins

A **protein** is a type of nutrient that is needed to build, repair, and maintain body cells and tissues. Your skin, hair, blood, muscles, and vital organs are all made of proteins. During the teen years, you need proteins to help your body grow and develop to its adult size.

MATH YOU CAN USE

Count Calories

Tony is trying to eat 2,700 calories per day, and would like to consume ⅓ of those calories at each meal. For lunch, he eats a large bag of potato chips (380 calories), a cheeseburger with mustard and ketchup (545 calories), and a can of soda (155 calories). What fraction of his total daily calories did Tony consume for lunch? Was this more or less than ⅓?

Math Concept **Comparing Fractions** To compare two fractions with different denominators, rewrite each one as an equivalent fraction with a common denominator. For example, to compare ⅚ and ¾, you would rewrite them as 10/12 and 9/12.

Starting Hint Add up the calories for the chips, cheeseburger, and soda. Write this total as the numerator of a fraction, with 2,700 as the denominator. Reduce to lowest terms. Then, compare that fraction to ⅓ by rewriting each fraction with common denominators.

Math *For more math help, go to the Math Appendix located at the back of this book.*

Combine "Food Groups
Combining "different foods will provide the essential amino acids your body needs. *Why are amino acids important to your health?*

Even after you stop growing, you still need proteins to help your body repair itself. Billions of worn-out body cells are replaced every day, and proteins are used to make those new cells.

Each protein is a different combination of amino acids. **Amino acids** are the building blocks that make up proteins. Your body manufactures some amino acids. Others, called essential amino acids, cannot be produced by your body. They must come from the food you eat.

Some foods contain all the essential amino acids. These foods, such as meat, fish, poultry, milk, cheese, and eggs, are called complete proteins. Other foods are good sources of protein, but they lack one or more of the essential amino acids. These foods, called incomplete proteins, come from plants and include dry beans, nuts, and grains.

By combining proteins from grains with proteins from dry beans or nuts, you can get all the essential amino acids that your body needs.

Carbohydrates, Fiber, and Whole Grains

Carbohydrates (,kär-bō-'hī-,drāts) are the starches and sugars that give the body most of its energy. Starches are found in grains, such as oats, rice, and wheat. Foods made from grain, including bread, tortillas, pasta, and cereals, also provide starch. Potatoes, corn, dry beans, and nuts are additional sources of starch.

Natural sugars are found in fruits and milk, which are also high in other nutrients. Candy, cake, and soft drinks also contain sugar, but they are high in calories and low in other nutrients. They should be eaten less often than fruits and milk.

Almost all carbohydrates come from plant sources, which also provide fiber. **Fiber** is plant material that your body cannot digest. Although fiber is not a nutrient, eating the right amount of fiber-rich foods helps the body function normally. Fiber provides bulk, which helps move food through your digestive system. It also helps your body eliminate waste. A diet rich in high-fiber foods can reduce the risk for certain diseases, such as colon cancer.

Fiber Source Fruits and vegetables are good sources of fiber. *Why is eating enough fiber important?*

Good sources of fiber include foods made from whole grains. **Whole grains** are foods that contain the entire edible grain. Whole wheat breads, whole wheat cereals, and popcorn are whole grain foods. Fruits and vegetables, especially those with edible skins, stems, and seeds, also contain fiber.

Fats

Like carbohydrates, fats are an important source of energy. Fats contain twice as many calories as carbohydrates. There are 9 calories in 1 gram of fat. Saturated fats are the least healthful type of fat. Read labels to find out how much fat is in the foods you eat.

Your body relies on fat cells to store energy and to help regulate body temperature. Your skin needs fats to stay smooth, and your nervous system needs them to work properly. Fats also carry several vitamins needed by the body.

Saturated fats are found in food from animal sources, such as meats, egg yolks, cheese, and butter. Saturated animal fats contain a waxy substance called **cholesterol** (kə-'les-tə-,rōl). Your body produces all the cholesterol it needs, so you do not need to add cholesterol to your diet. In fact, diets high in cholesterol have been linked to an increased risk of heart disease. Unsaturated fats come from plants. These fats are found mainly in vegetable oils, such as olive, corn, or canola oil. No more than 30 percent of the calories you consume should come from fat, with the majority being unsaturated fats.

Vitamins

A **vitamin** is a substance that is needed in small quantities to help regulate body functions. **Figure 19.2** on page 427 lists different vitamins and describes the ways in which these vitamins benefit your body.

The essential vitamins include A, B-complex, C, D, and E. Your body cannot make most vitamins, so you must get them from the foods you eat. These nutrients can easily be obtained from a variety of delicious foods.

Vitamin A Have you ever walked into a dark room after being in the bright sunlight? Vitamin A helps your eyes to adjust to the dark. It also helps keep your skin healthy and helps your body resist infection. Dark green, leafy vegetables, deep yellow vegetables, and dairy products are good sources of vitamin A.

Safety Check

Dietary Supplements
It may seem easy to fill in nutritional gaps with vitamin and mineral pills, but they are not risk-free. If you do choose to supplement your diet, follow these tips:

- Do not mix supplements with prescription medication.
- Talk to a pharmacist or doctor about which ones are right for you.
- Avoid supplements that promise you will lose weight, or prevent or cure illness.
- Only take the recommended amount.

Vitamin Source Dark green, leafy vegetables contain vitamin A. *Why is important to eat foods containing vitamin A?*

B-Complex Vitamins: Thiamine, Niacin, and Riboflavin

B-complex vitamins give you energy by helping your body use calories from carbohydrates, fats, and proteins. Riboflavin, found in dairy products, helps keep your eyes and skin healthy. Thiamine and niacin, found in meat, dry beans, and grain products, promote a healthy nervous system. B-complex vitamins come from many different foods. When selecting grain products, such as flour and bread, try to choose whole-grain or enriched foods.

Vitamin C Ascorbic acid, also called vitamin C, helps your body fight infection and helps wounds heal. It also helps to keep your gums healthy. Good sources of vitamin C include oranges, melons, berries, and dark green, leafy vegetables, such as spinach and broccoli.

Vitamin D Vitamin D helps your body absorb and use minerals, such as calcium and phosphorus. It is essential for normal bone and tooth development. Your body can make its own vitamin D when your skin is exposed to sunlight. Foods that provide vitamin D include fortified milk, fish oils, beef, butter, and egg yolks.

Vitamin E To keep red blood cells healthy, your body needs vitamin E. You can find it in vegetable oils, yellow vegetables, grains, nuts, and green leafy vegetables.

Minerals

Food also contains **minerals**, which are elements needed in small amounts for strong bones and teeth, healthy blood, and regular elimination of body wastes. Like vitamins, minerals are essential to good health.

Every day your body uses minerals. Minerals such as iron, zinc, and iodine, are needed only in small amounts. Calcium, phosphorus, and magnesium are needed in greater amounts. **Figure 19.2** describes the minerals your body needs and the various foods in which they can be found.

Calcium Young people need calcium to develop strong teeth and bones. Calcium is also necessary throughout life to reduce the risk of **osteoporosis** (ˌäs-tē-ō-pə-ˈrō-səs), a condition in which bones gradually lose their mineral content. Bones can become weak and brittle, or easy to break. Calcium also helps your muscles move and your heart beat.

🔊 **Milk and Calcium** Milk is a good source of calcium. *What are some other sources of calcium?*

© Ingram Publishing/SuperStock

Figure 19.2 Vitamins and Minerals

Give Your Body What it Needs Vitamins and minerals are essential to good health. *Why is it better to get vitamins and minerals from healthful foods than to replace foods with vitamin and mineral supplements?*

Vitamins	Function and Benefits	Food Sources
Vitamin A	Promotes healthy skin, eyes, nose, mouth, throat	Dark green vegetables, deep yellow vegetables, fruits, eggs, dairy products
B-Complex Vitamins	Help carbohydrates, fats, and proteins produce energy	Whole-grain foods, pork, organ meats, dry beans, peas
■ **Thiamine**	Promotes healthy growth, appetite, digestion, nervous system	Whole-grain foods, pork, organ meats, dry beans, peas
■ **Riboflavin**	Promotes healthy skin, eyes	Milk, cheese, yogurt, eggs, organ meats, poultry, fish, enriched breads, cereals
■ **Niacin**	Promotes healthy digestive tract, nervous system, skin	Whole-grain foods, liver, meat, fish, poultry, nuts
Vitamin C (also called ascorbic acid)	Helps the body fight infection and heal wounds; promotes healthy gums	citrus fruits, berries, melon, broccoli, spinach, potatoes, tomatoes, green pepper, cabbage
Vitamin D	Works with calcium to build strong bones and teeth	Fortified milk, fish liver oil
Vitamin E	Keeps oxygen from destroying other nutrients and cell membranes	Vegetable oil, salad dressing, margarine, grains, fruits, some vegetables
Vitamin K	Helps blood clot	Green leafy vegetables, egg yolks
Minerals	Function and Benefits	Food Sources
Calcium	Promotes healthy teeth, bones, heart function, muscles, soft tissue, nerves, blood clotting	Milk, cheese, yogurt, green leafy vegetables, fish with edible bones
Fluoride	Helps make teeth strong	Drinking water
Iodine	Helps the thyroid gland work properly	Saltwater fish, iodized salt
Iron	Aids in the body's use of oxygen	Meat, liver, eggs, dry beans, dried fruits, whole-grain foods, spinach
Magnesium	Promotes and regulates many body functions and produces energy	Nuts, peanut butter, seeds, dry beans and peas, whole-grain foods, milk, fish, green leafy vegetables, bananas
Phosphorus	Promotes healthy bones and teeth; helps the body produce energy	Milk, yogurt, cheese, egg yolk, meat, fish, poultry
Potassium	Helps regulate body fluids and heart function	Orange juice, bananas, meat, nuts, dried fruits
Zinc	Promotes wound healing; affects growth, taste, appetite, smell	Meat, organ meats, eggs, poultry, seafood, cheese, milk
Sodium	Helps regulate body fluids and muscle function	Table salt, cured meats, pickles, many processed foods

When you bleed, calcium aids vitamin K in helping your blood clot. Calcium also helps keep your nerves and soft tissues healthy. The best sources of calcium are dairy products and dark green, leafy vegetables.

Iron Like calcium, iron is one of the most important nutrients. Iron is an essential component of blood. It helps carry oxygen to your brain, your muscles, and all of your body's cells. Oxygen helps your body produce energy for physical activity. Females need about twice as much iron as males. The best sources of iron are meat, poultry, dry beans, dried fruits, and dark green, leafy vegetables.

Water

Water helps regulate your body functions and carries nutrients to body cells. It aids in digestion, removes wastes, and helps control your body temperature. Water is lost through perspiration and urine, so you must replace it. You should drink at least eight glasses of water each day. When you play basketball, tennis, or engage in other physical activities, your body produces sweat, and you need even more water.

Section 19.1 After You Read

Review What You Have Learned

1. **Explain** how you can achieve a high level of wellness.
2. **Identify** good sources of Vitamin A.

Practice Academic Skills

English Language Arts

3. Create an informative pamphlet that communicates the importance of minerals in a healthful meal plan. Use information from the chapter for your pamphlet. Find clip art, graphics, or photos to make your pamphlet attractive, informative, and easy to read.

Social Studies

4. Think about how food plays a part in tradition and culture. Name one of your family's traditions which includes food. Does the food serve a purpose other than nutrition? Be prepared to share your findings and conclusions with the class.

• •

➤ **Check Your Answers** Check Your Answers at connectED.mcgraw-hill.com.

Section **19.2** Healthful Eating

Before You Read

Use Notes When you come across an unfamiliar section or term, write down the word or a question. After you finish the section, look up the terms or try to answer your questions based on what you have read.

Read to Learn

Key Concepts

✓ **Explain** how MyPlate can help you have a healthy lifestyle.

✓ **Name** the consequences of being overweight.

✓ **Identify** examples of healthful snacks.

✓ **Describe** how to choose your meals when dining out.

Main Idea

Use the Dietary Guidelines from MyPlate to promote a balanced diet.

Content Vocabulary

○ MyPlate
○ portion
○ diabetes
○ sodium

Academic Vocabulary

■ component
■ refined

Graphic Organizer

As you read, write down eight topics from the Dietary Guidelines. Use a graphic organizer like the one shown to help you organize your information.

Dietary Guidelines	
1.	5.
2.	6.
3.	7.
4.	8.

Graphic Organizer Go to connectED. mcgraw-hill.com to download this graphic organizer.

With so many food options, it is easy to see how it is sometimes difficult to choose the right foods to eat. Tempting advertisements for fast food and soda are often directed at young people. However, you can use the MyPlate as a guideline for eating right. By following its suggestions, you can live a healthy lifestyle.

As You Read

Connect Think about your weight. What are some of the influences that affect the way you see yourself?

 **Vocabulary**

You can find definitions in the glossary at the back of this book.

MyPlate and the Dietary Guidelines

MyPlate is organized to look like a dinner plate, with a glass on the side, labeled dairy. The plate is divided into four sections. Each section is labeled with a food group. The size of each section provides guidance in selecting how much food you should eat from each food group. For example, based on MyPlate, your overall diet should contain more vegetables and grains than proteins, fruits, and dairy. When you create a weekly menu, keep in mind that the overall eating plan should contain more vegetables and grains than other foods. MyPlate shows the five food groups, which include Protein (or meats and beans), Vegetables, Fruits, Grains, and Dairy. Four of the food groups are shown on MyPlate. Dairy is shown alongside the plate in a cup. MyPlate does not include oils or fats. Oils and fats are not a food group. They should be consumed in small amounts. Visit the MyPlate Web site, www.choosemyplate.gov, for free food and exercise recommendations. Also, as you can see in **Figure 19.3**, nutrition requirements change depending on your age and what stage of life you are in. The important point to remember is that you need to eat foods from all the food groups to get the nutrients you need.

MyPlate MyPlate uses a place setting to remind you to make healthier food choices. Use it to think about building a healthful plate at meal and snack times. *What steps can you take to eat more healthfully?*

U.S. Department of Agriculture

Figure (19.3) Nutrition Across the Life Span

Nutrition Stages There are different nutrition requirements for every age. *What are the nutrition requirements for your age group?*

Life Span Period	Nutrition Requirements
Pregnancy (includes nursing mothers)	Approximately 300 additional calories are required each day for increased energy needs.
Infancy (Birth-1 year)	Most of the infant's nutritional needs during the first year are met through human milk or infant formula.
Early Childhood (2-5 years)	Breakfast is especially important, and nutritious snacks help meet the child's daily nutrient needs.
Middle Childhood (6-11 years)	Snack foods may need to be monitored because consumption of sugary foods and empty calorie foods increases during this stage.
Adolescence (12-19 years)	An increased need for calcium occurs due to rapid bone growth. Teens need to increase their intake of foods from the milk group.
Young Adulthood (19-39 years)	Eating a well-balanced diet and exercising on a regular basis are good beginnings for young adults. Iron and calcium intakes are very important.
Middle Adulthood (40-65)	Eat a variety of foods, maintain desirable weight, avoid too much fat and cholesterol, increase fiber intake, avoid too much sugar and sodium, exercise regularly, refrain from smoking, and limit stress.
Older Adulthood (over 65 years)	A healthy diet can help reduce some of the effects of aging. Vitamins B_6, B_{12}, C, D, E, and thiamin, calcium, iron, and zinc are important. Regular exercise is needed.

How can you make sure that your diet contributes to your wellness? **Figure 19.4** on page 432 describes the Dietary Guidelines, which take into account the important effect diet has on your health.

By following the Dietary Guidelines, you can ensure that you are eating the right types of foods. You can also reduce your chances of developing certain health problems. Of course, food alone cannot make you healthy. Good health also depends on your heredity and environment. Your exercise habits also play an important role in your health. Following the Dietary Guidelines can help keep you healthy, and perhaps even help improve your health.

Reading Check *Explain* What are the benefits to following the Dietary Guidelines?

Figure 19.4   Dietary Guidelines

Improve Your Health To ensure you are eating the right types of foods, follow these Dietary Guidelines. *What else can you do to maintain and improve your health?*

- **Get enough nutrients within your calorie needs.** Choose a variety of nutritious foods and beverages from the basic food groups.
- **Maintain a healthy weight.** To maintain body weight in a healthy range, balance your intake of calories from food and beverages with the calories you burn in physical activities.
- **Be physically active every day.** Regular physical activity promotes health, well-being, and a healthy body weight. Teens should be physically active for at least 60 minutes every day.
- **Choose whole grains, fruits, vegetables, and milk.** Choose a healthy eating plan that emphasizes fruits, vegetables, whole grains, and fat-free or low-fat milk and milk products.
- **Limit fats and cholesterol.** For teens, total fat intake should only be 25 to 35 percent of the total calorie intake. Most fats should come from sources such as fish, nuts, and vegetable oils.
- **Be choosy about carbohydrate foods.** Choose fiber-rich fruits, vegetables, and whole grains often. Look for foods and beverages low in added sugars.
- **Reduce sodium (salt) and increase potassium.** Choose and prepare foods with less salt. Eat plenty of potassium-rich foods, such as fruits and vegetables.
- **Keep food safe.** Know how to prepare, handle, and store food safely to keep you and your family safe.

Maintain a Healthy Weight

A person who is at a healthy weight is not overweight or too thin. Being overweight is linked with illnesses such as high blood pressure, heart disease, stroke, cancer, and diabetes. **Diabetes** is a condition in which the body cannot control blood sugar properly. Although being too thin is less common, it is also linked with disease and a greater risk of early death.

How can you know if your weight is "healthy"? You should not compare your weight with that of your friends. There are differences among people of the same age and even the same height. For example, people with a large body frame usually weigh more than people of the same height with a smaller body frame. Also, people with a lot of muscle may also weigh more than people of the same height with less muscle. There are many different healthy weights for people of the same height. At this time in your life, growing and gaining weight are normal. To determine if your weight is right for you, consult your doctor. He or she can consider all the factors that contribute to a healthy weight for you.

Reading Check   *Examine* *How can you determine if your weight is right for you?*

How To...

Measure Food Portions

Actual portion sizes can be deceiving. When you fill your bowl with ice cream, you actually may be eating several helpings. Follow these guidelines to judge the right portion when a measuring cup is not handy. These estimates apply if you are 14–18 years old and get 30 minutes of daily physical activity beyond normal activities.

½ cup of fruit juice
= size of a 4-oz juice box

1 small apple = 1 cup
= size of a baseball

½ cup of sliced fruit
= size of a small computer mouse

1½ to 2
cups
Fruit
Group

½ cup of carrots or other vegetables
= size of a small computer mouse

10 medium fries count as ½ cup
= size of a deck of cards

1 cup of raw vegetables
= size of a baseball

2½ to 3
cups
Vegetable
Group

1 cup of milk
= an 8-oz carton of milk

1 cup of yogurt
= size of a baseball

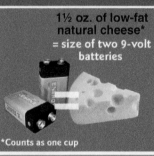

1½ oz. of low-fat natural cheese*
= size of two 9-volt batteries

*Counts as one cup

2 to 3
cups
or equivalent
Dairy
Group

2-3 oz of meat, poultry, or fish
= size of a deck of cards

1 tablespoon of peanut butter counts as 1 oz
= size of one 9-volt battery

½ cup of beans counts as 2 oz = size of a small computer mouse

5 to 6½
ounces
or equivalent
Protein
Food
Groups

½ cup of cooked pasta = 1 oz
= size of a small computer mouse

1 cup of dry cereal = 1 oz
= size of a baseball

1 slice of bread counts as 1 oz = size of a CD*
*About the thickness of 10 CDs (1/2 inch)

6 to 8
ounces
or equivalent
Grains
Group

Eat Right

Eating the right foods can help you live a long and healthy life. It is important to check the labels of foods before you buy them. Not all foods labeled low fat or sugar-free are healthful. For instance, cereals made with whole grains may also be higher in fat than another cereal, but can still be very healthful. Compare several brands of an item to see which one is really most healthful.

Fats and Cholesterol

Fat is an important nutrient that provides energy. However, health experts recommend a diet that is low in fat and cholesterol. The amount of fat in your diet depends on what you eat over several days, not in one meal or type of food. For example, if you like a small amount of butter on your baked potato, you will not be getting too much fat as long as you limit the amount of other fats you eat. Some foods that contain fats and cholesterol, such as meats, milk, cheese, and eggs, also contain high-quality protein and important vitamins and minerals. Choose low-fat versions of these foods such as non-fat or low-fat milk and cheese. Eating meals and snacks low in fat and cholesterol can help lower your risk of obesity and heart disease.

Healthy Weight Different body types have different healthy weights. *What are some of the factors that affect what a person's healthy weight is?*

Cholesterol is carried through your bloodstream by lipoproteins. Two of the main kinds are high-density lipoprotein (HDL) and low-density lipoprotein (LDL). The cholesterol carried by HDL is sometimes called "good" cholesterol. That is because HDL helps remove cholesterol from the blood and may reduce the risk of heart disease. The "bad" LDL cholesterol builds up in the arteries and may increase the risk of heart disease.

Vegetables, Fruits, and Grains

These foods are an essential part of a varied and healthful diet. They contain complex carbohydrates, fiber, and other nutrients that contribute to good health. In addition, these foods are usually low in fats. If you eat the suggested amounts of these foods, you are also likely to decrease the fat that you are eating and get more fiber. Fiber is found naturally in whole-grain breads and cereals, dry beans and peas, vegetables, and fruits.

Sugar

Sugar is a type of carbohydrate that is found in many foods. Sugar provides calories, and most people like the way it tastes. Eating too much sugar is not healthful, but it is not necessary to avoid sugar entirely. Fruit contains natural sugar. Many foods such as cookies, some cereals, and soft drinks, contain refined, or chemically processed, sugar. Natural sugar is preferable to refined sugar so try to make most of your sugar intake natural sugar.

Salt and Sodium

Salt contains **sodium**, a mineral that helps regulate the amount of fluid in our bodies. You need some sodium to stay healthy. However, most Americans take in more sodium than they need. Too much sodium can lead to high blood pressure, heart attack, and stroke. These risks increase as you get older. To reduce the amount of sodium you eat, flavor your food with herbs and spices instead of salt. Avoid salty snacks, and choose processed food made with less sodium.

SCIENCE YOU CAN USE

Hidden Sodium

Salt may be hidden in foods that do not taste salty, such as cake or bread. Many cereal manufacturers add salt to cereal to bring out the taste of the sugar.

Procedure Survey your own cupboard. Choose one type of food, such as canned soup or cereal. Scan the ingredient lists for salt. The closer to the beginning of the list of ingredients, the more salt there is in the food product. Read the nutrition label to find out how much salt is in each serving.

Analysis Write down your findings. Note the amount of sodium (salt) listed on the nutrition label per serving. Indicate where in the ingredients list salt is listed.

Nutrition Source
Dining out can provide good sources of nutrition as well as time to spend with friends. *What sources of nutrition can be found in pizza?*

Snacks

Consume empty-calorie snacks in very limited amounts. Empty-calorie foods are foods that are high in calories but low in nutrients. Potato chips, candy, and soft drinks are examples of empty-calorie foods. They often contain large amounts of sugar, salt, and fat, but little nutrition. Select whole-grain items from the bread group. A wide variety of nutrient-dense snacks can be found in the fruit group and vegetable group. For example, blend orange juice and a banana with non-fat yogurt and ice cubes to make a healthful fruit smoothie. Mix nuts, raisins, pretzels, and dry cereal to form a healthful grab-and-go snack.

Reading Check *Identify* What are some examples of foods that are high in calories but low in nutrients?

Dining Out

Do you enjoy dining out? Maybe you like getting together with friends over a meal. Perhaps your family enjoys eating at a restaurant to try new foods. When you dine out, remember to choose your meals with the same attention to nutrition as when you eat at home.

As you look at a menu, the most important point to remember is to choose foods from all of the food groups. Here are some tips for ordering when you dine out:

- Eat only until you feel satisfied. Overeating is more common when dining out.
- Most portion sizes are larger than a serving. Bring leftovers home.
- Select dishes that are low in fat, sugar, salt, and calories. For example, baked potatoes have much less fat than French fries.
- Choose nutrient-dense dishes. For example, order whole-wheat or vegetable pasta. Instead of soft drinks or milk shakes, order juice or milk.
- Remember that sauces and salad dressings add calories. Choose sauces made with tomatoes, rather than sauces made with butter and cream. Ask for dressing on the side of your salad, so you can control the amount.
- Limit desserts. Consider sharing one dessert with your dining companions.

Section 19.2 After You Read

Review What You Have Learned

1. **Explain** what the different sizes of plates in MyPlate represents.
2. **Determine** the best way to know if your weight is right for you.
3. **Identify** the effect of too much sodium in your diet.
4. **Describe** tips for ordering when you are dining out.

Practice Academic Skills

English Language Arts

5. Prepare a presentation for younger children about how to use MyPlate. Use information from the chapter and other resources to best communicate how younger children can make good choices for eating. Be ready to share your presentation with elementary students.

Social Studies

6. Conduct research to learn about environmental factors that can affect food production. Is there any way we can anticipate these and plan for them? If an environmental event negatively affects food production, is there anything we can do to improve the situation? Write a summary of your discoveries.

✈ **Check Your Answers** Check Your Answers at connectED.mcgraw-hill.com.

Discovering Careers

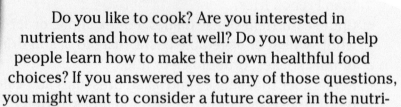

Focus on Careers in Food and Nutrition ▼

Do you like to cook? Are you interested in nutrients and how to eat well? Do you want to help people learn how to make their own healthful food choices? If you answered yes to any of those questions, you might want to consider a future career in the nutrition field. The following chart explores several careers in nutrition.

Job Title	Job Description
Nutritionist	Develops nutrition education materials and classes. Teaches nutrition education courses. Counsels pregnant women on proper nutrition.
Dietitian	Plans therapeutic diets. Oversees preparation and service of meals. Consults with health care personnel to determine nutritional needs and diet restrictions.
Food and Drug Inspector	Inspects establishments where foods, drugs, and cosmetics are manufactured. Investigates handling of consumer products. Enforces legal standards of sanitation.
Hospital Chef	Oversees food preparation for hospital patients. Trains and supervises kitchen staff. Uses safe food-handling procedures. Develops menus for the special requirements of patients.

Career Activities ▼

At School

1 Select three of the careers listed. Research the education, training, and work experience required for each career. Write a summary of your results.

At Home

2 Prepare a dinner menu for your family using MyPlate as your guideline.

At Work

3 Name five ways you can practice good nutrition and wellness in the workplace. Share your findings with your classmates.

In the Community

4 Contact and interview someone in your community who works in nutrition. Ask this person to describe what his or her typical work day is like. Share what you learned with your class.

Chapter Summary

Section 19.1 Nutrients for Health
You can have an appetite without being hungry. Eating a diet low in fat and cholesterol can lower your risk for obesity and heart disease. Proteins are needed to build, maintain, and repair your body. Carbohydrates provide energy. Fats provide energy, keep skin smooth, and help your nervous system work. Vitamins, minerals, and water help regulate your body functions. All contribute to your good health.

Section 19.2 Healthful Eating
MyPlate and the Dietary Guidelines help promote a balanced diet. A person who is at a healthy weight is not overweight or underweight. Eating the right foods can help you live a long and healthy life. Vegetables, fruits, and grains are an essential part of a varied and healthful diet. Empty-calorie snacks and desserts should be limited. When you dine out, choose your meals carefully.

Words You Learned

1. Use each of these content and academic vocabulary words in a sentence.

Content Vocabulary
- wellness (p. 421)
- nutrient (p. 421)
- appetite (p. 422)
- calorie (p. 422)
- protein (p. 423)
- amino acid (p. 424)
- carbohydrate (p. 424)
- fiber (p. 424)
- whole grain (p. 425)
- cholesterol (p. 425)
- vitamin (p. 425)
- mineral (p. 426)
- osteoporosis (p. 426)
- MyPlate (p. 430)
- portion (p. 430)
- diabetes (p. 432)
- sodium (p. 435)

Academic Vocabulary
- adequate (p. 421)
- brittle (p. 426)
- component (p. 430)
- refined (p. 435)

Review Key Concepts

2. Distinguish the difference between hunger and appetite.

3. Describe the functions of proteins, carbohydrates, and fats in the human body.

4. Explain how MyPlate can help you have a healthy lifestyle.

5. Name the consequences of being overweight.

6. Identify examples of healthful snacks.

7. Describe how to choose your meals when dining out.

Critical Thinking

8. Determine if there are any fast-foods or beverages that you enjoy that are healthful.

9. Evaluate your diet for a week based on MyPlate and the Dietary Guidelines.

Real-World Skills and Applications

Problem-Solving

10. Choosing Restaurants Compile nutrition information from three different restaurants in your area. Using information from MyPlate and the Dietary Guidelines, make a list of the top three main dishes from each restaurant. Suggest healthful appetizers, side dishes, beverages, and dessert options.

Technology Applications

11. Create a Spreadsheet Using spreadsheet software, create a spreadsheet to keep track of the fruits and vegetables you eat. Record the number of servings of each fruit and vegetable you eat every day for one week. At the end of the week, show the varieties and your total servings. Review your results, then decide if you are eating enough fruits and vegetables, or if you need to add more to your meals and snacks.

Financial Literacy

12. Comparison Shopping Packaging and processing makes food items more expensive. You may be surprised to find what the cost of processed snacks and foods is. With your family, write out a shopping list for one week of meals at your home. Make your usual list, and then create another list that includes only foods that meet MyPlate and the Dietary Guidelines. Choose healthful foods and snacks such as fruits and vegetables instead of processed or sugar-filled snacks. Take both lists to the grocery store and track the cost for each list. What is the difference in cost? Which list is the most expensive? What changes could you and your family make based on the results of your findings? How can you live a healthier lifestyle?

13. State of Nutrition Draw or print out a map that shows the outlines of a region in the United States, such as the Southwest, the Pacific Northwest, or the Eastern Seaboard. For each state in your selected region, find out what foods are produced there. For example, Wisconsin is known for its cheese products. Draw a picture of the food product in the outline of the state that produces it.

14. Wellness Organizations Conduct research to find out about government and community organizations that help people with nutrition and wellness issues. Make a list of low-cost or no-cost organizations that provide people with information about such topics as prenatal care, nutrition assistance, or food delivery for individuals who cannot leave their homes. Prepare a brief presentation on your findings to the class.

15. Organic Foods With permission from your parents or teacher, go online to find information about organic foods. What does organic mean? What kinds of organic food products can you find in grocery stores? How much do they cost in comparison to non-organic foods? Include your list in your Life Skills Binder.

Academic Skills

English Language Arts

16. Write an Advertisement You have been asked to create a full-page advertisement for your local newspaper that shows how to apply the guidelines from MyPlate into daily eating habits. The advertisement needs to appeal to a variety of readers with colorful graphics, catchy phrases, and photos. Use poster board to create the advertisement and share with your class.

Social Studies

17. Research Family Food Choose a cultural background from your own family history. Research the kinds of food that the culture has eaten historically. How has the diet of this particular culture affected its health and life span? How do you incorporate this lifestyle and diet into your family today? Write an overview of what you have found about your family's cultural background.

Mathematics

18. Limiting Fat Jennifer's health class inspired her to start a more healthful eating plan. Her doctor recommended that she consume 2,200 calories a day. Yesterday, she calculated that she consumed 110 grams of fat during the day. What percent of Jennifer's total calories came from fat? If she wishes to reduce her fat intake to 30% of her daily calories, how many grams of fat should she have per day?

Math Concept **Calculating Percents** To find what percent a number is of another number, divide the first number by the second number, multiply by 100, and add the % symbol.

Starting Hint There are 9 calories in one gram of fat. Jennifer's total fat calories equal 110×9. Divide that total by 2,200 and multiply by 100 to find her current fat percentage. Reverse the process using the 30% amount to determine her optimal fat intake in grams.

Standardized Test Practice

Essay

Read the writing prompt and write an essay using details and examples to illustrate your points.

Test-Taking Tip Plan out your essay before you begin writing. Jot down the main points or details you want to focus on in the margins of your test. Refer to these points frequently as you write. This will help you remain focused.

19. Living a healthy lifestyle is a goal we should all have. Write an essay describing a person you know who is living a healthy lifestyle. Specifically describe the choices that person makes and how he or she lives a healthy lifestyle. Your essay should inspire readers to make their lifestyle healthier.

Chapter 20

Health and Fitness

Section 20.1

Physical Activity

■ **Main Idea** Choosing to include physical activity in your daily routine can improve your overall state of wellness.

Section 20.2

Body Weight and Health

■ **Main Idea** The best way to maintain a healthy body weight is to balance nutritious meals with physical activity.

Explore the Photo

Think about the phrase "Move more and sit less." *How do you think increasing your physical activity can improve your life?*

Advertisement

Physical Fitness is Fun Write an advertisement for elementary-age children in your community, encouraging them to start being physically fit now. Consider activities they would enjoy. Make suggestions about how they can begin. Convince them that being physically fit is fun and important. Include graphics or clip art to support your text.

Writing Tips Follow these steps to write an advertisement:

1. Consider your audience. What is important to them? How can you appeal to them?
2. Make your language concise, clear, and age appropriate.
3. Emphasize the benefits of what you are advertising.

Section 20.1 Physical Activity

Reading Guide

Before You Read

Preview Look at the photos and figures in this chapter and read their captions. Begin thinking about how physical activity benefits overall health

Read to Learn

Key Concepts

✓ **Explain** how fitness affects your daily activites.

✓ **Describe** Describe what is needed to reach and maintain a healthy body weight.

Main Idea

Choosing to include physical activity in your daily routine can improve your overall state of wellness.

Content Vocabulary

○ fitness
○ stamina
○ aerobic

Academic Vocabulary

■ obtain   ■ flexible

Graphic Organizer

As you read, identify five ways physical activity affects your body and your weight. Use a graphic organizer like the one shown to help you organize your information.

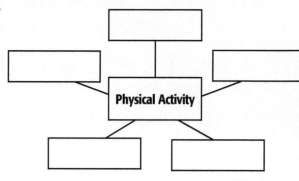

Graphic Organizer Go to connectED. mcgraw-hill.com to download this graphic organizer.

Schoolwork takes up much of Aaron's time. He has chores to do at home, and he has an after-shool job delivering flyers for local restaurants. Aaron also spends time with friends. Even though Aaron is busy, he still finds time to be physically active and to eat well. He stays fit by riding his bike, skating, and swimming at the community pool. What do you do to stay healthy and fit?

Wellness, Fitness, and Your Health

As You Read

Connect Think about the physical activities you enjoy most. How can you make them part of your fitness routine?

Wellness is taking positive steps toward your overall good health. Wellness has two main goals. One is to keep you healthy, and the other is to help you prevent disease and illness. When you choose wellness, you choose to take care of yourself. It is important that you make the effort now to become informed and to make smart choices that can help protect you for the rest of your life.

When you are physically fit, you look and feel your best. A healthy, fit body means you take care of yourself. **Fitness** is the ability to handle daily events in a healthy way. Fitness means that you:

- Have the energy to do your schoolwork and chores, with enough leftover to have fun too.
- Are confident about your abilities.
- Make physical activity and exercise a part of your life every day.
- Keep your weight at the right level for you.
- Can better deal with stress and the ups and downs of life.
- Are more able to do what you want to do in life.

 **Vocabulary**

You can find definitions in the glossary at the back of this book.

SUCCEED IN SCHOOL!

Build Self-Esteem Make Friends Make an effort to develop close friendships. These friends will offer support when you need it. It is important to have good friends and also to be a good friend.

• • • • • • • • • • • • •

Get Outdoors Outdoor sports are ways to have fun while staying healthy and fit. *What types of outdoor physical activity do you enjoy?*

Design Pics/Stock Foundry

Hands-On LAB

Walking as Exercise

In this activity you will learn how to incorporate walking into your regular activities. A brisk walk can burn up to 300 calories an hour. Before you begin, read through the entire Hands-On Lab assignment. Write down any questions that you have about the activity. Reread the text or ask your teacher for help if you need it.

Supplies
- ✓ Comfortable clothes
- ✓ Shoes designed for walking
- ✓ Notebook
- ✓ Digital step counter (optional)
- ✓ Water and snacks

Develop Your Plan
- Decide how far you want to walk.
- Consider the weather conditions.
- Find routes outdoors and indoors, such as a shopping mall.
- Determine where you can walk safely.

Implement Your Plan
- Dress in comfortable clothes appropriate for weather conditions.
- Wear comfortable walking shoes and socks.
- Walk the route or routes you chose.
- If possible, walk with a friend, family member, or pet.

- Walk 10 minutes a day to start.
- Increase your frequency and distance each week for a month.
- Keep a log of your distance and time walked.
- Record any changes you notice in your physical fitness.

Evaluate Your Results

How did you decide where to you walk? How far and for how long did you walk the first time? How much distance and time did you add to your walks? What differences did you notice in your physical fitness? Write one or more paragraphs to explain your answers.

Projects and Activities Go to connectED.mcgraw-hill.com.

Colin Hawkins/Getty Images

You cannot be fit unless you are physically active. By exercising regularly you will enjoy all the benefits of fitness:

- You can feel more positive about yourself. Knowing you are taking care of your body is good for your self-esteem.
- You can look your best. Physical activity helps you control weight and gives you a healthy appearance.
- Day-to-day tasks may seem easier because your energy level may improve.
- Relax and sleep more easily.
- Your physical and mental stamina may increase. **Stamina** is the ability to focus on or perform a single activity for a long time. For example, you may be able to dance without getting too tired, and you may be able to pay more attention in class and learn more.

There are plenty of enjoyable, inexpensive ways to exercise. What is important is that you make physical activity a regular part of your life. For example, Jennifer walks to school instead of taking the bus. Her friend Nick plays on a softball team and enjoys getting together with friends to play volleyball on weekends.

Financial Literacy

Exercise Classes

Lucy has recently signed up for a membership at her local gym. She enjoys using the gym's strength and cardio equipment, but she is also interested in the classes the gym offers, such as aerobics, yoga, and kickboxing. However, the classes are not included in Lucy's regular membership. She has the option of paying $2.50 for each class she takes. Another option is to upgrade her membership and take an unlimited number of classes for an extra $15 each month. How many classes would she need to take each month to make the $15 per month upgrade plan the less expensive option?

Math Concept Solving Algebraic Equations
Use a variable such as x to represent an unknown quantity. Rearrange the equation step by step so that the variable is on one side of the equals sign, and all other numbers are on the other.

Starting Hint Let x stand for the number of classes. To find the number of classes where the prices of both options are the same, write an equation: $2.50x = 15$. Solve for x by dividing both sides by $2.50.

 For math help, go to the Math Appendix at the back of the book.

Reading Check *Name What are the two main goals of wellness?*

Exercise and Physical Activity

Physical activity is essential if you want to obtain, or reach, and maintain a healthy body weight. Whether you want to lose weight, gain weight, or maintain your weight, physical activity has many benefits.

Calories Physical activity burns calories. During physical activity, your body burns up calories from the food you eat. A calorie is a unit of energy. By using calories for energy, your body will store fewer calories as body fat. **Figure 20.1** shows how activities you may be doing can help you burn calories.

D. Hurst/Alamy

Stay Hydrated

Be sure to drink plenty of water (but not too much) while working out. Fluids must be replaced to prevent dehydration, or loss of body fluid.

- Drink water before you feel thirsty.

- Watch for signs of dehydration, including fatigue, headache, nausea, and light-headedness.

There is no way to burn fat in a specific area of the body. Physical activity burns calories and fat from all parts of the body. That is why a variety of physical activity helps your overall appearance.

Heart and Lungs Staying physically active helps your heart and lungs work at peak function. **Aerobic** (ˌer-ˈō-bik) activities are continuous, rhythmic activities that improve the efficiency of your heart and lungs. Aerobic activities such as running, bicycling, and swimming increase your intake of oxygen and help improve circulation.

Flexibility Being flexible allows you to kneel, bend, turn, and throw. It also helps reduce your risk of injury. You can improve your flexibility by doing activities that involve stretching and bending.

Appetite Control Physical activity can help relieve stress and tension, which can trigger a desire to eat more or less than you normally would.

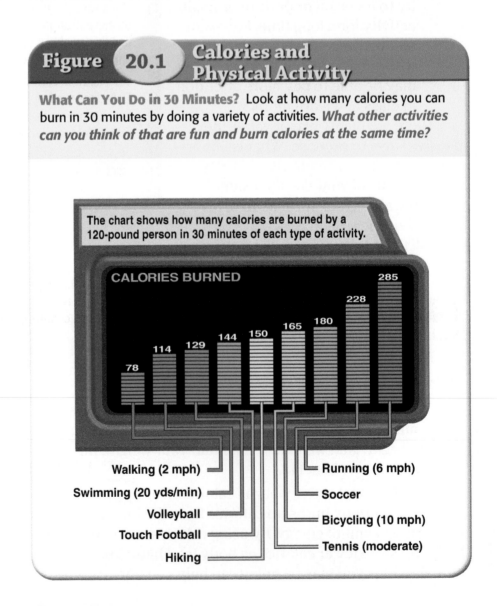

Figure 20.1 Calories and Physical Activity

What Can You Do in 30 Minutes? Look at how many calories you can burn in 30 minutes by doing a variety of activities. *What other activities can you think of that are fun and burn calories at the same time?*

The chart shows how many calories are burned by a 120-pound person in 30 minutes of each type of activity.

CALORIES BURNED

Activity	Calories
Walking (2 mph)	78
Swimming (20 yds/min)	114
Volleyball	129
Touch Football	144
Hiking	150
Running (6 mph)	165
Soccer	180
Bicycling (10 mph)	228
Tennis (moderate)	285

Choose an Exercise Routine

To exercise regularly, you need to find an exercise routine that suits you and that you enjoy. From walking to dancing to team sports, the options are endless.

Organized Exercise Volleyball, baseball, basketball, and soccer are just a few types of organized ways to participate in physical activity. Sign up to be a part of a team, or organize your friends for a regular game.

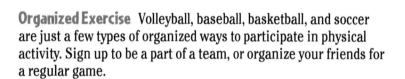

Indoor Exercise You can lift small hand weights or work out on larger machines to build muscle and bone density. You can also use cardio machines indoors, such as a treadmill, elliptical, or stationary bike.

Outdoor Exercise Walking, running, swimming, biking, and skating are activities you can enjoy outdoors. Being out in the fresh air and sunshine can be very motivating. Find an outdoor activity that you look forward to.

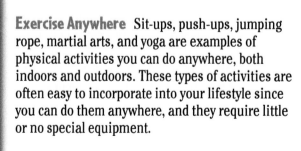

Exercise Anywhere Sit-ups, push-ups, jumping rope, martial arts, and yoga are examples of physical activities you can do anywhere, both indoors and outdoors. These types of activities are often easy to incorporate into your lifestyle since you can do them anywhere, and they require little or no special equipment.

Be More Active

There are many ways to put more movement into your life. You do not have to be an athlete to be active. Aim for at least 60 minutes of physical activity every day. You can do it all at once, or spread it out in 15- or 20-minute periods. Try these ideas:

Use your feet. When possible, walk instead of getting a ride.

Use your wheels. Skating and biking are great ways to get moving.

Take the stairs. Avoid elevators and escalators. Get your energy up by using the stairs.

Let music get you moving. Dance alone or with friends.

Do chores. Many chores, such as dusting, raking leaves, and taking out the trash can get you moving.

Help others. See if you have neighbors who need help with chores, pet walking, or yard work.

Play and have fun! Do what you enjoy, as long as it involves movement.

Section 20.1 After You Read

Review What You Have Learned

1. **Explain** the positive ways fitness helps you handle daily events.
2. **Identify** the benefits of exercise.

Practice Academic Skills

English Language Arts

3. Write an essay that encourages teens to be fit. Include benefits of fitness with specific examples of how fitness helps you look and feel your best.

Social Studies

4. Research the benefits of organized exercise versus more individual exercise. How can each aid in the development of not only a person's fitness and lifelong commitment to exercise, but also other important characteristics? Be prepared to share your findings with your classmates.

. . . .

Check Your Answers Check Your Answers at connectED.mcgraw-hill.com.

Section 20.2 Body Weight and Health

Knowing what is healthful for you and your body is a life-long commitment. Though some teens may use celebrities or sports figures as models for the perfect body, it is important for everyone to accept the body they have and work to make it the best it can be. The best way to keep your body healthy is to eat well and exercise regularly.

Healthy Body Weight

Are you happy with your weight? Do you think that you are too heavy or too thin? People who maintain a healthy body weight are neither overweight nor underweight. Being overweight can lead to obesity. **Obesity** is a condition in which a person's weight is 20 percent or more above his or her healthy weight. Obese people are at greater risk for such illnesses as diabetes and heart disease.

Vocabulary

You can find definitions in the glossary at the back of this book.

Being underweight is unhealthy, too. People who are underweight often are not eating enough or properly. This means that they are not getting the nutrients they need.

Reading Check **Distinguish** *How is being underweight considered unhealthy?*

Build Self-Esteem

Help Others Part of developing self-esteem is knowing that you can help others. You feel good about yourself when you offer support to your family or friends, or when you take part in community activities such as visiting the elderly or working with children.

● ● ● ● ● ● ● ● ● ● ●

Healthy Weight Your healthy body weight depends on your height and body type. *How does being overweight or underweight affect your health?*

Thinkstock/Stockbyte/Getty Images

Healthy and Unhealthy Weight Loss

Think of controlling your weight as a balancing act. You have to balance the calories you get from the foods you eat with the calories you **expend**, or use, for energy. You gain weight when you consume more calories than your body uses. You lose weight when your body uses more calories than you consume. To maintain your weight, you must make sure that the calories you eat equal those you burn as energy.

Many teens think that they need to lose or gain weight. They believe that they have to eat or avoid certain foods or skip meals. It is important to eat a balanced diet. Include foods you enjoy, but limit the amount of fats, oils, and sweets. The most healthful way to lose excess weight is to take in fewer calories and participate in more physical activities.

Fad Diets

Achieving a healthy body weight through physical activity and a well-balanced diet takes time. Only a balanced meal plan combined with physical activity will work for healthy weight loss or maintenance, and long-term success. If you are overweight or obese, you might be tempted to lose weight quickly by going on a fad diet. A **fad diet** promises quick weight loss through unrealistic or unhealthful means. Fad dieting usually results in muscle and water loss, but not in the loss of fat.

COMMUNITY CONNECTIONS

Be a Role Model
Volunteer with a youth agency that coordinates physical activities for younger children. Be a trail guide, a coach, or a role model for children to be fit and healthy.

Discover International...
Fitness

Yoga
The word yoga means union in Sanskrit, the language of ancient India where yoga began. The union is the relationship between the mind, body, and spirit. In the western world, yoga is most commonly understood as physical exercises and stretching. However, yoga is more than just stretching. It is about creating balance in the body through developing both strength and flexibility. This is done through the performance of poses or postures, each of which has specific physical benefits.

Yoga [ˌyō-gə] a system of exercises, breathing, and meditation for achieving bodily or mental control and well-being.

chrisgramly/Getty Images

Balance Calories You can still eat your favorite foods, such as ice cream or potato chips, if you balance physical activity, healthful foods, and calories. *How does exercising affect the amount of calories you can consume?*

Avoid any diet that encourages:

- **Consuming only liquids.** A low-calorie, all-liquid diet does not offer the food energy, fiber, or nutrients that you need.
- **Fasting.** If you fast, or stop eating, even for a short period, your body will not get the nutrients and energy needed to function properly. When you starve yourself, your body will burn up muscle, not fat, in order to get the protein it needs for growth.
- **The use of diet pills.** Diet pills contain drugs that can temporarily suppress, or hold back, your desire to eat. However, the drugs can cause harmful side effects like a rapid heart rate, anxiety, and addiction.

Fad diets are rarely successful in controlling weight. Most people who lose weight on a fad diet gain the weight back and sometimes more. Fad diets are often unbalanced, which means that they do not provide all of the nutrients you need. Some may even cause physical harm.

Steroids

Steroids are prescription drugs used for specific medical conditions. Steroids should not be used as bodybuilding supplements. Steroids can damage your skin and even cause a heart attack or stroke. Also, steroids can make you irritable and restless.

The most sensible and healthy way to control your weight is to combine a nutritious and balanced meal plan with physical activity. In the long run, you will be more likely to maintain a healthy weight.

Reading Check   *Predict* *What are some of the dangers of diet pills?*

Eating Disorders

Some people can develop an **eating disorder**, which is an extreme eating behavior that can lead to depression, anxiety, and even death. Eating disorders are psychological problems that are related to food. Both males and females can suffer from eating disorders. Teens with eating disorders often try to hide them. If left untreated, eating disorders will damage your body.

Anorexia Nervosa

Anorexia nervosa (ˌa-nə-ˌrek-sē-ə (ˌ)nər-ˈvō-sə) is an eating disorder in which a person feels an extreme fear of gaining weight. A person suffering from anorexia nervosa severely limits eating in an attempt to either lose weight or keep from gaining weight. No matter how thin the person becomes, he or she still feels overweight. Dieting turns into self-starvation. Someone suffering from anorexia nervosa may cut food into tiny pieces, chew food for a long time, or constantly rearrange food. An anorexic person also may exercise for dangerously long periods of time. He or she may also spend less time with friends. Anorexia can cause heart disease, stunted growth, brain damage, and even death.

SCIENCE YOU CAN USE

Target Heart Rate

When exercising, it is important to know how hard you may be working or how much harder you can work safely. Knowing your target heart rate zone is a good way to measure this. By measuring your heart rate during exercise, you can work to keep your heart rate in the correct zone.

Procedure During exercise, take your heart rate by putting your index finger to your neck or wrist. Count the beats for 15 seconds. Multiple that number of beats by 4.

Analysis Note your level of exertion. Now, try different types of exercise for different lengths of time (for example, walk quickly up a flight of stairs, run for 5 minutes, run for 2 minutes, walk for 10 minutes, do 50 jumping jacks). Find your heart rate during at least five different types of physical activity and then compare them. Is there consistency with your heart rate and how tired you are? If you exercised longer or harder, did your heart rate increase? What is your heart rate range?

Bulimia Nervosa

Bulimia nervosa (bü-'lē-mē-ə (,)nər-'vō-sə) is an eating disorder in which a person eats very large amounts of food, then vomits or uses laxatives to get rid of the eaten food. Bulimia patients often suffer from depression and often become dependent on drugs. Bulimia is a secret ritual and can be hard to recognize. Bulimics usually weigh within 15 pounds of a healthy weight. A bulimic person often has stained teeth and swollen cheeks due to damage to the teeth, gums, and esophagus. Without help to control the disorder, bulimia can lead to kidney problems, heart failure, throat cancer, and even death.

Binge Eating

Binge eating is an eating disorder in which a person eats large quantities of food at one time. A binge eater has a lack of control over his or her eating habits and cannot stop eating. Binge eaters do not exercise excessively. People with a binge eating disorder may be overweight or they may gain and lose weight frequently. Binging often results in weight gain, high blood pressure, heart disease, and diabetes.

Reading Check *Connect* *What health problems can be caused by eating disorders or extreme eating behaviors?*

L. Mouton/PhotoAlto

Self-Concept and Fitness You are much more than the size or shape of your body. *What can you do every day to keep feeling good about yourself?*

Take Care of Yourself

Eating disorders can be caused by low self-esteem, depression, troubled relationships, poor body image, and chemical imbalances in the brain. If you think you or someone you know has an eating disorder, talk to a parent, teacher, or counselor. It almost always takes medical, nutritional, and psychological counseling to defeat an eating disorder. A key part of preventing eating disorders is educating yourself. You need be aware of the symptoms and be informed about where you can get help. It is also important to remember that your worth as a person is much deeper than your body size.

Remember that you are unique. Do not compare your body type to anyone else. Resist media images of "perfect" body types, such as those of supermodels, movie stars, and professional athletes. There is no such thing as a "perfect" body. Work to maintain a positive attitude about yourself and your life. Be the very best you can be by following a healthy meal plan and enjoying lots of physical activity.

Section 20.2 After You Read

Review What You Have Learned

1. **Define** obesity.
2. **Summarize** the relationship between the amount of calories you consume and the amount of physical activity you get.
3. **Name** the three most common eating disorders.
4. **Explain** what you should do if you think someone has an eating disorder.

Practice Academic Skills

English Language Arts

5. Write a letter to a friend who you think may have an eating disorder. Explain what the signs are and what the long-term effects could be. Encourage him or her to find support and help in dealing with the problem.

Social Studies

6. Choose one of the common eating disorders mentioned in the chapter and research about how it develops, what contributes to its development, and how it is treated. Write an overview of what you discover about the disorder.

Check Your Answers Check Your Answers at connectED.mcgraw-hill.com.

Discovering Careers

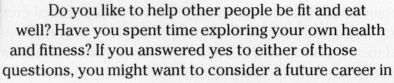

Do you like to help other people be fit and eat well? Have you spent time exploring your own health and fitness? If you answered yes to either of those questions, you might want to consider a future career in health and fitness. The following chart explores several careers in the health and fitness industry.

Job Title	Job Description
Weight-Loss Counselor	Assists people in devising and carrying out a weight-loss plan. Discusses eating habits that encourage good nutrition.
Sports Trainer	Works with athletes and sports teams to support injuries and training challenges for individuals. Creates plans for training to avoid injury.
Exercise Physiologist	Develops exercise programs. Promotes physical fitness. Records patient's heart activity during exercise under physician's supervision. Checks physical condition of client.
Personal Trainer	Develops personalized training programs based on client's goals and aspirations. Provides motivation, support, and assistance while clients work out.
Eating Disorders Therapist	Provides individual, group, and family therapy. Treats physical symptoms, psychological issues, social concerns, and nutritional problems. Works with dietitians and medical professionals to develop meal plans and food shopping strategies.

Career Activities ▼

At School

1 Select three of the careers listed. Research the education, training, and work experience required for each career. Write a summary of your results.

At Home

2 Create a log of your family's physical activity for a week. Then talk about how you and your family could improve your health and fitness.

At Work

3 Name three ways healthy employees benefit the workplace. Share your findings with your classmates.

In the Community

4 Contact and interview someone in your community who works in health and fitness. Ask this person to describe what his or her typical work day is like. Share what you learned with your class.

Ingram Publishing

Chapter Summary

Section 20.1 Physical Activity
Wellness is taking positive steps toward your good health, including physical activity. When you are physically fit, you look and feel your best. A healthy, fit body means you take care of yourself. Fitness is the ability to handle daily events in a healthy way. By exercising regularly you can enjoy all the benefits of fitness. Physical activity is necessary if you want to reach and maintain a healthy body weight. There are many activities you can add to your daily routine to get more movement.

Section 20.2 Body Weight and Health
People who maintain a healthy body weight are neither overweight nor underweight. You have to balance the calories you eat with the calories you use for energy. The most sensible and healthy way to control your weight is to combine a nutritious and balanced meal plan with physical activity. Some people develop eating disorders, or extreme eating behaviors, that can lead to depression, anxiety, disease, and even death. Work to maintain a positive attitude about yourself and your life.

Words You Learned

1. Create a fill-in-the-blank sentence for each of these vocabulary terms. The sentence should contain enough information to help determine the missing word.

Content Vocabulary
- fitness (p. 445)
- stamina (p. 447)
- aerobic (p. 448)
- obesity (p. 452)
- fad diet (p. 453)
- eating disorder (p. 455)
- anorexia nervosa (p. 455)
- bulimia nervosa (p. 456)
- binge eating (p. 456)

Academic Vocabulary
- obtain (p. 447)
- flexible (p. 448)
- expend (p. 453)
- fast (p. 454)

Review Key Concepts

2. **Explain** how fitness affects your daily activities.

3. **Describe** what is needed to reach and maintain a healthy body weight.

4. **List** the risks associated with obesity.

5. **Explain** the most healthful way to lose excess weight.

6. **Identify** how eating disorders can destroy your health.

7. **Recognize** the causes of eating disorders.

Critical Thinking

8. **Compare and contrast** how being overweight and underweight affects the body.

9. **Propose** your own plan for balancing diet and exercise.

Real-World Skills and Applications

Problem-Solving

10. Prioritize For some people, it is often difficult to carve out time for exercise, yet it is something you need to do in order to be healthy. Look at your own daily schedule for a week. Make exercise a priority. Come up with a schedule where exercise is a high priority.

Interpersonal and Collaborative

11. Healthful Alternatives Follow your teacher's directions to form groups. In your group, cut out advertisements for junk food. Then create your own advertisement for a healthful alternative made with fruits or vegetables. Cut out pictures or draw your own. Write your own advertisement to convince people to buy your product. Use descriptive language to explain the benefits, including taste and nutrition. Share your advertisements with the other groups.

Financial Literacy

12. Exercise More, Spend Less Many people decide that the best way to commit to working out on a regular basis is signing up for a gym membership. Health clubs have many advantages: they offer a wide array of exercise classes and state-of-the-art fitness equipment. Many people also like working out in a group setting, and the opportunity to work with personal trainers. However, a gym membership can be very expensive. Think about some of the ways you can get some of the same benefits without purchasing a health club membership. Make a list of five low-cost (or no-cost) ways you can get strength training, cardiovascular training, and/or other fitness activities (like those offered in exercise classes) without signing up at a health club.

ACTIVE LEARNING

13. Fitness Picnic Take a group of friends to the park. Fly kites, play baseball, toss a football, run laps, do sit-ups and push-ups, or other simple physical activities. Picnic on delicious yet healthful snacks, such as fresh fruits and vegetables, breads, and cheeses after you have had a good workout. How did you feel after the fitness picnic? How was it better for you than other activities? Share the benefits of the picnic with your class.

14. Research a Fruit or Vegetable Choose a fruit or vegetable that you may not know much about. Research its history, how and where it is grown, who eats it, and the ways it can be prepared. Prepare a brief presentation on what you find to the class. Can you find an unusual recipe that incorporates your fruit or vegetable?

NET Connection

15. Calorie Burning With permission from your teacher or parents, go online and search for a calorie-burning calculator. Calculate how many calories you can burn doing different types of exercise. Record your findings in your Life Skills Binder and refer to them when you exercise.

D. Hurst/Alamy

Academic Skills

English Language Arts

16. Other Benefits Physical activity is great for the body, but it also benefits your mental health. It can help improve your perspective, or the way you look at life. Write a short essay to explain the ways physical fitness and good nutrition can improve more than just your physical health.

Science

17. Cross Training Cross training is an important aspect of exercising. Using the same muscles over and over again makes your body accustomed to the activity and can leave you open to injury. It is important to do different types of exercise which use different muscle groups in different ways.

Procedure List different physical activities and how they work your body's muscles. Consider how you could add variety to your workouts.

Analysis Plan a physical fitness program that includes a variety of physical activities for cross training.

Mathematics

18. Fitness Goal Sheldon is planning to try out for his school's swim team. He does not have a pool at home, and the community pool is closed for repairs. Since jogging is easy and free, he decided to improve his health and stamina by setting a goal of jogging 20 minutes a day. Sheldon has most of the summer to get ready for the tryouts, so he plans to jog every weekday until school starts. If he jogs for 16 minutes on Monday, 30 minutes on Tuesday, 20 minutes on Wednesday, and 14 minutes on Thursday, how long should he jog on Friday to reach his average?

Math Concept **Calculating Mean** When you have a series of values, calculate the mean, or average, by finding the sum of all of the values, and dividing that sum by the number of values.

Starting Hint The sum of five values, divided by 5, equals 20. Write an algebraic equation to find the missing value: $(16 + 30 + 20 + 14 + x) \div 5 = 20$. Solve for x.

Standardized Test Practice

Multiple Choice
Choose the letter of the best answer.

> **Test-Taking Tip** Eat well before taking a test. Have a good breakfast or lunch and avoid junk food. Studies show that you need good nutrition to concentrate and perform your best.

19. If I spend 6% of my time doing physical activity over 4,000 hours, how much time have I spent?
 a. 240 hours
 b. 600 hours
 c. 24 hours
 d. 200 hours

Play with Your Food!

Eating well and exercising are good ways to keep healthy. Your doctor can give you advice to follow for your age and size. Participating in sports and walking are ways to keep active. This project will help you explore ways to stay healthy.

My Journal Complete the journal entry from page 417, and refer to it to select and research your play's topic.

Project Assignment ▼

In this project, you will:

- List topics about health issues in your age group.
- Research facts about a health topic of your choice.
- Write a short play about nutrition and exercise.
- Interview an expert on physical fitness.
- Act out your play for your class.
- Include this project in the ninth section of your personal Life Skills binder.

 Step 1 Select and Research Your Topic

Choose a health issue related to nutrition and fitness. Use the textbook to start your research. Look for more information from magazine articles, health books, or Web sites. Write a summary of your research.

Step 2 Write a Play About Taking Care of Your Body

Invent two characters and imagine a scene in which they talk about your topic. Write a dialogue that uses the facts you have researched to make a point. The play should last about two minutes. Use these questions to help you write the dialogue:

✔ Are your characters explaining the facts we need to know?
✔ Have you picked a situation for the characters that best illustrates the issue?
✔ Is the dialogue natural and understandable?
✔ Does the ending make a strong point?

Step 3 Interview An Expert on Nutrition and Fitness

Read your play to a health expert like a doctor, nurse, nutritionist, or personal trainer. Then ask these questions:

✔ Please give an example of how you handle my topic in your job.
✔ How effective is the play I wrote?
✔ What changes can I make so that I make my point clearly?

Use these interviewing skills when conducting your interview and these writing skills when writing the summary of notes from your interview.

Interviewing Skills
- Record interview responses and take notes.
- Listen attentively.

Writing Skills
- Use complete sentences.
- Use correct spelling and grammar.

Life Skills Project Checklist

Research Nutrition and Fitness

✅ Gather facts about your chosen topic.

✅ Imagine a scene that would demonstrate the important ideas and facts of your topic.

✅ Interview a doctor, nutritionist, or other health professional.

Writing Skills

✅ List the facts about your chosen topic.

✅ Write the facts into the dialogue of a play.

✅ Write a summary from your interview with a health professional.

Present Your Findings

✅ Memorize the lines of your play, and partner with another classmate to perform it.

✅ Invite the students of the class to ask any questions they may have. Answer these questions with responses that respect their perspectives.

✅ Add this project to your Life Skills binder.

Academic Skills

✅ Conduct research to gather information.

✅ Communicate effectively.

✅ Organize your presentation so the audience can follow along easily.

✅ Thoroughly express your ideas.

Step 4 Perform Your Play for Your Class

Use the Life Skills Project Checklist on the right to plan, memorize your lines, and perform your play for the class.

Use these speaking skills when presenting your final report.

Speaking Skills

- Speak clearly and concisely.
- Be sensitive to the needs of your audience.
- Use standard English to communicate.

Step 5 Evaluate Your Presentation

Your project will be evaluated based on:

✔ The detail and organization of your research on the health issue you chose.

✔ The written dialogue of the play.

✔ The impact of your performance and memorization of lines.

✔ The summary written from interview notes.

✔ Grammar and sentence structure.

✔ Presentation to the class.

✔ Creativity and neatness.

🖈 **Evaluation Rubric** Go to connectED. mcgraw-hill.com for a rubric you can use to evaluate your final project.

Chapter 21
Working in the Kitchen

Chapter 22
Prepare to Cook

Chapter 23
Cooking Basics

Unit Preview

This unit is about kitchen safety and cooking basics. In this unit, you will learn about:

- Safe kitchen and food-handling practices.
- Preventing accidents in the kitchen.
- Meal preparation and food shopping.
- Reading and following recipes.
- Choosing the best ingredients.
- A variety of cooking techniques.

Explore the Photo
Cooking can be a fun and delicious experience which allows you to be creative. *What dishes or favorite meals do you know how to cook?*

A Meal from Your Culture

When you are done studying this unit, you will complete a project in which you will:

✓ Prepare a dish that reflects your heritage.

✓ Interview a member of your cultural community about the recipe.

✓ Share your meal with the class, explaining why it is important to your family or culture.

The prewriting activity below will help you get started.

My Journal

Prewriting Activity
Locate Information

Conduct research to find recipes for meals or foods that reflect your cultural heritage. Choose two or three dishes that you enjoy with your family, or meals that have special memories for you. Add recipes for these dishes to your journal and include answers to these questions:

● Besides being tasty, what makes these meals or foods important to you?

● What makes these meals or foods unique to your family or culture?

● What memories are associated with these meals or foods?

Chapter **21**

Working in the Kitchen

Thinkstock / Alamy

Explore the Photo

There are many things you need to keep in mind in order to stay safe in the kitchen. *What can happen if you do not pay attention to what you are doing while you cook or prepare a meal?*

Write a Personal Narrative

Remember When Choose a vivid memory from your childhood about an event or situation that happened in the kitchen. Narrate the events related to this memory so that your readers will understand why the event was important and memorable.

Writing Tips Follow these steps to write a personal narrative:

1. Use a strong point of view. The reader should be able to imagine what you are describing.
2. Begin with your thesis statement that communicates your memory, the point you want to make, and why the event was so memorable.
3. Tell a story.

467

Reading Guide

Before You Read

Use Color As you read this section, try using different colored pens to take notes, using a different color for each different type of information. This is a visual trick that can help you learn new material and study for tests. For example, you could use red for vocabulary words, blue for explanations, and green for examples.

Read to Learn

Key Concepts

✓ **Name** two types of bacteria that cause food poisoning.

✓ **Explain** how to keep leftovers from spoiling.

Main Idea

Food contamination occurs when food is handled improperly. Learn techniques to keep your kitchen and food clean and safe.

Content Vocabulary

○ foodborne illness ○ salmonella
○ contamination ○ perishable
○ E. coli

Academic Vocabulary

■ minimize ■ promptly

Graphic Organizer

As you read, write down three ways to help prevent food contamination. Use a graphic organizer like the one shown to help you organize your information.

Prevent Food Contamination
1.
2.
3.

Graphic Organizer Go to connectED. mcgraw-hill.com to download this graphic organizer.

As You Read

Connect Think about the foods and beverages in your refrigerator. Is there anything that should be thrown out?

When you get home from school, do you remember to wash your hands before eating? Sometimes you may be in a hurry and grab a snack without thinking about washing your hands. Eating unsafe food can make you very sick. Do you practice food and kitchen safety?

Foodborne Illness

Foodborne illness, also called food poisoning, is an illness caused by unsafe food. Food can become unsafe because of bacteria, parasites, fungi, viruses, or harmful chemicals. The symptoms of foodborne illnesses can sometimes feel like a mild flu. Symptoms such as diarrhea, nausea, stomach pain, headache, muscle pain, and fatigue usually appear within four to forty-eight hours after eating unsafe food. Get rest and drink plenty of fluids. If you have symptoms for more than one or two days, call a doctor. The safe handling of food and utensils can prevent most food-borne illnesses.

 **Vocabulary**
You can find definitions in the glossary at the back of this book.

Reading Check *Identify* *What are the symptoms of foodborne illnesses?*

Keep Food Safe

Contamination occurs when food becomes infected with harmful bacteria. If you follow some simple procedures when you handle and prepare food, you can minimize, or decrease, the risk of food contamination. In mild cases, people who eat contaminated food may experience headaches, stomach cramps, and fever. In more severe cases, however, medical attention may be necessary.

A few types of bacteria cause most food poisoning. **E. coli** is the most deadly form of food poisoning. E. coli bacteria are found in contaminated water, raw or rare ground beef, and unpasteurized milk. For this reason, you should only eat hamburgers that have been fully cooked. Another common type of food poisoning is caused by salmonella bacteria. **Salmonella** (ˌsal-mə-ˈne-lə) bacteria are often found in raw or undercooked foods, such as meat, eggs, fish, and poultry. Salmonella grow quickly at room temperature and can be spread by hands and cooking utensils. Thoroughly cook all meat, poultry, fish, and eggs. Wash your hands, knife, and cutting board with soap and hot water whenever you cut raw meat, fish, or poultry.

You should always clean up the kitchen as you cook. Wipe up spills immediately and clean off the countertops. As you finish using pots, pans, and cooking utensils, wash them in hot, soapy water. By keeping the kitchen clean, it will be a more healthful and pleasant place to work.

Stay Alert
Snooze or Lose
If you are too tired, you will not be able to concentrate well in class. Not getting enough sleep can lead to poor school performance. Balance your time in order to get enough sleep.
• • • • • • • • • • • • •

Handling Food

Another way to reduce the risk of food poisoning is to handle perishable foods carefully. Foods that are **perishable** are likely to spoil quickly. Perishable foods include meat, poultry, fish, eggs, fresh fruits and vegetables, leftovers, and dairy products. Hot foods such as hamburgers should be kept hot, and cold foods such as yogurt should be kept cold until they are eaten. Keep hot foods at 140°F (60°C) or above, and cold foods at 40°F (4°C) or below. Otherwise bacteria might grow.

Foods that have been cooked should not stand at room temperature for more than two hours. For a packed lunch or picnic, use cold packs and a cooler to keep the cold foods cold.

Storing Leftovers

To keep leftovers from spoiling, refrigerate or freeze them promptly, or immediately after the meal. Put leftovers in a tightly covered shallow container, and store them in the refrigerator. Many leftovers can also be frozen for use at a later date. When freezing leftovers, pack them in an airtight container, and label them with the name of the food and the date. Freezing food keeps bacteria from growing until the food is thawed. Most foods can be stored in the freezer for several months.

Freezer Storage

You can keep packaged frozen foods, meat, poultry, fish, bread, and home-prepared mixed dishes fresh and appealing by properly freezing them. Some foods do not freeze well, such as cooked egg whites, lettuce, and foods with mayonnaise or salad dressing.

Here are some storage guidelines:

- Store frozen foods in their original packages.
- Wrap foods properly so they do not spoil or get freezer burn. Freezer burn is harmless, but it causes unappealing, dried-up white areas on food. To prevent freezer burn, keep foods airtight in freezer paper, heavy-duty foil, freezer-quality plastic bags, or plastic freezer containers.
- Label frozen foods with the name, date frozen, and serving amount.

MATH YOU CAN USE

+ − × ÷ ENTER

Thaw a Turkey

The safest way to thaw a frozen turkey is in the refrigerator. Allow 24 hours of thawing time for every 5 pounds (2 kg) of turkey. On what day do you need to start defrosting a 20-pound (9 kg) turkey for Thanksgiving, which falls on a Thursday?

Math Concept **Selecting Units of Measure** Converting measurements into more manageable equivalents makes problem solving easier. For example, 24 hours = 1 day.

Starting Hint First, determine the number of days needed to defrost the turkey. Then, count backward from Thursday. Remember: the turkey will need to be cooked starting Thanksgiving morning!

 For more math help, go to the Math Appendix located at the back of this book.

Prevent Food Contamination

To avoid getting sick from the foods you eat, you need to follow some basic guidelines for handling food. These guidelines will help you care for your health and the health of others.

(l)Ken Karp/McGraw-Hill Education; (r)Photodisc/Alamy

Keep Your Kitchen and Utensils Clean Keep hands, counters, and utensils clean. If you spill something on the floor, wipe it up immediately with a paper towel, cloth, or mop. Wash cutting boards, utensils, and hands after handling raw meat, poultry, or seafood. Use separate towels for drying hands and drying dishes.

Prepare Food Properly When you are ill, it is best not to prepare food for others. Thaw frozen foods in the refrigerator or microwave oven. Keep raw meat, poultry, and seafood separate from other foods. Wash raw foods thoroughly. Keep your hair out of the food.

Serve and Store Food Safely Keep hot foods hot and cold foods cold. Serve cold and cooked food immediately. Refrigerate leftovers immediately. Use a separate spoon for tasting food. After you have used it for tasting, wash the spoon.

Food Safety and Shopping When shopping for food, put raw meat, poultry, and fish in plastic bags so they will not drip on other food. Check package labels for "use by" dates and directions for storage and cooking. Choose chilled, high-quality fresh produce. Refrigerated foods should feel cold and frozen foods should be solid. Avoid discolored or mushy frozen packages. Ice crystals signal thawed, refrozen food. Shop for refrigerated, frozen, and deli foods last. They will have less time to warm up. Avoid food packages with holes, tears, or broken safety seals. Pick canned goods without dents, bulges, rust, or leaks. Bulging cans signal that a food has been contaminated with dangerous organisms. Take groceries home right away. If getting groceries home takes more than 30 minutes, bring an insulated cooler for perishable foods.

🔼 **Store Leftovers** Put away leftovers without delay. *Why is it important to store leftovers properly?*

Refrigerator Storage

A refrigerator keeps perishable foods fresh for one day to several weeks. Even properly stored foods will not keep forever. Keep your refrigerator as cold as possible without freezing foods. Safe temperatures range from 32°F to 40°F (0°C to 4°C). Inside shelves and drawers stay colder than door shelves. Refrigerator storage guidelines include:

- Use foil, plastic wrap, zippered plastic bags, or airtight containers to cover and protect food.
- Put meat, poultry, fish, milk, and eggs on inside shelves. Use door shelves for most condiments, such as ketchup, mustard, and relish.
- Place raw meat, poultry, and fish on a plate or in a plastic bag, on the bottom shelf so they do not drip onto other foods.
- Leave space for cold air to circulate around food.
- Wipe spills immediately. Sanitize drawers. Throw away spoiled foods.

Dry Storage

Keep nonperishable foods in a cabinet or pantry. This includes grains such as rice, cereal, flour, and crackers. Oils, dry herbs, and unopened cans and jars can also be stored safely in a cabinet or pantry. Dry storage areas should be clean, dry, dark, and cool (below 85°F or 29°C). Tips for dry storage include:

- Do not store foods above the refrigerator or stove, or near a furnace outlet.
- Do not keep food under a sink. Openings around pipes cannot be sealed. Pests and moisture from pipes can spoil food.
- Do not store cleaning products or trash near food. Cleaners, detergents, and other household chemicals can contaminate food.
- Read the labels on food packaging. Some foods need refrigeration after being opened.

SUCCEED IN SCHOOL!

Stay Alert
Snack Attack Hunger dulls the brain. If you are thinking about food, you will not be able to pay attention as well in class. One way to avoid hunger is to be sure to eat a healthful breakfast every morning.

Section 21.1 After You Read

Review What You Have Learned

1. **Identify** places where E. coli bacteria can develop.
2. **Describe** freezer burn and how to prevent it.

Practice Academic Skills

English Language Arts

3. Write a step-by-step kitchen safety guide for someone who is just starting out in the kitchen. Provide guidelines for keeping the kitchen and food safe. Be sure to include what tools or supplies they will need.

Social Studies

4. Research food safety regulations for restaurants in your community. What are the guidelines for clean kitchens and cooking? How often are restaurants checked for following guidelines? How do the guidelines contribute to public safety? Write a short overview of what you discover.

✦ **Check Your Answers** Check Your Answers at connectED.mcgraw-hill.com.

Section 21.2 Kitchen Essentials

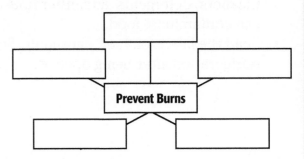
As You Read

Connect Being in the kitchen can be dangerous. What are the potential dangers in your family's kitchen?

Your home may seem like a safe place to be. However, if you do not take precautions to avoid accidents, your home can become very dangerous. The kitchen is a common place for accidents. How do you keep yourself safe when you cook or help others in the kitchen?

Kitchen Safety

The most common kitchen accidents include falls, burns, fires, cuts, and electric shocks. These types of accidents are usually preventable if you develop good, safe work habits. In general, keep hair, loose clothing, jewelry, and apron strings out of the way. They could catch fire or become tangled in appliances. Always pay attention to your tasks, and use the right tools for each job.

Falls

To prevent falls, follow these guidelines:

- Stand on a short stepladder or a sturdy step stool with a waist-high hand bar to get at high or hard-to-reach items. Do not use chairs because they tip over too easily.
- Turn pot and pan handles toward the center of the stove or counter so that the pots or pans will not get knocked over.
- Clean up spilled foods or liquids immediately.
- Keep cupboard doors and drawers closed when not in use.
- Choose kitchen rugs with a nonskid backing.
- Never walk on a wet floor. Clear away floor clutter.
- Store heavy items within easy reach.

© Adam Gault/age fotostock

Avoid Kitchen Falls Clean up spilled food and liquids right away to avoid slips and falls. *What else can you do to avoid falls in the kitchen?*

Stay Alert
Talk It Through
Being stressed can be a distraction. If you are worried about something, you might have trouble focusing on your schoolwork. If something is really bothering you, find someone to talk to about it, like a friend, parent, teacher, or counselor.

Burns

Several kitchen **hazards**, or dangers, can burn you. You can prevent most burns in the kitchen by following these safety precautions:

- Use dry potholders when cooking hot foods and liquids or removing them from the stove, oven, or microwave.
- Turn pot and pan handles toward the center of the range. This helps keep someone from bumping a hot pan off the range.
- When cooking, remove pan lids by tilting them away from you. This allows steam to escape safely at the back of the pot, away from your hands and face.
- Use medium or low temperatures to cook greasy foods, such as French fries or fried chicken, to avoid splattering hot oil.
- Wait until appliances cool down before cleaning them.

Fires

Fires can happen easily in the kitchen. Follow these safety precautions, or actions taken in advance:

- Keep a fire extinguisher in the kitchen where you can reach it quickly and safely. Be sure that you know how to use it properly.
- Do not wear clothing with long, loose-fitting sleeves when cooking. The sleeves can easily catch fire.
- If your hair is long, tie it back.
- Keep all flammable objects, such as paper bags, potholders, kitchen towels, curtains, and plastic containers, away from the stove. **Flammable** means capable of burning easily.
- Do not leave the kitchen while food is cooking. Fire can spread in seconds.
- If a grease fire starts, turn off the heat and smother the fire with a tight-fitting lid. Never use water. Water causes a grease fire to spread.
- Keep aerosol cans away from heat. They can explode if heated. Also, the spray from aerosol cans may be flammable.

 **Vocabulary**

You can find definitions in the glossary at the back of this book.

Cuts

Kitchen knives have specific purposes, from trimming and peeling fruits and vegetables to slicing meat.

To prevent cuts from knives and other hazards, observe the following safety rules:

- Keep knives sharp. Sharp knives are often safer than dull ones, since a dull knife will force you to use more force, which can lead to the knife slipping and cutting you.
- Cut food away from your body. Use a cutting board for all cutting jobs, even if it is only a single apple. Do not hold food in your hand to cut.
- Wash knives and sharp objects separately from other utensils.
- Store knives in a special compartment in the drawer or in a knife holder. Put them away immediately after cleaning them.
- If you drop a knife, let it fall. Do not try to catch it.
- Never pick up broken glass with bare hands. Sweep it into a dustpan immediately. Then wipe the floor with several thicknesses of damp paper towels, put the broken pieces into a paper bag, and place the bag in a trash can.
- Throw away chipped or cracked plates and glasses.

Safety Check

Fire Extinguishers
Every kitchen should be equipped with a fire extinguisher. To use one, follow these steps:

- Pull the ring and stand back several feet from the fire. Aim the nozzle at the base of the flames.
- Squeeze the handle.
- Spray back and forth across the base of the fire.

Knife Safety To cut safely, use the right knife for the job. Hold your hand so your fingertips are under your knuckles, and be careful of the thumb holding the food. *What else can you do to avoid accidental cuts?*

© Hero/age fotostock

Electric Shocks

Electrical appliances make kitchen tasks easier, but they can also cause electric shocks. To prevent shocks, take the following precautions:

- Avoid using any appliance with a frayed, or worn, cord.
- Dry your hands before using electrical equipment.
- Disconnect appliances by pulling out the plug directly, not by tugging on the cord.
- Keep portable appliances unplugged when not in use.
- Always unplug a toaster before trying to pry food from it. Forks, knives, or other metal utensils can **conduct**, or carry, electricity and cause an electrical shock.

Reading Check *List What are some flammable kitchen items?*

Small Equipment

Not all kitchen tools and cookware are essential. For example, you do not have to have a vegetable peeler to peel a carrot. You can also do the job with a paring knife. However, a kitchen equipped with basic tools and cookware makes food preparation much easier.

Kitchen Equipment
Tools and small equipment for the kitchen are designed for specific purposes. *Why is it important to have basic tools and cookware in the kitchen?*

© Thinkstock/Alamy

Figure (21.1) Kitchen Tools and Cookware

The Right Tool for the Right Job Having the right tools is an important part of being a successful cook. *Which of these tools would you use to turn chicken on a grill?*

Rubber Scraper

Vegetable Peeler

Rotary Beater

Wire Whisk

Tongs

Paring Knife

Chef's Knife

Bread Knife

Metal Spatula

Kitchen Fork

Large Spoon

Tube Pan

Grater

Mixing Bowls

Colander

Sifter

Loaf Pan

Muffin Pan

Cookie Sheet

Casseroles

Saucepan

Pie Pan

Square Cake Pan

Cake Pan

Double Boiler

Roasting Pan

🔼 **Microwave Oven** Convenience and speed are the advantages of microwave cooking. *What kinds of foods would not cook well in a microwave?*

Many types of utensils and cookware are available. A **utensil** is a tool or container used in the kitchen. **Figure 21.1** illustrates many common kitchen items. You can cook just about anything if you have basic kitchen utensils, cookware, and appliances and know how to use them. Preparing food will be easier, more enjoyable, and safer when you select the right tools for the job. The most commonly used utensils include those for cooking, mixing, and slicing or cutting. Commonly used small appliances include toasters, hand mixers, food processors, and blenders. The best cookware to use depends on the type of food you are cooking and where you are cooking it. For instance, you could use a metal cake pan to bake cookies in a conventional oven, but not in a microwave oven. You should never put metal in a microwave oven. Metal in a microwave creates sparks which could result in a fire.

Reading Check *Recall Can you use a metal cake pan to bake cookies in a microwave oven? Why or why not?*

Large Equipment

Large kitchen appliances, such as stoves, refrigerators, convection ovens, microwave ovens, and dishwashers, add convenience, speed, and ease to the kitchen. Compare appliances before you buy them. Check the prices, features, and energy efficiency of different models so you can get the best value for your money. Read the owner's manual to learn how to safely use and care for appliances. You can also learn about how each feature works, and what to do if the appliance stops working. Keep the owner's manuals for reference.

Ingram Publishing

The cost of large kitchen equipment varies, depending on extra features they may include. For example:

- **Refrigerators** may have the freezer on the side, on the top, or on the bottom. Some are self-defrosting and have extra features, such as additional freezer space, ice makers, or ice cube and water dispensers.
- **Dishwashers** vary in the number and depth of racks they contain. Quiet-running and energy-efficient models tend to be more expensive.
- **Stoves or ranges** usually come with conventional ovens. Some stoves also include microwave ovens, while others include convection ovens.
- **Convection ovens** use a high-speed fan to circulate hot air throughout the oven, evenly and continuously, which speeds up the cooking. Conventional ovens may be self-cleaning or continuous cleaning. An automatic timer that can turn the oven on or off is another possible feature.
- **Microwave ovens** are fast, convenient, and easy to use. They come in a variety of sizes and have a range of power settings.

Section 21.2 After You Read

Review What You Have Learned

1. **Describe** ways to avoid falls in the kitchen.
2. **Name** some commonly used small appliances.
3. **Explain** why you should keep the owner's manuals that come with appliances.

Practice Academic Skills

English Language Arts

4. Choose one of the most common kitchen accidents, and create a poster that communicates how to avoid that type of accident. Use photos, clip art, graphics, and attention-grabbing text to show how to avoid this type of accident in the kitchen.

Social Studies

5. Choose a small appliance that is used in the kitchen. Research the history of the appliance, including who created it and how it has changed and developed over the years. Be prepared to give a short presentation to your classmates.

Check Your Answers Check Your Answers at connectED.mcgraw-hill.com.

Discovering Careers

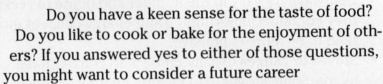

Do you have a keen sense for the taste of food? Do you like to cook or bake for the enjoyment of others? If you answered yes to either of those questions, you might want to consider a future career in food inspection or serving. The following chart explores several careers in food service.

Job Title	Job Description
Flavorist	Identifies the chemical compounds in food flavors. Conducts experiments to test different flavors. Blends and creates flavors.
Head Server	Supervises and trains wait staff to take guests' orders, clear tables, and present checks. Suggests menu items and answers questions regarding foods.
Caterer	Provides food for parties, special dinners, and receptions. Meets with clients to discuss menus. Delivers and serves food.
Cake Decorator	Designs cakes and pastries for sale. Creates decorations on specialty cakes, birthday cakes, and wedding cakes.
Restaurant Kitchen Manager	Organizes procedures for cooking and cleaning. Schedules employees for work. Makes sure policies regarding safe cooking are followed.

Career Activities ▼

At School

 1 Select two of the careers listed. Research the education, training, and work experience required for each career. Write a summary of your results.

At Home

2 With a parent, write out the procedures that you and your family follow when cooking. How safe is your home kitchen?

At Work

3 Can you think of all the different types of jobs there are, working in a restaurant? Do some research if necessary.

In the Community

4 Contact and interview someone in your community who works in food service. Ask this person to describe what his or her typical work day is like. Share what you learned with your class.

Chapter Summary

Section 21.1 Food Safety
Foodborne illness, also called food poisoning, is an illness caused by unsafe food. Food can become unsafe because of bacteria, parasites, fungi, viruses, and harmful chemicals. Keeping food safe can prevent food from becoming infected with harmful bacteria. By following some simple procedures when handling and preparing food, you can reduce the risk of food contamination. Store food properly and quickly after you are finished eating, and cook meat fully before serving.

Section 21.2 Kitchen Essentials
The most common kitchen accidents include falls, burns, fires, cuts, and electric shocks. These types of accidents are usually preventable if you develop good, safe work habits. For your kitchen, many types of utensils and cookware are available. The best cookware to use depends on the type of food you are cooking and where you are cooking it. Large kitchen equipment such as stoves, convection ovens, microwave ovens, refrigerators, and dishwashers, can also make food preparation easier.

Words You Learned

1. Use at least six of these content and academic vocabulary words in a short essay about food and kitchen safety.

Content Vocabulary
- foodborne illness (p. 469)
- contamination (p. 469)
- E. coli (p. 469)
- salmonella (p. 469)
- perishable (p. 470)
- flammable (p. 476)
- utensil (p. 480)
- convection oven (p. 481)

Academic Vocabulary
- minimize (p. 469)
- promptly (p. 470)
- hazard (p. 476)
- conduct (p. 478)

Review Key Concepts

2. **Name** two types of bacteria that cause food poisoning.

3. **Explain** how to keep leftovers from spoiling.

4. **Identify** the five most common kitchen accidents.

5. **Describe** the benefit of having basic tools and cookware.

6. **List** five examples of large kitchen appliances.

Critical Thinking

7. **Formulate** a plan for keeping food safe in your home.

8. **Evaluate** the safety of your kitchen at home. If there are safety issues, suggest how these can be fixed.

9. **Compare and contrast** conventional ovens with convection ovens.

Real-World Skills and Applications

Problem-Solving

10. First Aid in the Kitchen You and your older sister prepared a meal for your parents' 15th wedding anniversary. Everything was going well until your sister accidentally knocked over a pan on the stove. The liquid in the pan caused a minor burn on the top of her foot. Write a paragraph to explain the proper first-aid procedure, and include the list of supplies you would need.

Interpersonal and Collaborative

11. Kitchen Safety Guidelines Follow your teacher's directions to form groups. Design a brochure about kitchen safety. The brochure should include illustrations and written safety guidelines. Post your team's brochure in the classroom. Remember to share them with family members at home.

Financial Literacy

12. Appliances and Energy Use When comparing costs for large kitchen and household appliances, you should consider both the purchase price and the ongoing electricity costs of operating the appliance. The government requires most major new appliances to have a yellow EnergyGuide sticker that shows typical energy usage and costs for that model, and how it compares to other models. Imagine that you are comparing two similar refrigerators. Model A costs $595, and uses $58 worth of electricity a year. Model B costs $715, but uses $35 in electricity a year. If a refrigerator lasts 15 years, which model will end up being the least expensive?

13. Design a Kitchen With all the options these days for a kitchen, you can have any type of kitchen you want. Design a kitchen that is safe, convenient, and well-equipped. Begin with a list of what you would want in your kitchen. Then design your kitchen for the most efficient use. Create a diagram of your kitchen that shows where appliances will be placed and where utensils will be found for your perfect kitchen. Include where the cupboards, counters, sink, dishwasher and refrigerator will be. Share your diagram with the class.

14. Research Disease Choose either E.coli or salmonella, and research to find additional, in-depth information on one of these illnesses. Find out how it is caused, the symptoms, and ways to prevent it. Prepare a brief presentation on what you find to the class.

15. Set the Table With permission from your teacher or a parent, go online to search for information on proper table settings. On plain paper, illustrate different ideas and save them for reference. Label according to the appropriate kind of function, for example, picnic, holiday, or family meal. Compile the different table settings to include in your Life Skills Binder.

Academic Skills

English Language Arts

16. Establish Safety Procedures Imagine that your class is having a dinner party for the parents. Your job is to make sure that the food served is safe to eat. Write down all the procedures you would follow to make the food safe. Present the procedures in an easy-to-follow list of steps.

Social Studies

17. Research Food Safety Food safety has changed and developed throughout history. Choose a historical period and find examples of how safety was addressed in the kitchen. Did different social groups follow different procedures for food safety? Were men and women involved in food preparation? What were the biggest risks that people of this period had to address? Present your findings to the class.

Mathematics

18. Storing Food Marco has just finished cooking 2 quarts (115.5 cubic inches) of vegetable soup that he would like to store in the freezer for later use. He is trying to decide if all of that soup will fit inside one resealable container. The container he would like to use is cylindrical, and measures 8 inches wide and 4 inches tall. Can Marco fit 2 quarts of soup in the container?

Math Concept **Volume of a Cylinder** A cylinder is a solid with a circular base and top. Calculate the volume (V) of a cylinder as $V = \pi r^2 h$, where r is the radius of the circular base, and h is the cylinder's height. Use 3.14 for π.

Starting Hint The height (h) of the container is 8 inches. Since a circle's radius equals ½ of its diameter, the radius (r) of the top and bottom of the container is ½ x 4 inches = 2 inches. Plug these numbers into the volume formula to find the volume in cubic inches.

Standardized Test Practice

Mathematics

Choose the letter of the best answer. Write the letter for the answer on a separate sheet of paper.

Test-Taking Tip Study for tests over a few days or weeks, and continually review class material. Do not wait until the night before to try and learn everything.

19. If the formula for converting from Celsius to Fahrenheit is F = 9/5C + 32, what is the formula for converting from Fahrenheit to Celsius?
  a. C = 5/9(F − 32)
  b. C = 5/9(F − 32)
  c. C = 32 − 9/5F
  d. C = 9/5(F − 32)

Chapter 22

Prepare to Cook

Section 22.1

Meal Preparation

■ **Main Idea** Plan your meals ahead of time, before you shop for food or begin preparing the meal.

Section 22.2

Recipe Basics

■ **Main Idea** Good cooking begins with learning different recipe formats and the meanings of recipe terms and abbreviations.

BJI/Blue Jean Images/Getty Images

Explore the Photo

Before you can start cooking, you need to plan your meal. *How do you decide what to buy when you go to the supermarket for food?*

First Draft

Cooking Your Favorite Recipe
Everyone likes to share a recipe for their favorite dish. Write a draft about how to make a favorite recipe you and your family enjoy. Include what is involved with making the dish and what ingredients you need.

Writing Tips Follow these steps to write a first draft:

1. Just write. Do not think too much about what you are writing.

2. Include details. You can always take out what you do not need later.

3. Do not worry about spelling or punctuation. You will fix these later.

Section 22.1 Meal Preparation

Reading Guide

Before You Read

Two-Column Notes Two column notes are a useful way to study and organize what you have read. Divide a piece of paper into two columns. In the left column, write down main ideas. In the right column, list supporting details.

Read to Learn

Key Concepts

✓ **Identify** the food groups you should include when planning nutritious meals.

✓ **Describe** the information you can find on food labels.

✓ **List** the elements that can destroy nutrients in foods.

Main Idea

Plan your meals ahead of time, before you shop for food or begin preparing the meal.

Content Vocabulary

○ appetizer
○ equivalent
○ meal patterns
○ garnish
○ texture
○ vegetarian
○ unit pricing
○ grade labeling

Academic Vocabulary

■ complement
■ economize

Graphic Organizer

As you read, write down descriptions for national brand, store brand, and generic brand. Use a graphic organizer like the one shown to help you organize your information.

Type of Brand	Description
National Brand	
Store Brand	
Generic Brand	

 Graphic Organizer Go to **connectED.mcgraw-hill.com** to download this graphic organizer.

Whether you are throwing a birthday party for a friend or cooking a meal for your family, it is best to start by making a plan. Serving tasty, attractive, and nutritious meals requires more than just being a good cook. Planning meals, reading recipes, and shopping for food put your management skills to use.

As You Read

Connect When was the last nice dinner party you were invited to? What did you notice about the dinner that made it special?

Meal Planning

As you plan, think of meals that are simple and nutritious. Include a variety of foods, and consider your skills, time, and money. For good nutrition, plan meals that include foods from each food group from MyPlate.

The Proteins Group includes all meats, poultry, fish, legumes, eggs, nuts, and seeds. Growing teens need approximately 5½ ounces every day. Foods from this group are usually served as the main dish in a meal.

The Grain Group includes cereal, rice, pasta, breads, and grits. You need 6 ounces every day. Some foods in this group, such as brown rice, whole-wheat bread, and oatmeal are whole grains. You should try to eat at least 3 ounces of whole grains every day.

The Vegetable Group includes broccoli, carrots, spinach, lettuce, asparagus, and green beans. Teens need 2½ cups every day. Raw vegetables can be eaten in salads, as a snack, or as an **appetizer**, a dish served before the main meal. Raw or cooked vegetables can also be served as a side dish.

The Fruit Group includes apples, oranges, tomatoes, avocados, blueberries, plums, and grapes. You need 2 cups of fruit every day. These may include fresh, frozen, dried, and canned fruit as well as fruit juice. Fruit can be part of any meal.

 **Vocabulary**

You can find definitions in the glossary at the back of this book.

Meal Plan Plan meals by using a variety of nutritious foods. *Why is using a variety of food in your diet important?*

Corbis Premium RF / Alamy

SUCCEED IN SCHOOL!

Balance Your Life

All Work and No Play

Studying and doing homework are important, but it is equally important to maintain balance in your life. If you are overworked, you will not be healthy and happy. Be sure to mix in fun with obligation.

The Milk Group includes milk, yogurt, and cheese. As a growing teen, you need 3 cups, or the equivalent of 3 cups, every day. **Equivalent** refers to a food that has equal value, such as consuming a cup of yogurt in place of a cup of milk. Foods from this group can be served with any meal.

Oils Healthful oils are not a food group, but many foods from the five food groups contain healthful oils. Healthful oils include fish oil, vegetable oil, and olive oil.

Meal Pattern

Most people follow **meal patterns**, which are habits that determine when and what they eat each day. They usually select similar types of foods each day for breakfast, lunch, dinner, and snacks. For example, your meal pattern for one day might be:

- **Breakfast** Cereal with fruit and nuts, juice, milk
- **Lunch** Sandwich, fruit or vegetable, dessert, milk
- **Dinner** Meat or poultry, vegetable, rice or pasta, milk
- **Snack** Fresh fruit

Meal planning is easy when you are aware of your meal patterns and choose nutritious foods. Simply choose a combination of foods from the food groups that fit your meal pattern. To plan a lunch for the meal pattern above, you might choose a tuna salad sandwich, carrot sticks, oatmeal cookies, and milk.

Meal patterns should be flexible. You may be trying to gain or lose weight. You may be invited to eat at a friend's home. There may be a special occasion that requires specific food, such as birthday cake, or you may go to a restaurant which limits options.

Variety

Including a variety of foods in each meal makes eating more interesting. Eating many different foods from all of the food groups also makes it easier to get all the nutrients you need. Meals planned with variety in mind look and taste better.

One way to add variety is to vary the way foods are prepared. Another way is to choose foods that provide different colors, sizes and shapes, textures, flavors, and temperatures.

Trans Fat

Trans fat has been connected to increasing LDL cholesterol (the "bad" cholesterol) and lowering HDL cholesterol (the "good" cholesterol). It is important to read labels to know what is in the food you eat. Take a trip to your local grocery store to find what foods have trans fat.

Procedure Use a spreadsheet to track the foods that contain trans fat. Write down the name of the product and the amount of trans fat contained in it.

Analysis What foods did you find that most often had trans fat? Did any of these foods surprise you? What amounts of trans fat did these foods contain? Do you see a pattern in the types of food? What alternatives are there?

- **Color** Choosing foods of different colors will make the meal look more interesting. For instance, have a salad with tomatoes and carrots to add color to your meal. Add a garnish to provide more color. A **garnish** is a small amount of a food or seasoning to decorate the meal. Parsley, lemon wedges, orange slices, and paprika are examples of garnishes.
- **Size and Shape** Varying the sizes and shapes of foods will give you a much more appealing meal.
- **Texture** Foods with different textures add variety to a meal. **Texture** is the way something feels when touched. For example, raw vegetables are usually crisp, while pudding tends to feel smooth. One way to vary the textures of foods is by preparing them in different ways. For example, think of the difference in texture between raw carrots and cooked carrots.
- **Flavor** Combine flavors that complement each other. Steak, mushrooms, broccoli, and cheese are some flavors that go well together.
- **Temperature** Vary the temperatures of food in a meal. Plan some hot food items and some cold food items.

Meal Pattern Knowing your meal patterns can help you plan meals. *What can you do to add variety to your regular meals?*

Gather Your Resources

As you plan your meals, take time to read through the recipes carefully and make sure that you have all of the resources you will need.

- **Skills** If you are a beginning cook, you may want to avoid complicated recipes. Could you choose convenience foods for part of the meal? For instance, you might make a dessert from a mix rather than make it from scratch.
- **Equipment** Some recipes will require a specific utensil. Make sure that you have all of the necessary tools and equipment before you start cooking.
- **Ingredients** Make sure you have all the ingredients the recipe calls for before you start cooking.
- **Money** Do the ingredients fit your food budget? Can you economize, or save money, with coupons or use foods that are less expensive because they are in season?
- **Time** When you know that you will be working within a time frame, such as having only one hour to cook dinner, choose foods that can be prepared within the time allowed.

 **Packaged Mixes** Using packaged mixes is a good way to learn the basics of cooking. *What are the benefits of using packaged mixes?*

It is also important to make sure that all foods are ready to serve at the right time. Some dishes take longer than others to prepare, and some foods take longer than others to cook. For this reason, you must know what to do first and when to do it. See **Figure 22.1** for a sample time schedule.

Special Dietary Needs

You may need to take into account special diet considerations for a family member, friend, or even yourself. When cooking for guests, ask in advance if anyone has any special diet needs. For example, someone with high blood pressure would need to limit salt and sodium intake. It is also possible that someone could be a **vegetarian** who eats only vegetables, fruits, grains, nuts, and sometimes eggs or dairy products. Many cookbooks are available with special diet recipes. You can also find recipes online.

Reading Check *Plan* What preparation should you do before you plan a meal?

Smart Shopping

Learning how to find the best buys is an important part of being a smart shopper. Some brands are better buys than others. Store brands and generic brands are usually less expensive than national brands.

- **National Brands** Products that you see advertised on television or in newspapers or magazines are known as national brands. These products often cost more than others because the manufacturer spends a great deal of money on packaging and advertising. These costs are added to the price of the product.

Figure (22.1) Set a Time Schedule

Make Your Meal a Success Using a time schedule can help you organize your meal so that all the foods are ready to serve at the same time. *What might happen if you do not use a schedule when preparing a meal?*

Sample Time Schedule

- 4:30 Start preparing chicken.
  4:45 Turn on oven.
- 5:00 Place chicken in oven.
  5:15 Wash and chop broccoli.
- 5:30 Begin cooking rice.
- 5:40 Set table.
  5:50 Steam broccoli in microwave.
  5:55 Remove broccoli, rice, and chicken.
- 6:00 Serve the meal.
- 6:45 Wash dishes and clean up kitchen.

Step 1–First list the job that will take longest to do. Then list in order the other jobs to be done until you have listed them all.

Step 2–Some foods take longer to cook than others, so you must plan what to do first and when to do it.

Step 3–Besides cooking time, consider that some dishes take longer to prepare than others.

Step 4–Do not forget to allow time for setting the table, serving the food, and cleaning up.

Step 5–Plan a time schedule backward, from the end to the beginning. First decide at what time you will serve the meal. Then figure out how much time you will need to prepare each of the different foods.

- **Store Brands** Products that have the store's name or another name used only by that store on the label are called store brands. They usually cost less because there is little or no advertising cost. They often have the same ingredients and nutrients as national brands.
- **Generic Brands** Products with labels listing only the product name and nutritional information are generic brands. These often cost even less than store brand products.

Products will vary in price, quality, and taste. Price alone is not an indicator of quality or taste. You will want to compare national brands, store brands, and generic brands to see which ones you prefer.

Read Food Labels

Food labels give you valuable nutrition information and shopping information. See **Figure 22.2** for explanations of the items listed on food labels. By law, food labels must provide the following information:

- The name of the food.
- The name and address of the product's manufacturer.
- The nutritional content, including serving size, calories, and nutrient amounts per serving.
- A list of ingredients in order of amount. For example, a box of dry cereal might list oat flour first, then sugar, followed by other ingredients, to show that oat flour is the main ingredient, then sugar, and then the rest of the ingredients, in order.
- The total weight. For example, which is a better value: a 1-lb. (500-gram) bag of tortilla chips for $1.99 or an 11-oz. (300-gram) bag for $1.49?
- The trans fat amounts.

Unit Pricing

Unit pricing means showing the cost of the product per unit. Examples of units include ounces, pounds, grams, liters, and gallons. Look for the unit pricing label on the edge of the store shelf. It will give you the product name, the size, and the price per unit. You can easily decide which size is the best buy.

Grade Labeling

Understanding and using grade labeling can also help you when you shop. **Grade labeling** is a measurement of food quality using standards set by the government. Many food items including eggs, poultry, and meat are graded. The highest grade is the highest in quality. For example, Grade AA eggs are of higher quality than Grade A eggs.

Reading Check *Define* What are unit pricing and grade labeling?

Figure 22.2 Nutrition Facts

Food Labels Nutrition Facts on food labels can help you decide whether or not you want to purchase the item based on nutrients and ingredients. *There are 2 servings in this can. How many calories does the entire can contain?*

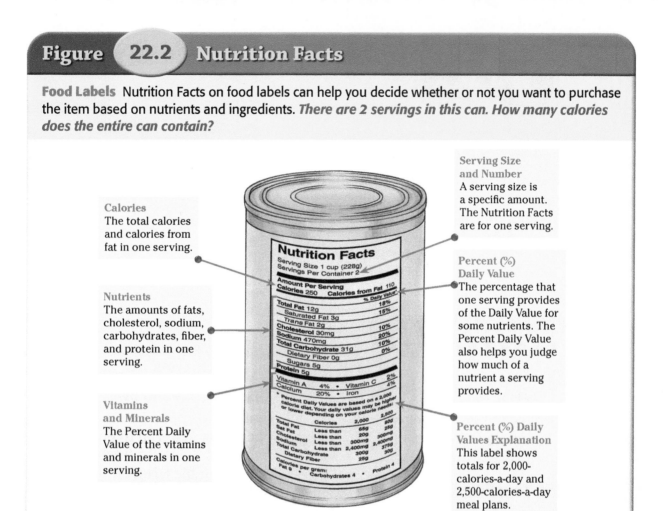

Calories
The total calories and calories from fat in one serving.

Nutrients
The amounts of fats, cholesterol, sodium, carbohydrates, fiber, and protein in one serving.

Vitamins and Minerals
The Percent Daily Value of the vitamins and minerals in one serving.

Serving Size and Number
A serving size is a specific amount. The Nutrition Facts are for one serving.

Percent (%) Daily Value
The percentage that one serving provides of the Daily Value for some nutrients. The Percent Daily Value also helps you judge how much of a nutrient a serving provides.

Percent (%) Daily Values Explanation
This label shows totals for 2,000-calories-a-day and 2,500-calories-a-day meal plans.

Food Storage

When you get home from the supermarket, you will need to store the food you bought. Heat, light, time, and moisture destroy nutrients. They can also affect the flavor and spoil foods. Storing foods properly helps them maintain their freshness and flavor.

Many food items need special treatment to stay fresh. Items you cannot use before the expiration date can be saved by freezing. Here are a few food storage tips:

- Keep butter and margarine covered in the refrigerator, so they do not absorb odors.
- Keep baking powder tightly covered, so it will not lose its strength.
- Slice and freeze fruits and vegetables that you will not use right away.
- Green bananas will ripen at room temperature within a couple of days. After that they can be stored in the refrigerator for three to five days.

Plan a Shopping Trip

In this activity you will plan a shopping trip for groceries. Before you begin, read through the entire Hands-On Lab assignment. Write down any questions that you have about the activity. Reread the text or ask your teacher for help if you need it.

Supplies

✓ Shopping List

✓ Coupons and newspaper

✓ Calculator

Develop Your Plan

- Make a weekly meal plan and list the grocery items needed.

- Review your shopping list for staple foods such as milk, eggs, bread, and salt.

- Clip coupons, and check your local newspaper for sale items.

Implement Your Plan

- Review the recipes in your meal plan to see what ingredients you need.

- Make a shopping list. Identify items that are less important in case you exceed your budget. You can put these items back.

- Discuss the budget with your parent or another adult, and take a calculator with you so you can keep track of what you are spending.

- Use the information on product labels and unit pricing to help you select items.

- Look for meat, poultry, and fish that are wrapped in undamaged packaging material to ensure freshness. Look for fresh fruits and vegetables. Never buy dented or bulging cans because the food may be spoiled. Keep raw foods away from cooked and ready-to-eat foods. Choose frozen and refrigerated foods last.

Evaluate Your Results

Did you forget any items on your shopping list? What did you learn about food shopping and your food budget? How would you make your next shopping trip different? Write one or more paragraphs to explain your answer.

Projects and Activities Go to connectED.mcgraw-hill.com.

Corbis Super RF/Alamy

- Store onions and potatoes separately. Potatoes will spoil faster when stored near onions.
- Store a container of ice cream inside a heavy, brown bag to prevent freezer burn.
- Freeze leftover broth in ice cube trays. Pop out the broth cubes and store them in a freezer bag for later use.
- Cook fresh meat and freeze it for use at a later meal.

Handle Leftovers Properly

Just like fresh foods, you must also store leftover foods properly to keep them safe. Follow these rules for keeping leftovers:

- Throw away food that has been kept out too long.
- Refrigerate or freeze leftovers as soon as the meal is done.
- Eat refrigerated leftovers within three to four days.
- Reheat leftover solid foods to 165°F (74°C).
- Boil leftover soups, sauces, and gravies before eating.

When you practice food safety procedures, you will help yourself and those in your home stay healthier, enjoy food more, and even save money.

Section 22.1 After You Read

Review What You Have Learned

1. **Describe** ways to add variety to your food.
2. **List** ways to save money when you shop.
3. **Identify** the benefit of proper food storage.

Practice Academic Skills

English Language Arts

4. Imagine you are going to have a dinner party for close friends and family. Create a formal invitation that includes what you will serve, what time your guests need to arrive, attire to wear, and the place. Use graphics and attention-grabbing text to make your invitation exciting. Clearly communicate the theme you have chosen. Share your invitation with your classmates.

Social Studies

5. What are some meals and foods that are unique to your family? Talk with family members to find out the story behind the foods that you and your family eat that is unique. Bring in a sample menu and recipe. Explain the origin of the food your family enjoys with the class.

Check Your Answers Check Your Answers at connectED.mcgraw-hill.com.

Section 22.2 Recipe Basics

Reading Guide

Before You Read

Study with a Buddy It can be difficult to review your own notes and quiz yourself on what you have just read. Studying with a partner, even for just a short period of time, can help you study better.

Read to Learn
Key Concepts

✓ **Explain** the importance of following recipes.

✓ **Identify** the different ways to mix food.

✓ **Suggest** additions to a recipe's ingredients for better nutrition.

Main Idea

Good cooking begins with learning different recipe formats and the meanings of recipe terms and abbreviations.

Content Vocabulary

○ recipe ○ ingredient

Academic Vocabulary

■ assemble ■ abbreviation

Graphic Organizer

As you read, identify three guidelines for following recipes. Use a graphic organizer like the one shown to help you organize your information.

Recipe Guidelines
1.
2.
3.

 Graphic Organizer Go to **connectED.mcgraw-hill.com** to download this graphic organizer.

There will always be occasions to cook for other people. To make the best impression, you want the food to be delicious and come out the way you planned. In order for this to happen, you need to know how to follow a recipe that includes specific cooking terms. The more you cook, the better you will become. You will learn something new with every recipe you try, and you may find that friends and family are lining up to eat your food!

Recipes

Almost all cooks use recipes. A **recipe** is a list of directions for preparing a specific food. If you know how to read and follow recipes, you will greatly increase your chances of success in the kitchen.

Some recipes are easier to follow than others. Look at **Figure 22.3** to see which type of recipe format works better for you. While you are learning to cook, look for easy-to-read recipes that do the following:

- State the amount of each component or part. These are the **ingredients**.
- Provide step-by-step instructions on how to combine the ingredients.
- Mention the sizes of pans that will be needed.
- Specify the cooking time and temperature.
- Estimate the number of servings the recipe should produce.

In whatever format a recipe appears, the procedure for following the recipe remains the same. Some general guidelines for using recipes are on the next page.

As You Read

Connect Think of a recipe you used or saw recently. Was the recipe easy to use? If so, what about the recipe made it easy to use for you?

◇ Vocabulary

You can find definitions in the glossary at the back of this book.

Figure 22.3 Recipe Formats

Reading Recipes Recipes are written in different formats, or styles. *Which do you like better? Why?*

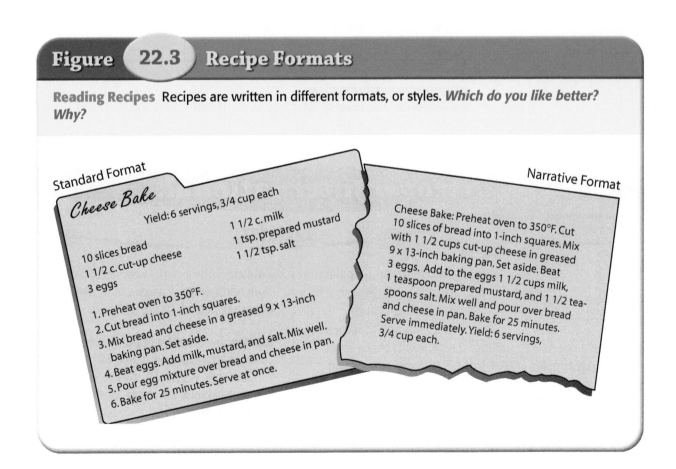

Standard Format

Cheese Bake

Yield: 6 servings, 3/4 cup each

10 slices bread
1 1/2 c. cut-up cheese
3 eggs
1 1/2 c. milk
1 tsp. prepared mustard
1 1/2 tsp. salt

1. Preheat oven to 350°F.
2. Cut bread into 1-inch squares.
3. Mix bread and cheese in a greased 9 x 13-inch baking pan. Set aside.
4. Beat eggs. Add milk, mustard, and salt. Mix well.
5. Pour egg mixture over bread and cheese in pan.
6. Bake for 25 minutes. Serve at once.

Narrative Format

Cheese Bake: Preheat oven to 350°F. Cut 10 slices of bread into 1-inch squares. Mix with 1 1/2 cups cut-up cheese in greased 9 x 13-inch baking pan. Set aside. Beat 3 eggs. Add to the eggs 1 1/2 cups milk, 1 teaspoon prepared mustard, and 1 1/2 teaspoons salt. Mix well and pour over bread and cheese in pan. Bake for 25 minutes. Serve immediately. Yield: 6 servings, 3/4 cup each.

• Read through the entire recipe. Make sure that you understand all the terms and abbreviations.
• **Assemble**, or bring together, all the ingredients and equipment before you start.
• Do any necessary preparation, such as preheating the oven or greasing a pan.

Recipe Abbreviations

Recipes often show measurements in shortened form to save space. To follow the recipe, it is essential to understand what each **abbreviation**, or shortened word, means. Can you imagine how your vegetable soup would taste if you added two tablespoons of salt instead of two teaspoons?

Here are some of the most common abbreviations used in recipes:

t. or tsp.	teaspoon	**lb.**	pound
T. or Tbsp.	tablespoon	**°F**	degrees Fahrenheit
oz.	ounce	**°C**	degrees Celsius
c.	cup	**mL**	milliliter
pt.	pint	**L**	liter
qt.	quart	**g**	gram
gal.	gallon		

Reading Check   *Prepare What can you do to get ready to use a recipe?*

Discover International...
Dining

Italy
Many Italian foods are popular in the United States. In fact, when you eat spaghetti or pizza, you may forget that these foods are not American! Italians generally make these foods in a simpler style. Olive oil, tomato sauces, and vegetables make many Mediterranean foods heart-healthy, especially those from southern Italy. Pasta is usually the first dish in a meal, followed by meat, fish, or a vegetable dish. Traditional foods in northern Italy use more butter and creamy sauces. Polenta, risotto, and hearty bean soups are popular in Italy.

Polenta [pō-ˈlen-tə] a cornmeal dish from northern Italy, which can be eaten as a mush or cooled, sliced, and fried.

Risotto [ri-ˈsó-tō] a rice dish with a creamy texture, often flavored with chicken, fish, sausage, vegetables, cheese, or wine. It is usually made with a special short-grain rice called Arborio rice.

Cooking and Mixing Terms

Every recipe for hot food has some type of cooking instructions. To follow the recipe, you need to become familiar with some common cooking terms and know what they mean. Here are some cooking terms you are most likely to read:

Bake Cook in the oven without a cover.

Boil Cook in liquid hot enough to bubble rapidly.

Braise Simmer gently in a small amount of liquid in a covered pan. The food may be browned first.

Broil Cook under direct heat.

Brown Cook in a small amount of fat over high heat to brown the surface.

Chill Put in the refrigerator until cold.

Cook Prepare food by dry heat or moist heat.

Cook By Dry Heat Cook food uncovered without adding any liquid.

Cook By Moist Heat Cook in a covered pan with liquid added.

Deep-Fat Fry Cook in hot fat deep enough to cover the food.

Fry Cook in hot fat.

Roast Cook in the oven in dry heat.

Sauté Fry in a small amount of fat until done.

Scald Heat milk until it steams and just begins to bubble around the edge of the pan.

Simmer Cook to just below the boiling point so the liquid barely bubbles.

Steam Cook over boiling water.

Stew Cook slowly in liquid.

Stir fry Cook quickly in a small amount of fat at high heat.

Preheat Heat the oven to the right temperature before putting in the food.

 Steamed Foods A steamer holds food above boiling water for moist cooking. *What types of food might you steam?*

(t)D.Hurst/Alamy; (b)Len Rizzi/National Cancer Institute

Financial Literacy

Find the Best Buy

Emily drinks an 8-ounce glass of orange juice every morning. She can buy a 64-fluid-ounce carton of orange juice at the grocery store for $3.75, or a 16-fluid-ounce bottle of fresh-squeezed orange juice for $1.99. She can also buy a 12-ounce can of frozen orange juice concentrate for $2.15. If a can of orange juice concentrate makes 48 fl. oz. of juice, which type of juice is cheapest per ounce?

Math Concept **Calculate Unit Price** The unit price of an item indicates the cost for every 1 unit of measurement. Calculate unit price by dividing the price of an item by the quantity. Round your answer to the nearest cent.

Starting Hint: Calculate the unit price (price per ounce) of the three containers of orange juice by dividing price by the number of ounces of juice that come from the container.

For math help, go to the Math Appendix at the back of the book.

Figure 22.4 Mixing Terms and Techniques

Mix It Up You can mix food in a variety of ways. *What is the difference between blending and creaming?*

Whip Beat fast with an electric mixer, rotary beater, or wire whip to add enough air to make the mixture fluffy.

Blend Stir until the ingredients are completely mixed.

Cream Blend until smooth and fluffy.

Stir Move the ingredients in a circular motion to mix or to prevent burning.

Toss Tumble ingredients lightly with a spoon and fork.

Combine Mix two or more ingredients together.

Beat Mix or stir quickly, bringing the contents of the bowl to the top and down again.

It is equally important to understand mixing terms. For example, do you know how to blend pudding? **Figure 22.4** illustrates basic mixing terms and techniques.

Adjust Recipes for Nutrition and Flavor

Nutrition and flavor are linked. Use proper techniques for preparing food to help keep nutrients and flavor. Nutrients can be lost during preparation. Some are destroyed by heat or by oxygen in the air. You can modify many dishes for nutrition without giving up flavor. Some recipes can be adjusted to lower the calories or fat, or increase the fiber, calcium, iron, and other nutrients. Follow these guidelines to make common recipes more nutritious and to retain nutrients:

- **Add More Vegetables** Add more cut-up vegetables to casseroles, pasta dishes, and other mixed dishes. Pare or trim as little from fruits and vegetables as possible.

- **Increase Calcium** Add calcium-fortified tofu to salads and stir-fries.
- **Reduce Fat** Use less of high-fat ingredients such as butter, margarine, salad dressing, and peanut butter.
- **Add More Fiber** Add fiber-rich dry beans and peas to soups and mixed dishes.
- **Reduce Added Sugar** Use vanilla, cinnamon, and other spices to bring out food's natural sweetness instead of using sugar.
- **Reduce Sodium** Cut down on the salt. Use herbs, spices, and citrus to enhance flavor.
- **Keep Foods Whole** Use whole or large pieces when possible.
- **Use the Correct Temperature** Cook food for the right length of time and serve it at the right temperature
- **Use the Microwave** By microwaving foods, in little or no liquid, you keep more vitamins in the food.

Balance Your Life
Look Ahead Preparation is important. If you have a big paper due at the end of a semester, it is better to work on it a little at a time than to try to cram it all into a week or a few days. If you have a school break coming up, do some extra work ahead of time so you can be carefree and relaxed during your break.

Section 22.2 After You Read

Review What You Have Learned

1. **Explain** what can greatly increase your success in the kitchen.
2. **List** five common cooking terms.
3. **Summarize** ways to save nutrients and enhance flavor.

Practice Academic Skills

English Language Arts

4. Write a letter to a good friend who has requested a recipe from you. Explain how to make the dish that she or he is requesting in a step-by-step way. Include ingredients, instructions, baking time, servings, and any other information about the recipe. You might want to explain why this recipe is special to you.

Social Studies

5. Think about dishes that your grandparents or family members may fix on a regular basis without using an actual recipe. Watch them cook the dish, and ask for the ingredients and instructions. Write them down on recipe cards for other members of your family, including yourself. Consider this to be a part of your family history.

Check Your Answers Check Your Answers at connectED.mcgraw-hill.com.

Discovering Careers

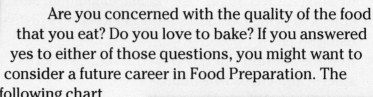

Are you concerned with the quality of the food that you eat? Do you love to bake? If you answered yes to either of those questions, you might want to consider a future career in Food Preparation. The following chart explores several careers in the food science industry.

Career Activities ▼

At School

1 Select two of the careers listed. Research the education, training, and work experience required for each career. Write a summary of your results.

At Home

2 Look through two or three different brands of the same type of food at your home. How are the ingredients the same? How are they different?

At Work

3 Give three examples of how technology has changed the food prepared and served in the workplace. Compare findings with your classmates.

In the Community

4 Contact and interview someone in your community who works in the food science industry. Ask this person to describe what his or her typical work day is like. Share what you learned with your class.

Job Title	Job Description
Agricultural Engineer	Applies engineering technology and knowledge of biological sciences to agricultural problems. Concerned with machinery, structures, conservation, and agricultural products' processing.
Agronomist	Studies crop production and soil and plant sciences. Develops new methods of growing crops for more efficient production, higher yield, and improved quality.
Health Inspector	Visits food service locations to document health conditions. Evaluates areas for food safety hazards. Recommends safe food-handling practices to restaurant managers.
Food Technologist	Conducts new product research for the development of foods. Involved in the quality control, packaging, processing, and use of foods.
Food Tester	Performs tests to determine physical or chemical properties of food or beverage products. Ensures compliance with quality and safety standards.

Cultura Creative/Alamy

Chapter Summary

Section 22.1 Meal Preparation

As you plan a meal, think of options that are simple and nutritious. Consider your skills, time needed, ingredients and supplies, and money when choosing your meals. Including a variety of foods in each meal makes eating more interesting and also makes it easier to get the nutrients you need. Learning how to find the best buys is an important part of being a smart shopper. Food labels give you valuable nutrition and shopping information.

Section 22.2 Recipe Basics

A recipe is a list of directions for preparing a specific food. Read through the entire recipe before you begin. Make sure that you understand all the terms and abbreviations. Assemble all the ingredients and equipment. Do any necessary preparation. To be able to follow the recipe, you need to become familiar with some common cooking and mixing terms and abbreviations. Many recipes can be modified to improve nutritional value.

Words You Learned

1. Label each of these content and vocabulary terms as a noun, verb, or adjective.

Content Vocabulary

- appetizer (p. 489)
- equivalent (p. 490)
- meal patterns (p. 490)
- garnish (p. 491)
- texture (p. 491)
- vegetarian (p. 492)
- unit pricing (p. 494)
- grade labeling (p. 494)
- recipe (p. 499)
- ingredient (p. 499)

Academic Vocabulary

- complement (p. 491)
- economize (p. 491)
- assemble (p. 500)
- abbreviation (p. 500)

Review Key Concepts

2. **Identify** the food groups you should include when planning nutritious meals.

3. **Describe** the information you can find on food labels.

4. **List** the elements that can destroy nutrients in foods.

5. **Explain** the importance of following recipes.

6. **Identify** the different ways to mix food.

7. **Suggest** additions to a recipe's ingredients for better nutrition.

Critical Thinking

8. **Analyze** a cookbook recipe. Highlight food preparation terms in the recipe. What will you need to follow this recipe? What do you need to do before you start preparing this recipe?

9. **Evaluate** the variety of foods you ate yesterday. Write down everything you ate, and assess if you are eating balanced meals from each of the food groups.

Real-World Skills and Applications

Problem-Solving

10. Obtain Information Look through your cabinets and pantry at home to find five foods that you regularly eat. Read the labels on the products and write down information about serving size, nutritional content, calories, and the list of ingredients. Are these healthful foods? How can you tell? For the items that are not healthful, what alternatives could you add to your next shopping trip?

Interpersonal and Collaborative

11. Host a Potluck Do you know what a potluck is? A potluck is a meal to which each person brings one dish that is shared by everyone. Follow your teacher's directions to form groups. Plan a potluck. Choose recipes that you and your group can prepare for a meal. Come up with a plan for each person to contribute a dish for your meal. Bring your food to school and eat lunch together, sharing your recipe and the steps you took to prepare the dish.

Financial Literacy

12. Saving at the Supermarket There are many ways to save money on groceries, including using coupons, looking for sales, buying items in larger quantities, and switching to store or generic brands. Michael needs to make sandwiches for a picnic he is planning to attend with his basketball team. The coach gave him a budget for buying ingredients. Michael found good deals on bread and jam, but he is having a difficult time deciding which peanut butter is the best value. He can buy a 28-ounce jar for $4.89, or a 40-ounce jar for $5.99. The 17-ounce jars are normally $3.50 each, but as part of an in-store sale, he can buy two of them for $5.00. He has a coupon that will let him save 50 cents on any size jar, but he cannot use the coupon on sale items. If 1 ounce of peanut butter constitutes one serving, how can Michael get the lowest cost per serving?

13. Recipe Round Up It is fun to share what we like to cook or eat. Create a class cookbook by having everyone contribute a favorite recipe. Make sure that all the recipes are in a step-by-step format and use the correct abbreviations. Collect the recipes in a binder and create a decorative cover.

14. Research Recipes Choose a food that is somewhat common such as bread, pasta, rice, or beef. Research the origin of the food. Find recipes from the past that include that food. How have the food and its preparation evolved? Prepare a brief presentation on what you find to the class.

15. Find an Appetizer Snacks and appetizers are very popular, especially before dinner, at parties, or while watching sports or movies. With permission from a teacher or parent, go online to search for healthful appetizer ideas. Compile what you find and include your list in your Life Skills Binder.

D.Hurst/Alamy

Academic Skills

English Language Arts

16. Dining Together Write a letter to the local newspaper in your community about the importance of families eating meals together at home on a regular basis. Include examples of what families gain by eating together.

Science

17. Chemical Reactions For bread to rise and bake into a loaf, there are ingredients that are needed for the chemical reaction that allows the bread to rise.

Find recipes for different types of bread that require yeast.

Procedure Determine what ingredients are needed for the chemical reaction that makes a loaf of bread.

Analysis What is the list of ingredients that are needed for the chemical reaction? How do they work together to create bread?

Mathematics

18. Changing Recipe Yield Daphne would like to prepare homemade granola using a recipe that calls for 4 cups of rolled oats, 1½ cups of wheat germ, ½ cup of almonds, ½ cup of coconut, ½ cup of raisins, 1 cup of honey, and ¼ cup of oil. The recipe makes 8 cups of granola, but that is too much for Daphne. Rewrite the recipe so that it yields 6 cups instead.

Math Concept **Multiplying Fractions** To multiply fractions, first convert any mixed or whole numbers to improper fractions. Then multiply all numerators to get the new numerator, and multiply the denominators to get the new denominator. Reduce to lowest terms.

Starting Hint The new recipe yields ⅛, or ¾, of the original recipe. To reduce each ingredient by the same proportion, multiply each ingredient amount by ¾.

Standardized Test Practice

Short Answer

Write two or three sentences to answer each question.

19. Why do you need to learn how to read a recipe?

20. What is the advantage of planning meals for a whole week in advance?

Test-Taking Tip Put as much information into your answer as possible. Use easy-to-read, short sentences that define key words. Also give an example that explains your answer.

Chapter 23

Cooking Basics

Hero/Corbis/Glow Images

Explore the Photo
Recipes show you a variety of ways to cook and flavor to foods. It all depends on the food and the results you want. *Why are recipes useful?*

Compare and Contrast

Finding Similarities and Differences
Think about two dishes that you enjoy eating. Compare and contrast the two dishes, focusing on what about them is the same and what is different. Use specific examples to show the similarities and differences.

Writing Tips Follow these steps to write a compare and contrast report:

1. Write a topic sentence that includes what you will compare.

2. Use specific examples and details to show the similarities and differences.

3. Use transition words and phrases between comparisons and contrasts.

Section 23.1 Choose Your Ingredients

Reading Guide

Before You Read

Get Your Rest The more well-rested and alert you are when you sit down to study, the more likely you will remember the information later. Studying in the same state of mind as when you are likely to take a test, fully rested and mentally sharp, can help to ensure your best performance.

Read to Learn
Key Concepts
- ✓ **Explain** Why herbs and spices are important.
- ✓ **Describe** how fruit may be processed.
- ✓ **Name** a benefit of convenience foods.

Main Idea
Herbs, spices, fruit, and vegetables all contribute to preparing delicious meals.

Content Vocabulary
- ○ produce
- ○ processed
- ○ antioxidant
- ○ convenience food

Academic Vocabulary
- ■ crucial
- ■ seasonal

Graphic Organizer
Vegetables come from many different parts of plants. As you read, name eight plant parts that produce the vegetables you eat. Use a graphic organizer like the one shown to help you organize your information.

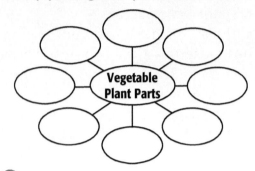

Vegetable Plant Parts

Graphic Organizer Go to **connectED.mcgraw-hill.com** to download this graphic organizer.

Just about everyone knows how to cook something. Maybe you are a whiz at scrambled eggs or pancakes. Perhaps you are already in charge of preparing entire meals for your family. Whatever level of experience you have in the kitchen, you can improve your cooking skills with a few tips and guidelines.

As You Read

Connect Think about a dish that you recently prepared for your family or friends. What was involved in the preparation?

Basic Ingredients

When cooking, the success of your dish depends in part on following step-by-step instructions. As you learn to cook, you will notice that some common ingredients are found in many recipes. Some of these basic ingredients are flour, sugar, shortening or butter, milk, eggs, and spices. Each ingredient in a recipe is used for a specific purpose.

Herbs and Spices

Herbs and spices are the special ingredients that separate average cooks from great cooks. Herbs and spices add taste, color and aroma, or scent, to foods. They are the special ingredients that make some recipes better than others. Herbs and spices are crucial, or very important, to the flavor of a dish. There are many varieties of herbs and spices. Learning which herbs and spices to use, and how much to use, is based on experience. Here are some common herbs and spices:

- **Basil** This popular herb has a mild flavor. It is often used in soups, salads, and pizzas.
- **Parsley** Often used as a garnish, this herb is also found in green sauces, such as pesto. It has a soothing effect on your taste buds.
- **Chives** This herb has a mild onion flavor. It is often used as a garnish or to add flavor to soups and dips.
- **Cilantro** This herb has a unique flavor and aroma. It is often used in salsas, Mexican dishes, and dips.
- **Dill Weed** This herb has a delicate flavor. It is often used in dips and fish dishes.
- **Cinnamon** This spice comes from the bark of the laurel tree. Ground cinnamon is common in cakes, cookies, and specialty drinks.
- **Nutmeg** This spice comes from the fruit of the nutmeg tree. It has a nutty, mild flavor. It is used often in pies and puddings.
- **Cumin** Commonly found ground or as a whole seed, this spice is somewhat hot. It is often used in marinades and sauces.
- **Saffron** This yellow spice comes from the crocus plant. It is used to give its yellow color and flavor to foods.
- **Garlic** This strong herb is a dried root from the lily family. It grows in a bulb that is then minced or chopped.

◆ **Vocabulary**

You can find definitions in the glossary at the back of this book.

Extra Flavor Herbs and spices give foods unique flavors. *Instead of seasoning with salt, what herbs or spices might taste good with potatoes or green beans?*

©Space Images/Blend Images LLC

Figure 23.1 Measurement Equivalents

Accurate Measuring It is important to measure accurately when preparing meals. *What would happen if you used 2 cups of milk instead of 1 cup for your mashed potatoes?*

Customary	Customary Equivalent	Approximate Metric Equivalent
1 teaspoon	*none*	5 milliliters (mL)
1 tablespoon	3 teaspoons	15 milliliters
½ cup	8 tablespoons	125 milliliters
1 cup	16 tablespoons 8 fluid ounces	250 milliliters
2 cups	1 pint	500 milliliters
4 cups	1 quart	1000 milliliters or 1 liter (L)
1 pound	16 ounces	500 grams (g)

Measure Ingredients

By measuring accurately, using the proper measuring tools, and following directions, you will ensure that your recipes are consistent and turn out the same way every time you use them.

When you cook, you will probably use customary measurements such as cups for volume and pounds for weight. The customary measurement system is the measurement system commonly used in the United States. However, the metric system can also appear in recipes, so you may need to know how to convert between the two systems. The metric system is a system of weights and measures based on multiples of ten and is used in most other countries. See **Figure 23.1** for measurement equivalents.

Cooking Temperature

The customary system measures temperature in degrees Fahrenheit (°F). The metric system measures in degrees Celsius (°C). Many thermometers show both. Recipes sometimes include length measurements, such as the length and width of a pan or the size of a vegetable. The customary system measures length in inches (in.), while metrics uses millimeters (mm) or centimeters (cm).

Reading Check *Confirm How can you make sure that your recipe will come out the way you want?*

Fruits and Vegetables

Fruits and vegetables, also called **produce**, are full of essential nutrients. Vegetables can fit into your eating plan in many ways. Serve them as side dishes, main dishes, salads, and garnishes. Like vegetables, fruits are easy to include in your eating plan. Fruits come in a variety of forms, such as fresh, frozen, canned, dried, and as a juice. Many fruits have skins you can eat, such as apples and pears, which can add fiber to your snacks.

Fruits

Besides tasting great, fruit provides important vitamins and minerals, carbohydrates, and fiber. It is easy to get the recommended number of daily servings because fruits go well with any meal and make great snacks. Try adding dried fruit, such as apples or apricots, on your breakfast cereal. Freeze grapes or berries and use them in place of ice cubes in juices and teas.

Some produce, like strawberries, is seasonal, or readily available at certain times of the year. Seasonal food is less expensive than food that is not in season. When you buy produce in-season, you get the best possible quality and also save money. Out-of-season produce may be less nutritious because it is often artificially ripened, or shipped a long distance. If fresh fruits are not available, you might choose processed fruits. **Processed** means that a food is changed from its raw form before being sold. Fruits that are frozen, canned, or dried are considered processed.

Vegetables

Vegetables are a delicious part of a well-balanced diet. They are also valuable sources of carbohydrates, fiber, and important vitamins and minerals. New varieties are developed each year. Like fruits, vegetables are most nutritious when they are fresh. Vegetables are seasonal, but most are available year-round. You can choose frozen, canned, dried, or fresh vegetables.

MATH YOU CAN USE

Probability

Juanita has baked three dozen cupcakes for a party. Fifteen of the cupcakes have a fresh strawberry filling, another twelve are vanilla, and the remaining 9 are banana. However, Juanita covered each cupcake with the same white vanilla frosting, and now she cannot tell them apart. If she selects one at random, what is the probability it will be strawberry? Vanilla? Banana?

Math Concept **Finding Theoretical Probability** Mathematical probability is a number between 0 and 1 that measures the likelihood of an event occurring. The higher the number, the more likely the event will occur. To find an event's probability, write a fraction (in lowest terms) with the number of ways the event can occur as the numerator and the total number of possible outcomes as the denominator.

Starting Hint Since there are 36 total cupcakes, there are 36 possible outcomes when Juanita goes to pick one cupcake, so use 36 as the denominator of each fraction.

 For more math help, go to the Math Appendix located at the back of this book.

Measuring Correctly

In this activity you will use tools to measure different ingredients accurately. Before you begin, read through the entire Hands-On Lab assignment. Write down any questions that you have about the activity. Reread the text or ask your teacher for help if you need it.

Supplies

✓ Flour sifter
✓ Dry and liquid measuring cups and spoons
✓ Metal spatula
✓ Rubber scraper
✓ Flour
✓ Shortening
✓ Oil
✓ Baking soda

Develop Your Plan

■ Gather measuring utensils.
■ Gather ingredients.
■ Measure ingredients.

Implement Your Plan

■ Gather your measuring utensils and ingredients.
■ Sift and measure 1 cup of flour.
■ Press shortening into a dry measuring cup, making sure there are no air pockets. Level it with a metal spatula. Remove shortening with a rubber scraper.

■ Place the liquid measuring cup on a flat surface. Pour oil up to the ½ cup line. Check it at eye level.
■ Pour ¼ teaspoon of baking soda into the measuring spoon. Level the top with a metal spatula.

Evaluate Your Results

Why must you measure ingredients exactly? What could happen if you do not measure ingredients correctly? Write down three tips that you learned from this experience. Write one or more paragraphs to explain your answer.

➤ **Projects and Activities** Go to connectED.mcgraw-hill.com.

Vegetables actually come from many different parts of plants. Vegetables can be:

- Fruits, such as tomatoes, eggplants, and peppers.
- Flowers, such as broccoli and cauliflower.
- Stems, such as asparagus and celery.
- Roots, such as beets, carrots, and turnips.
- Tubers (underground stems), such as potatoes.
- Bulbs, such as onions and garlic.
- Leaves, such as cabbage, greens, kale, and spinach.
- Seeds, such as beans, corn, and peas.

Fresh vegetables need to be refrigerated until you are ready to use them. For best results, they should be used within a few days after you buy them. Before serving fresh vegetables, wash them carefully under cold running water. If you plan to eat them raw, you may want to peel the vegetables and blot them dry. To keep raw vegetables crisp, do not wash them too far in advance of serving time. Raw vegetables can be enjoyed alone, or you can try dipping carrots, cauliflower, or broccoli in low-fat ranch dressing for a refreshing and healthful snack.

Many vegetables contain antioxidants. An **antioxidant** ('an-tē-'äk-sə-dənt) is a substance that protects cells from oxidation, a chemical reaction that causes cell damage. Antioxidants may help prevent heart disease, cancer, and other ailments. Antioxidants include vitamins C and E, beta-carotene, and the mineral selenium.

Reading Check   *Identify*   *What is an antioxidant?*

Fresh Fruit   Choose the freshest fruit you can in order to get the best flavor and highest nutritional value. *How much fruit should you eat every day?*

© Pascal Broze/SuperStock

Convenience Foods

There may be occasions when you will want to prepare meals in a hurry. **Convenience foods** are already prepared or partially prepared to save you time. For instance, you might buy a bag of tossed salad instead of purchasing all the ingredients and cutting them up yourself. A common type of convenience food is a mix such as cake and muffin mixes. Other convenience foods include frozen pizza, canned chili, and soup. Be careful when you use convenience foods as they tend to cost more than fresh foods. Additionally, they may not taste as fresh. They may contain preservatives, which are chemicals added to make foods last longer. However, once in a while it may be worth the extra cost to save time and avoid wasting food.

Always follow the directions given on the package. Make sure in advance that you have all the ingredients and utensils you will need and that you understand all the instructions. When using a general-purpose baking mix, use only the recipes provided on the box. Do not try to substitute the mix for ingredients in another recipe.

Section 23.1 After You Read

Review What You Have Learned

1. **List** the common, basic ingredients found in many recipes.
2. **Name** ways to use vegetables in your food.
3. **Explain** a drawback of using convenience foods.

Practice Academic Skills

English Language Arts

4. Use clip art, illustrations or pictures from magazines to create a pamphlet encouraging people to buy spices. Discuss the benefits of spices, using specific examples of spices and the dishes in which they can be used. Share your pamphlet with the class.

Social Studies

5. Use poster board to create a map that shows where fruits and vegetables are most commonly grown in the United States. Use graphics, clip art, or your own drawings to show the region and the produce grown there.

Check Your Answers Check Your Answers at connectED.mcgraw-hill.com.

Section 23.2 Cooking Techniques

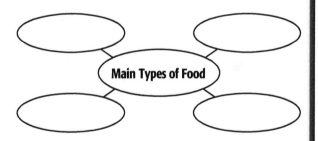
There are many different ways to prepare food. To get what you want from your meals, it is important to know how to cook bread and grains, fruits and vegetables, milk products, and meat, poultry, and fish.

Cooking Grains

Grains include cereal, rice, pasta, and bread. These go well with vegetables, fruits, cheese, meat, chicken, fish, and beans.

Breads

Breads are made from whole wheat, rye, white, or corn flour. Other ingredients are added to give each type of bread a particular flavor, texture, and appearance.

As You Read

Connect Think about a recent meal you cooked for yourself, or a meal that was cooked for you. How was each item cooked or prepared?

Quick Breads and Yeast Breads

Quick breads are breads in which the leavening agent is baking powder or baking soda. Baking powder and baking soda cause the air bubbles to form, making the bread rise quickly as it bakes. It is important to mix the **batter**, a liquid or semiliquid mixture, usually containing flour, milk, and eggs, just long enough to blend the ingredients. Too much mixing makes quick breads flat and heavy. Air bubbles, which form during baking, make quick breads light and fluffy.

Yeast breads are breads in which the leavening agent is yeast. They take longer to prepare than quick breads. Most sandwich breads, French and Italian breads, and hamburger buns are yeast breads.

A dough made with yeast must rise twice. First, you must let it rise in a warm place outside the oven for an hour or more. Then you punch it down, shape it, and let it rise in the pan before baking. You can also buy frozen yeast dough. Let the dough warm to room temperature and rise until it is ready to be baked.

International Sandwiches Sandwiches are more than just slices of ham on wheat bread. Greek gyros and the Asian spring rolls in this photo are also types of sandwiches. *What other types of sandwiches do you enjoy?*

Copyright © FoodCollection

Sandwiches

A sandwich is any filling put in or on bread or another edible wrapper. You can use any type of bread or a wrap, such as pita or a tortilla. Then add a spread, such as mustard, mayonnaise, honey, pesto, butter, or margarine. Fillings can include peanut butter, fruit preserves, tuna, chicken salad, meat or cheese. Finally, use lettuce, spinach, avocado, relish, sprouts, tomatoes, peppers, and olives for extra flavor. Try a tuna melt by putting tuna and cheese on a bagel or bread and melting the cheese. Peanut butter with banana slices on oatmeal bread provides foods from three of the five food groups.

Cereal, Rice and Pasta

Some breakfast cereals, rice, and pasta must be cooked before you eat them. Some of the cooking techniques are similar because they all contain corn starch.

Cereal can be enjoyed with cold milk or cooked and eaten hot such as instant oatmeal, grits, and wheat cereals. They can be cooked with water or milk on top of the stove or in a microwave oven. Try adding raisins or sliced bananas to hot cereal to add texture, flavor, and sweetness.

Rice is a grain that must be cooked. Rice should be simmered in water, not boiled. When cooked properly, rice is light and fluffy, not heavy or gummy. Do not rinse rice, because rinsing removes nutrients. Use a little oil in the cooking water to help the grains separate and to prevent foaming. Keep the lid on while cooking and do not drain. Fluff the rice with a fork before serving. Before you cook rice, read the directions on the package.

Pasta is made from wheat flour, water, and sometimes eggs and other flavorings. It comes in many shapes and sizes, from long strands to corkscrews to shells. Pasta is another grain that must be cooked before it is eaten. To make your pasta slippery and not sticky, use plenty of water, about 4 quarts (4L) of water per pound of pasta. Heat the water to a boil before adding the pasta. Keep it boiling during the cooking time. Do not cover the pot. Stir the pasta occasionally to prevent clumping. Cook the pasta just long enough so that it is tender, or easily chewed or cut, but slightly firm. Use the package instructions to guide cooking times. Drain the pasta carefully by pouring the pasta into a colander placed in the sink.

Reading Check *Follow Directions* *What are some tips for cooking rice?*

SUCCEED IN SCHOOL!

Handle Criticism
Accept Constructive Criticism Not all criticism is bad. In fact, some can be very helpful and positive. Criticism given in a fair, respectful way is actually a useful tool in helping people improve and avoid mistakes in the future.

Cooking Fruits and Vegetables

When you think of the kinds of fruit you enjoy, you probably think of eating raw fruit, such as apples, grapes, and bananas. However, fruits are used in many cooked dishes, too. Like fruit, vegetables can be enjoyed raw or cooked. Some vegetables, such as potatoes, winter squash, and artichokes, must be cooked before you eat them.

Baked fruit can be used for desserts such as baked apples and baked pears. Recipes include fruit, butter, sugar, cream, and spices such as cinnamon or nutmeg. Fruits can be baked in a conventional oven or a microwave oven or cooked in a pan on the stove.

Fruits taste and look best when they are cooked properly. During cooking, small amounts of some vitamins are lost. Some dissolve in water and some are destroyed by heat and air. To minimize nutrient loss, use low heat and as little water as possible.

Like fruits, vegetables can retain, or keep, their nutrients and keep their texture and flavor if they are cooked properly. Cook vegetables until they are tender and crisp, not soft. To prevent vitamin and mineral loss during cooking, add as little water as possible, use a lid to speed cooking time and avoid overcooking. Vegetables that are cooked properly have a somewhat brighter color than raw ones. For example, green beans are bright green when they are done, and olive green when they have cooked too long.

Vegetables can be cooked and served as a side dish or added to other ingredients to make a casserole. A **casserole** is a one-dish meal that is baked and often reheated after cooking. The most common ways to cook vegetables are:

- **Simmering** Cook vegetables in a small amount of liquid, just below the boiling point. Cover the pan with a tight-fitting lid.
- **Steaming** Place vegetables inside a steamer over simmering water inside a covered pan. The vegetables should not touch the water.
- **Baking** Vegetables, such as potatoes, are baked in their skins. Before baking, pierce the skins several times so they do not burst.
- **Stir-frying** Cook vegetables quickly over high heat while stirring them in a small amount of oil.

Reading Check *Explain How can you prevent vitamin and mineral loss when cooking vegetables.*

Cooking with Milk Products

Milk or cream can be used to make soups, sauces, puddings, and custards. Milk and buttermilk are often used in cakes, pies, breads, and muffins.

Thick, creamy sauces add flavor to many dishes. A basic white sauce made with milk can be served over vegetables or noodles. For extra flavor, add cheese or herbs to the sauce.

When cooking with milk products, it is important to be especially careful. Milk burns, or scorches, easily if the temperature is too high or if it is cooked too long. To cook milk you need to **scald** it, or bring it slowly to a temperature just below the boiling point. Never let milk boil. Heat only until little bubbles begin to appear around the edge of the pan.

Milk may curdle if you do not handle it properly. When milk **curdles**, it separates into little particles or curds. Adding tomatoes or fruit juices to milk may cause curdling, as they contain acid. To avoid this, add ingredients very slowly and stir the milk constantly.

Cheese is an important ingredient in many recipes. Cheese is supposed to melt, not cook, so heating cheese too long or at high temperatures may cause it to burn or become rubbery or stringy. When cooking with cheese, use low to medium heat. Grate or shred hard cheeses, such as cheddar, before adding them to other ingredients. The cheese will blend faster and more evenly. Add cheese at the end of the cooking time so that the cheese will not become overcooked.

Try sprinkling grated cheese on soups, chili, baked potatoes, or burritos. For an easy snack, eat cheese with crackers, crusty bread, or fresh fruit.

Reading Check *Describe* What can you do to keep cheese from burning or becoming rubbery or stringy when you cook with it?

Macaroni and Cheese A popular favorite among children is macaroni and cheese. *What ingredients could you add to this dish to make it appealing to adults?*

Avoiding Steam Burns

Moisture can build up inside a pot or pan and create steam. When the steam hits the air to escape, it can cause severe burns.

- Carefully remove lids from pots and pans when cooking.
- Use a potholder to remove the lid.

Cooking Meat, Poultry, and Fish

Protein-rich foods such as meat, poultry, and fish are popular main dishes. They can be prepared in a variety of ways. When cooking meat, poultry, or fish, the two basic methods you will use are moist heat and dry heat (See **Figure 23.2**). The method you choose depends on the recipe you are following and the tenderness of the meat or poultry.

Moist Heat

When you boil, stew, braise, or simmer meat, you are using moist heat. Moist-heat cooking is cooking food slowly in a covered container, usually with water, broth, or a sauce. When cooked, some of the meat juices will flow into the cooking liquid. Moist-heat cooking methods are good choices to use with less expensive, tougher cuts of meat. When cooked slowly in liquid, meats become more tender and flavorful. Use moist heat to cook chuck roast, corned beef, pork blade steak, pot roast, poultry, round steak, spareribs, and stew meat.

Dry Heat

Dry-heat cooking is cooking without liquid. Broiling, char-broiling, roasting, baking, pan frying, and deep frying are dry heat cooking methods. This method is used for tender cuts of meat such as beef rib roast, fish, ground beef, pork, turkey, ham, lamb, pork chops, poultry and sirloin steak.

Reading Check List *What are some dry-heat cooking methods?*

Figure 23.2 Cooking Methods for Meat

Dry Heat or Moist Heat? Dry-heat cooking is used for tender pieces of meat, while moist-heat cooking is used to help make tough cuts more tender. *What types of meat would benefit from moist-heat cooking?*

Dry Heat Methods

Roasting and Baking

Frying

Broiling

Moist Heat Methods

Stewing

Braising

Other Proteins

Other high-protein foods can be used as the main dish instead of meat, poultry, or fish. Beans and eggs are two good substitutes. They are high in protein, vitamins, and minerals and low in cost. They are two of the most nutritious foods you can cook. They are also both vegetarian options.

Legumes are dry beans and peas which come in a variety of tastes and textures. Red kidney beans, black beans, white beans, lentils, lima beans, split peas, and black-eyed peas offer healthful alternatives to meat, poultry, and fish dishes. You can make baked beans or roll them in tortillas with rice and cheese to make burritos.

Eggs can also be a main dish. Eggs can be hard-boiled, scrambled, fried, or used in quiches and omelets. A **quiche** ('kēsh) is a main-dish pie filled with eggs, cheese, and other ingredients such as ham, spinach, and mushrooms. An **omelet** is a well-beaten egg that is first cooked in a frying pan without stirring. Then it is filled with other ingredients, such as mushrooms, peppers, and cheese.

Section 23.2 After You Read

Review What You Have Learned

1. **Describe** the process for making yeast bread.
2. **Name** the most common ways to cook vegetables.
3. **Explain** the best ways to cook with cheese.
4. **Identify** two sources of protein other than meat.

Practice Academic Skills

English Language Arts

5. Write a letter to someone who is trying to cut back on sugar intake. Tell him or her that fruit is an easy, healthful, convenient, and delicious substitute for candy or cookies. Use information from this chapter, but write in your own words.

Social Studies

6. Choose a historical period and research a cooking technique addressed in the section. Compare and contrast the cooking technique with what we do today. How was cooking different? How have techniques changed? Has the technique improved? Share your information with the class.

Check Your Answers Check Your Answers at connectED.mcgraw-hill.com.

Discovering Careers

Do you like to try new cooking techniques? Are you interested in how food is prepared before it arrives in markets or restaurants? If you answered yes to either of those questions, you might want to consider a future career in food preparation. The following chart explores several careers in the food industry.

Job Title	Job Description
Menu Planner	Works closely with executive chef to select menu items. Participates in cost control, ordering of supplies, and some food preparation.
Pastry Chef	Prepares a wide variety of pastries and desserts. Supervises pastry cooks. Plans work schedules. Orders supplies.
Farmer	Raises both crops and livestock. Determines crops to be grown and livestock to be bred. Monitors market conditions and weather.
Baker	Uses raw ingredients to bake breads and pastries for sale. Offers specialty breads for a variety of events.
Food Critic	Evaluates restaurants based on standards for cooking techniques, flavor, and service. Writes column or blog with recommendations.

Career Activities ▼

At School

❶ Select three of the careers listed. Research the education, training, and work experience required for each career. Write a summary of your results.

At Home

❷ Plan a dinner with your family. Each of you should take responsibility for one portion of the meal (for example, main dish, side dish, dessert, appetizer, sauce). What techniques did each of you use to cook your part of the meal?

At Work

❸ Plan three nutritious brown-bag lunches that you could take to work. Compare your examples with those of your classmates.

In the Community

❹ Contact and interview someone in your community who works in the food industry. Ask this person to describe what his or her typical work day is like. Share what you learned with your class.

Chapter Summary

Section 23.1 Choose Your Ingredients
The success of your dish depends in part on following step-by-step instructions. By measuring accurately, using the proper measuring tools and following directions, you ensure that your recipes turn out the same every time. Herbs and spices add taste, color, and aroma to foods. Fruits and vegetables are a delicious part of a well-balanced meal plan. Convenience foods can save you time.

Section 23.2 Cooking Techniques
There are many techniques for cooking food. Grain products like rice, pasta, and oatmeal are cooked in water. Some foods made from grains must be cooked before you eat them. Like fruit, vegetables can be enjoyed raw or cooked. Vegetables retain their nutrients and keep their texture and flavor when cooked properly. When cooking meat, poultry, or fish, you can use moist heat or dry heat.

Words You Learned

1. Create a fill-in-the-blank sentence for each of these vocabulary terms. The sentence should contain enough information to help determine the missing word.

Content Vocabulary
- produce (p. 513)
- processed (p. 513)
- antioxidant (p. 515)
- convenience food (p. 516)
- quick bread (p. 518)
- batter (p. 518)
- yeast bread (p. 518)
- casserole (p. 520)
- scald (p. 521)
- curdle (p. 521)
- legume (p. 523)
- quiche (p. 523)
- omelet (p. 523)

Academic Vocabulary
- crucial (p. 511)
- seasonal (p. 513)
- tender (p. 519)
- retain (p. 520)

Review Key Concepts

2. **Explain** why herbs and spices are important.
3. **Describe** how fruit may be processed.
4. **Name** a benefit of convenience foods.
5. **Name** two types of breads.
6. **Explain** how fruits and vegetables are a part of a well-balanced diet.
7. **Describe** ways to use milk products in cooking.
8. **Identify** two basic methods of cooking meat, poultry, or fish.

Critical Thinking

9. **Explain** how you can retain the nutrients in vegetables when you cook them.

Real-World Skills and Applications

Problem-Solving

10. Quick and Nutritious Meal You have 30 minutes to prepare a nutritious dinner for you and your family. You have chicken breasts as the main ingredient. What cooking methods could you use to prepare dinner? What could you add to the meal to increase its nutritional value?

Technology Applications

11. Herb and Spice Guide Use a spreadsheet or word-processing software to make a reference guide for cooking with herbs and spices. With permission from a teacher or parent, go online to search for information to add to what you learned in this chapter. Include information about how herbs and spices work together. Also look for examples of foods that work best with specific herbs and spices.

Financial Literacy

12. Buying Convenience Foods As their name implies, convenience foods can save busy home cooks a great deal of shopping and cooking time versus preparing meals and baked goods from scratch. However, convenience foods can be less nutritious than home-cooked foods, and you can pay a lot for all that convenience. Find a simple cake recipe. Determine the cost of all the ingredients you would need to purchase to make that cake from scratch. Then, determine the cost of making a similar cake using a cake mix. Finally, determine the cost of purchasing a finished cake from a bakery or grocery store. How do the prices compare? What are the pros and cons of each type of cake?

13. A Nutritious Gift Snack and fruit baskets are so popular that there are stores and Web sites devoted to creating and selling them as gifts. Create a snack or fruit basket to give to a friend, teacher, or family member as a gift. Include an attractive collection of fruits and tasty, nutritious snacks. Also, find a few recipes for healthful treats. Compile them into a small booklet and create a cover for it, and include the booklet in the basket.

14. Spice Origins What is your favorite spice? Is it sweet like cinnamon or hot like curry? Conduct research to learn where your favorite spice originated. What is the spice made from? What was it originally used for? How is it used today? Can the spice be used for something other than adding flavor to food? Present your information in a brief report.

15. Cancer-fighting Foods According to the National Cancer Institute, antioxidants are plentiful in fruits and vegetables, as well as in other foods such as nuts, grains and some meats, poultry, and fish. Researchers continue to study the effect of antioxidants on cancer prevention. With permission from your parents or teacher, go online to search for foods that may help prevent cancer. Make a list of at least 10 foods and explain how you can add them to your meals. Include this information in your Life Skills Binder.

D.Hurst/Alamy

Academic Skills

English Language Arts

16. Cooking Vegetables Creative preparation can make it easier and more enjoyable to add vegetables to your meals. Having many different options for cooking them will give you more variety in your meals. Create a poster that explains six possible ways to cook vegetables. Include graphics, photos, and clear instructions for each cooking technique. Display your posters in your classroom.

Social Studies

17. Research a Family Recipe Families often have a recipe that has been handed down from one generation to another. Often the recipe has not been written down but is communicated orally from mother or father to daughter or son. Choose a family recipe that has been handed down, and research to find out its origins, the ingredients, and its importance to your family heritage and culture. Write an overview of what you find.

Mathematics

18. Slicing Bread Katherine needs to slice two loaves of fresh-baked bread. The sourdough loaf is 12 in. long, and she would like each slice to be ¾ in. thick. A rye loaf is 13 ½ in. long, and she would like each slice to be ½ in. thick. How many slices will she get out of each loaf?

Math Concept **Dividing with Fractions** To divide when a fraction is involved, first convert any mixed or whole numbers to improper fractions. Multiply the first fraction by the reciprocal of the second fraction. Reduce your answer to lowest terms.

Starting Hint For the sourdough, you will need to divide 12 by ¾, which requires you to multiply 12/1 by the reciprocal of ¾, or 4/3. For the rye loaf, first convert 13 ½ into an improper fraction by multiplying 13 × 2 and adding that number to 1 to get the new numerator.

Standardized Test Practice

Math Word Problem

Read the word problem and possible answers. Then choose the correct answer.

Test-Taking Tip Solve a word problem in two steps. First, translate the words into an equation of numbers and variables. Then solve each equation in order to get the correct answer.

19. You are getting ready to check out of the grocery store. The store is offering a 22% discount for students shopping for their parents. Your total amount is $112.53. After you deduct the discount, what will your amount be?
a. $22.51
b. $90.02
c. $101.00
d. $165.04

A Meal from Your Culture

Preparing food from your own culture is a way to explore your identity. Your family may have favorite dishes that they make on holidays and special occasions. Recipe books are often specific to a culture, nationality, or heritage. This project will help you explore food from your background.

My Journal Complete the journal entry from page 465, and refer to it to complete your recipe collection.

Project Assignment ▼

In this project, you will:

- Gather recipes of dishes common to your background.
- Write about a recipe that means something to your family.
- Prepare a dish that reflects your culture.
- Interview someone who shares your heritage.
- Present your findings to your class.
- Include this project in the tenth section of your personal Life Skills binder.

 Step 1 Gather Recipes from Your Culture

Ask family members or friends if they have recipes that reflect your heritage. Read cookbooks to find more ideas. Compile the recipes you gather, and write a summary of your research that identifies common ingredients and preparation methods.

Step 2 Choose a Recipe and Prepare a Dish

Pick a recipe you can make. Gather the ingredients, and follow instructions carefully. If you need help, ask a parent or friend. Then write two or more paragraphs that answer these questions:

- ✔ What were the key ingredients?
- ✔ What was the most challenging part of the preparation process?
- ✔ Is there any method you use today that an ancestor might have done differently, for example, using a microwave instead of an open fire?
- ✔ What is the traditional way to serve this dish?

Step 3 Interview a Member of Your Culture

Interview someone in your community who is familiar with the traditions of your culture. Ask these questions:

- ✔ What does this dish mean to you?
- ✔ What is the history of this recipe?
- ✔ Tell me a story about a memorable meal that included this dish.

Use these interviewing skills when conducting your interview and these writing skills when writing the summary of notes from your interview.

Interviewing Skills
- Record interview responses and take notes.
- Listen attentively.

Writing Skills
- Use complete sentences.
- Use correct spelling and grammar.

Step 4 Serve and Present Your Cultural Dish

Use the Life Skills Project Checklist on the right to plan and serve your dish to the class and give an oral report on it.

Use these speaking skills when presenting your final report.

Speaking Skills
- Speak clearly and concisely.
- Be sensitive to the needs of your audience.
- Use standard English to communicate.

Step 5 Evaluate Your Presentation

Your project will be evaluated based on:

✔ Organization and cultural relevance of your collected recipes.
✔ The dish you prepared for the class.
✔ Description of your food preparation experience.
✔ The summary written from interview notes.
✔ Grammar and sentence structure.
✔ Presentation to the class.
✔ Creativity and neatness.

🖈 **Evaluation Rubric** Go to **connectED.mcgraw-hill.com** for a rubric you can use to evaluate your final project.

Life Skills Project Checklist

Research Cultural Recipes

✅ Collect traditional recipes from your family or friends.

✅ Read cookbooks about food from your background.

✅ Prepare a recipe from your heritage.

✅ Interview someone who is familiar with your culture.

Writing Skills

✅ Describe common ingredients and preparation methods of your culture.

✅ Describe your own food preparation experience.

✅ Write a summary from your interview with someone who shares your background.

Present Your Findings

✅ Prepare a short presentation to give before serving your dish to the class. Describe how your dish is important to your culture.

✅ Invite the students of the class to ask any questions they may have. Answer these questions with responses that respect their perspectives.

✅ Add this project to your Life Skills binder.

Academic Skills

✅ Conduct research to gather information.

✅ Communicate effectively.

✅ Organize your presentation so the audience can follow along easily.

✅ Thoroughly express your ideas.

Amos Morgan/Getty Images

Math Appendix

Number and Operations

▶ *Understand numbers, ways of representing numbers, relationships among numbers, and number systems*

Fraction, Decimal, and Percent

A percent is a ratio that compares a number to 100. To write a percent as a fraction, drop the percent sign, and use the number as the numerator in a fraction with a denominator of 100. Simplify, if possible. For example, $76\% = \frac{76}{100}$, or $\frac{19}{25}$. To write a fraction as a percent, convert it to an equivalent fraction with a denominator of 100. For example, $\frac{3}{4} = \frac{75}{100}$, or 75%. A fraction can be expressed as a percent by first converting the fraction to a decimal (divide the numerator by the denominator) and then converting the decimal to a percent by moving the decimal point two places to the right.

Comparing Numbers on a Number Line

In order to compare and understand the relationship between real numbers in various forms, it is helpful to use a number line. The zero point on a number line is called the origin; the points to the left of the origin are negative, and those to the right are positive. The number line below shows how numbers in fraction, decimal, percent, and integer form can be compared.

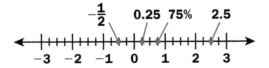

Percents Greater Than 100 and Less Than 1

Percents greater than 100% represent values greater than 1. For example, if the weight of an object is 250% of another, it is 2.5, or $2\frac{1}{2}$, times the weight.

Percents less than 1 represent values less than $\frac{1}{100}$. In other words, 0.1% is one tenth of one percent, which can also be represented in decimal form as 0.001, or in fraction form as $\frac{1}{1,000}$. Similarly, 0.01% is one hundredth of one percent or 0.0001 or $\frac{1}{10,000}$.

Ratio, Rate, and Proportion

A ratio is a comparison of two numbers using division. If a basketball player makes 8 out of 10 free throws, the ratio is written as 8 to 10, 8:10, or $\frac{8}{10}$. Ratios are usually written in simplest form. In simplest form, the ratio "8 out of 10" is 4 to 5, 4:5, or $\frac{4}{5}$. A rate is a ratio of two measurements having different kinds of units—cups per gallon, or miles per hour, for example. When a rate is simplified so that it has a denominator of 1, it is called a unit rate. An example of a unit rate is 9 miles per hour. A proportion is an equation stating that two ratios are equal. $\frac{3}{18} = \frac{13}{78}$ is an example of a proportion. The cross products of a proportion are also equal. $\frac{3}{18} = \frac{13}{78}$ and $3 \times 78 = 18 \times 13$.

Representing Large and Small Numbers

In order to represent large and small numbers, it is important to understand the number system. Our number system is based on 10, and the value of each place is 10 times the value of the place to its right.

The value of a digit is the product of a digit and its place value. For instance, in the number 6,400, the 6 has a value of six thousands and the 4 has a value of four hundreds. A place value chart can help you read numbers. In the chart, each group of three digits is called a period. Commas separate the periods: the ones period, the thousands period, the millions period, and so on. Values to the right of the ones period are decimals. By understanding place value you can write very large numbers like 5 billion and more, and very small numbers that are less than 1, like one-tenth.

Scientific Notation

When dealing with very large numbers like 1,500,000, or very small numbers like 0.000015, it is helpful to keep track of their value by writing the numbers in scientific notation. Powers of 10 with positive exponents are used with a decimal between 1 and 10 to express large numbers. The exponent represents the number of places the decimal point is moved to the right. So, 528,000 is written in scientific notation as 5.28×10^5. Powers of 10 with negative exponents are used with a decimal between 1 and 10 to express small numbers. The exponent represents the number of places the decimal point is moved to the left. The number 0.00047 is expressed as 4.7×10^{-4}.

Factor, Multiple, and Prime Factorization

Two or more numbers that are multiplied to form a product are called factors. Divisibility rules can be used to determine whether 2, 3, 4, 5, 6, 8, 9, or 10 are factors of a given number. Multiples are the products of a given number and various integers.

For example, 8 is a multiple of 4 because $4 \times 2 = 8$. A prime number is a whole number that has exactly two factors: 1 and itself. A composite number is a whole number that has more than two factors. Zero and 1 are neither prime nor composite. A composite number can be expressed as the product of its prime factors. The prime factorization of 40 is $2 \times 2 \times 2 \times 5$, or $2^3 \times 5$. The numbers 2 and 5 are prime numbers.

Integers

A negative number is a number less than zero. Negative numbers like –8, positive numbers like +6, and zero are members of the set of integers. Integers can be represented as points on a number line. A set of integers can be written {..., –3, –2, –1, 0, 1, 2, 3, ...} where ... means "continues indefinitely."

Real, Rational, and Irrational Numbers

The real number system is made up of the sets of rational and irrational numbers. Rational numbers are numbers that can be written in the form a/b where a and b are integers and $b \neq 0$. Examples are 0.45, $\frac{1}{2}$, and $\sqrt{36}$. Irrational numbers are non-repeating, non-terminating decimals. Examples are $\sqrt{71}$, π, and 0.020020002....

Complex and Imaginary Numbers

A complex number is a mathematical expression with a real number element and an imaginary number element. Imaginary numbers are multiples of i, the "imaginary" square root of –1. Complex numbers are represented by $a + bi$, where a and b are real numbers and i represents the imaginary element. When a quadratic equation does not have a real number solution, the solution can be represented by a complex number. Like real numbers, complex numbers can be added, subtracted, multiplied, and divided.

Vectors and Matrices

A matrix is a set of numbers or elements arranged in rows and columns to form a rectangle. The number of rows is represented by m and the number of columns is represented by n. To describe the number of rows and columns in a matrix, list the number of rows first using the format $m \times n$. Matrix A below is a 3×3 matrix because it has 3 rows and 3 columns. To name an element of a matrix, the letter i is used to denote the row and j is used to denote the column, and the element is labeled in the form $a_{i,j}$. In matrix A below, $a_{3,2}$ is 4.

$$\text{Matrix A} = \begin{pmatrix} 1 & 3 & 5 \\ 0 & 6 & 8 \\ 3 & 4 & 5 \end{pmatrix}$$

A vector is a matrix with only one column or row of elements. A transposed column vector, or a column vector turned on its side, is a row vector. In the example below, row vector b' is the transpose of column vector b.

$$b = \begin{pmatrix} 1 \\ 2 \\ 3 \\ 4 \end{pmatrix}$$

$$b' = (1 \quad 2 \quad 3 \quad 4)$$

▶ *Understand meanings of operations and how they relate to one another*

Properties of Addition and Multiplication

Properties are statements that are true for any numbers. For example, $3 + 8$ is the same as $8 + 3$ because each expression equals 11. This illustrates the Commutative Property of Addition. Likewise, $3 \times 8 = 8 \times 3$ illustrates the Commutative Property of Multiplication.

When evaluating expressions, it is often helpful to group or associate the numbers. The Associative Property says that the way in which numbers are grouped when added or multiplied does not change the sum or product. The following properties are also true:

- **Additive Identity Property:** When 0 is added to any number, the sum is the number.

- **Multiplicative Identity Property:** When any number is multiplied by 1, the product is the number.

- **Multiplicative Property of Zero:** When any number is multiplied by 0, the product is 0.

Rational Numbers

A number that can be written as a fraction is called a rational number. Terminating and repeating decimals are rational numbers because both can be written as fractions.

Decimals that are neither terminating nor repeating are called irrational numbers because they cannot be written as fractions. Terminating decimals can be converted to fractions by placing the number (without the decimal point) in the numerator. Count the number of places to the right of the decimal point, and in the denominator, place a 1 followed by a number of zeros equal to the number of places that you counted. The fraction can then be reduced to its simplest form.

Writing a Fraction as a Decimal

Any fraction $\frac{a}{b}$, where $b \neq 0$, can be written as a decimal by dividing the numerator by the denominator. So, $\frac{a}{b} = a \div b$. If the division ends, or terminates, when the remainder is zero, the decimal is a terminating decimal. Not all fractions can be written as terminating decimals. Some have a repeating decimal. A bar indicates that the decimal repeats forever. For example, the fraction $\frac{4}{9}$ can be converted to a repeating decimal, $0.\overline{4}$

Adding and Subtracting Like Fractions

Fractions with the same denominator are called like fractions. To add like fractions, add the numerators and write the sum over the denominator. To add mixed numbers with like fractions, add the whole numbers and fractions separately, adding the numerators of the fractions, then simplifying if necessary. The rule for subtracting fractions with like denominators is similar to the rule for adding. The numerators can be subtracted and the difference written over the denominator. Mixed numbers are written as improper fractions before subtracting. These same rules apply to adding or subtracting like algebraic fractions. An algebraic fraction is a fraction that contains one or more variables in the numerator or denominator.

Adding and Subtracting Unlike Fractions

Fractions with different denominators are called unlike fractions. The least common multiple of the denominators is used to rename the fractions with a common denominator. After a common denominator is found, the numerators can then be added or subtracted. To add mixed numbers with unlike fractions, rename the mixed numbers as improper fractions. Then find a common denominator, add the numerators, and simplify the answer.

Multiplying Rational Numbers

To multiply fractions, multiply the numerators and multiply the denominators. If the numerators and denominators have common factors, they can be simplified before multiplication. If the fractions have different signs, then the product will be negative. Mixed numbers can be multiplied in the same manner, after first renaming them as improper fractions. Algebraic fractions may be multiplied using the same method described above.

Math Appendix

Dividing Rational Numbers

To divide a number by a rational number (a fraction, for example), multiply the first number by the multiplicative inverse of the second. Two numbers whose product is 1 are called multiplicative inverses, or reciprocals. $\frac{7}{4} \times \frac{4}{7} = 1$. When dividing by a mixed number, first rename it as an improper fraction, and then multiply by its multiplicative inverse. This process of multiplying by a number's reciprocal can also be used when dividing algebraic fractions.

Adding Integers

To add integers with the same sign, add their absolute values. The sum takes the same sign as the addends. An addend is a number that is added to another number (the augend). The equation $-5 + (-2) = -7$ is an example of adding two integers with the same sign. To add integers with different signs, subtract their absolute values. The sum takes the same sign as the addend with the greater absolute value.

Subtracting Integers

The rules for adding integers are extended to the subtraction of integers. To subtract an integer, add its additive inverse. For example, to find the difference $2 - 5$, add the additive inverse of 5 to 2: $2 + (-5) = -3$. The rule for subtracting integers can be used to solve real-world problems and to evaluate algebraic expressions.

Additive Inverse Property

Two numbers with the same absolute value but different signs are called opposites. For example, −4 and 4 are opposites. An integer and its opposite are also called additive inverses. The Additive Inverse Property says that the sum of any number and its additive inverse is zero. The Commutative, Associative, and Identity Properties also apply to integers. These properties help when adding more than two integers.

Absolute Value

In mathematics, when two integers on a number line are on opposite sides of zero, and they are the same distance from zero, they have the same absolute value. The symbol for absolute value is two vertical bars on either side of the number. For example, $|-5| = 5$.

Multiplying Integers

Since multiplication is repeated addition, $3(-7)$ means that −7 is used as an addend 3 times. By the Commutative Property of Multiplication, $3(-7) = -7(3)$. The product of two integers with different signs is always negative. The product of two integers with the same sign is always positive.

Dividing Integers

The quotient of two integers can be found by dividing the numbers using their absolute values. The quotient of two integers with the same sign is positive, and the quotient of two integers with a different sign is negative. $-12 \div (-4) = 3$ and $12 \div (-4) = -3$. The division of integers is used in statistics to find the average, or mean, of a set of data. When finding the mean of a set of numbers, find the sum of the numbers, and then divide by the number in the set.

Adding and Multiplying Vectors and Matrices

In order to add two matrices together, they must have the same number of rows and columns. In matrix addition, the corresponding elements are added to each other. In other words $(a + b)_{ij} = a_{ij} + b_{ij}$. For example,

$$\begin{pmatrix} 1 & 2 \\ 2 & 1 \end{pmatrix} + \begin{pmatrix} 3 & 6 \\ 0 & 1 \end{pmatrix} = \begin{pmatrix} 1+3 & 2+6 \\ 2+0 & 1+1 \end{pmatrix} = \begin{pmatrix} 4 & 8 \\ 2 & 2 \end{pmatrix}$$

Matrix multiplication requires that the number of elements in each row in the first matrix is equal to the number of elements in each column in the second. The elements of the first row of the first matrix are multiplied by the corresponding elements of the first column of the second matrix and then added together to get the first element of the product matrix. To get the second element, the elements in the first row of the first matrix are multiplied by the corresponding elements in the second column of the second matrix then added, and so on, until every row of the first matrix is multiplied by every column of the second. See the example below.

$$\begin{pmatrix} 1 & 2 \\ 3 & 4 \end{pmatrix} \times \begin{pmatrix} 3 & 6 \\ 0 & 1 \end{pmatrix} = \begin{pmatrix} (1\times3)+(2\times0) & (1\times6)+(2\times1) \\ (3\times3)+(4\times0) & (3\times6)+(4\times1) \end{pmatrix} = \begin{pmatrix} 3 & 8 \\ 9 & 22 \end{pmatrix}$$

Vector addition and multiplication are performed in the same way, but there is only one column and one row.

Permutations and Combinations

Permutations and combinations are used to determine the number of possible outcomes in different situations. An arrangement, listing, or pattern in which order is important is called a permutation. The symbol P(6, 3) represents the number of permutations of 6 things taken 3 at a time. For P(6, 3), there are $6 \times 5 \times 4$ or 120 possible outcomes. An arrangement or listing where order is not important is called a combination. The symbol C(10, 5) represents the number of combinations of 10 things taken 5 at a time. For C(10, 5), there are $(10 \times 9 \times 8 \times 7 \times 6) \div (5 \times 4 \times 3 \times 2 \times 1)$ or 252 possible outcomes.

Powers and Exponents

An expression such as $3 \times 3 \times 3 \times 3$ can be written as a power. A power has two parts, a base and an exponent. $3 \times 3 \times 3 \times 3 = 3^4$. The base is the number that is multiplied (3). The exponent tells how many times the base is used as a factor (4 times). Numbers and variables can be written using exponents. For example, $8 \times 8 \times 8 \times m \times m \times m \times m \times m$ can be expressed 8^3m^5. Exponents also can be used with place value to express numbers in expanded form. Using this method, 1,462 can be written as $(1 \times 10^3) + (4 \times 10^2) + (6 \times 10^1) + (2 \times 10^0)$.

Squares and Square Roots

The square root of a number is one of two equal factors of a number. Every positive number has both a positive and a negative square root. For example, since $8 \times 8 = 64$, 8 is a square root of 64. Since $(-8) \times (-8) = 64$, -8 is also a square root of 64. The notation $\sqrt{}$ indicates the positive square root, $-\sqrt{}$ indicates the negative square root, and $\pm\sqrt{}$ indicates both square roots. For example, $\sqrt{81} = 9$, $-\sqrt{49} = -7$, and $\pm\sqrt{4} = \pm2$. The square root of a negative number is an imaginary number because any two factors of a negative number must have different signs, and are therefore not equivalent.

Math Appendix

Logarithm

A logarithm is the inverse of exponentiation. The logarithm of a number x in base b is equal to the number n. Therefore, $b^n = x$ and $\log_b x = n$. For example, $\log_4(64) = 3$ because $4^3 = 64$. The most commonly used bases for logarithms are 10, the common logarithm; 2, the binary logarithm; and the constant e, the natural logarithm (also called $ln(x)$ instead of $\log_e(x)$). Below is a list of some of the rules of logarithms that are important to understand if you are going to use them.

$$\log_b(xy) = \log_b(x) + \log_b(y)$$
$$\log_b(x/y) = \log_b(x) - \log_b(y)$$
$$\log_b(1/x) = -\log_b(x)$$
$$\log_b(x)y = y\log_b(x)$$

▶ Compute fluently and make reasonable estimates

Estimation by Rounding

When rounding numbers, look at the digit to the right of the place to which you are rounding. If the digit is 5 or greater, round up. If it is less than 5, round down. For example, to round 65,137 to the nearest hundred, look at the number in the tens place. Since 3 is less than 5, round down to 65,100. To round the same number to the nearest ten thousandth, look at the number in the thousandths place. Since it is 5, round up to 70,000.

Finding Equivalent Ratios

Equivalent ratios have the same meaning. Just like finding equivalent fractions, to find an equivalent ratio, multiply or divide both sides by the same number. For example, you can multiply 7 by both sides of the ratio 6:8 to get 42:56. Instead, you can also divide both sides of the same ratio by 2 to get 3:4. Find the simplest form of a ratio by dividing to find equivalent ratios until you can't go any further without going into decimals. So, 160:240 in simplest form is 2:3. To write a ratio in the form *1:n*, divide both sides by the left-hand number. In other words, to change 8:20 to *1:n*, divide both sides by 8 to get 1:2.5.

Front-End Estimation

Front-end estimation can be used to quickly estimate sums and differences before adding or subtracting. To use this technique, add or subtract just the digits of the two highest place values, and replace the other place values with zero. This will give you an estimation of the solution of a problem. For example, 93,471 − 22,825 can be changed to 93,000 − 22,000 or 71,000. This estimate can be compared to your final answer to judge its correctness.

Judging Reasonableness

When solving an equation, it is important to check your work by considering how reasonable your answer is. For example, consider the equation $9\frac{3}{4} \times 4\frac{1}{3}$. Since $9\frac{3}{4}$ is between 9 and 10 and $4\frac{1}{3}$ is between 4 and 5, only values that are between 9×4 or 36 and 10×5 or 50 will be reasonable. You can also use front-end estimation, or you can round and estimate a reasonable answer. In the equation 73×25, you can round and solve to estimate a reasonable answer to be near 70×30 or 2,100.

Algebra

▶ *Understand patterns, relations, and functions*

Relation

A relation is a generalization comparing sets of ordered pairs for an equation or inequality such as $x = y + 1$ or $x > y$. The first element in each pair, the x values, forms the domain. The second element in each pair, the y values, forms the range.

Function

A function is a special relation in which each member of the domain is paired with exactly one member in the range. Functions may be represented using ordered pairs, tables, or graphs. One way to determine whether a relation is a function is to use the vertical line test. Using an object to represent a vertical line, move the object from left to right across the graph. If, for each value of x in the domain, the object passes through no more than one point on the graph, then the graph represents a function.

Linear and Nonlinear Functions

Linear functions have graphs that are straight lines. These graphs represent constant rates of change. In other words, the slope between any two pairs of points on the graph is the same. Nonlinear functions do not have constant rates of change. The slope changes along these graphs. Therefore, the graphs of nonlinear functions are *not* straight lines. Graphs of curves represent nonlinear functions. The equation for a linear function can be written in the form $y = mx + b$, where m represents the constant rate of change, or the slope. Therefore, you can determine whether a function is linear by looking at the equation. For example, the equation $y = \frac{3}{x}$ is nonlinear because x is in the denominator and the equation cannot be written in the form $y = mx + b$. A nonlinear function does not increase or decrease at a constant rate. You can check this by using a table and finding the increase or decrease in y for each regular increase in x. For example, if for each increase in x by 2, y does not increase or decrease the same amount each time, the function is nonlinear.

Linear Equations in Two Variables

In a linear equation with two variables, such as $y = x - 3$, the variables appear in separate terms and neither variable contains an exponent other than 1. The graphs of all linear equations are straight lines. All points on a line are solutions of the equation that is graphed.

Quadratic and Cubic Functions

A quadratic function is a polynomial equation of the second degree, generally expressed as $ax^2 + bx + c = 0$, where a, b, and c are real numbers and a is not equal to zero. Similarly, a cubic function is a polynomial equation of the third degree, usually expressed as $ax^3 + bx^2 + cx + d = 0$. Quadratic functions can be graphed using an equation or a table of values. For example, to graph $y = 3x^2 + 1$, substitute the values -1, -0.5, 0, 0.5, and 1 for x to yield the point coordinates $(-1, 4)$, $(-0.5, 1.75)$, $(0, 1)$, $(0.5, 1.75)$, and $(1, 4)$.

Math Appendix

Plot these points on a coordinate grid and connect the points in the form of a parabola. Cubic functions also can be graphed by making a table of values. The points of a cubic function form a curve. There is one point at which the curve changes from opening upward to opening downward, or vice versa, called the point of inflection.

Slope

Slope is the ratio of the rise, or vertical change, to the run, or horizontal change of a line: slope = rise/run. Slope (m) is the same for any two points on a straight line and can be found by using the coordinates of any two points on the line:

$$m = \frac{y_2 - y_1}{x_2 - x_1}, \text{ where } x_2 \neq x_1$$

Asymptotes

An asymptote is a straight line that a curve approaches but never actually meets or crosses. Theoretically, the asymptote meets the curve at infinity. For example, in the function $f(x) = \frac{1}{x}$, two asymptotes are being approached: the line $y = 0$ and $x = 0$. See the graph of the function below.

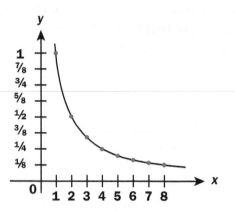

▶ Represent and analyze mathematical situations and structures using algebraic symbols

Variables and Expressions

Algebra is a language of symbols. A variable is a placeholder for a changing value. Any letter, such as x, can be used as a variable. Expressions such as $x + 2$ and $4x$ are algebraic expressions because they represent sums and/or products of variables and numbers. Usually, mathematicians avoid the use of i and e for variables because they have other mathematical meanings ($i = \sqrt{-1}$ and e is used with natural logarithms). To evaluate an algebraic expression, replace the variable or variables with known values, and then solve using order of operations. Translate verbal phrases into algebraic expressions by first defining a variable: Choose a variable and a quantity for the variable to represent. In this way, algebraic expressions can be used to represent real-world situations.

Constant and Coefficient

A constant is a fixed value unlike a variable, which can change. Constants are usually represented by numbers, but they can also be represented by symbols. For example, π is a symbolic representation of the value 3.1415…. A coefficient is a constant by which a variable or other object is multiplied. For example, in the expression $7x^2 + 5x + 9$, the coefficient of x^2 is 7 and the coefficient of x is 5. The number 9 is a constant and not a coefficient.

Monomial and Polynomial

A monomial is a number, a variable, or a product of numbers and/or variables such as 3×4. An algebraic expression that contains one or more monomials is called a polynomial. In a polynomial, there are no terms with variables in the denominator and no terms with variables under a radical sign. Polynomials can be classified by the number of terms contained in the expression. Therefore, a polynomial with two terms is called a binomial ($z^2 - 1$), and a polynomial with three terms is called a trinomial ($2y^3 + 4y^2 - y$). Polynomials also can be classified by their degrees. The degree of a monomial is the sum of the exponents of its variables. The degree of a nonzero constant such as 6 or 10 is 0. The constant 0 has no degree. For example, the monomial $4b^5c^2$ had a degree of 7. The degree of a polynomial is the same as that of the term with the greatest degree. For example, the polynomial $3x^4 - 2y^3 + 4y^2 - y$ has a degree of 4.

Equation
An equation is a mathematical sentence that states that two expressions are equal. The two expressions in an equation are always separated by an equal sign. When solving for a variable in an equation, you must perform the same operations on both sides of the equation in order for the mathematical sentence to remain true.

Solving Equations with Variables
To solve equations with variables on both sides, use the Addition or Subtraction Property of Equality to write an equivalent equation with the variables on the same side. For example, to solve $5x - 8 = 3x$, subtract $3x$ from each side to get $2x - 8 = 0$. Then add 8 to each side to get $2x = 8$. Finally, divide each side by 2 to find that $x = 4$.

Solving Equations with Grouping Symbols
Equations often contain grouping symbols such as parentheses or brackets. The first step in solving these equations is to use the Distributive Property to remove the grouping symbols. For example $5(x + 2) = 25$ can be changed to $5x + 10 = 25$, and then solved to find that $x = 3$.

Some equations have no solution. That is, there is no value of the variable that results in a true sentence. For such an equation, the solution set is called the null or empty set, and is represented by the symbol $\varnothing$ or {}. Other equations may have every number as the solution. An equation that is true for every value of the variable is called the identity.

Inequality
A mathematical sentence that contains the symbols < (less than), > (greater than), ≤ (less than or equal to), or ≥ (greater than or equal to) is called an inequality. For example, the statement that it is legal to drive 55 miles per hour or slower on a stretch of the highway can be shown by the sentence $s \leq 55$. Inequalities with variables are called open sentences. When a variable is replaced with a number, the inequality may be true or false.

Solving Inequalities
Solving an inequality means finding values for the variable that make the inequality true. Just as with equations, when you add or subtract the same number from each side of an inequality, the inequality remains true. For example, if you add 5 to each side of the inequality $3x < 6$, the resulting inequality $3x + 5 < 11$ is also true. Adding or subtracting the same

number from each side of an inequality does not affect the inequality sign. When multiplying or dividing each side of an inequality by the same positive number, the inequality remains true. In such cases, the inequality symbol does not change. When multiplying or dividing each side of an inequality by a negative number, the inequality symbol must be reversed. For example, when dividing each side of the inequality $-4x \geq -8$ by -2, the inequality sign must be changed to $\leq$ for the resulting inequality, $2x \leq 4$, to be true. Since the solutions to an inequality include all rational numbers satisfying it, inequalities have an infinite number of solutions.

Representing Inequalities on a Number Line

The solutions of inequalities can be graphed on a number line. For example, if the solution of an inequality is $x < 5$, start an arrow at 5 on the number line, and continue the arrow to the left to show all values less than 5 as the solution. Put an open circle at 5 to show that the point 5 is *not* included in the graph. Use a closed circle when graphing solutions that are greater than or equal to, or less than or equal to, a number.

Order of Operations

Solving a problem may involve using more than one operation. The answer can depend on the order in which you do the operations. To make sure that there is just one answer to a series of computations, mathematicians have agreed upon an order in which to do the operations. First simplify within the parentheses, often called graphing symbols, and then evaluate any exponents. Then multiply and divide from left to

right, and finally add and subtract from left to right.

Parametric Equations

Given an equation with more than one unknown, a statistician can draw conclusions about those unknown quantities through the use of parameters, independent variables that the statistician already knows something about. For example, you can find the velocity of an object if you make some assumptions about distance and time parameters.

Recursive Equations

In recursive equations, every value is determined by the previous value. You must first plug an initial value into the equation to get the first value, and then you can use the first value to determine the next one, and so on. For example, in order to determine what the population of pigeons will be in New York City in three years, you can use an equation with the birth, death, immigration, and emigration rates of the birds. Input the current population size into the equation to determine next year's population size, then repeat until you have calculated the value for which you are looking.

▶ Use mathematical models to represent and understand quantitative relationships

Solving Systems of Equations

Two or more equations together are called a system of equations. A system of equations can have one solution, no solution, or infinitely many solutions. One method for solving a system of equations is to graph the equations on the same coordinate plane. The coordinates of the point where the graphs intersect is the solution. In other words, the solution of a system is the ordered pair that is a solution of all equations. A more accurate way to solve a system of two equations is by using a method called substitution. Write both equations in terms of y. Replace y in the first equation with the right side of the second equation. Check the solution by graphing. You can solve a system of three equations using matrix algebra.

Graphing Inequalities

To graph an inequality, first graph the related equation, which is the boundary. All points in the shaded region are solutions of the inequality. If an inequality contains the symbol $\leq$ or $\geq$, then use a solid line to indicate that the boundary is included in the graph. If an inequality contains the symbol $<$ or $>$, then use a dashed line to indicate that the boundary is not included in the graph.

▶ Analyze change in various contexts

Rate of Change

A change in one quantity with respect to another quantity is called the rate of change. Rates of change can be described using slope:

$$\text{slope} = \frac{\text{change in } y}{\text{change in } x}$$

You can find rates of change from an equation, a table, or a graph. A special type of linear equation that describes rate of change is called a direct variation. The graph of a direct variation always passes through the origin and represents a proportional situation. In the equation $y = kx$, k is called the constant of variation. It is the slope, or rate of change. As x increases in value, y increases or decreases at a constant rate k, or y varies directly with x. Another way to say this is that y is directly proportional to x. The direct variation $y = kx$ also can be written as $k = \frac{y}{x}$. In this form, you can see that the ratio of y to x is the same for any corresponding values of y and x.

Slope-Intercept Form

Equations written as $y = mx + b$, where m is the slope and b is the y-intercept, are linear equations in slope-intercept form. For example, the graph of $y = 5x - 6$ is a line that has a slope of 5 and crosses the y-axis at $(0, -6)$. Sometimes you must first write an equation in slope-intercept form before finding the slope and y-intercept. For example, the equation $2x + 3y = 15$ can be expressed in slope-intercept form by subtracting $2x$ from each side and then dividing by 3: $y = -\frac{2}{3}x + 5$, revealing a slope of $-\frac{2}{3}$ and a y-intercept of 5. You can use the slope-intercept form of an equation to graph a line easily. Graph the y-intercept and use the slope to find another point on the line, then connect the two points with a line.

Math Appendix

Geometry

▶ *Analyze characteristics and properties of two- and three-dimensional geometric shapes and develop mathematical arguments about geometric relationships*

Angles

Two rays that have the same endpoint form an angle. The common endpoint is called the vertex, and the two rays that make up the angle are called the sides of the angle. The most common unit of measure for angles is the degree. Protractors can be used to measure angles or to draw an angle of a given measure. Angles can be classified by their degree measure. Acute angles have measures less than 90° but greater than 0°. Obtuse angles have measures greater than 90° but less than 180°. Right angles have measures of 90°.

Triangles

A triangle is a figure formed by three line segments that intersect only at their endpoints. The sum of the measures of the angles of a triangle is 180°. Triangles can be classified by their angles. An acute triangle contains all acute angles. An obtuse triangle has one obtuse angle. A right triangle has one right angle. Triangles can also be classified by their sides. A scalene triangle has no congruent sides. An isosceles triangle has at least two congruent sides. In an equilateral triangle all sides are congruent.

Quadrilaterals

A quadrilateral is a closed figure with four sides and four vertices. The segments of a quadrilateral intersect only at their endpoints. Quadrilaterals can be separated into two triangles. Since the sum of the interior angles of all triangles totals 180°, the measures of the interior angles of a quadrilateral equal 360°. Quadrilaterals are classified according to their characteristics, and include trapezoids, parallelograms, rectangles, squares, and rhombuses.

Two-Dimensional Figures

A two-dimensional figure exists within a plane and has only the dimensions of length and width. Examples of two-dimensional figures include circles and polygons. Polygons are figures that have three or more angles, including triangles, quadrilaterals, pentagons, hexagons, and many more. The sum of the angles of any polygon totals at least 180° (triangle), and each additional side adds 180° to the measure of the first three angles. The sum of the angles of a quadrilateral, for example, is 360°. The sum of the angles of a pentagon is 540°.

Three-Dimensional Figures

A plane is a two-dimensional flat surface that extends in all directions. Intersecting planes can form the edges and vertices of three-dimensional figures or solids. A polyhedron is a solid with flat surfaces that are polygons.

Polyhedrons are composed of faces, edges, and vertices and are differentiated by their shape and by their number of bases. Skew lines are lines that lie in different planes. They are neither intersecting nor parallel.

Congruence

Figures that have the same size and shape are congruent. The parts of congruent triangles that match are called corresponding parts. Congruence statements are used to identify corresponding parts of congruent triangles. When writing a congruence statement, the letters must be written so that corresponding vertices appear in the same order. Corresponding parts can be used to find the measures of angles and sides in a figure that is congruent to a figure with known measures.

Similarity

If two figures have the same shape but not the same size they are called similar figures. For example, the triangles below are similar, so angles A, B, and C have the same measurements as angles D, E, and F, respectively. However, segments AB, BC, and CA do not have the same measurements as segments DE, EF, and FD, but the measures of the sides are proportional.

For example, $\dfrac{\overline{AB}}{\overline{DE}} = \dfrac{\overline{BC}}{\overline{EF}} = \dfrac{\overline{CA}}{\overline{FD}}$.

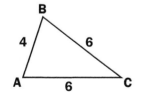

Solid figures are considered to be similar if they have the same shape and their corresponding linear measures are proportional. As with two-dimensional figures, they can be tested for similarity by comparing corresponding measures. If the compared ratios are proportional, then the figures are similar solids. Missing measures of similar solids can also be determined by using proportions.

The Pythagorean Theorem

The sides that are adjacent to a right angle are called legs. The side opposite the right angle is the hypotenuse.

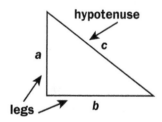

The Pythagorean Theorem describes the relationship between the lengths of the legs a and b and the hypotenuse c. It states that if a triangle is a right triangle, then the square of the length of the hypotenuse is equal to the sum of the squares of the lengths of the legs. In symbols, $c^2 = a^2 + b^2$.

Sine, Cosine, and Tangent Ratios

Trigonometry is the study of the properties of triangles. A trigonometric ratio is a ratio of the lengths of two sides of a right triangle. The most common trigonometric ratios are the sine, cosine, and tangent

Math Appendix

ratios. These ratios are abbreviated as *sin*, *cos*, and *tan*, respectively.

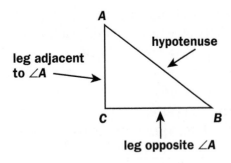

If ∠A is an acute angle of a right triangle, then

$$\sin \angle A = \frac{\text{measure of leg opposite } \angle A}{\text{measure of hypotenuse}},$$

$$\cos \angle A = \frac{\text{measure of leg adjacent to } \angle A}{\text{measure of hypotenuse}}, \text{ and}$$

$$\tan \angle A = \frac{\text{measure of leg opposite } \angle A}{\text{measure of leg adjacent to } \angle A}.$$

▶ *Specify locations and describe spatial relationships using coordinate geometry and other representational systems*

Polygons

A polygon is a simple, closed figure formed by three or more line segments. The line segments meet only at their endpoints. The points of intersection are called vertices, and the line segments are called sides. Polygons are classified by the number if sides they have. The diagonals of a polygon divide the polygon into triangles. The number of triangles formed is two less than the number of sides. To find the sum of the measures of the interior angles of any polygon, multiply the number of triangles within the polygon by 180. That is, if *n* equals the number of sides, then (*n* − 2) 180 gives the sum of the measures of the polygon's interior angles.

Cartesian Coordinates

In the Cartesian coordinate system, the *y*-axis extends above and below the origin and the *x*-axis extends to the right and left of the origin, which is the point at which the *x*- and *y*-axes intersect. Numbers below and to the left of the origin are negative. A point graphed on the coordinate grid is said to have an *x*-coordinate and a *y*-coordinate. For example, the point (1,−2) has as its *x*-coordinate the number 1, and has as its *y*-coordinate the number −2. This point is graphed by locating the position on the grid that is 1 unit to the right of the origin and 2 units below the origin.

The *x*-axis and the *y*-axis separate the coordinate plane into four regions, called quadrants. The axes and points located on the axes themselves are not located in any of the quadrants. The quadrants are labeled I to IV, starting in the upper right and proceeding counterclockwise. In quadrant I, both coordinates are positive. In quadrant II, the *x*-coordinate is negative and the *y*-coordinate is positive. In quadrant III, both coordinates are negative. In quadrant IV, the *x*-coordinate is positive and the *y*-coordinate is negative. A coordinate graph can be used to show algebraic relationships among numbers.

▶ *Apply transformations and use symmetry to analyze mathematical situations*

Similar Triangles and Indirect Measurement

Triangles that have the same shape but not necessarily the same dimensions are called similar triangles. Similar triangles have corresponding angles and corresponding sides. Arcs are used to show congruent angles. If two triangles are similar, then the corresponding angles have the same measure, and the corresponding sides are proportional. Therefore, to determine the measures of the sides of similar triangles when some measures are known, proportions can be used.

Transformations

A transformation is a movement of a geometric figure. There are several types of transformations. In a translation, also called a slide, a figure is slid from one position to another without turning it. Every point of the original figure is moved the same distance and in the same direction. In a reflection, also called a flip, a figure is flipped over a line to form a mirror image. Every point of the original figure has a corresponding point on the other side of the line of symmetry. In a rotation, also called a turn, a figure is turned around a fixed point. A figure can be rotated 0°–360° clockwise or counterclockwise. A dilation transforms each line to a parallel line whose length is a fixed multiple of the length of the original line to create a similar figure that will be either larger or smaller.

▶ *Use visualizations, spatial reasoning, and geometric modeling to solve problems*

Two-Dimensional Representations of Three-Dimensional Objects

Three-dimensional objects can be represented in a two-dimensional drawing in order to more easily determine properties such as surface area and volume. When you look at the triangular prism, you can see the orientation of its three dimensions, length, width, and height. Using the drawing and the formulas for surface area and volume, you can easily calculate these properties.

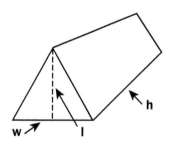

Another way to represent a three-dimensional object in a two-dimensional plane is by using a net, which is the unfolded representation. Imagine cutting the vertices of a box until it is flat then drawing an outline of it. That's a net. Most objects have more than one net, but any one can be measured to determine surface area. Below is a cube and one of its nets.

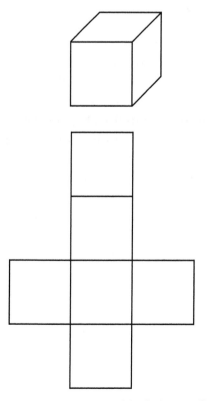

Math Appendix

Measurement

▶ **Understand measurable attributes of objects and the units, systems, and processes of measurement**

Customary System

The customary system is the system of weights and measures used in the United States. The main units of weight are ounces, pounds (1 equal to 16 ounces), and tons (1 equal to 2,000 pounds). Length is typically measured in inches, feet (1 equal to 12 inches), yards (1 equal to 3 feet), and miles (1 equal to 5,280 feet), while area is measured in square feet and acres (1 equal to 43,560 square feet). Liquid is measured in cups, pints (1 equal to 2 cups), quarts (1 equal to 2 pints), and gallons (1 equal to 4 quarts). Finally, temperature is measured in degrees Fahrenheit.

Metric System

The metric system is a decimal system of weights and measurements in which the prefixes of the words for the units of measure indicate the relationships between the different measurements. In this system, the main units of weight, or mass, are grams and kilograms. Length is measured in millimeters, centimeters, meters, and kilometers, and the units of area are square millimeters, centimeters, meters, and kilometers. Liquid is typically measured in milliliters and liters, while temperature is in degrees Celsius.

Selecting Units of Measure

When measuring something, it is important to select the appropriate type and size of unit. For example, in the United States it would be appropriate when describing someone's height to use feet and inches. These units of height or length are good to use because they are in the customary system, and they are of appropriate size. In the customary system, use inches, feet, and miles for lengths and perimeters; square inches, feet, and miles for area and surface area; and cups, pints, quarts, gallons or cubic inches and feet (and less commonly miles) for volume. In the metric system use millimeters, centimeters, meters, and kilometers for lengths and perimeters; square units millimeters, centimeters, meters, and kilometers for area and surface area; and milliliters and liters for volume. Finally, always use degrees to measure angles.

▶ **Apply appropriate techniques, tools, and formulas to determine measurements**

Precision and Significant Digits

The precision of measurement is the exactness to which a measurement is made. Precision depends on the smallest unit of measure being used, or the precision unit. One way to record a measure is to estimate to the nearest precision unit. A more precise method is to include all of the digits that are actually measured, plus one estimated digit. The digits recorded, called significant digits, indicate the precision of the measurement. There are special rules for determining significant digits. If a number contains a decimal point, the number of significant digits is found by counting from left to right, starting with the first nonzero digit.

If the number does not contain a decimal point, the number of significant digits is found by counting the digits from left to right, starting with the first digit and ending with the last nonzero digit.

Surface Area

The amount of material needed to cover the surface of a figure is called the surface area. It can be calculated by finding the area of each face and adding them together. To find the surface area of a rectangular prism, for example, the formula $S = 2lw + 2lh + 2wh$ applies. A cylinder, on the other hand, may be unrolled to reveal two circles and a rectangle. Its surface area can be determined by finding the area of the two circles, $2\pi r^2$, and adding it to the area of the rectangle, $2\pi rh$ (the length of the rectangle is the circumference of one of the circles), or $S = 2\pi r^2 + 2\pi rh$. The surface area of a pyramid is measured in a slightly different way because the sides of a pyramid are triangles that intersect at the vertex. These sides are called lateral faces and the height of each is called the slant height. The sum of their areas is the lateral area of a pyramid. The surface area of a square pyramid is the lateral area $\frac{1}{2}bh$ (area of a lateral face) times 4 (number of lateral faces), plus the area of the base. The surface area of a cone is the area of its circular base (πr^2) plus its lateral area (πrl, where l is the slant height).

Volume

Volume is the measure of space occupied by a solid region. To find the volume of a prism, the area of the base is multiplied by the measure of the height, $V = Bh$. A solid containing several prisms can be broken down into its component prisms. Then the volume of each component can be found and the volumes added. The volume of a cylinder can be determined by finding the area of its circular base, πr^2, and then multiplying by the height of the cylinder. A pyramid has one-third the volume of a prism with the same base and height. To find the volume of a pyramid, multiply the area of the base by the pyramid's height, and then divide by 3. Simply stated, the formula for the volume of a pyramid is $V = \frac{1}{3}bh$. A cone is a three-dimensional figure with one circular base and a curved surface connecting the base and the vertex. The volume of a cone is one-third the volume of a cylinder with the same base area and height. Like a pyramid, the formula for the volume of a cone is $V = \frac{1}{3}bh$. More specifically, the formula is $V = \frac{1}{3}\pi r^2 h$.

Upper and Lower Bounds

Upper and lower bounds have to do with the accuracy of a measurement. When a measurement is given, the degree of accuracy is also stated to tell you what the upper and lower bounds of the measurement are. The upper bound is the largest possible value that a measurement could have had before being rounded down, and the lower bound is the lowest possible value it could have had before being rounded up.

Math Appendix

Data Analysis and Probability

▶ *Formulate questions that can be addressed with data and collect, organize, and display relevant data to answer them*

Histograms

A histogram displays numerical data that have been organized into equal intervals using bars that have the same width and no space between them. While a histogram does not give exact data points, its shape shows the distribution of the data. Histograms also can be used to compare data.

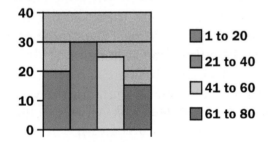

- 1 to 20
- 21 to 40
- 41 to 60
- 61 to 80

Box-and-Whisker Plot

A box-and-whisker plot displays the measures of central tendency and variation. A box is drawn around the quartile values, and whiskers extend from each quartile to the extreme data points. To make a box plot for a set of data, draw a number line that covers the range of data. Find the median, the extremes, and the upper and lower quartiles. Mark these points on the number line with bullets, then draw a box and the whiskers. The length of a whisker or box shows whether the values of the data in that part are concentrated or spread out.

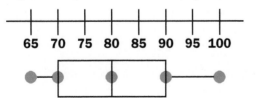

Scatter Plots

A scatter plot is a graph that shows the relationship between two sets of data. In a scatter plot, two sets of data are graphed as ordered pairs on a coordinate system. Two sets of data can have a positive correlation (as x increases, y increases), a negative correlation (as x increases, y decreases), or no correlation (no obvious pattern is shown). Scatter plots can be used to spot trends, draw conclusions, and make predictions about data.

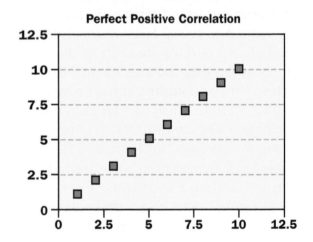

Perfect Positive Correlation

Randomization

The idea of randomization is a very important principle of statistics and the design of experiments. Data must be selected randomly to prevent bias from influencing the results. For example, you want to know the average income of people in your town but you can only use a sample of 100 individuals to make determinations about everyone. If you select 100 individuals who are all doctors, you will have a biased sample. However, if you chose a random sample of 100 people out of the phone book, you are much more likely to accurately represent average income in the town.

Statistics and Parameters

Statistics is a science that involves collecting, analyzing, and presenting data. The data can be collected in various ways—for example through a census or by making physical measurements. The data can then be analyzed by creating summary statistics, which have to do with the distribution of the data sample, including the mean, range, and standard error. They can also be illustrated in tables and graphs, like box-plots, scatter plots, and histograms. The presentation of the data typically involves describing the strength or validity of the data and what they show. For example, an analysis of ancestry of people in a city might tell you something about immigration patterns, unless the data set is very small or biased in some way, in which case it is not likely to be very accurate or useful.

Categorical and Measurement Data

When analyzing data, it is important to understand if the data is qualitative or quantitative. Categorical data is qualitative and measurement, or numerical, data is quantitative. Categorical data describes a quality of something and can be placed into different categories. For example, if you are analyzing the number of students in different grades in a school, each grade is a category. On the other hand, measurement data is continuous, like height, weight, or any other measurable variable. Measurement data can be converted into categorical data if you decide to group the data. Using height as an example, you can group the continuous data set into categories like under 5 feet, 5 feet to 5 feet 5 inches, over 5 feet five inches to 6 feet, and so on.

Univariate and Bivariate Data

In data analysis, a researcher can analyze one variable at a time or look at how multiple variables behave together. Univariate data involves only one variable, for example height in humans. You can measure the height in a population of people then plot the results in a histogram to look at how height is distributed in humans. To summarize univariate data, you can use statistics like the mean, mode, median, range, and standard deviation, which is a measure of variation. When looking at more than one variable at once, you use multivariate data. Bivariate data involves two variables. For example, you can look at height and age in humans together by gathering information on both variables from individuals in a population. You can then plot both variables in a scatter plot, look at how the variables behave in relation to each other, and create an equation that represents the relationship, also called a regression. These equations could help answer questions such as, for example, does height increase with age in humans?

▶ Select and use appropriate statistical methods to analyze data

Measures of Central Tendency

When you have a list of numerical data, it is often helpful to use one or more numbers to represent the whole set. These numbers are called measures of central tendency. Three measures of central tendency are mean, median, and mode. The mean is the sum of the data divided by the number of items in the data set. The median is the middle number of the ordered data (or the mean of the two middle numbers). The mode is the number

Math Appendix

or numbers that occur most often. These measures of central tendency allow data to be analyzed and better understood.

Measures of Spread
In statistics, measures of spread or variation are used to describe how data are distributed. The range of a set of data is the difference between the greatest and the least values of the data set. The quartiles are the values that divide the data into four equal parts. The median of data separates the set in half. Similarly, the median of the lower half of a set of data is the lower quartile. The median of the upper half of a set of data is the upper quartile. The interquartile range is the difference between the upper quartile and the lower quartile.

Line of Best Fit
When real-life data are collected, the points graphed usually do not form a straight line, but they may approximate a linear relationship. A line of best fit is a line that lies very close to most of the data points. It can be used to predict data. You also can use the equation of the best-fit line to make predictions.

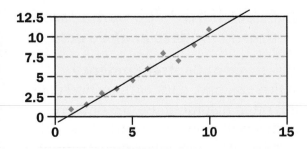

Stem and Leaf Plots
In a stem and leaf plot, numerical data are listed in ascending or descending order. The greatest place value of the data is used for the stems. The next greatest place value forms the leaves. For example, if the least number in a

set of data is 8 and the greatest number is 95, draw a vertical line and write the stems from 0 to 9 to the left of the line. Write the leaves from to the right of the line, with the corresponding stem. Next, rearrange the leaves so they are ordered from least to greatest. Then include a key or explanation, such as $1|3 = 13$. Notice that the stem-and-leaf plot below is like a histogram turned on its side.

```
0|8
1|3 6
2|5 6 9
3|0 2 7 8
4|0 1 4 7 9
5|1 4 5 8
6|1 3 7
7|5 8
8|2 6
9|5
```
Key: **1|3 = 13**

▶ Develop and evaluate inferences and predictions that are based on data

Sampling Distribution
The sampling distribution of a population is the distribution that would result if you could take an infinite number of samples from the population, average each, and then average the averages. The more normal the distribution of the population, that is, how closely the distribution follows a bell curve, the more likely the sampling distribution will also follow a normal distribution. Furthermore, the larger the sample, the more likely it will accurately represent the entire population. For instance, you are more likely to gain more representative results from a population of 1,000 with a sample of 100 than with a sample of 2.

Validity

In statistics, validity refers to acquiring results that accurately reflect that which is being measured. In other words, it is important when performing statistical analyses, to ensure that the data are valid in that the sample being analyzed represents the population to the best extent possible. Randomization of data and using appropriate sample sizes are two important aspects of making valid inferences about a population.

▶ *Understand and apply basic concepts of probability*

Complementary, Mutually Exclusive Events

To understand probability theory, it is important to know if two events are mutually exclusive, or complementary: the occurrence of one event automatically implies the non-occurrence of the other. That is, two complementary events cannot both occur. If you roll a pair of dice, the event of rolling 6 and rolling doubles have an outcome in common (3, 3), so they are not mutually exclusive. If you roll (3, 3), you also roll doubles. However, the events of rolling a 9 and rolling doubles are mutually exclusive because they have no outcomes in common. If you roll a 9, you will not also roll doubles.

Independent and Dependent Events

Determining the probability of a series of events requires that you know whether the events are independent or dependent. An independent event has no influence on the occurrence of subsequent events, whereas, a dependent event does influence subsequent events. The chances that a woman's first child will be a girl are $\frac{1}{2}$, and the chances that her second child will be a girl are also $\frac{1}{2}$ because the two events are independent of each other. However, if there are 7 red marbles in a bag of 15 marbles, the chances that the first marble you pick will be red are $\frac{7}{15}$ and if you indeed pick a red marble and remove it, you have reduced the chances of picking another red marble to $\frac{6}{14}$.

Sample Space

The sample space is the group of all possible outcomes for an event. For example, if you are tossing a single six-sided die, the sample space is {1, 2, 3, 4, 5, 6}. Similarly, you can determine the sample space for the possible outcomes of two events. If you are going to toss a coin twice, the sample space is {(heads, heads), (heads, tails), (tails, heads), (tails, tails)}.

Computing the Probability of a Compound Event

If two events are independent, the outcome of one event does not influence the outcome of the second. For example, if a bag contains 2 blue and 3 red marbles, then the probability of selecting a blue marble, replacing it, and then selecting a red marble is $P(A) \times P(B) = \frac{2}{5} \times \frac{3}{5}$ or $\frac{6}{25}$.

If two events are dependent, the outcome of one event affects the outcome of the second. For example, if a bag contains 2 blue and 3 red marbles, then the probability of selecting a blue and then a red marble without replacing the first marble is $P(A) \times P(B \text{ following } A) = \frac{2}{5} \times \frac{3}{4}$ or $\frac{3}{10}$. Two events that cannot happen at the same time are mutually exclusive. For example, when you roll two number cubes, you cannot roll a sum that is both 5 and even. So, $P(A \text{ or } B) = \frac{4}{36} + \frac{18}{36}$ or $\frac{11}{18}$.

MAKING CAREER CHOICES

A career differs from a job in that it is a series of progressively more responsible jobs in one field or a related field. You will need to learn some special skills to choose a career and to help you in your job search. Choosing a career and identifying career opportunities require careful thought and preparation. To aid you in making important career choices, follow these steps:

STEPS TO MAKING A CAREER DECISION

1. Conduct a self-assessment to determine your:
   - values
   - lifestyle goals
   - interests
   - skills and aptitudes
   - personality
   - work environment preferences
   - relationship preferences

2. Identify possible career choices based on your self-assessment.

3. Gather information on each choice, including future trends.

4. Evaluate your choices based on your self-assessment.

5. Make your decision.

After you make your decision, plan how you will reach your goal. It is best to have short-term, medium-term, and long-term goals. In making your choices, explore the future opportunities in this field or fields over the next several years. What impact will new technology and automation have on job opportunities in the next few years? Remember, if you plan, you make your own career opportunities.

PERSONAL CAREER PORTFOLIO

You will want to create and maintain a personal career portfolio. In it you will keep all the documents you create and receive in your job search:

- Contact list
- Résumé
- Letters of recommendation
- Employer evaluations
- Awards
- Evidence of participation in school, community, and volunteer activities
- Notes about your job search
- Notes made after your interviews

CAREER RESEARCH RESOURCES

In order to gather information on various career opportunities, there are a variety of sources to research:

- **Libraries.** Your school or public library offers good career information resources. Here you will find books, magazines, pamphlets, films, videos, and special reference materials on careers.

In particular, the U.S. Department of Labor publishes three reference books that are especially helpful: the *Dictionary of Occupational Titles (DOT)*, which describes about 20,000 jobs and their relationships with data, people, and things; the *Occupational Outlook Handbook (OOH)*, with information on more than 200 occupations; and the *Guide for Occupational Exploration (GOE)*, a reference that organizes the world of work into 12 interest areas that are subdivided into work groups and subgroups.

- **The Internet.** The Internet is becoming a primary source of research on any topic. It is especially helpful in researching careers.

- **Career Consultations.** Career consultation, an informational interview with a professional who works in a career that interests you, provides an opportunity to learn about the day-to-day realities of a career.

- **On-the-Job Experience.** On-the-job experience can be valuable in learning firsthand about a job or career. You can find out if your school has a work-experience program, or look into a company or organization's internship opportunities. Interning gives you direct work experience and often allows you to make valuable contacts for future full-time employment.

THE JOB SEARCH

To aid you in your actual job search, there are various sources to explore. You should contact and research all the sources that might produce a job lead, or information about a job. Keep a contact list as you proceed with your search. Some of these resources include:

- **Networking with family, friends, and acquaintances.** This means contacting people you know personally, including school counselors, former employers, and professional people.

- **Cooperative education and work-experience programs.** Many schools have such programs in which students work part-time on a job related to one of their classes. Many also offer work-experience programs that are not limited to just one career area, such as marketing.

- **Newspaper ads.** Reading the Help Wanted advertisements in your local papers will provide a source of job leads, as well as teach you about the local job market.

- **Employment agencies.** Most cities have two types of employment agencies, public and private. These employment agencies match workers with jobs. Some private agencies may charge a fee, so be sure to know who is expected to pay the fee and what the fee is.

- **Company personnel offices.** Large and medium-sized companies have personnel offices to handle employment matters, including the hiring of new workers. You can check on job openings by contacting the office by telephone or by scheduling a personal visit.

- **Searching the Internet.** Cyberspace offers multiple opportunities for your job search. Web sites, such as Hotjobs.com or Monster.com, provide lists of companies offering employment. There are tens of thousands of career-related Web sites, so the challenge is finding those that have jobs that interest you and that are up-to-date in their listings. Companies that interest you may have a Web site, which will provide valuable information on their benefits and opportunities for employment.

APPLYING FOR A JOB

When you have contacted the sources of job leads and found some jobs that interest you, the next step is to apply for them. You will need to complete application forms, write letters of application, and prepare your own résumé. Before you apply for a job, you will need to have a work permit if you are under the age of 18 in most states. Some state and federal labor laws designate certain jobs as too dangerous for young workers. Laws also limit the number of hours of work allowed during a day, a week, or the school year. You will also need to have proper documentation, such as a green card if you are not a U.S. citizen.

JOB APPLICATION

You can obtain the job application form directly at the place of business, by requesting it in writing, or over the Internet. It is best if you can fill the form out at home, but some businesses require that you fill it out at the place of work.

Fill out the job application forms neatly and accurately, using standard English, the formal style of speaking and writing you learned in school. You must be truthful and pay attention to detail in filling out the form.

PERSONAL FACT SHEET

To be sure that the answers you write on a job application form are accurate, make a personal fact sheet before filling out the application:

- Your name, home address, and phone number
- Your Social Security number
- The job you are applying for
- The date you can begin work
- The days and hours you can work
- The pay you want
- Whether or not you have been convicted of a crime
- Your education
- Your previous work experience
- Your birth date
- Your driver's license number if you have one
- Your interests and hobbies, and awards you have won
- Your previous work experience, including dates
- Schools you have attended
- Places you have lived
- Accommodations you may need from the employer
- A list of references—people who will tell an employer that you will do a good job, such as relatives, students, former employers, and the like

LETTERS OF RECOMMENDATION

Letters of recommendation are helpful. You can request teachers, counselors, relatives, and other acquaintances who know you well to write these letters. They should be short, to the point, and give a brief overview of your assets. A brief description of any of your important accomplishments or projects should follow. The letter should end with a brief description of your character and work ethic.

LETTER OF APPLICATION

Some employees prefer a letter of application, rather than an application form. This letter is like writing a sales pitch about yourself. You need to tell why you are the best person for the job, what special qualifications you have, and include all the information usually found on an application form. Write the letter in standard English, making certain that it is neat, accurate, and correct.

RÉSUMÉ

The purpose of a résumé is to make an employer want to interview you. A résumé tells prospective employers what you are like and what you can do for them. A good résumé summarizes you at your best in a one- or two-page outline. It should include the following information:

1. **Identification.** Include your name, address, telephone number, and e-mail address.

2. **Objective.** Indicate the type of job you are looking for.

3. **Experience.** List experience related to the specific job for which you are applying. List other work if you have not worked in a related field.

4. **Education.** Include schools attended from high school on, the dates of attendance, and diplomas or degrees earned. You may also include courses related to the job you are applying for.

5. **References.** Include up to three references or indicate that they are available. Always ask people ahead of time if they are willing to be listed as references for you.

A résumé that you put online or send by e-mail is called an *electronic résumé*. Some Web sites allow you to post them on their sites without charge. Employers access these sites to find new employees. Your electronic résumé should follow the guidelines for a regular one. It needs to be accurate. Stress your skills and sell yourself to prospective employers.

COVER LETTER

If you are going to get the job you want, you need to write a great cover letter to accompany your résumé. Think of a cover letter as an introduction: a piece of paper that conveys a smile, a confident hello, and a nice, firm handshake. The cover letter is the first thing a potential employer sees, and it can make a powerful impression. The following are some tips for creating a cover letter that is professional and gets the attention you want:

- **Keep it short.** Your cover letter should be one page, no more.

- **Make it look professional.** These days, you need to type your letter on a computer and print it on a laser printer. Do not use an inkjet printer unless it produces extremely crisp type. Use white or buff-colored paper; anything else will draw the wrong kind of attention. Type your name, address, phone number, and e-mail address at the top of the page.

- **Explain why you are writing.** Start your letter with one sentence describing where you heard of the opening. "Joan Wright suggested I contact you regarding a position in your marketing department," or "I am writing to apply for the position you advertised in the Sun City Journal."

- **Introduce yourself.** Give a short description of your professional abilities and background. Refer to your attached résumé: "As you will see in the attached résumé, I am an experienced editor with a background in newspapers, magazines, and textbooks." Then highlight one or two specific accomplishments.

- **Sell yourself.** Your cover letter should leave the reader thinking, "This person is exactly what we are looking for." Focus on what you can do for the company. Relate your skills to the skills and responsibilities mentioned in the job listing. If the ad mentions solving problems, relate a problem you solved at school or work. If the ad mentions specific skills or knowledge required, mention your mastery of these in your letter. (Also be sure these skills are included on your résumé.)

- **Provide all requested information.** If the Help Wanted ad asked for "salary requirements" or "salary history," include this information in your cover letter. However, you do not have to give specific numbers. It is okay to say, "My wage is in the range of $10 to $15 per hour." If the employer does not ask for salary information, do not offer any.

- **Ask for an interview.** You have sold yourself, now wrap it up. Be confident, but not pushy. "If you agree that I would be an asset to your company, please call me at [insert your phone number]. I am available for an interview at your convenience." Finally, thank the person. "Thank you for your consideration. I look forward to hearing from you soon." Always close with a "Sincerely," followed by your full name and signature.

- **Check for errors.** Read and re-read your letter to make sure each sentence is correctly worded and there are no errors in spelling, punctuation, or grammar. Do not rely on your computer's spell checker or grammar checker. A spell check will not detect if you typed "tot he" instead of "to the." It is a good idea to have someone else read your letter, too. He or she might notice an error you overlooked.

INTERVIEW

Understanding how to best prepare for and follow up on interviews is critical to your career success. At different times in your life, you may interview with a teacher or professor, a prospective employer, a supervisor, or a promotion or tenure committee. Just as having an excellent résumé is vital for opening the door, interview skills are critical for putting your best foot forward and seizing the opportunity to clearly articulate why you are the best person for the job.

RESEARCH THE COMPANY

Your ability to convince an employer that you understand and are interested in the field you are interviewing to enter is important. Show that you have knowledge about the company and the industry. What products or services does the company offer? How is it doing? What is the competition? Use your research to demonstrate your understanding of the company.

PREPARE QUESTIONS FOR THE INTERVIEWER

Prepare interview questions to ask the interviewer. Some examples include:

- "What would my responsibilities be?"
- "Could you describe my work environment?"
- "What are the chances to move up in the company?"
- "Do you offer training?"
- "What can you tell me about the people who work here?"

DRESS APPROPRIATELY

You will never get a second chance to make a good first impression. Nonverbal communication is 90 percent of communication, so dressing appropriately is of the utmost importance. Every job is different, and you should wear clothing that is appropriate for the job for which you are applying. In most situations, you will be safe if you wear clean, pressed, conservative business clothes in neutral colors. Pay special attention to grooming. Keep makeup light and wear very little jewelry. Make certain your nails and hair are clean, trimmed, and neat. Do not carry a large purse, backpack, books, or coat. Simply carry a pad of paper, a pen, and extra copies of your résumé and letters of reference in a small folder.

EXHIBIT GOOD BEHAVIOR

Conduct yourself properly during an interview. Go alone; be courteous and polite to everyone you meet. Relax and focus on your purpose: to make the best possible impression.

- Be on time.
- Be poised and relaxed.
- Avoid nervous habits.
- Avoid littering your speech with verbal clutter such as "you know," "um," and "like."
- Look your interviewer in the eye and speak with confidence.
- Use nonverbal techniques to reinforce your confidence, such as a firm handshake and poised demeanor.
- Convey maturity by exhibiting the ability to tolerate differences of opinion.
- Never call anyone by a first name unless you are asked to do so.
- Know the name, title, and the pronunciation of the interviewer's name.
- Do not sit down until the interviewer does.
- Do not talk too much about your personal life.
- Never bad-mouth your former employers.

BE PREPARED FOR COMMON INTERVIEW QUESTIONS

You can never be sure exactly what will happen at an interview, but you can be prepared for common interview questions. There are some interview questions that are illegal. Interviewers should not ask you about your age, gender, color, race, or religion. Employers should not ask whether you are married or pregnant, or question your health or disabilities.

Take time to think about your answers now. You might even write them down to clarify your thinking. The key to all interview questions is to be honest, and to be positive. Focus your answers on skills and abilities that apply to the job you are seeking. Practice answering the following questions with a friend:

- "Tell me about yourself."
- "Why do you want to work at this company?"
- "What did you like/dislike about your last job?"
- "What is your biggest accomplishment?"
- "What is your greatest strength?"
- "What is your greatest weakness?"
- "Do you prefer to work with others or on your own?"
- "What are your career goals?" or "Where do you see yourself in five years?"
- "Tell me about a time that you had a lot of work to do in a short time. How did you manage the situation?"
- "Have you ever had to work closely with a person you didn't get along with? How did you handle the situation?"

AFTER THE INTERVIEW

Be sure to thank the interviewer after the interview for his or her time and effort. Do not forget to follow up after the interview. Ask, "What is the next step?" If you are told to call in a few days, wait two or three days before calling back.

If the interview went well, the employer may call you to offer you the job. Find out the terms of the job offer, including job title and pay. Decide whether you want the job. If you decide not to accept the job, write a letter of rejection. Be courteous and thank the person for the opportunity and the offer. You may wish to give a brief general reason for not accepting the job. Leave the door open for possible employment in the future.

FOLLOW UP WITH A LETTER

Write a thank-you letter as soon as the interview is over. This shows your good manners, interest, and enthusiasm for the job. It also shows that you are organized. Make the letter neat and courteous. Thank the interviewer. Sell yourself again.

ACCEPTING A NEW JOB

If you decide to take the job, write a letter of acceptance. The letter should include some words of appreciation for the opportunity, written acceptance of the job offer, the terms of employment (salary, hours, benefits), and the starting date. Make sure the letter is neat and correct.

STARTING A NEW JOB

Your first day of work will be busy. Determine what the dress code is and dress appropriately. Learn to do each task assigned properly. Ask for help when you need it. Learn the rules and regulations of the workplace.

You will do some paperwork on your first day. Bring your personal fact sheet with you. You will need to fill out some forms. Form W-4 tells your employer how much money to withhold for taxes. You may also need to fill out Form I-9. This shows that you are allowed to work in the United States. You will need your Social Security number and proof that you are allowed to work in the United States. You can bring your U.S. passport, your Certificate of Naturalization, or your Certificate of U.S. Citizenship. If you are not a permanent resident of the United States, bring your green card. If you are a resident of the United States, you will need to bring your work permit on your first day. If you are under the age of 16 in some states, you need a different kind of work permit.

You might be requested to take a drug test as a requirement for employment in some states. This could be for the safety of you and your coworkers, especially when working with machinery or other equipment.

IMPORTANT SKILLS AND QUALITIES

You will not work alone on a job. You will need to learn skills for getting along and being a team player. There are many good qualities necessary to get along in the workplace. They include being positive, showing sympathy, taking an interest in others, tolerating differences, laughing a little, and showing respect. Your employer may promote you or give you a raise if you show good employability skills.

There are several qualities necessary to be a good employee and get ahead in your job:

- be cooperative
- possess good character
- be responsible
- finish what you start
- work fast but do a good job

- have a strong work ethic
- work well without supervision
- work well with others
- possess initiative
- show enthusiasm for what you do
- be on time
- make the best of your time
- obey company laws and rules
- be honest
- be loyal
- exhibit good health habits

LEAVING A JOB

If you are considering leaving your job or are being laid off, you are facing one of the most difficult aspects in your career. The first step in resigning is to prepare a short resignation letter to offer your supervisor at the conclusion of the meeting you set up with him or her. Keep the letter short and to the point. Express your appreciation for the opportunity you had with the company. Do not try to list all that was wrong with the job.

You want to leave on good terms. Do not forget to ask for a reference. Do not talk about your employer or any of your coworkers. Do not talk negatively about your employer when you apply for a new job.

If you are being laid off or face downsizing, it can make you feel angry or depressed. Try to view it as a career-change opportunity. If possible, negotiate a good severance package. Find out about any benefits you may be entitled to. Perhaps the company will offer job-search services or consultation for finding new employment.

TAKE ACTION!

It is time for action. Remember the networking and contact lists you created when you searched for this job. Reach out for support from friends, family, and other acquaintances. Consider joining a job-search club. Assess your skills. Upgrade them if necessary. Examine your attitude and your vocational choices. Decide the direction you wish to take and move on!

Glossary

How to Use This Glossary

- Content vocabulary terms in this glossary are words that relate to this book's content. They are **highlighted yellow** in your text.
- Words in this glossary that have an asterisk (*) are academic vocabulary terms. They help you understand your school subjects and are used on tests. They are **boldfaced blue** in your text.
- Some of the vocabulary words in this book include pronunciation symbols to help you sound out the words. Use the pronunciation key to help you pronounce the words.

Pronunciation Key		
a . . . . **a**t	**ô** . . . . **f**o**r**k, **a**ll	**th** . . . **th**in
ā . . . . **a**pe	**oo** . . . w**oo**d, p**u**t	**th** . . . **th**is
ä . . . . f**a**ther	**o͞o** . . . f**oo**l	**zh** . . . trea**s**ure
e . . . . **e**nd	**oi** . . . **oi**l	**ə** . . . . **a**go, tak**e**n, penc**i**l, lem**o**n, circ**u**s
ē . . . . m**e**	**ou** . . . **ou**t	**ˈ** . . . . indicates primary stress (symbol in front of and *above* letter)
i . . . . **i**t	**u** . . . . **u**p	**ˌ** . . . . indicates secondary stress (symbol in front of and *below* letter)
ī . . . . **i**ce	**ū** . . . . **u**se	
o . . . . h**o**t	**ü** . . . . r**u**le	
ō . . . . h**o**pe	**u̲** . . . . p**u**ll	
ȯ . . . . s**aw**	**ŋ** . . . . si**ng**	

A

***abbreviation** A shortened form of a written word or phrase used in place of the whole. (p. 500)

abstinence (ˈab-stə-nən(t)s) The decision to avoid high-risk behaviors, including sexual activity and the use of tobacco, alcohol, and other drugs. (p. 63)

***acceptance** To acknowledge as satisfactory; to approve. (p. 60)

accessory An interesting item added to make a space or outfit more personal. (p. 296)

***accommodation** The providing of what is needed or desired for convenience; adaptation; adjustment. (p. 170)

***accomplish** To bring about a result by effort; to succeed in reaching; to achieve. (p. 121)

acne A common skin condition that occurs when pores are clogged with oil, dead skin cells, and bacteria. (p. 19)

acquaintance (ə-kwān-tᵊn(t)s) A person one greets or meets fairly often, but with whom one does not have a close relationship. (p. 53)

***adapt** To change; to modify; to adjust. (p. 41)

addiction A person's physical or mental dependence on a drug or other substance. (p. 63)

***adequate** Enough to meet a need or to qualify for something. (p. 421)

adolescence (a-də-ˈle-sᵊn(t)s) The period of great growth and change between childhood and adulthood. (p. 16)

***advance** Before a deadline or an anticipated event; ahead of time. (p. 45)

advertisement A message that persuades consumers to buy a product or service. (p. 236)

aerobic (ˌer-ˈō-bik) Continuous, rhythmic activities that improve heart and lung efficiency. (p. 448)

alteration A change made to clothing, often to modify the style and give it a fresh, new look. (p. 328)

***alternate** Not the same as; distinct; different. (p. 266)

alternative A choice between two or more different things or actions. (p. 124)

amino acid The building block that makes up proteins. (p. 424)

analogous (ə-ˈna-lə-gəs) Alike; comparable; equivalent; similar. (p. 337)

anorexia nervosa (ˌa-nə-ˌrek-sē-ə (ˌ) nər-ˈvō-sə) An eating disorder in which a person feels an extreme fear of gaining weight and severely limits eating. (p. 455)

antioxidant (ˌan-tē-ˈäk-sə-dənt) A substance that protect cells and the immune system from damage by harmful chemicals. (p. 515)

appetite The desire to eat. (p. 422)

appetizer A dish served before a meal. (p. 489)

***appreciate** To value or admire highly; to be thankful for. (p. 215)

apprentice Someone who works under the guidance of a skilled professional in order to learn an art, craft, or trade. (p. 142)

aptitude A natural talent or ability for something. (p. 140)

***assemble** To bring together; to convene. (p. 500)

assertive Able to express one's views clearly and respectfully in a positive way. (p. 64)

attention span The length of time during which one is able to concentrate or remain interested. (p. 200)

attitude The way one feels about something. (p. 120)

autocratic leader Leader who takes complete control of projects, activities, and decisions. (p. 107)

B

batter A liquid or semiliquid mixture, usually containing flour, milk, and eggs. (p. 518)

benefit Help; useful aid; advantage. (p. 54)

bias A line diagonal to the grain of a fabric. (p. 393)

binge eating An eating disorder in which a person eats large quantities of food at one time. (p. 456)

biodegradable Able to be broken down and absorbed by the environment. (p. 314)

blend Two or more fibers combined to create a fabric. (p. 347)

body language Nonverbal communication through gestures, facial expressions, behaviors, and posture. (p. 78)

brand name A trademark used by a manufacturer to identify its products. (p. 356)

***brittle** Easy to break; fragile; weak. (p. 426)

budget The amount of money that is available for or assigned to a particular purpose; a plan for using one's money. (p. 250)

bulimia nervosa (bü-ˈlē-mē-ə (ˌ) nər-ˈvō-sə) An eating disorder in which a person eats very large amounts of food and then vomits or uses laxatives to get rid of the eaten food. (p. 456)

bully A person who physically or verbally abuses someone with the intent to cause injury or discomfort. (p. 65)

C

calorie A unit that measures the energy used by the body and the energy that food supplies to the body. (p. 422)

carbohydrate (ˌkär-bō-ˈhī-ˌdrāt) Any starch or sugar that provides the body with energy. (p. 424)

casing A fabric tunnel made to enclose elastic or a drawstring. (p. 403)

Glossary

casserole A mix of food cooked and served in a covered pot or dish. (p. 520)

cavity An area of decay in a tooth. (p. 20)

child abuse Physical, emotional, or sexual injury to children. (p. 190)

child neglect Failure to meet a child's physical and emotional needs. (p. 190)

childproof Made safe for children to play and explore. (p. 209)

cholesterol (kə-'les-tə-ˌrōl) The waxy substance contained in saturated animal fats. (p. 425)

citizen A member of a community such as a city, state, or country. (p. 97)

citizenship The way one handles one's responsibilities as a citizen. (p. 98)

color scheme A system of arranging colors in a pleasing manner. (p. 294)

colorfast Able to keep its original color through many washings. (p. 355)

***commitment** An agreement or pledge to do something in the future; a promise. (p. 185)

communication The process of sending and receiving messages about ideas, feelings, and information. (p. 77)

comparison shopping Evaluating similar items to check quality and price. (p. 244)

***complement** To complete or go well with something else. (p.491)

complementary (ˌkäm-plə-'men-t(ə-)rē) Contrasting or opposite colors. (p. 337)

***component** Ingredient; element; part. (p. 430)

comprehend To grasp the nature, significance, or meaning of; to understand. (p.160)

compromise ('käm-prə-ˌmīz) An agreement in which each person gives up something in order to reach a solution that satisfies everyone. (p. 56)

***conduct** The act, manner, or process of carrying on. (p. 478)

cone A cylinder used to hold large spools of thread. (p. 407)

***confide** To tell secrets to; to trust. (p. 56)

conflict A disagreement or struggle between two or more people. (p. 84)

consequence (ˌkän(t)-sə-ˌkwen(t)s) The result of a choice. (p. 126)

conservation The saving of resources. (p. 307)

***consistent** Reacting the same way to a situation each time it occurs; free from variation; regular; steady. (p. 190)

constructive criticism Helpful advice meant to help one grow and improve. (p. 11)

consumer A person who buys goods and services. (p. 235)

contamination Becoming infected with harmful bacteria. (p. 469)

convection oven An oven having a fan that circulates hot air evenly and continuously around food. (p. 481)

convenience food Food already prepared or partially prepared to save time. (p. 516)

***convenient** Suited to personal comfort or to efficient performance; easier to manage. (p. 283)

cooperative play Playing together with one or two other children and sharing toys. (p. 201)

***coordinate** To make suitable for fitting together; to mix and match; to harmonize. (p. 356)

***coordination** The harmonious functioning of parts for effective results; movement. (p. 199)

***cope** To adjust to difficult and stressful situations. (p. 269)

***credit** Honor; praise or recognition; acknowledgment. (p. 151)

credit A method of payment allowing one to buy now and pay later. (p. 251)

***crucial** Very important; significant; essential. (p. 511)

culture Ways of thinking, acting, dressing, and speaking shared by a group of people. (p. 8)

curdle To separate into little particles or curds. (p. 521)

D

*dart A tapered, V-shaped seam used to give shape to a garment. (p. 379)

decision Something that one chooses or makes up one's mind about after thinking over all possible choices. (p. 123)

decompose To break down and become part of the soil. (p. 312)

*delegate To assign responsibility or authority; to hand over. (p. 104)

democratic leader A leader who involves everyone in the decision-making process. (p. 107)

dermatologist A doctor who treats skin disorders. (p. 19)

design principle A rule that directs how the elements of design are organized. (p. 295)

design The art of combining elements in a pleasing way. (p. 293)

*determine To come to a decision by investigation, reasoning, or calculation; to figure out. (p. 396)

developmental task An achievement expected at specific ages and stages of growth. (p. 194)

diabetes A condition in which the body cannot control blood sugar properly. (p. 434)

diplomacy (də-'plō-mə-sē) The ability to be honest without being hurtful; tact. (p. 82)

disability A permanent or temporary physical, mental, or emotional condition. (p. 44)

discipline ('di-sə-'plən) The task of teaching a child which behaviors are acceptable and which are not. (p. 190)

discrimination (dis-ˌkri-mə-'nā-shən) The unfair treatment of people based on age, gender, race, or religion. (p. 169)

*dispose To throw away; to get rid of. (p. 312)

diverse Made up of many different parts. (p. 55)

divorce The legal end to a marriage. (p. 43)

*durability Ability to exist for a long time without significant damage or wear. (p. 20)

E

E. coli The most deadly form of food poisoning, found in contaminated water, raw or rare ground beef, and unpasteurized milk. (p. 469)

ease The amount of fullness added to clothing for movement and comfort. (p. 396)

eating disorders An extreme eating behavior that can lead to depression, anxiety, and even death. (p. 455)

*economize To save money. (p. 491)

*efficient Productive without waste; effective. (p. 307)

*elect To select by vote for an office, position, or membership; to choose. (p. 104)

*element Portion; aspect; part. (p. 293)

emphasis Special weight placed upon something considered important; stress; accent. (p. 295)

employability skill A skill which helps one function in life and at work. (p. 159)

*endorse To approve openly; to recommend. (p. 236)

energy The power or ability to be active. (p. 261)

*enrich To make better by the addition of some desirable quality or ingredient; to improve. (p. 33)

*entitled Having a right or claim to something; allowed to expect. (p. 97)

entrepreneur (ˌän-trə-p(r)ə-'nər) A person who starts and runs his or her own business. (p. 151)

environment The conditions by which one is surrounded. (p. 31)

equivalent Something which has equal value as something else. (p. 490)

*escalate To increase in number, amount, or intensity; to get worse. (p. 85)

Glossary

*essential Of the utmost importance; absolutely necessary; fundamental; vital. (p. 163)

*exchange The act of giving or taking one thing in return for another; a trade; sharing. (p. 80)

expectation A person's idea about what should be or should not be. (p. 57)

*expend To make use of for a specific purpose; utilize. (p. 453)

expenses The goods and services on which one spends one's money. (p. 250)

*expire To come to an end; to conclude. (p. 247)

F

fad A fashion that is very popular for a short time. (p. 328)

fad diet A diet which promises quick weight loss through unrealistic or unhealthful means. (p. 453)

fashion A style of clothing that is popular at a particular time. (p. 328)

*fast To stop eating. (p. 454)

feed dog The part of the sewing machine that positions the fabric for the next stitch. (p. 400)

feedback Evaluative or corrective information about an action, event, or process; a response. (p. 80)

fiber (1) A tiny strand or thread, many of which combine to make fabric; (2) Plant material that one's body cannot digest. (pp. 347, 424)

fitness The ability to handle daily events in a healthy way. (p. 445)

flammable Capable of burning easily. (p. 476)

*flexible The body's ability to kneel, bend, turn, and throw. (p.448)

flexibility The ability to adjust to new conditions. (p. 170)

floor plan A drawing of a room and how its furniture is arranged. (p. 284)

foodborne illness An illness caused by unsafe food; food poisoning. (p. 469)

fossil fuel A fuel, such as coal, oil, or natural gas, which comes from the remains of prehistoric plants and animals. (p. 306)

franchise ('fran-ˌchīz) An agreement or license to sell a company's products or to operate a business that carries that company's name. (p. 151)

functional Useful and convenient. (p. 284)

G

garnish A small amount of a food or seasoning, such as parsley, lemon wedges, orange slices, or paprika, used to decorate food. (p. 491)

gesture ('jes-chər) The use of body movements to communicate meaning or emotion. (p. 78)

goal Something one wants to achieve or accomplish. (p. 117)

gossip To talk to people about someone else's personal life or private business. (p. 81)

grade labeling A measurement of food quality using standards set by the government. (p. 494)

grain The direction the threads run in a fabric. (p. 348)

grooming The things one does to care for one's physical appearance. (p. 19)

guarantee ('gär-ən-tē) A manufacturer's written promise to repair or replace a product if it does not work as claimed. (p. 245)

guidance Direction caregivers need to give children so they can learn basic rules for behavior. (p. 188)

guide sheet A set of step-by-step instructions for sewing a pattern. (p. 394)

H

harassment Offensive behavior which violates people's rights; uninvited and unwelcome verbal or physical behavior. (p. 170)

*hazard Something that is potentially dangerous. (p.476)

hem An edge made by folding fabric over and stitching it down. (p. 374)

heredity (hə-'re-də-tē) The passing on of traits, or characteristics and qualities, from parents to their children. (p. 8)

hue Colors, the three basic of which are red, yellow, and blue. (p. 334)

hygiene Keeping oneself clean. (p. 19)

I

*imitate To follow as a pattern, model, or example; to copy. (p. 222)

impulse buying Making a sudden decision to buy something one did not plan to purchase. (p. 242)

incineration The disposal of waste by burning. (p. 312)

income The amount of money one earns or receives regularly. (p. 250)

independent play Playing alone and showing little interest in interacting with others. (p. 200)

ingredient A part of a combination or mixture; a recipe component. (p.499)

*integrity Sticking to a code of moral values; honor and truthfulness. (p. 127)

intensity The brightness or dullness of a color. (p. 334)

interfacing Fabric sewn between two layers of a garment for strength or to prevent stretching around necklines, closures, and buttonholes. (p. 385)

interlock To lock together; to form closely fitted stitches. (p. 373)

intruder Someone who uses force to get into a home. (p. 210)

*inventory An itemized list; a summary. (p. 330)

J

jealousy When a person feels unhappy about someone else's possessions, accomplishments, or luck. (p. 58)

job satisfaction A feeling of accomplishment from a job well done. (p. 146)

job shadowing Spending time with someone to observe him or her on the job. (p. 141)

K

*key Important; fundamental; necessary. (p. 305)

knit fabric Stretchy fabric made by looping threads together. (p. 348)

L

landfill A large pit where waste is buried between layers of earth. (p. 312)

layout A diagram of how pattern pieces should be placed on fabric. (p. 394)

leader A person with the ability to guide and motivate others. (p. 104)

leadership The direction or guidance that helps a group accomplish its goals. (p. 104)

legume The fruit or seed of plants, such as peas or beans, used for food. (p. 523)

long-term goal A goal that may take months or even years to reach. (p. 117)

looper The rounded part that holds the thread inside a serger. (p. 407)

M

management The skillful use of resources to accomplish a task. (p. 259)

marking Symbols located on pattern pieces. (p. 394)

*material Things which are not necessary for survival like food, shelter, and water, but which can make life easier and more enjoyable. (p. 262)

meal patterns Habits that determine when and what people eat each day. (p. 490)

media A form of conveyance or expression; communication that advertisers use. (p. 237)

mentor Someone with experience who supports, advises, and encourages the progress of a less experienced person. (p. 143)

*merchandise Products available to buy. (p. 243)

mineral An element needed in small amounts for sturdy bones and teeth, healthy blood, and regular elimination of body wastes. (p. 426)

Glossary

*minimize To reduce; to decrease. (p. 469)

modesty The belief about the proper way to cover the body with clothes. (p. 327)

*modify To make different; to change; to alter. (p. 139)

monitor To watch carefully over someone or something. (p. 210)

monochromatic (mä-nə-krō-'ma-tik) Having or consisting of one color or hue. (p. 337)

motivate To make someone feel enthusiastic, interested, and committed to a project or task. (p. 104)

multi-tasking Doing more than one job at the same time. (p. 265)

MyPlate A colorful representation of how to make healthful food choices and increase physical activity. (p. 430)

N

nap A fabric with a one-way texture, such as corduroy. (p. 382)

natural fiber Fibers, such as cotton, linen, silk, and wool, which are made from plant and animal products. (p. 347)

natural resource A material that is supplied by nature. (p. 305)

negotiation (ni-,go-shē-'a-shən) The process of talking about a conflict and deciding how to reach a compromise. (p. 87)

networking Using personal connections to help achieve one's goals. (p. 142)

*neutral Not engaged on either side; indifferent. (p. 87)

*notice Warning of something; an announcement. (p. 173)

notions Additional materials needed to complete a sewing project, such as thread and buttons. (p. 379)

nutrient ('nü-trē-ənt) A substance in food that is important for the body's growth and maintenance. (p. 421)

O

obesity A condition in which a person's weight is 20 percent or more above his or her healthy weight. (p. 452)

*obtain To gain or attain usually by planned action or effort; to reach. (p. 447)

omelet A well-beaten egg that is first cooked in a frying pan without stirring, then topped with other ingredients, such as mushrooms, peppers, and cheese, and finally folded over. (p. 523)

*operate To perform a function; to work. (p. 373)

*opinion A view or judgment formed in the mind about a particular matter. (p. 22)

orientation (,òr-ē-ən-'tā-shən) A meeting during which an employee is given details about pay, benefits, and job expectations, and is often given a tour as well. (p. 167)

osteoporosis (,as-tē-ō-pə-'ro-səs) A condition in which bones gradually lose their mineral content and become weak. (p. 426)

*outcome Something that follows as a result or consequence. (p. 124)

*outline A line that marks the outer limits of an object or figure; boundary; shape; form. (p. 293)

P

parenting The process of caring for children and helping them to grow and learn. (p. 185)

pattern A plan for making a garment or project. (p. 378)

peer A person of the same age. (p. 56)

peer mediation A process in which peers help other students find a solution to a conflict before it becomes more serious. (p. 88)

peer pressure The influence one feels to go along with the behavior of one's peers. (p. 60)

perception (pər-'sep-shən) Using one's senses to get information about one's environment. (p. 80)

perishable Likely to spoil quickly. (p. 470)

*permanent Continuing without change; lasting; long-term. (p. 314)

*persuade To move by argument to a belief, position, or course of action; to convince. (p. 160)

pollution The changing of air, water, and land from clean and safe to dirty and unsafe. (p. 305)

portfolio A neatly organized collection of one's skills, experiences, and qualifications. (p. 140)

portion An appropriate amount of food for one person. (p. 430)

*potent Having force, authority, or influence; powerful. (p. 261)

*potential Best chance for success; existing in possibility; capable of development into actuality. (p. 14)

*precaution A measure taken beforehand to prevent harm or secure good; safety measure. (p. 209)

prejudice ('pre-jə-dəs) An opinion about people that is formed without facts or knowledge. (p. 84)

*pressed Smoothed; ironed. (p. 359)

*primary Basic; fundamental. (p. 334)

priority Something ranked high in importance. (p. 120)

proactive Thinking ahead about possible decisions or problems and taking action right away. (p. 124)

processed Changed from raw form before being sold; subjected to a special treatment. (p. 513)

procrastinate (prə-ˌkras-tə-ˌnāt) To wait until the last minute to do something; to put off. (p. 267)

produce Fruits and vegetables. (p. 513)

*product The result of something; item; merchandise; output. (p. 409)

promotion A move into a job with more responsibility. (p. 172)

*promptly Readily; quickly; immediately. (p. 470)

proportion The relation of one part to another. (p. 295)

protein A type of nutrient that is needed to build, repair, and maintain body cells and tissues. (p. 423)

Q

quiche (ˌkēsh) A main-dish pie filled with eggs, cheese, and other ingredients such as ham, spinach, and mushrooms. (p. 523)

quick bread Bread in which the leavening agent is baking powder or baking soda. (p. 518)

R

ravel When loose threads pull out of the cut edge of fabric. (p. 382)

*raw Not being in a polished or processed form; unfinished. (p. 374)

recipe A list of directions for preparing a specific food. (p. 499)

recycling Turning waste items into products that can be used. (p. 310)

redirect To change the course or direction of; to turn attention to something else. (p. 221)

reference A responsible adult who can tell an employer about one's character and quality of work. (p. 164)

*refined Chemically processed to remove impurities. (p. 435)

refusal skills Communication tools that can help one say no when one feels pushed to take part in activities that are unsafe, unhealthful, or that go against one's values. (p. 61)

*reinforce To strengthen by additional assistance, material, or support. (p. 384)

reliable Able to be counted on; dependable. (p. 217)

*reserved Restrained in words and actions; shy; less expressive. (p. 32)

resign To decide to leave a job; to give up one's position; to quit. (p. 172)

*resist To place opposite or against something; to fight; to oppose. (p. 61)

Glossary

resource Something or someone that is a source of help or information. (p. 261)

*respect Value; high or special regard. (p. 11)

responsible Dependable; making wise choices. (p. 38)

*restrict To confine within boundaries; to restrain; to limit. (p. 211)

*result Consequence; end product; outcome; conclusion; effect. (p. 407)

résumé ('re-zə-ˌmā) A document which summarizes one's qualifications, work experience, education, and interests. (p. 164)

*retain To hold secure or intact; to keep. (p. 520)

*reveal To open up to view; to display; to show. (p. 140)

*routine Habitual; mechanical; established; regular. (p. 285)

rumor A statement spread from one person to another without knowing whether or not it is true. (p. 81)

S

salmonella (ˌsal-mə-'ne-lə) Bacteria often found in raw or undercooked foods, such as meat, eggs, fish, and poultry. (p. 469)

scald To bring slowly to a temperature just below boiling point. (p. 521)

*seasonal Foods more readily available and less expensive at certain times of the year. (p. 513)

self-actualization (self-ˌak-ch(ə-w)ə-lə-'zā-shən) Reaching one's full potential. (p. 14)

self-concept A mental picture of oneself. (p. 10)

self-esteem A sense of confidence and self-worth. (p. 11)

selvage The tightly woven edge of the fabric that has no visible loose threads. (p. 393)

*sequence Order of succession; continuity of progression; order. (p. 194)

*service Work performed for others. (p. 235)

sew-through button A button, used when the joined materials need to lie flat, which has two or four holes through it and no loop on the back. (p. 406)

shade The dark value of a hue. (p. 334)

shank button A button, used with thick fabrics, which has a stem on the back. (p. 406)

shelter A structure built to protect people from weather and extreme temperatures. (p. 283)

shoplifting Taking items from a store without paying for them. (p. 247)

short-term goal A goal that can be reached quickly, perhaps in a few days or weeks. (p. 117)

sibling A brother or a sister. (p. 33)

sign language A system of hand signs used by or for people who have hearing impairments. (p. 78)

*signal To show, communicate, or indicate. (p. 78)

*slant To take a diagonal course; to slope; to angle. (p. 348)

sodium A mineral that helps regulate the amount of fluid in our bodies. (p. 435)

soil The loose material in which plants grow. (p. 306)

stamina The ability to focus on or perform a single activity for a long time. (p. 447)

static cling When electricity builds up in the dryer and causes clothing to stick to itself or to one's body. (p. 358)

*status Rank in relation to others; position in society. (p. 327)

staystitch A row of stitching made very near the seamline within the seam allowance. (p. 400)

stereotype An idea about the qualities or behavior of a certain group. (p. 32)

*strategy A careful plan or method; a way to prepare. (p. 352)

stress The body's reaction to changes around it. (p. 268)

style The distinctive quality or form of something; the design of a garment. (p. 328)

synthetic fiber Fibers, such as rayon, nylon, and polyester, which are made from manufactured substances. (p. 347)

T

tail chain A length of thread shaped like a chain, made by pressing on the presser foot without placing fabric under the needle. (p. 409)

teamwork When a group works together to reach a goal. (p. 108)

***technology** A manner of accomplishing a task using specialized processes, methods, or knowledge; equipment and machinery. (p. 150)

***tender** Easily crushed, chewed, or cut; fragile. (p. 519)

texture (1) The feel and appearance of a fabric's surface; (2) The way something feels when touched or tasted. (pp. 339, 491)

***thrive** To survive and improve; to prosper; to flourish. (p. 100)

time management The development of practices and skills that increase how quickly and effectively one can do something. (p. 265)

tint The light value of a hue. (p. 334)

trade-off Something that one gives up in order to get something else. (p. 120)

tradition A custom or belief. (p. 32)

traffic pattern The path people take to move around within a room as well as enter and exit the room. (p. 284)

***transfer** To move to a different place; to shift; to convey. (p. 398)

trend A temporary fashion or product; a current style or preference. (p. 236)

U

unit pricing The cost of a product per unit. (p. 494)

utensil A tool or container used in a household, especially a kitchen; cookware. (p. 480)

V

***value** Relative lightness or darkness of a color; luminosity. (p. 334)

vegetarian A person who does not eat meat; one whose diet consists wholly of vegetables, fruits, grains, nuts, and sometimes eggs or dairy products. (p. 492)

vitamin A substance that is needed in small quantities to help regulate body functions. (p. 425)

volunteer To give one's time and energy without pay to help others. (p. 98)

W

wellness One's best level of health; the quality or state of being in good health. (p. 421)

whole grain Foods that contain the entire edible grain. (p. 425)

work ethic A personal commitment to doing one's very best. (p. 172)

***worth** The value of something measured by its qualities. (p. 120)

woven fabric Fabric made by interlacing lengthwise and crosswise yarns, which are several fibers twisted together, on a loom. (p. 347)

Y

yeast bread Bread in which the leavening agent is yeast. (p. 518)

Glossary

Index

Index

Index

Index

Index

Index